# IN THE NAME OF THE NATION

# IN THE NAME
# OF THE NATION

*India and Its Northeast*

SANJIB BARUAH

STANFORD UNIVERSITY PRESS
STANFORD, CALIFORNIA

STANFORD UNIVERSITY PRESS
Stanford, California

Printed in the United States of America on acid-free, archival-quality paper

Library of Congress Cataloging-in-Publication Data

Names: Baruah, Sanjib, author.
Title: In the name of the nation : India and its northeast / Sanjib Baruah.
Description: Stanford, California : Stanford University Press, 2020. |
     Series: South Asia in motion | Includes bibliographical references and index.
Identifiers: LCCN 2019018060 (print) | LCCN 2019019807 (ebook) |
     | ISBN 9781503610705 | ISBN 9781503610705 (cloth: alk. paper) |
     ISBN 9781503611283 (pbk.: alk. paper) | ISBN 9781503611290 (ebook)
Subjects: LCSH: India, Northeastern—Politics and government. | Insurgency—
     India, Northeastern—History. | India—Relations—India, Northeastern. |
     India, Northeastern—Relations—India. | India—Politics and
     government—1947–
Classification: LCC DS483.62 (ebook) | LCC DS483.62 .B37 2020 (print) | DDC
     954/.105—dc23
LC record available at https://lccn.loc.gov/2019018060

Cover design: Rob Ehle

Typeset by Kevin Barrett Kane in 10.75/15 Adobe Caslon Pro

*To the memory of my mother,*
RENU BARUA,
*who passed away on November 9, 2018,*
*as I was completing this manuscript*

# CONTENTS

# PREFACE

INDIA'S EFFORTS TO BUILD a multilingual, multireligious, and multi-cultural democratic society, and the conflicts that arise along its many fault lines, attract significant scholarly and media attention. But the experience of Northeast India—a region that includes vast tracts of borderland space fringing Bhutan, China's Tibetan areas, Myanmar, Bangladesh, and Nepal—stands out as distinctive and different. A profusion of small language communities, "tribes," and "subtribes" inhabit certain parts of this region, and this can convey the impression of an almost opaque multiplicity. But cultural boundaries in those areas are in fact quite fluid. The census numbers paint a religious landscape where Hindus are a majority; Islam, Christianity, and Buddhism have a strong presence; and local religious traditions and practices remain influential. Christians make up a majority in three of eight northeastern states and a significant minority in two other states.

The region is an anomalous zone in the republic, where certain basic rules and norms of democracy are rendered ineffective for long periods—or they can be suspended on short notice. Ethnic militias and armed groups have flourished there for decades. But these militarized organizations coexist comfortably with functioning electoral institutions. Special security laws produce severe democracy deficits that are now almost as old as the republic. The brunt of these laws falls on relatively small areas, and politically sensitive and media-intensive urban areas are left out of their jurisdiction. This is partly what has allowed the unhappy status quo to continue—to the chagrin of local rights activists.

This book is about postcolonial India's troubled relations with this region—commonly referred to as just "the Northeast." The ambivalence associated with borderlands, representational practices that reproduce and reinforce a relation of hierarchy, and a center-periphery interactional dynamic are all part of this story. Many from the region who live in India's capital city of Delhi and other metropolitan areas complain of being objects of a racialized gaze. But the book goes beyond these specificities. It takes the history of this troubled relationship as a vantage point to reflect on how the generalization of the territorially circumscribed nation-form, and of the sovereignty of the nation-state, has played out since decolonization. I reject the evolutionism that makes these political forms seem inevitable rather than highly contingent artifacts. Can democracy be sustained and deepened under conditions prevailing in the region? This concern informs the book's core arguments. Its focus is on contemporary history, but the continuities and ruptures between colonial and postcolonial institutions and practices are an important part of my argument. The text therefore reaches back into the British colonial period from time to time.

My tone is academic, but I have a personal connection to the region. I was born in Shillong, in Northeast India, and I grew up in the region. But it became a focus of my intellectual interest much later—after I completed my doctoral work and began teaching at a liberal arts college in the United States. My work on Northeast India has not been formed in an academic discipline or an area studies program.[1] I rely not only on academic research but also on personal memory for some of the events covered herein. Some key moments in the region's postcolonial transition are part of my childhood and teenage memories. Writing about those junctures gave me the feeling of recalling a time not unlike what historian Eric Hobsbawm once called "a twilight zone between history and memory."[2]

I have been writing on Northeast India for the past three decades: a period of considerable public and political upheaval in the region. The years coincide with the book's temporal focus. I have traveled extensively in the region during this time—sometimes walking familiar paths and renewing old connections but mostly traveling to familiar yet unknown places: meeting new people and making new friends. These personal connections have sustained my affection and empathy for the people. I make a special effort to heed the many unheard and frequently misunderstood political voices from the region. Misperceptions and misjudgments about the conflicting political sentiments that prevail in the region have cost Indian democracy dearly.

This book could not have been imagined without the stimulation and challenge of friends, colleagues, and students. The work progressed mainly through conversations in a variety of contexts. Some of the underlying arguments were developed in the course of my teaching classes on political economy and on the workings of the nation-state at Bard College. The initial formulations of the ideas set forth here were prepared as texts of university and public lectures and conference papers. I owe a debt of gratitude to those who invited me to speak on these subjects: Amit Baishya, Meenaxi Barkataki-Ruscheweyh, Urvashi Butalia, Eric de Maaker, Prasenjit Duara, Thomas Blom Hansen, B. G. Karlsson, Åshild Kolås, Yasmin Saikia, Joëlle Smadja, Aparna Sundar, Nandini Sundar, Willem van Schendel, and Mélanie Vandenhelsken. A number of recent invitations gave me the opportunity to present and discuss nearly complete chapters of the book. For these occasions I am thankful to Gudrun Bühnemann, Lalita du Perron, Monirul Hussain, Christophe Jaffrelot, Simi Malhotra, Chandan Kumar Sharma, Dina M. Siddique, H. Srikanth, and Jyotirmoy Talukdar. I owe a special thanks to Preeti Gill, at whose behest I began writing this book, though it took a different course and direction from what we envisaged.

Xonzoi (Sanjay) Barbora has been a consistent and most generous interlocutor. Conversations—either face-to-face or by email—with Arindam Barkataki, Eric Beverley, Tarun Bharatiya, Mario Bick, Diana Brown, Kanchan Chandra, Arup Jyoti Das, Richard H. Davis, Rohan D'Souza, Thomas Bloom Hansen, Soibam Haripriya, Jane Huber, Yengkhom Jilangamba, Rakhee Kalita, Bengt G. Karlsson, David Kettler, Leela Khanna, Dolly Kikon, Amrith Lal, Babloo Loitongbam, Michelle Murray, Ankur Tamuli Phukan, Yasmin Saikia and Radhika (Radz) Subramaniam made me rethink and recast parts of the book's argument. I am grateful to the two readers for Stanford University Press for their attentive reading of the manuscript. Their thoughtful critiques and suggestions have done much to improve the book. Finally, I would like to express my gratitude to Marcela Maxfield, the commissioning editor at Stanford University Press, for much kind advice and support. Needless to say, none of these people bears any responsibility for errors and omissions or for the analysis and interpretations presented here.

I accomplished a significant part of the work presented here during my time as Distinguished Visiting Professor at the Omeo Kumar Das Institute of Social Change and Development in Guwahati, India, and as Global Fellow at the Peace Research Institute in Oslo, Norway. I am grateful to the faculties and staffs of those institutions for their many acts of kindness and assistance.

I have been engaged both personally and professionally with the ideas and themes developed in this book over a long period. Previous iterations of some of the arguments have appeared in other publications. I am grateful to the publishers and to the editors of journals and edited volumes for permission to use portions of previously published pieces in this book.

My debt to Zilkia Janer is of a different order. Our many conversations led me to engage with ideas and debates in culinary history and in the intellectual world of Latin America. In quite unexpected ways, they helped my understanding of the modern history of a part of the world very far from the Americas. She was first to read these pages, and the book benefited from her comments, suggestions, and help in countless ways.

MAP 1. *Map of Northeast India*

IN THE NAME OF THE NATION

# INTRODUCTION

> It was time for me to try and discover what on earth this strange
> country to which I had been sent was. . . . I had come from an
> environment . . . where the unit of account was the nation state and
> the problems, if they could possibly have been given a monetary
> value, were worth trillions of dollars. What I was faced with here
> was incredibly tiny groups of separate identities with problems so
> small that I could not grasp why they should be bothered about.
> —B. K. Nehru, *Nice Guys Finish Second*

WHEN USING A DIRECTIONAL NAME, it is perhaps always a good idea to ask, "Where is it we really start from, where is the place that enunciates this itinerary"?[1] In Northeast India, or just "the Northeast"[2]— a common way for Indians to refer to the region today—the point of reference is clear: it is the Indian heartland. It is not a long vernacularized directional name like the Maghreb (the place where the sun sets, or the West in Arabic, since the area was once the western-most area conquered by the Arabs), Norway (north way), or Austria (eastern realm). Northeast India is a postcolonial coinage that took root in the 1970s. Unlike informal or vernacular names like North India or South India—or the Midwest in the United States, most of which is located in the country's eastern half—Northeast India is an officially organized and named region—an artifact of deliberate policy. But if this name was expected to stick in vernacular practice—as a form of self-identification—it has not.[3] One rarely hears anyone saying: "As a Northeasterner, I . . . ," though people would say "as a Manipuri," "a Naga," "a Khasi," or "a businesswoman," "a journalist," or "an engineer."[4] There is, however, some evidence of an incipient Northeastern identity coming into existence in recent years.

There has been some effort to give the directional name a Hindu-accented cultural makeover. Prime Minister Narendra Modi likes to talk about the auspiciousness of the northeastern direction in the *Vastu Shastra*—the traditional Indian system of architecture and design. The "*ishan kon* of a house *should be taken care of,*" he says—using the Vastu Shastra's word for the northeastern direction: the direction of Gods that Vastu practitioners recommend as an ideal location for a *pujaghar* (household shrine)—so the Northeast should be developed to ensure the country's well-being.[5] The directional place-name highlights the peculiar relation that has developed between this region and the nation over the seven decades since decolonization.[6] The commonly used derivative term *Northeasterner* functions not only to describe a person's geographical provenance; it expresses a certain hierarchy and relation of power. The term, as I will explain below, has a racial inflection as well.

This official region was once a part of British Imperial India's "frontier system."[7] The political-legal structure of the colonial province of Assam paralleled that of another frontier province of British Imperial India: the North West Frontier Province [NWFP]. Located in present-day Pakistan, it was renamed Khyber Pakhtunkhwa in 2010. The Federally Administered Tribal Area (FATA) was located between the "settled districts" of the NWFP and the international border with Afghanistan. This is similar to the North East Frontier Tracts, which is most of the contemporary state of Arunachal Pradesh and a part of the state of Nagaland—located between the settled districts of Assam and the international border with Tibet and Burma. *Northeast India*, as an official place-name, carries with it the weight of a number of haphazard and poorly thought-out decisions made by managers of the postcolonial Indian state as they were trying to turn an imperial frontier space into the national space of a "normal sovereign state."[8] National security was uppermost in the minds of the officials making those decisions. The area borders China, Myanmar, Bangladesh, and Bhutan. That 98 percent of the region's borders are international is a cliché one hears endlessly in India. National security-minded writers never tire of using the metaphor of a "chicken-neck" when referring to the fourteen-miles-wide land corridor in Siliguri in northern Bengal. It supposedly underscores the region's extreme security vulnerability. An obsessive use of the language of national geopolitics naturalizes the sub-continent's post-1947 political map. The imagined borders between the "inside" and the "outside" fix the region in terms of official India's national security anxieties. A fact of political geography—a product of the Partition of 1947—has been naturalized.

I begin by interrogating this regional identifier because the region itself—its dominant representations and discordant political history—renders inadequate so much accepted knowledge about India as a successful postcolonial democracy on an upward and inclusive economic trajectory. The collection of paradoxes that is the Northeast stands as an exceptional example of the shortcomings and failures of the territorially circumscribed postcolonial nation-state as an institutional complex, and understanding how this region came to be what it is today is crucial to understanding that larger story.

## DEMOCRACY DEFICITS

Northeast India has had a long history of armed conflicts,[9] though in international forums Indian officials avoid using this locution to reference this fact. They prefer to use the word *insurgency*. That the language of insurgency and counterinsurgency has become commonplace in Indian official discourse is remarkable. This contrasts with the practice of at least one major democracy: the United Kingdom, where *insurgency* and *counterinsurgency* were taboo words carefully avoided in reference to the conflict in Northern Ireland. It was feared that the use of this language could be taken to mean that it is "an expeditionary or colonial mission" or a case of "overseas military deployment, a war."[10] The situation in Northern Ireland was therefore commonly referred to as "the Troubles." Despite the liberal use of the term *insurgency*, the idea of an armed rebellion with mass support—the focus of conventional counterinsurgency theory—bears almost no relation to Northeast India's armed conflicts.[11] It would be hard to argue that the vast majority of armed political groups pose any kind of a strategic threat to the Indian state.[12] As a former officer of the Indian Army once said mockingly, "The moment they fired a few shots and were organized into a violent movement . . . powerful government functionaries came running from the Centre. The funds increased, the allocations increased."[13] Most groups using the language of armed resistance as a form of claims-making do not draw their strength from the advantages traditionally associated with guerilla groups; they take advantage of gaps in the rule of law, and they all maintain ties with mainstream actors in politics, administration, and business.[14] Even when a group proclaims independent and sovereign statehood as its goal, the challenges it presents have little in common with guerilla groups that were the focus of the canonical works on counterinsurgency warfare. Laldenga, for example, led the powerful Mizo rebellion in the 1960s and 1970s. But he "had always held the avenue of negotiations open even at the time of declaring independence."[15]

This history of armed conflicts and the discourse of insurgency surrounding it have had a formative role in shaping the way Northeast India is governed.[16] The armed conflicts provide both the backdrop and the rationale for the Armed Forces Special Powers Act (AFSPA)—a law that has been in effect in the region for nearly six decades. The Indian Parliament first adopted this law as far back as 1958, during the early days of the Naga rebellion. It has since been amended a number of times to accommodate the names of the new northeastern states created since then.[17] It allows civilian authorities to call on the armed forces to come to the assistance of civil powers. Once a state—or a part of a state—is declared "disturbed" under AFSPA, the armed forces are empowered to make preventive arrests, search premises without warrants, and even shoot and kill civilians. Legal action against an officer for abusing those powers requires the prior approval of the central government—a rule that has effectively meant de facto immunity from prosecution.[18] A disturbed area proclamation under AFSPA has uncanny similarities with emergencies or states of exception—including martial law and a state of siege. Critics of AFSPA charge that it effectively suspends fundamental freedoms and creates a de facto emergency regime. The powers granted under AFSPA, says a 2013 report of the UN Human Rights Council, "are in reality broader than that allowable under a state of emergency as the right to life may effectively be suspended under the Act and the safeguards applicable in a state of emergency are absent."[19]

The persistence of such an exceptionally harsh security regime cannot be explained by the putative challenge of powerful and unending "insurgencies." Decisions to proclaim an area disturbed under AFSPA are made with remarkable casualness. Officials rarely offer much by way of justification.[20] In recent years the familiar flow of news about armed conflicts in Northeast India have been punctuated by reports of ceasefires, ceremonial arms surrenders, peace talks and signing of Suspension of Operations agreements, and peace accords. It has become routine for senior government functionaries to announce that the door is open for militants to forsake violence and join the "national mainstream." Yet in these efforts to end armed conflict, one hears little about getting rid of AFSPA. Evidently few believe that an outbreak of peace is on the horizon. A writer on Indian security affairs describes the state of affairs: "Northeast continues to remain a tinderbox, but insurgent capacity to challenge the might of the state has continuously declined."[21] Most security experts typically talk of the situation having improved selectively, and they attribute it mostly to the elimination of sanctuaries for rebel groups in Bangladesh and Bhutan. "The multiple insurgencies of India's Northeast," says the head of India's major security research and monitoring organization, "have seen dramatic deceleration and disintegration." The incidents of violence have declined "to some of the lowest levels in the past two and a half decades." But "cyclic surges and recessions in insurgent activities," he warns, have occurred in the past as well.[22] Significantly, the lists of "Terrorist, Insurgent and Extremist Groups" regularly updated by this organization make a distinction between "active" and "inactive" armed groups. There are, in addition, "proscribed" armed groups and armed groups in "peace talks/ceasefire." Assam, for instance, is listed as having seven active and thirty-six inactive armed groups, as well as three proscribed armed groups. Thirteen armed groups are described as being either in "peace talks" or under "ceasefire agreements." Even peaceful Mizoram has one active and one inactive group.[23] In the eyes of India's national security bureaucrats and security experts, the situation in the region remains in a permanent state of flux. They can never be sure when an inactive armed group crosses over to the active category, or the other way around, or when a "proscribed" armed organization becomes "un-proscribed," enters into a ceasefire, and becomes a partner in peace with state actors. Thus, in February of 2018, as authoritative an official as the chief minister of Manipur provided a curious explanation for the extortions and kidnappings taking place in his state. He said they were occurring because negotiations with organizations under Suspension of Operations agreements had been slow to start.[24] The democratically elected chief minister of Nagaland once explained to a reporter that since Naga armed groups do not receive government subsidies—unlike other armed groups in the region—they are "bound to collect tax from the people for their survival."[25] During their fieldwork in the Naga-dominated Ukhrul District of Manipur in 2016, Shalaka Thakur and Rajesh Venugopal found that "when talking of the government . . . there is often confusion about who is being referred to." The district's main urban center hosts the institutions of both the Indian state and those of the Government of the People's Republic of Nagaland/Nagalim (GPRN), run by the NSCN-IM, currently engaged in peace negotiations with the Indian government. An official of the GPRN told them that they collect "taxes to feed armed cadres and run the administration. We run the people's government."[26] In July of 2018 a report of a committee of the Indian Parliament noted that Assam today tops the country in certain categories of violent crime. The parliamentary standing committee on home affairs, headed by former home minister Palaniappan Chidambaram, said in its report that it "is perplexed that despite a waning trend in insurgency, violent crimes and kidnappings have been on a rise." Among possible reasons, says the report, is the "poor rehabilitation and settlement of former insurgents who may be indulging in such crimes for ransom."[27] This pattern—a prolongation of durable disorder[28]—may not be an intended effect of Indian policy, but that the ceasefire and negotiations policy in place since the 1990s would produce such an outcome should not be surprising.[29]

After six decades, it is hard for anyone to claim that AFSPA is designed as an "exception" to serve a restorative function for India's democratic order.[30] In fact, Northeast India today suffers from serious democracy deficits because of this law and the culture of impunity it fosters. Indeed, the culture of impunity has become so entrenched that many in the region now believe that even repealing AFSPA "will be no panacea."[31] AFSPA may be at the center of this special security order, but it is by no means reducible to it. I will use the phrase "the AFSPA regime" to emphasize this reality. In the history of security legislations in India, there are examples of a controversial security law being repealed but another law being soon adopted giving state institutions similar powers.[32] An attempt at such a cosmetic quick fix of the AFSPA regime is unlikely in the immediate future, but it cannot be ruled out indefinitely. Moreover, it is important to recognize that even when an armed conflict has ended in the region, it has had no visible effect on the trend of a continually expanding footprint of the Indian Army and of other centrally controlled security forces. This is partly because their deployment in Northeast India serves both internal and external security ends, and, increasingly, the two have become indistinguishable. The increase of large military and security facilities built in the region points to the long-term nature of their deployment. Monirul Hussain, the author of a book on involuntary removal and resettlement of displaced people in the region, points out the irony of some of these military and police installations developed by land acquisition through eminent domain laws having luxury golf courses inside them.[33] The Indian military establishment, though, is careful not to formally call them golf courses. Thus, the Rangapahar golf course (Spear Golf Club) in Dimapur, Nagaland, is called the Army Spear Environmental Park and Training Area. The Narengi golf course in Guwahati is called the Rhino Environmental Park and Training Area (REPTA).[34]

There are many unintended effects of the AFSPA regime. The resultant decision-making environment, says a former head of the police of the state of Karnataka—observing conditions in the state of Manipur—is like that of a man with a hammer as his only tool: every problem looks like a nail to be hit on the head.[35] Arguably, all across Northeast India the AFSPA regime has become a major obstacle to innovative problem solving. Significant numbers of armed conflicts in the world—as becomes apparent from large data sets—do not end in victory or defeat or peace but in a draw.[36] In the actually existing world of postcolonial sovereignty—with a large number of nominally sovereign "quasi-states"[37]—armed conflicts are not always about a clash of wills over the monopoly of the legitimate use of violence between armed groups and states.[38] It is rare in Northeast India for a peace deal between the government and an armed group to be followed by comprehensive and transparent demobilization of ex-combatants. These peace settlements—flawed at the point of conception—are examples of such ambiguous political outcomes. To a careful observer, signs of future trouble would be apparent from the start. When flawed peace accords turn "former insurgents" into partners in the exercise of state power, their demonstrated military prowess becomes a part of local political equations. These arrangements have the making of hybrid political regimes where state and nonstate armed entities are in de facto informal partnership. The authority of such hybrid regimes does not depend on the actual use of violence: an armed group's reputed capacity for violence can do the job, and there may be vigilante groups engaging in violence from time to time with the acquiescence of state actors. The fear of physical harm in the hands of former militants—with the complicity of state actors—props up these hybrid regimes.[39]

Indian security experts talk of a "politician-insurgent nexus." Corruption scandals arise from time to time that implicate government officials, mainstream politicians, and leaders of armed groups. They point to the prevalence of such hybrid regimes. As recently as August of 2018, in a case involving the theft of guns from Manipur Police armory, India's National Investigation Agency arrested a number of people, including elected members of the Manipur state legislature, police officials, and leaders of an armed group that had signed a Suspension of Operations Agreement with the government. "Despite the decrease in insurgent violence," observed a security analyst following those arrests, "the nexus of militants with Government officials and politicians feeds an underground economy of violence and prevents any final resolution of the multiple conflicts in India's Northeast."[40] There are elements of a hybrid political regime in these so-called "nexuses." They have affinity with the phenomena of "shadow states" or "war-lord rule." It is hardly surprising that the perceived need for the continuation of AFSPA never really goes away.

Equally predictably, the use of AFSPA in this political climate extends beyond the actual conduct of counterinsurgency operations. Multiple state and nonstate armed actors operate under its shadow. For instance, in Assam in the 1990s, death squads—or "secret killers" as they were called—carried out a wave of extrajudicial killings. They could not have occurred without the cover of AFSPA. Anthropologist Dolly Kikon narrates an episode involving the Central Industrial Security Force (CISF)—a force designed to protect the country's economic infrastructure, including airports. It is unlikely that anyone ever intended to include the CISF within the meaning of "armed forces" in AFSPA. Yet this law was in the background when CISF personnel in 2007 shot and killed a person in an area where it was responsible for guarding oil installations. The incident did not take place at an installation guarded by the CISF. The victim was a local activist, Nilikesh Gogoi, known for his opposition to the government's appropriation of private lands "to expand plantations and oil exploration sites." While AFSPA was not explicitly invoked, CISF officials said in defense of their action that it was a case of "mistaken identity" and blamed the incident on the extra vigilance that it has to maintain in the region because of the poor security conditions that supposedly prevail. Local citizens initially protested the killing, but soon family members accepted monetary compensation, and the public mood changed in favor of moving on. The AFSPA regime, Kikon observes, creates "different expectations and concepts of justice."[41] This security culture probably explains why Assam's Kaziranga National Park has acquired a reputation as "the park that shoots people to protect rhinos." A reporter of the British Broadcasting Corporation found that the park's rangers have "the kind of powers to shoot and kill normally only conferred on armed forces policing civil unrest."[42]

Official squeamishness about the use of the term *armed conflict*—and preference for the term *insurgency*—is largely explained by India's well-known defense in international forums of the sanctity of the principle of state sovereignty and the complementary principle of noninterference in the domestic affairs of states. Official India appears to associate the term *armed conflict* with regimes of external intervention: the meddling in the internal affairs of states by foreign governments and nongovernmental humanitarian and human rights organizations. The prospect apparently provokes the deepest of anxiety among Indian officials. Thus the Indian government once declared: "There are no situations of 'armed conflict' within the territory of India." The context was a discussion of the United Nations Security Council Resolution 1325, which recommends the participation of women in institutions and processes of conflict resolution and "post-conflict reconstruction." The UN Committee on the Elimination of Discrimination Against Women had queried governments about the implementation of the resolution in their countries. Indian officials were concerned that acknowledging the incidence of armed conflicts in the country might pave the way for international meddling. The protestation that "India has no armed conflicts" was therefore followed by the statement: "hence the Security Council Resolution 1325 relating to Women in Armed Conflict is not applicable to India."[43] The assertion that there is no internal armed conflict in India is not empirically tenable. But one can hardly begrudge Indian officials their cleverness and inventiveness. For, to paraphrase the novelist Amitav Ghosh, it could well be said that sovereignty in our time resides precisely where UN peacekeepers and humanitarian and international human rights actors do not: "the reason why the UN is probably never going to intervene in Ulster or Tibet is because it will be excluded by actual, as opposed to nominal, sovereignty."[44] Of course, India has not been able to convince UN bodies of its official position based on factual evidence, nor has it tried to. Thus, following a visit to India in 2012, the UN Human Rights Council's Special Rapporteur on Extrajudicial, Summary or Arbitrary Executions, South African jurist Christof Heyns, said that it was hard to reconcile what he observed in the country "with India's insistence that it is not engaged in an internal armed conflict."[45] Privately, Indian officials would probably agree with UN officials. They take a radically different position on the subject when speaking in domestic forums, including legal arenas. For example, in December of 2015 India's attorney general described the situation in Manipur as "warlike." He told a Supreme Court bench while defending the Indian Army against charges of extrajudicial killings that, "We are fighting an enemy." It may not be a conventional war, but there is "a constant war-like situation," where "a number of people, including security personnel, are being killed." In confronting armed groups seeking secession, said democratic India's principal legal spokesman, "we don't count bullets. [The] Army does not collect empty shells. We have to fire. We have to save ourselves, save the country and its people."[46]

The AFSPA regime makes Northeast India "an anomalous zone" within the republic "in which certain legal rules, otherwise regarded as embodying fundamental policies and values of the larger legal system, are locally suspended."[47] Crime and punishment in a "disturbed area" under AFSPA takes a very different form than in places under ordinary law. Consider section 144 of the Indian Penal Code (IPC), which prohibits public gatherings of more than four people in times of civil unrest. Local state authorities can impose this restriction in any part of India; and under the IPC an offense is punishable by six months in prison or fine or both. But the same offense in a disturbed area under AFSPA, as Wajahat Habibullah, a distinguished Indian civil servant with extensive experience in such matters, points out, becomes in effect punishable by death.[48] What AFSPA effectively does, writes political theorist Ananya Vajpeyi, is to "create an entirely separate space within India, a sort of second and shadow nation."[49] The situation is similar to what political scientist Guillermo O'Donnell once described as "undemocratic sub-national regimes" coexisting with "national-level democratic regimes." The foundation of a high-quality democracy, says O'Donnell, is "a truly democratic rule of law" and "not simply a rule of law in the minimal, historical sense." It would be difficult to claim that in a disturbed area under AFSPA, "all public and private agents are subject to appropriate, legally established controls on the lawfulness of their acts," which defines a democratic rule of law regime.[50]

There is often a tendency to assume that high voter turnout in regularly held elections, which is the case in Northeast India, is a sign of consent to India's democratic institutions.[51] But consent is never given over to some idealized and abstract notion of democracy and the rule of law; it is given to an actually existing political order. The local face of democracy in some parts of Northeast India can be the hybrid political regimes that I have described. For instance, in Nagaland, observes the anthropologist Jelle J. P. Wouters, "inhabitants often distance themselves (and are distanced from) ideas of India and 'Indianness'" and "a resistance movement against the Indian state continues to hold sway, eliciting considerable local support." Yet voter turnout in elections is often as high as 80 percent—significantly higher than the national average.[52] Indeed, armed groups in Northeast India are often enthusiastic participants in elections—certainly after signing a "peace accord" but before as well. They have a track record of successfully claiming a share of development funds—with the complicity of elected and appointed public officials. Who wins an election has always mattered to leaders of armed groups. They successfully navigate the electoral landscape and pursue alliances with elected politicians and appointed officials. Peace settlements usually bring with them a state commitment to substantially increase funds to promote development. Leaders of armed organizations—in their new role as a local governing authority—can then acquire control over significant public resources. Such arrangements blur the boundary between "state and society, between public and private."[53]

There is a long history of resistance to AFSPA in Northeast India. Especially memorable was the sixteen-year hunger strike by Manipuri civil disobedience campaigner Irom Sharmila to focus national attention on the devastating effects on civilian life of a disturbed area proclamation under AFSPA. But the protests had little resonance in the rest of India. What has enabled the persistence of this security regime is the othering of the people of Northeast India, and of the region, and the uncertain place they occupy vis-à-vis the affective boundaries of the nation.

## THE INSCRIPTION OF OTHERNESS

Imagined as an internal other, Northeast India is often represented in ways that reek of exoticism and internal orientalism. As recently as 2008, the Australian scholar Duncan McDuie-Ra observed multiple billboards for a museum in the region urging visitors to come and see "all the tribes of the Northeast under one roof."[54] They featured photographic representations of people in "traditional tribal" attire, one for each state. Six of the states were "embodied" as exotically dressed women dancers. The other two images, he writes, were of "a novice monk from Sikkim smiling shyly . . . and a Naga elder with a skull necklace and chest tattoos; the quintessential warrior." He found that the same eight images were reproduced in many tourism brochures.[55] A widely held image of Mizoram, write the authors of a social history of the state, is of "a faraway Shangri-La of green hills, bamboo groves and quaintly dressed, innocent exotics who danced a lot . . . , a happy land that was an asset to India but needed guardianship, guidance and uplift." This, they speculate, is the result of the way Mizos had been represented in choreographed performances of "unity in diversity" at celebrations of India's official nationalism.[56]

There is ample expression in contemporary Indian popular culture of the Northeast as a place of danger located outside the affective boundaries of the nation. The commonly used phrase "Northeast policy" is itself quite telling. Philosopher Mrinal Miri, who was born in the region, once asked: "To whom, or for whom, do you have a policy? The Northeast is a part of this country and at the same time we think that the people of the Northeast should be made the object of a policy." Human beings do not have a policy toward family members or friends. To be made an object of policy implies that the peoples of the region are not in a relationship of "human concerns such as love, friendship, understanding of the other" but in a relationship of manager and managed.[57]

A career in Northeast India is among their least preferred options for Indians entering the elite Indian Administrative Service. A young woman officer told anthropologist Dalel Benbabaali during her research on India's civil service that her parents wanted her to "marry within the caste, but . . . no well-settled man from my community would leave everything and go with me to the North-East. Life is difficult there, even for me." Another officer told her that when his mother heard about his appointment in Assam, "she started crying." The only time the poor woman had apparently heard of Assam was "in a Telugu movie in which the hero punishes the villain by putting him on a train to Assam."[58]

Military garrisons—increasingly "a fixture of everyday life" in Northeast India[59]—tend to reproduce the region's psychological and emotional separation from the mainland.[60] Sociologist Sanjay Barbora describes life inside military garrisons:

> Within their confines, soldiers and their families live in colonies that seek to provide them a semblance of the homes they have left behind in order to serve in counterinsurgency operations in the region. There are schools, cinema halls, canteens and clubs for servicemen that provide all the grocery and liquor available in other parts of India. Many have their families with them and the self-contained, secure parameters of the garrison do not require their families to ever leave. . . . The ability to reproduce a quality of life that is denied to those outside it is a remarkable achievement of the garrison.[61]

Outside those garrisons lies the world of "civilians—a term that is slightly pejorative in army talk—hence, not so important in the larger part of life that involves the garrison." The nonmilitary engagement of soldiers with the world outside is limited. Among the few occasions when they venture out could be a visit by "the officer in command (or his socially conscious spouse) . . . to local women's collectives or a self-help group that has been in the news locally.[62]

In journalist Anil Yadav's book on his travels through the region in the early 2000s, we read of a fellow traveler on a train to Assam offering him advice on the "country" he was going to visit. This copassenger is a soldier in India's Border Security Force (BSF). His native village in the Ghazipur District of Uttar Pradesh is not far from Yadav's own hometown. Assigned to a battalion in Assam, he was returning to work after two weeks on furlough at home. Here is Yadav's account of the advice he gets:

> Now that you're on your way, avoid the women and the mosquitoes there. Only then can you return to Ghazipur. "Damn! Is that even a country, Sir?" This was his catchphrase. He told me that in the BSF, personnel are made to line up, struck on their mouths and forced to swallow quinine tablets. There is also a standing order that they should sleep inside mosquito nets; there is a fine for defying that order. Life is always fragile, as if it were suspended upon a leaf, because who knows when the ULFA and Bodo wallas will arrive and start shooting. Militants freely roam among crowds of people, he said, like fish in water. Their presence would be known only after a few people were gunned down.[63]

Yadav points out that the border security man did not use the word *des* (country) to include the Northeast in the larger unity of India. Instead, "he was travelling from his 'des' to 'pardes' [abroad] to work there." He uses his copassenger's catchphrase "Damn! Is that even a country, Sir?" (*Wah Bhi Koi Des Hai Maharaj*) as the title of his travel book.[64] It is likely, however, that the Hindi words *des* and *pardes* have a less literal meaning here: they do not necessarily point to a distinction between home and abroad. As suggested by Aditya Nigam in a different context, this usage of these terms testifies to the fact that the common people in India negotiate their everyday lives "through a very different set of categories from the ones that the idea of nationhood accustoms us to."[65]

A significant part of Northeast India's population—majorities in Mizoram, Meghalaya, and Nagaland—are Christians. Christianity in this region—as in many other parts of the world—is seen as "our" religion, not a foreign religion. "We do not take Christianity as foreign religion," declared the Naga nationalist leader Angami Zapu Phizo in 1951, "any more than we consider the light of the sun as foreign."[66] Western missionaries may have pioneered proselytization and conversion during European colonization, but the agents of proselytization have for a long time been locals and other Indians. Many Rabhas of western Assam, for example, converted to Baptist Christianity because of efforts by Mizo missionaries. Ironically, this happened after the Indian government had expelled a group of Australian missionaries from the area, allegedly for their "anti-national activities." The missionaries from the Mizo Hills—regional neighbors of the Rabhas—turned out to be far more persuasive proselytizers than their Australian forerunners.[67] This is typical. Christian denominations with a significant presence in Northeast India include some that emphasize missionary work as essential to their faith. Northeasterners today may account for a significant proportion of Indian-born Christian missionaries in the world. Unfortunately, such facts do not fit well with resurgent Hindu cultural nationalist ideas about India's national space and territory. Hindu nationalism's majoritarian thrust equates India with Hinduism. Its discourse dwells on Hinduism's sacred geography—the stories of Hindu gods and heroes that link mountains, rivers, forests, and villages and turn them into a living landscape.[68] Certain extreme strands tend to define modern Hinduism as the religion of the Indian nation. Anyone living on "Hindu" territory is part of the "Hindu nation." Islam and Christianity, despite their long history in India, are "foreign" religions. Hindu majoritarian nationalists believe that Christian missionaries destabilize the nation by converting poor and marginalized communities to Christianity.[69] But their discourse of conversion, which focuses on the supposed gullibility of poor Indians falling prey to the machinations of foreign missionaries, strains credibility in the context of Christianity in Northeast India. In this part of the world, Christianity's appeal lies primarily in being what James C. Scott has called "a powerful, alternate and to some degree oppositional, modernity."[70] The phenomenon is best understood in the context of a long history of the peoples of the hills adopting religious identities that differed from those of the people of the valley states whose cultures had stigmatized them.

The large concentration of tribal people and the region's sizable Muslim and Christian populations have made Northeast India a priority area for Hindu nationalist organizations. The Hindu majoritarian Rashtriya Swayamsevak Sangh (RSS)—which describes itself as a "cultural organization"—and its affiliates have made significant inroads into the region. According to one estimate, they grew from about 650 branches in 1995 to more than 6,000 in 2017.[71] They have been a key force behind the spate of recent electoral successes of the Bharatiya Janata Party (BJP). Thus, the region today is simultaneously othered and incorporated. An illustrative example is these comments by the manager of a production facility being built in Assam of a multibillion-dollar Ayurvedic (traditional system of Indian medicine) products company owned by a billionaire yogi close to the Hindu nationalist establishment. The company conducted hundreds of workshops in Assam to train employees for its planned facility. Explaining the goals of the workshops to an American journalist, he said, "We are mentally conditioning them," teaching them a "value system." The people of Assam have "bad habits," and among them he listed their nonvegetarian food ethos and "a lack of proper respect for the nation."[72]

Ideologues of Hindu cultural nationalism have been deploying narratives of India's geographical unity as a sacred landscape partly to push back against the narratives of autonomy and self-determination that have dominated the politics of the region in recent years. They like to tell stories from the Mahabharata that revolve around female characters that were supposedly from this region and, according to certain myths, matrimonially related to Hindu gods and heroes. These are the "other" women of the Mahabharata.[73] Thus, Ulupi and Chitrangada—two women married to Arjuna—were supposedly Naga and Manipuri princesses; Krishna's consort Rukmini, a Mishimi girl from Arunachal Pradesh; and Bhima's wife Hidimba, a Dimasa woman from Assam. While these may be myths, says Mohan Bhagwat—the chief of the RSS—"the role of *Dharma* is to turn them into articles of faith, and to get people to believe in them."[74] This is consistent with the organization's perception of itself as the "archetypical collective guru, a contemporary depersonalized analogue of the Raj guru, who acts as counselor to official bearers of power." The RSS sees itself as guru not just to the BJP, with which it has long-standing political ties, but also to the nation as a whole.[75]

## Race and the Politics of Naming

There is perhaps no better evidence of the region's othering than the normalization of the racialized category *Northeasterner*. India's Home Ministry used the euphemism "the concerns of the people of the North East living in other parts of the country" to define the mandate of a committee formed in 2014 (the Bezbaruah Committee) to address racially motivated attacks on Northeasterners in the nation's capital.[76] Official India's reluctance to attach the word *race* to the lived experience of "people of the North East living in other parts of the country" is quite telling. The phenotypic traits that Indians seem to associate with Northeasterners[77]—as two anthropologists describe them—are "the epicanthic fold, high cheekbones and yellowish skin tones."[78] This perceived phenotypic difference could be traced back to the German naturalist J. F. Blumenbach's idea of the "Mongolian variety"—his name for the "race type" of the people of eastern Asia, including China and Japan.[79] The phrase "Mongolian fringe," coined by Olaf Caroe—the foreign secretary of British India in Delhi—in some ways foreshadows the term *Northeasterner*.[80] The divide between "Mongolians" and inhabitants of "India proper" seemed self-evident to British imperial geopolitical thinkers and colonial administrators.

To Foreign Secretary Caroe, the Mongolian fringe was British Imperial India's inner ring of defense.[81] In the official note where the phrase appears, he tries to show that China regards Tibet and certain neighboring areas as unredeemed lands. Caroe included in the Mongolian fringe Nepal, Sikkim, Bhutan, and the "North East Frontier Tracts" of what was then the frontier province of Assam.[82] In 1943 the North East Frontier Tracts was renamed the North East Frontier Agency (NEFA) as part of a plan to reorganize the British presence and gradually extend control up to the McMahon Line.[83] This territorial inheritance from the Raj, however, remained mostly "un-administered, if not unexplored," even at the time of decolonization; it "existed primarily in maps." There were no state institutions in many of these "frontier tracts" until the 1950s—even as late as the 1960s.[84] The name NEFA remained in use until 1972, when it was changed to Arunachal Pradesh. In 1957 the district of Nagaland of Assam and the Tuensang Frontier Tract—a part of NEFA until then—was combined into a new territorial unit: the Naga Hills–Tuensang Area. This territory became the state of Nagaland in 1963. China considers Arunachal Pradesh—the bulk of the North East Frontier Tracts of the colonial era—as a disputed territory and calls it "China's Southern Tibet." In India's unresolved border dispute with China, there are clear echoes of the geopolitical anxieties articulated by Caroe in the 1940s.

The people who in the eyes of British colonial officials were racially Mongolian inhabited not only the North East Frontier Tracts; they lived in many other parts of the colonial frontier province as well. In making the Mongolian fringe argument, Caroe, as he explained, included the tribes north of the Assam Valley because they were "inter-posed between India and Tibet, or as the Chinese would have it are part of Tibet and so part of China."[85] But he left out "tribes such as the Nagas"—in his words, "more interesting in many ways, which fringe the India-Burma border south of the Assam Valley, for that is a territory which leads to another part of the Empire, namely Burma."[86] A comment by Robert Reid, governor of Assam from 1937 to 1942, indicates that the entire hill population and parts of the plains population of this frontier province were racially Mongolian in British colonial eyes. The Assam Valley, said Reid, "contains a substratum of Mongolian population similar to that of the hills." He was building the case that the "backward areas" of Assam should not be grouped with those of the Central Indian Plateau. "The culture of the Mongolian areas," he said, "is different from, rather than lower than, that of the 'backward areas' of India proper, to which they neither historically nor racially belong."[87]

There were clear signs during the years immediately after decolonization that major Indian nationalist leaders had inherited the racialized gaze of colonial officialdom. Thus, Home Minister Vallabhbhai Patel, independent India's first home minister, wrote about the implications of the Chinese takeover of Tibet: "All along the Himalayas in the north and north-east, we have, on our side of the frontier, a population ethnologically and culturally not different from Tibetans or Mongoloids [*sic*]. The undefined state of the frontier and the existence on our side of a population with its affinities to Tibetans or Chinese have all the elements of the potential trouble between China and ourselves."[88] The racial ideas held by British colonial officials like Caroe and Reid no longer enjoy the respectability they once did. But it seems that people in most parts of the world still like to find ways to talk about the phenotypic traits of fellow humans that they see as different. Northeasterners have long complained of being subjected to racial slurs based on phenotypic stereotypes.[89] Evidently the visual phenotypes that Indians associate with Northeasterners have not found "a place in common imaginaries of the 'Indian Face.'" Many Northeasterners find themselves "nonrecognized and misrecognized, mirrored back by the wider Indian society as foreigners, hailing from such places as China, Nepal, Thailand, or Japan and on a visit to India, or as 'lesser Indians' rather than as equal citizens."[90]

A large number of Northeasterners now live in India's major metropolitan cities. Since India's official population data do not provide the places of origin of migrants, there is no reliable data on their numbers. But according to McDuie-Ra, it becomes "clear from qualitative research in Delhi and throughout the Northeast that more people are leaving the region than ever before and that the majority travel to Delhi."[91] Many of the niches they occupy in the service sectors of metropolitan India are related to their being perceived as less Indian and more foreign. Their "un-Indian looks and English language skills," write Bengt G. Karlsson and Dolly Kikon, have been key to their ability to find relatively high paying jobs in India's global services economy.[92] McDuie-Ra describes the elite consumer spaces in Delhi employing Northeasterners as "denationalised and de-Indianised spaces." Many of them are crafted as global spaces "stripped of overt Indian-ness." In high-end restaurants in Delhi, he writes, Northeastern waiting staff, dressed "authentically" to look Chinese or Korean as the occasion demands, lend an air of "East Asian cool." But not all sectors of India's new economy that attract Northeasterners valorize "visual orientalism." In the call centers of Delhi and elsewhere, it is not their looks but the fact that they do not speak Indian-accented English that makes Northeasterners attractive to employers.[93] English language proficiency is higher and more widespread in states like Meghalaya, Mizoram, Nagaland, and parts of Manipur than in most parts of mainland India. This is because of the long history of educational institutions established by Christian missionaries and the value attached to English language. Northeasterners have a competitive edge in entry-level service sector jobs where proficiency in English is a necessary skill. These relatively low-paying jobs do not attract mainlanders with the same level of proficiency in English since, historically, access to English education in mainland India has been restricted to relatively privileged groups.

Northeast Indian migrants to the mainland, however, come from more diverse economic backgrounds than what the examples above may suggest. Many of them occupy lower status and lower-paying jobs as well. Proficiency in English is, indeed, a crucial determinant in whether they are "able to enter the better-paid, up-scale service economy or end up in lower-end jobs in construction manufacturing or agriculture/plantations."[94] The two groups are on different migratory paths. Surveying the electoral landscape of Assam in 2016, researchers from the Centre for Policy Research in Delhi commented on the large-scale youth migration from the state. "Throughout our travels," they wrote, "we met many families who have at least one son serving as a security guard somewhere in Bengaluru or a plywood factory in Kerala or Tamil Nadu."[95]

Estimates of the number of Northeasterners living in Delhi vary widely. The Bezbaruah Committee cited the figure of more than two hundred thousand,[96] while some newspaper accounts put the number as high as seven hundred thousand.[97] The estimated number in Bengaluru is more than three hundred thousand. There are substantial numbers of people from Northeast India living in cities such as Hyderabad, Chennai, Pune, Mumbai, and Kolkata.[98] Some occupy certain distinct labor market niches in the country's globalized consumer spaces. In India's airlines industry and in up-market restaurants, shopping malls, hotels, and spas of Delhi, the English-speaking skills and "Oriental" looks of young Northeasterners—and of women in particular—are in great demand. It is not accidental that the upscale consumer spaces project a "global aesthetic" that seeks to satisfy the upper-middle-class Indians' desire to "live abroad in India."[99] Northeasterners have become essential accessories in some of these spaces. The trend is not limited to Delhi. Indeed, one of the paradoxes of India's economic globalization may be that Indians whose looks do not fit the stereotypes of the Indian face held by many Indians occupy a large share of front-line customer-facing positions in the hospitality and travel industries. The economic opportunities in India's growing service economy now draw thousands of young Northeasterners to the India mainland. The term *Northeasterner* has now acquired new resonance, partly because of this wave of migration. The lived experience of occupying a "minoritized space"[100] in the nation's capital—of being subjected to a racial gaze, racial taunts, and race-based discrimination—has led those living in Delhi to slowly forge "a nascent pan-Northeast identity."[101] A category based on a racialized regime of visuality,[102] however, can hardly be expected to be precise. Not every person from Northeast India inherits the phenotypic traits supposedly typical of a Northeasterner, nor are those facial features found only among people from that region. In a city like Delhi, for example, many Northeasterners are likely to share these facial traits with fellow residents from the rest of Caroe's Mongolian fringe, as well as with Indians of Tibetan or Chinese ancestry. Thus, Sunita Akoijam, a Manipuri author who has lived in both Delhi and Kathmandu, writes touchingly of her memories of Delhi, where she fought "a bitter battle against exclusion from India";

but of Kathmandu she remembers only "the sweet amusement of fighting off attempts at inclusion into Nepal."[103]

*National Belonging and Unbelonging*

In the summer of 2012, India came face-to-face with the race-based insecurity that people from the Northeast feel in the mainland. A rally in Mumbai to protest violence against Muslims in Burma and Assam precipitated rumors of reprisal attacks against Northeasterners circulated through social media. There was an exodus of panicked Northeasterners from cities like Bengaluru, Pune, and Chennai. Thousands headed to the security of their "home" region. A woman waiting for a train in Bengaluru to return "home" was quoted as saying, "We do not want to take any risk as nobody comes to our rescue when we are attacked."[104] Investigative reports in the media later revealed that manipulated photos and video footage circulating on social media were behind the exodus. Some of the most widely circulated images had their origins in events that occurred as far away as China and Thailand.[105] "Everyone who looks even vaguely northeastern—be it Nepalis, Assamese, Nagas or Mizos [was] quick to head to the train station."[106] A well-known Indian lawyer of Chinese descent—a resident of Bengaluru—wrote that during those days he suddenly became self-conscious of his physical features while in public spaces. "A miasma of fear, doubt and anxiety has descended on the city," wrote Lawrence Liang. "It is possible that much of this has been fueled by rumours and hearsay; and while the rumours may be false the fear sadly isn't."[107] The sight of thousands of Northeasterners fleeing major Indian cities in overloaded trains brought home the reality of the significant presence of "the Mongolian fringe" in metropolitan India. Many Indians would like to read this recent migration as pointing inexorably to the growing integration of the region with the "national mainstream." But the ethnicized, racialized, and gendered vulnerability that the exodus highlights tells a more complicated story of national belonging and unbelonging.

In January of 2014, the murder of a young man from Arunachal Pradesh in India's capital city, and the ensuing protests, led the Home Ministry to constitute the Bezbaruah Committee. Twenty-year-old Nido Taniam was killed in a brawl; racial insults were hurled at Taniam, and he refused to acquiesce. The incident, according to the veteran Delhi-based journalist and author Sanjoy Hazarika, marked a significant change of attitudes. A few years earlier, not many Northeasterners in Delhi would have dared to speak out against racial insults—"unsure of whether they would get support even from their peers." But that was no longer the case. "That is why when Nido reacted in fury to an insult and paid for it with his life, the outrage and mobilization at his death was spectacular."[108] The Bezbaruah Committee, to its credit, did not shy away from using the word *race*. It referred to a growing number of incidents of a "racial nature" involving Northeasterners in the National Capital Region—that is, Delhi and contiguous urban areas. The committee met groups and individuals who told of being subjected to racial slurs and abuse.[109] Delhi's fledgling North East Support Centre and Helpline reported in 2014 that it handles fifteen to twenty distress calls a month from victims and witnesses of such racial incidents.[110] Organizations representing residents with roots in Northeast India had long protested the refusal of the Delhi police to take these racial incidents seriously. After Taniam's murder, their cries received a more sympathetic response from the wider public. Leading national politicians attended the solidarity protests. Even Prime Minister Manmohan Singh met with Taniam's parents and assured them that the guilty would be punished. But reports of racial incidents have continued to appear in the press since then. In December of 2015, the Indian Supreme Court ruled on a petition regarding a number of hate crimes and issued a number of directives on the subject. The Bezbaruah Committee's report, it said, "should not, like innumerable instances of its ilk, languish on dusty shelves of long-forgotten archives." The Court was remarkably open about using the word *race* in this context. "The governments, both at the Centre and in the states, have a non-negotiable obligation to take positive steps to give effect to India's commitment to racial equality," said the ruling. It recommended the formation of a panel to receive and entertain complaints from individuals and groups of individuals who claim to be victims of racial abuse, racial atrocities, racial violence, and racial discrimination and forward them to the National Human Rights Commission and the state Human Rights Commissions and police stations for action.[111] But there has been no

legislative initiative so far to act on the key recommendation of the Bezba-
ruah Committee to amend the Indian Penal Code and the Code of Criminal
Procedure to recognize and punish the kind of hate crimes experienced by
Northeasterners.[112]

The epigraph of this chapter is from the autobiography of Braj Kumar
Nehru, a cousin of former prime ministers Jawaharlal Nehru and Indira
Gandhi, who was the governor of Assam and Nagaland during the time
when the region acquired its directional place-name. Nehru, before being
appointed governor, had held diplomatic positions, including India's
ambassador to the United States and high commissioner to the United
Kingdom. That was a world where, as he put it, he was engaged with
problems "worth trillions of dollars." To this cosmopolitan member of
the Indian elite, after life in London and Washington, DC, this "remote"
region of his home country was a "strange country."[113] As we have seen
in this chapter, he is by no means the only Indian to describe the region
as strange. But his explanation for this apparent strangeness—"incredibly
tiny groups of separate identities with problems so small that I could not
grasp why they should be bothered about"—provides an inadvertent clue
to why Northeast India has turned out such a convenient grouping: more
so than its creators could have imagined. The directional place-name and
its derivative *Northeasterner* have endured and gained in Indian popular
usage because they do more than just point to a relative geographical location; they stand in for a visual regime of racial profiling[114] and a relation
of unequal power.

CHAPTER 1

# THE INVENTION OF NORTHEAST INDIA

There were many efforts to pacify the Nagas, and through
concessions in 1963, the State of Nagaland was created. This
State was for a population of barely 500,000—less than the
population of many of the colonies of New Delhi—and yet all the
trappings that go with full Statehood, a Legislature, Cabinet, Chief
Minister, and later even Governor, went with this new status.
    —Lt. Gen. (Retd.) S. K. Sinha, Governor of Assam in 2001[1]

CERTAIN REGIONS OF THE WORLD may have roots in "deeply historical contexts of ethnonationalism," but others, writes geographer Anssi
Paasi, are "ad-hoc spatial units" put together for mundane administrative reasons or for purposes of economic planning. Northeast India belongs firmly to the latter category: regions that emerge "rapidly from the
desks of planners, politicians and business coalitions, . . . not from long
historical regionalization processes and the daily struggles of citizens."[2]
Embodied in this place-name, as I suggested in my introduction, is the
history of a series of ad hoc decisions made by national-security-minded
managers of the postcolonial Indian state. The cumulative effect of those
decisions was to institute a new governance structure that eventually replaced the administrative setup of a colonial frontier province. Five of the
eight states of what is called Northeast India now were part of colonial
Assam: Arunachal Pradesh, Assam, Meghalaya, Nagaland, and Mizoram.
Manipur and Tripura were "native" or "princely states," but the resident
British political officers or agents answered to the governor of Assam. The
history of one state—Sikkim—stands out from the other seven. It was
juridically independent during British colonial times but under British
paramountcy—or a part of Britain's informal empire.[3] With the end of
the Raj in 1947, Sikkim became an independent country. It was annexed

by India in 1975, and in 2001 Sikkim was made a member of the North Eastern Council—a statutory advisory body that consists of the member states of the regional formation—and thus formally a part of Northeast India. "Twins born out of a new vision for the Northeast" is how a former senior Indian civil servant who held top positions in the region and in India's Home Ministry describes two pieces of Indian parliamentary legislation of 1971: the North-Eastern Areas (Reorganization) Act and the North-Eastern Council Act. With these two laws, writes B. P. Singh, the region "emerged as a significant administrative concept . . . replacing the hitherto more familiar unit of public imagination, Assam."[4] It took a couple of decades longer for the racially inflected term *Northeasterner* to emerge. Since the new governance structure and its naming were the result of a process of muddling through—and not much thought was given to its possible consequences—it was perhaps inevitable that it would create as many new problems as it would solve.[5]

Northeast India's population is unevenly distributed across these eight states. Assam is by far the largest in terms of population. It has 69 percent of the region's population of 45.7 million. Tripura is the next most populous state, but it accounts for only 8 percent of the population.[6] The other six states are among the least populous in the country. The reasons are historical and geographical. Present-day Assam consists mostly of what were "the plains" and the "settled" districts of the colonial frontier province.[7] Ever since the beginnings of the tea, coal, and oil industries in the nineteenth century, the area has been a magnet for migrants from other parts of the subcontinent. It remains to this day the region's economic heartland. Colonial administrators did not expect the population density of the hill areas to ever become high. "In fact over half of Assam's total area of 67,000 square miles," said the Census Report for 1931, "consists of hilly and mountainous country which never did and never will support a dense population."[8] But this was before the advent of the postcolonial era of development. Still, the population density of these areas—which are now mostly full-fledged states—remains low. Tripura was a sparsely populated "princely state" in the British colonial era. But during and after the Partition of 1947, large numbers of Hindu refugees moved and settled there. This migration changed the state's demographic balance, which has had important political consequences.[9] The relatively low population of most Northeast Indian states has meant that they have little influence in national-level decision making. In India's quasi-federal dispensation,[10] the number of members of Parliament a state elects to India's national Parliament is determined by population. In the lower house of Parliament, Mizoram, Nagaland, and Sikkim have a single member each, while Arunachal Pradesh, Manipur, Meghalaya, and Tripura have two members each. The country's largest state, Uttar Pradesh, by contrast, has eighty members. The only state in the region with a parliamentary delegation comparable in number to some of the midsize states (in population) in the rest of India is Assam, which has fourteen members.

## THE EXCLUDED AREAS OF COLONIAL ASSAM

On a February evening in 1944, while the Second World War still raged, Robert Reid—a recently retired member of the Indian Civil Service— addressed a meeting of the Royal Geographical Society in London. The title of his lecture was "The Excluded Areas of Assam," but Reid also discussed what were called "Partially Excluded Areas." These territories are now a large part of today's Northeast India. The Southeast Asian front of the war at that time drew significant global attention to this frontier. While Reid emphasized the area's heterogeneity, the people of the Excluded Areas, he said, shared one thing in common: "neither racially, historically, culturally, nor linguistically [do] they have any affinity with the people of the plains, or with the people of India proper." If they were "tacked on as an Indian province," it was only a matter of historical accident and "a natural administrative convenience."[11] In British imperial ethnography, this point of view had by then become the conventional wisdom about that region.

Reid designed his lecture for the London audience as an introduction to the Excluded Areas and its peoples. He guided them through a map and showed photographs of the region's inhabitants. He spoke with great authority. Reid, after all, had until recently been the governor of Assam (from 1937 to 1942). He was forthright about placing people on a "civilizational" scale, and he confidently expressed his likes and dislikes. The "Dufflas, Akas, and Miris," he said, are "very primitive peoples, who respond hardly at all to the influences of civilization." While the Nagas of the Tirap Frontier Tract were "rather a degraded, backward type," in their "abode proper" they were "frank and independent by nature, often [exhibiting] a cheerful and hospitable disposition." Indeed, the qualities of "those picturesque people," said Reid, appealed to "the men who work there"—that is, the British colonial administrators who had "become devotedly attached to them."[12]

Phrases like "abode proper" and "backward and degraded type" underscore the British colonial inclination to fix "tribes" to their supposed natural habitats. This was in keeping with the old "anthropological construction of natives." The natives in anthropological discourse, as Arjun Appadurai puts it, are not only "persons who are from certain places, and belong to those places, but they are also those who are somehow incarcerated, or confined, in those places." They are always in their place—"a place to which explorers, administrators, missionaries, and eventually anthropologists, come."[13] But Reid did more than simply assume the "incarceration" of the natives in their place. To borrow Paul Gilroy's words, Reid had a "bio-cultural" notion of ethnic traits as "fixed, solid almost biological," and inheritable.[14] In Reid's construction, the natives of the Excluded Areas develop their "natural traits" in their "natural habitats." Because of the mixing of ethnicity with territory—what I would call a frame of ethnoterritoriality—colonial administrators made a distinction between "pure" and "impure" subtypes of what they determined to be a tribal group. In their minds, this paradigm explained the characteristics of people who did not conform to their ethnic stereotypes: those who stay in their assigned habitats versus those who presumably stray away. Here is an example of such thinking from a nineteenth-century colonial text: "On the side of the Burrail facing us, were villages belonging to a tribe we call Kutcha Nagas, a race inferior in fighting power to the Angamis, but not unlike them in appearance, though of inferior physique."[15] The Indic word *kutcha* means raw, uncooked, or unfinished; the implication of the name assigned to the group "Kutcha Nagas" is that they are not quite fully Naga.

Northeast India presented a peculiar set of conceptual problems to the British colonial scholar-administrator. Apart from the question of the phenotypic traits of the people, and the related issue of racialization discussed in the previous chapter, the "egalitarian" mores and habits of many of them—the absence of caste, in particular—did not conform to the British colonial idea of India as a "hierarchical" civilization with caste as its essential marker. Are these people inside the racial unity of India, or are they outside of it? There was no easy answer; the ethnic kin of the same people sometimes performed Hindu-like rituals a short distance away. Facts such as these had to be either assimilated into the master principle of caste or categorized as being outside the caste order and yet inside the racial unity of India. As anthropologist Matthew Rich argues, hills and plains emerged as the master oppositional binary as a solution to this problem.[16] The region's peoples came to be classified as belonging to either the hills or the plains; no one could belong to both. But neither the precolonial settlement patterns nor the political formations were bounded within these spaces. For instance, the Khasis—now regarded as native to the Khasi Hills of Meghalaya—were pushed to the hills only after confrontations between the East India Company and the "mountain Khasis and Bengali Khasis" of Sylhet in 1789. As historian David Ludden points out, the company, after its military victory over the Khasis, proclaimed "an absolute boundary at the base of the hills and prohibited Khasis from owning land in the plains, to vitiate future claims by Khasi rulers to Company land." This, says Ludden, is how "a modern border came into being, which would eventually separate Indian Meghalaya from Bangladeshi Sylhet. Khasi hills thus acquired an official ethnic identity, as hill Khasis became official aliens in the plains."[17]

Reid and many of his British colleagues in the civil service saw themselves as experts on the peoples and the cultures of this imperial frontier. Colonial civil servants in frontier regions typically persisted in their claim of "knowing their natives" till the last days of empire. They viewed the prospects of decolonization with disfavor—even alarm. In Northeast India a few launched a quiet opposition to decolonization even after the government in London had made up its mind to transfer power to Indian hands. Reid made little effort to hide his political preferences. Whatever India's future political dispensation may turn out to be, he had no doubt that the peoples of the Excluded Areas would have less "protection" or that protection may even be abolished. Appealing to the paternalism of his compatriots, he said: "We are responsible for the future welfare of a set of very loyal, primitive peoples, who are habituated to look to us for protection and who will get it from no other source." Reid made the case for continued British control of "a civil administrative unit comprising the Hill Areas along the north and east frontiers of Assam and taking in as well the similar areas in Burma itself."[18] Not all of his colleagues in the administration agreed with him. His successor as governor of Assam, Andrew Clow, thought it most unlikely that "a British Government which is prepared to set India and Burma on a self-governing footing should now undertake the financial and administrative responsibility for a patchwork of sparsely populated hills lying where these hills do." He rightly surmised that Indian opinion was sure to oppose such a move. Clow not only pointed to the obvious political difficulties; he objected to Reid's proposal on substantive grounds as well.[19]

Historians know this proposal as the Crown Colony scheme. In the emerging postwar world order there was little chance of a new British-controlled political entity coming up on the Indo-Burmese border. History was destined to prove Reid wrong. The principle of self-determination would soon become an international legal norm, not just a political ideal,[20] despite its restricted meaning to apply only to "non self-governing territories" as per the UN definition. Peoples of the Excluded Areas began participating in India's democratic institutions soon after India became independent in 1947. Contrary to Reid's fears, the safeguards to protect the peoples of those territories were mostly retained, and they were placed under the supervision of elected bodies. The results, however, as I will argue in Chapter 3, were mixed. Most of these territories that Reid talked about in his speech are now among the states of Northeast India. Though technically full-fledged units of the Union of India, they are states in a somewhat cosmetic sense.[21] This chapter's epigraph cites the condescending words of a former military general who was a governor of a Northeastern state describing one of these states, which nicely illustrates the view from New Delhi.

## THE POLITICAL GEOGRAPHY OF AN IMPERIAL FRONTIER

This debate during the last days of empire about the future of Excluded Areas reminds us that the colonial territories inherited by national elites in the last century were, in the words of legal historian Lauren Benton, often "politically fragmented; legally differentiated; and encased in irregular, porous, and sometimes undefined borders." All colonial powers, as she put it, created "semiautonomous spaces that were legally and politically differentiated from more closely controlled colonial territories."[22] The imperialist *par excellence* Viceroy George Nathaniel Curzon described the British Empire's frontier as threefold: there was an administrative border, a frontier of active protection, and an outer or advanced strategic frontier.[23] The colonial effort to establish direct rule—that is, modern property rights and a modern legal and administrative system—was limited to the territories located within the administrative border. These were the settled districts of the frontier province: most of present-day Assam and Sylhet, now in Bangladesh. With the production of tea, oil, and coal, this area had become an enclave of global capitalism by the closing decades of the nineteenth century.

The handover of large tracts of so-called wastelands to European tea planters subverted old economic and social networks and property regimes in the region. There were frequent attacks on the plantations by "tribesmen" protesting their dispossession during the early years of tea in Assam. Colonial writings portrayed them as marauding barbarians. The Inner Line—first introduced in 1873—was an attempt to fence off the plantations and cordon off areas of clear, cemented colonial rule. But the Inner Line was redrawn repeatedly "to accommodate the expansive compulsions of plantation capital, the recognition of imperfection in survey maps, the security anxiety of the state and the adaptive practices of internally differentiated local communities."[24] In effect, land was repeatedly transferred "between administration and un-administration."[25] The protocols of governance in these areas differed fundamentally from that of direct rule, under which the settled districts of Assam, which formed part of the "more closely controlled" parts of the empire,[26] were governed.

Beyond the indirectly ruled Excluded and Partially Excluded Areas were the Tribal Areas of Assam claimed as British territories. Viceroy Curzon called it a zone of "active protection." It consisted of "an immense tract of country," said Robert Reid, "over which we exercise [control], within the frontier though it be only the most shadowy control."[27] There was no interest in extending modern governmental institutions into those areas. Occasional military expeditions to teach the "primitive tribesmen" a lesson was considered adequate. A minimal administrative presence was gradually established in some of these areas, but even when British colonial rule came to an end, there were places with no state presence whatsoever. In the rest of this book, I will use the term *excluded areas* (in lower case) to include the territory that was called the Tribal Areas of Assam as well. Thus, unless otherwise indicated, excluded areas will include what in colonial times were three separate groups of territories: Excluded Areas, Partially Excluded Areas, and the Tribal Areas of Assam.

Beyond the Tribal Areas of Assam was Curzon's advanced "strategic" frontier. These territories, though technically independent, were expected to serve as buffer states. Both imperial diplomacy and military power were deployed for this purpose. This peculiar aspect of the imperial frontier system is the source of India's border dispute with China, which remains unresolved to this day. The McMahon Line, which defines the outer limits of Curzon's zone of "active protection," was supposed to be the boundary between India and Tibet, and Tibet was expected to function as a buffer state. An "intimate entanglement between the imperial and the national," writes historian Bérénice Guyot-Réchard, has shaped both Indian and Chinese policies in the eastern Himalayas. While the countries see themselves as victims of imperialism, their claims and governance methods are part of the inheritance of empire: the British in India's case, the Manchu in China's. "The tension between the two" imbues both countries "with a lasting sense of anxiety and vulnerability."[28] Guyot–Réchard's insight is useful for understanding India's Northeast policy more generally.

The institution of indirect rule developed in British colonial practice as a response to the perceived crisis of direct rule—that is, the demand for self-rule by the colonized. Direct rule created a volatile political configuration by racializing the identity of the rulers and the ruled—the former as a minority, the latter as the majority.[29] Indirect rule was designed as a response to this crisis. In effect, it meant abandoning the civilizational project of incorporating natives into Western modernity by governing them under a single law. Under indirect rule, each putative tribe was to be governed under its own set of "customary law." The political purpose was to circumvent the modernizing native elites and cultivate a set of pseudo-traditional elites, who were expected to shape the preferences of fellow tribesmen in a "traditional" direction. Indirect rule was an attempt to stabilize colonial rule through "a legal project that fractured the singular, racialized and majority identity, *native*, into several, plural, ethnicized, minority identities—called *tribes*."[30] We now know from works such as *The Camera as Witness*, by Joy Pachuau and Willem van Schendel, that indirect rule as a cultural project—of cultivating a pseudo-traditional elite—was unsuccessful. In the case of the Mizos, the rejection of this policy can be traced as far back as the beginning of the twentieth century. To a new Christian elite—exposed to European-style education in missionary schools—wearing Western dress became a way of expressing "a novel sense of modernity and sophistication, and it distinguished them from uneducated people."[31] As Julian Jacobs observes in the context of the Nagas, who inhabited another excluded area, they were "caught between two alternative Western views of what they should become: a missionary attitude which banned everything traditional, but which offered education, 'modern' aspirations, and freedom from the burden of communal obligations; and an administrative perspective which banned head-hunting but was passionately in favor of everything else traditional, and came close to advocating the isolation of Naga society in an unchanging primitive past."[32]

Colonial administrators in this region criticized the American Baptist missionaries for "strenuously imposing an alien Western culture on the converts." In his book *The Ao Nagas*, colonial administrator and ethnographer J. P. Mills complained that even though "no member of the Mission has ever studied Ao customs deeply, . . . nearly all have been eager to uproot what they neither understood nor sympathize with, and substitute for it a superficial civilization."[33] Writing when it was common to question the authenticity and finality of conversions to Christianity, Mills believed that the "authentic" Ao culture would reassert itself one day. Like most of his contemporaries, he failed to recognize the emergence of a new strain of cultural politics within the late colonial order: the struggle for equal membership within a modern world society.[34] Wearing European-style clothes was becoming a way of asserting the claim "to be respected by the Europeans and by one another as civilized, if humble, men, members of the new world society."[35] But while indirect rule as a cultural project may have failed, as a legal and political project it was an overwhelming success. In the administered excluded areas of Assam, customary laws that were reinforced by state power were able to impose group identities on individual subjects and institutionalize group life.[36] Until this day, they define the ethnic boundaries of groups defined as "tribes"—almost always in variance with the historical practices of these groups.[37] Not only have the legacies of indirect rule persisted under postcolonial rule; the protocols designed for the excluded areas have occasionally been extended to nonexcluded areas—that is, to territories that were part of the settled districts in colonial times.[38] Even in the "settled" districts of Assam, however, the legal and administrative structures in some ways were not always "direct." For instance, until 1926, Assam's tea plantations had an indenture system of labor recruitment. The labor contract was privately enforced, and plantation owners had the legal power to arrest absconding workers without a warrant if the nearest magistrate was more than ten miles away.[39] Although those penal clauses were repealed in 1908, and the indenture contract system was abolished in 1926, the arrest of absconders continued well after the 1908 repeal of the penal provisions. As historian Prabhu Mohapatra writes: "As late as 1930 the Royal Commission on Labour could see visible traces of the penal contract system on the backs of a few flogged laborers.... The penal legislation may have been abolished, but the huge unrelenting apparatus of surveillance and detention, carefully created since 1860, remained. So did labor resistance, reflected in high rates of desertion throughout the period, and in violent conflicts that broke out every year between the planters and the coolies. Assam had the most such conflicts of all the Asian plantation systems."[40]

When colonial rule came under siege in large parts of India, British residents of Assam were extremely aware of—and were immensely satisfied with—what indirect rule could accomplish in this frontier province, both in the excluded areas and in the settled districts. A tea planter in Assam, George M. Barker, described Assam in 1884 as "the last remaining district where any sort of respect is shown for Europeans; in all other parts of India the black man is as good as the white, a fact that is speedily brought home to a new comer." He continued: "It is here, in Assam, that nearly all the old rights of servility that were exacted by Europeans in the days of the East India Company, are still in existence, and flourish to the general better feeling amongst the whole community. Here no heavy babu swaggers past with his umbrella up, jostling you on the way; but with courtly mien, on seeing your pony coming along, furls up the umbrella, steps on one side, and salutes with a profound salaam."[41]

Historian Amalendu Guha had aptly described this exceptional political regime as a "planter Raj that tyrannised over the entire people."[42] During the final decades of British colonial rule, Indian nationalists raised objections to the excluded area regime. That insulating the people of the excluded areas from anticolonial ideas was one of the goals of this policy had become quite obvious by then. Moreover, the excluded areas were left outside the jurisdiction of the newly elected provincial governments that Indian nationalists had come to control.[43] But the Naga assertion of a separate national will at the very moment of India's independence became a warning signal to India's new rulers that the excluded areas under postcolonial rule would be vulnerable to political unrest. Suddenly, the surge of nationalism that had carried them to power seemed fragile. It became amply apparent that they lacked the political capital to reform the institutions of indirect rule in Northeast India. The Constituent Assembly decided to proceed with abundant political caution and made the fateful decision to live with important elements of the indirect rule regime, albeit with some modification. As a result, colonial territorialization—the Inner Line, as well as the other boundaries and hierarchies—remains firmly in place in postcolonial Northeast India to this day. Privileging those with state-backed ethnic credentials as indigene over those that colonial law regarded as settlers/migrants forms the foundation of the postcolonial political order of the colonial-era excluded areas. Class formation in these areas has followed a predictable trajectory. Two political scientists have argued that while indirect rule is conventionally thought of as a colonial form of governance, it did not always end with decolonization. Throughout the postcolonial world, they find "interactions between states and local elites, notables, and armed groups that reflect discrete indirect governance strategies."[44] This is certainly true of Northeast India, and it has had significant implications for the practice of citizenship in this region. Of course, the political history of Sikkim is not part of the set of events that I just outlined. But national security concerns did feature in the decision to bring this Himalayan kingdom into the ambit of Northeast India.

## OTHER LEGACIES OF THE IMPERIAL FRONTIER

The Himalayan kingdoms Nepal, Bhutan, and Sikkim—the last one now a part of Northeast India—were also part of the frontier system, a *cordon sanitaire* around British Imperial India.[45] In his 1940 note on the Mongolian fringe, Olaf Caroe described them as "the juridically independent State of Nepal, Sikkim, hitherto considered as an Indian State, and the Protectorate of Bhutan, a semi-independent State in special treaty relations with the government of India."[46] The ethnic Nepali population of this region—Bhutan, the Darjeeling District of West Bengal, Sikkim, and certain other parts of Northeast India—is a legacy of the informal empire. They are descendants of migrants from the hills of eastern Nepal. Not only were there no restrictions when they began migrating in the nineteenth century; migration was actively encouraged. Originally speakers of multiple languages, "the post-migration generations" speak Nepali as their primary language. By the time British colonial rule came to an end, ethnic Nepalis were the majority population in Sikkim, in five southern Dzonkhangs of Bhutan, and in the Indian district of Darjeeling—now in the state of West Bengal.[47] There are substantial ethnic Nepali communities in Assam and Meghalaya; however, as a result of the "illegality regimes"[48] introduced in the newly independent countries, suddenly the citizenship status of ethnic Nepalis in the entire region became vulnerable. This aspect of decolonization has not received much attention in the context of South Asia.[49] But it is extremely significant for Northeast India's postcolonial history.

Ethnic Nepali political assertion in Sikkim facilitated the Himalayan kingdom's merger with India in 1975. The ethnic Nepalis of Sikkim descend from migrants who were brought into this sparsely populated region after the British acquired political control over the territory in 1888. They are now Sikkim's dominant population, both numerically and politically. In the 1990s, ethnic Nepalis came under a harsh illegality regime in Bhutan. Nearly one hundred thousand Lhotshampas—southern Bhutanese in the Dzongkha language—were expelled. During the same period, they became victims of ethnic violence in Assam and Meghalaya. Ethnic Nepali political mobilization in this entire region has been an effort to assert citizenship rights in response to this growing sense of vulnerability. They form the social basis of the Gorkhaland movement in Darjeeling. Indeed, the use of the term *Gorkha* is itself "a means of claiming Indian citizenship."[50] Ethnic Nepali political activists prefer this term since it avoids the confusion between citizens of Nepal and ethnic Nepali citizens of independent India inherent in the term *Nepali*. The political developments in the states of Northeast India and in Darjeeling and Bhutan in the 1980s and 1990s had an interrelated chain of causation.

## ON THE MORROW OF INDEPENDENCE

Five of the eight states of the official region—Assam, Arunachal Pradesh (then the North East Frontier Agency), Nagaland, Meghalaya, and Mizoram—were part of Assam when India's new Constitution was inaugurated in 1950. In the version of colonial frontier administration that persisted beyond decolonization, the governor of Assam was given certain special powers, and an adviser on tribal affairs assisted him in this task. Two of the other states of the region—Manipur and Tripura—were "Part C states": a category made up of small "princely states" of the colonial era that became the Chief Commissioner's Provinces. The status of Manipur, however, remained ambiguous for a couple of years.[51] Its integration into India was anything but smooth, and it remains a persistent source of bitterness and controversy. As many Manipuri narratives would have it, full independence had returned to Manipur at the end of British colonial rule.[52] It adopted a democratic constitution based on the principles of Britain's constitutional monarchy, and a democratic assembly, based on male adult suffrage, was elected. But "under the new maneuvers by the succeeding Dominion of India ... Manipur was merged into the new state ... in October 1949, and the assembly was dissolved."[53] Indeed, all evidence points to the Maharaja of Manipur signing the agreement of merger with India under significant "duress" and "coercion."[54] Nearly every Manipuri account of the state's modern history, says long-term commentator on the region M. S. Prabhakara, "begins with a recital of the circumstances under which the territory lost its independent status and was merged into the Union of India. The thrust of all these accounts is that the merger of Manipur was accomplished with a combination of cajolement, promises that were not kept, and plain trickery." Indeed, this period of postcolonial history features prominently in the narratives of Manipuri political groups that speak the language of armed resistance today.[55] When Manipur was made into a Chief Commissioner's Province—a Part C state—following its controversial merger, the ancient kingdom of Manipur, says the highly respected Manipuri intellectual Lokendra Arambam, was reduced to "an obscure and backward part of the Indian Union."[56] Both princely states— Manipur and Tripura—first became Union Territories, and they became states of the Indian Union in 1972.

The Indian Constitution treated the excluded areas of Assam very differently from other areas of the country with concentrations of Scheduled Tribes (ST). Whereas the Fifth Schedule covers tribal areas in other parts of the country, the Sixth Schedule was designed for the excluded areas of Assam. Although the Constitution made extensive provisions for protective discrimination in favor of the STs all over the country, the provisions for STs in the excluded areas of Northeast India were different from those for STs in the rest of India. This is how the indirect rule regime of the colonial era was given a new lease of life.[57] The Sixth Schedule provided for autonomous districts and autonomous regions. These districts were to have elected councils empowered to levy some taxes and to constitute courts for the administration of customary law—justice involving tribals, and lawmaking powers on areas including land allotment, occupation or use of land, regulation of shifting cultivation, formation and administration of village and town committees, appointment of chiefs, inheritance of property, and marriage and social customs. But the formation of autonomous district councils did not proceed the way the Constitution makers had anticipated. The outbreak of the Naga rebellion meant that political conditions for holding elections to the Naga Hills District Council did not exist. So when the state of Nagaland was created in 1963, Article 371-A was inserted into the Constitution of India to extend similar protections to the people of Nagaland. According to this article, laws passed by the Indian Parliament that impinge on Naga customary practices—including matters of ownership and transfer of land—would not apply to Nagaland unless the Nagaland Assembly explicitly decided to do that. Since state institutions were nearly absent in most parts of the North East Frontier Agency (NEFA; today's Arunachal Pradesh and a part of Nagaland), the Sixth Schedule provisions could not be immediately put into effect. For a number of years after decolonization, this area was administered from New Delhi with the governor of Assam acting as the agent of the president of India. The Sixth Schedule was eventually supposed to be in place in this region. But because of the Indo-China war of 1962, the area went through a process of institutional reforms that differed dramatically from what the Constitution makers had had in mind.

## INDEPENDENCE AND THE POLITICS
## OF NATIONAL INSECURITY

During the first few years of India's Independence, a sense of national insecurity vis-à-vis the frontier province was almost palpable in the nation's capital. In my introduction I alluded to fears expressed by Home Minister Patel during the Chinese invasion of Tibet, about the undefined nature of India's border with Tibet, and the possible sympathies of people on the Indian side with those on the other side.[58] The Naga National Council headed by A. Z. Phizo boycotted India's first general elections in 1952; no Naga contested those elections. Naga nationalists set up a parallel government, and tensions with the government of India grew. The knowledge and experience inscribed into the institutional practices of the state played a key role in Indian decision making during this period.[59] This was certainly the case with the decision to respond militarily to the Naga rebellion. Nari Rustomji of the Indian Civil Service, who held a number of key positions in the region, including the position of adviser to the governor of Assam on tribal affairs, remembered the turn of events in the Naga Hills this way: "It may well be asked how such a ghastly tragedy could have been enacted at all with civilized and intelligent human beings at the helm of the administration. Part of the blame may be ascribed to the tradition of decision-making by precedent inherent in the administrative processes and inherited from the predecessor government. It was generally assumed during the early years of Independence, that the British technique of dealing with a situation was necessarily the correct technique, forgetting that the circumstances of the situation might be entirely different and necessitate a totally different approach."[60]

No one seems to have quite known how to think differently from the colonial administrators on matters affecting the colonial frontier province. A sense of insecurity that gripped the newly independent country's governing elite affected even decisions related to the location of strategic public sector industries. A controversy that arose over setting up of a public sector oil refinery is illustrative. The history of India's oil industry begins with the discovery of oil in Assam in the 1880s. Assam accounted for as much as half of India's total oil production during the first two decades after decolonization. The oil town of Digboi in Assam, in the words of an industry publication, "boasts two modern wonders of the world—a hundred-year-old oil field that is still producing and the world's oldest operating oil refinery, which produces in excess of its capacity."[61] Yet in the 1950s, national security concerns made the leaders of newly independent India extremely nervous about setting up a new public sector oil refinery in Assam. They decided to locate it in the state of Bihar instead—with a 1,400 km pipeline bringing crude from the oil fields of upper Assam. The decision became a source of contention between the state government and central government—both ruled by the Congress Party. "If Defence cannot undertake to protect the refinery located in Assam," asked Assam Chief Minister Bishnuram Medhi rhetorically in a letter to Prime Minister Nehru, "how will they protect the oil-fields and the transport system in the Eastern Region?" He called on the central government "not to think of protection of the refinery separately from the oil fields and the transport system, but to treat the refinery, oil fields and the lines of transport as parts of an integrated defence system."[62]

At the same time, some fresh thinking did begin to take place when leaders of independent India began facing the challenges of actually governing the region. Jawaharlal Nehru's notes during his first visit to the region as prime minister in 1952 are revealing. He commented on the radical difference between the conditions of the STs in the excluded areas of Assam and those in the rest of the country. The people of these areas, he said, referring to certain parts of the excluded areas, "never came in contact with our freedom movement. They were isolated and kept apart from it and, therefore, they were not prepared psychologically for the changes that have taken place. They had hardly come in contact with Indians as such and most of their dealings in the past, were with the British officers and foreign missionaries. Thus they lack the feeling of oneness with the rest of India or the Indian people and are greatly afraid that their small numbers will be swamped by others.... Their minds are full of apprehension about the future."[63]

Nehru's understanding was consistent with what we know about conditions in the excluded areas in the late colonial era. In the Mizo areas, for instance, the experience of colonialism was shorter and profoundly different from that of the settled areas. Middle-class educated Mizos did not feel they had much in common with Indians from the plains. Indian nationalism had almost no appeal, and colonial authorities were able to maintain control relatively easily.[64] The key challenge in these areas, concluded Nehru, was "how to remove this fear [of being swamped] and suspicion from their minds and how to make them feel at one with India.... Everything else is subordinate to this." He openly expressed doubts about whether the Sixth Schedule was robust enough to meet this challenge. If they cannot "remove the feeling of apprehension from the minds of these people," he said, he would not hesitate to change the Sixth Schedule.

"Generally speaking, tribal people," he wrote, "are in a questioning mood, trying to find out what is going to happen to them. . . . Their attitude thus is a mixture of hope and apprehension and every little incident emphasizes one or the other aspect." The Naga situation was already becoming a serious concern for Nehru: "The Nagas are definitely non-cooperative and even to some extent hostile," he wrote. "I refer particularly to the Nagas of the Hills Districts here and not to the Nagas elsewhere." His lack of sympathy for the rebel Nagas was quite evident in these notes. Yet Nehru seems to have developed some admiration for the organizing capacity and political savvy of the Naga National Council (NNC). Because of "their disciplined and . . . very effective non-cooperation," he wrote somewhat grudgingly, it had not been possible to form a District Council in the Naga Hills District as provided for in the Constitution's Sixth Schedule. But he did not particularly care for the Naga leader A. Z. Phizo. He said he had formed a "poor opinion" of Phizo, whom he had met twice by then: "His demand on behalf of Nagas is for independence. I have explained to him and to others in the clearest language that this is nonsense and we are not going to consider it. . . . I think we can ignore Zapu Phizo as a person." Nehru emphasized the need for "a very friendly approach on the one hand and firmness, where needed."[65]

A duality in the postcolonial state's approach to Northeast India was already beginning to take shape. If the disastrous military response to the Naga rebellion was an example of Nehruvian "firmness" at work, the experiments tried out in NEFA in the 1950s and 1960s under Verrier Elwin's leadership epitomized the "friendly approach." But the "friendly approach" was not necessarily a radical departure from colonial practice. Elwin's NEFA policies were, in fact, similar to a colonial mode of addressing "the contradiction between difference and improvement." Anthropologist Tania Murray Li calls it trusteeship: the effort to create "authentic otherness" by teaching "natives to be truly themselves" and "to improve native life ways by restoring them to their authentic state."[66] Not only were these policies firmly rejected by NEFA's inhabitants, but, as Guyot-Réchard has persuasively shown, they ultimately undermined nation-building and planted "the seed for future conflicts."[67]

## THE INVENTION OF NORTHEAST INDIA

The 1960s were turbulent years for postdecolonization India. A border war with China erupted in 1962, and the movement for Naga independence was in full swing. India and Pakistan fought a war in 1965, and the Mizo rebellion began the following year. After the 1962 war with China—and India's defeat—the fears expressed by Patel, about the challenge to national security if the country's external and domestic enemies were to join hands, became jarringly immediate. That the state of Nagaland was created a year after the China War is no accident. In retrospect, it turned out to be the first step toward replacing the administrative structure of the frontier province with a new structure of governance. By making Nagaland into a state, Indian officials hoped to create Naga stakeholders in the Indian dispensation that would help quell the Phizo-led rebellion. The epigraph of this chapter is from a speech by S. K. Sinha made in 2001. A retired general and veteran of counterinsurgency in Northeast India, he was then the governor of Assam. His use of the term *pacify*—a reminder of the horrors of colonial violence—is striking.[68] Others, however, have argued that the creation of Nagaland "not only proved the flexibility and the accommodative power of the Indian constitution, but also indicated that the Indian state, its repressive face notwithstanding, was also slowly learning to adjust itself to the autonomy demands of small nationalities."[69] The amendment to the Constitution, especially the insertion of clause 371-A, which gives special prerogatives to the state, writes political theorist Rajeev Bhargava, goes "a long way in protecting the Naga 'way of life.'" If the move failed to satisfy Naga aspirations, Bhargava believes it was partly because of the "pivotal role of timing in politics." The decision to grant autonomy to Nagaland came only "after an underground extremist movement for secession had already been strengthened." Furthermore, the formal autonomy granted to Nagaland was at odds with the actually existing governance structure that evolved because "the Indian governing elite and the army act ... differently with 'normal' and 'deviant' states."[70]

A number of moves followed the creation of Nagaland that eventually led to the dismantling of the remaining parts of the administrative setup of the colonial frontier province. The most comprehensive steps were taken in 1971: the year of B. P. Singh's "twins born out of a new vision for the Northeast."[71] This was the year when Pakistan broke up and Bangladesh emerged as an independent country. Significantly, India had intervened militarily in the Bangladesh Liberation War. All this was no coincidence. In subsequent years, almost all the territories that were part of the colonial frontier province of Assam under some form of indirect rule—including the princely states, or areas that were unadministered—became states of the Indian Union. At the same time, a parallel governance structure was put in place, giving India's national security establishment a decisive say in decision making on all matters related to the region.[72]

While Northeast India as a region with its peculiar governance structure is a 1970s invention, the directional term was familiar in British colonial practice. First, there was the North East Frontier of British Imperial India. But it did not refer to the same territory as contemporary Northeast India. It included the Himalayan kingdoms—the *cordon sanitaire* around British Imperial India. Second, there was once a proposal to name the short-lived province of eastern Bengal and Assam (1905 to 1911) "North Eastern Province." But the powerful lobby of European tea planters opposed the move. "Assam Tea" had by then achieved significant name recognition in global markets, and the tea lobby feared that eliminating the word *Assam* from the name of the province would hurt the industry. A few Assamese public intellectuals had also "raised an alarm at the prospect of the very name of Assam being obliterated for ever."[73] And third, there were the North East Frontier Tracts, which became the North East Frontier Agency. But it was only a part of the frontier province of Assam; the territory is now one of Northeast India's eight states.

OFFICIAL VISIONS OF THE FUTURE

The official Indian imagining of this region—as can be glimpsed from key government documents and everyday practices—is of a space that will, with the passage of developmental and nation-building time, catch up and become part of the "national mainstream."[74] It is generally assumed that New Delhi's tutelage would be necessary during this period of transition. The central government has a Ministry of Development of North Eastern Region (DONER). No other region has a central ministry dedicated to its development. DONER's vision, says its website, "is to accelerate the pace of socio-economic development of the Region so that it may enjoy growth parity with the rest of the country."[75] India's Ministry of Home Affairs has a separate North East Division to deal with the region's "developmental and security issues." Since it has two other divisions to deal with "internal security" matters, the armed conflicts and episodes of ethnic violence in Northeast India are clearly seen as belonging to a different category from those in mainland India. "Unlike other parts of the country," explains the Indian Home Ministry's website, "the North East holds an important position from a strategic point of view as these states share their borders with other countries like Bangladesh, Bhutan, Myanmar and China."[76]

The region has a "fragile security situation," proclaims this official website, attributing it to factors including "the terrain, the state of socio economic development and historical factors such as language/ethnicity, tribal rivalry, migration, control over local resources and a widespread feeling of exploitation and alienation." Apparently, all this results in "violence and diverse demands by various Indian Insurgent Groups." The implication is of an inherited structural condition, which is conflict- and violence-prone—seemingly incomprehensible and opaque. A number of factors are implicated: the region's borderland character, its imputed location in a prior stage of developmental temporality, and certain peculiarities of historical inheritance. For some mysterious reasons, the text seems to suggest, these factors conspire to produce a persistent perception among the people that they are exploited and alienated from the "national mainstream." Such an overdetermined political conjuncture makes serious inquiries into particular armed conflicts and their etiology seem redundant. The policy response that is outlined is similar to palliative medicine for illnesses for which there is no present cure, and managing and controlling symptoms are the only option. Only prodigious economic and social change will be able to alter the effects of such a stubborn set of structural factors. Until then, in order to keep this latecomer to the nation and to development safe from the nation's enemies, New Delhi has undertaken the mandate to manage and control symptoms. The AFSPA regime has become an essential tool for carrying on this peculiar set of self-imposed responsibilities.

## CHAPTER 2

# PARTITION'S LONG SHADOW
## *Nation and Citizenship in Assam*

The national order of things . . . usually also passes as the
normal or natural order of things. For it is self-evident that
"real" nations are fixed in space and "recognizable" on a map. . . .
One country cannot at the same time be another country.
— Liisa Malkki, "National Geographic: The Rooting of
Peoples and the Territorialization of National Identity"

INDIA'S PARTITION WAS NOT the inevitable culmination of struggles
by generations of anticolonialists.[1] Nor was it a conclusive one-time event.
The decision to formally and constitutionally divide British-ruled India
was made only ten weeks before the actual transfer of power on August
15, 1947. What it would mean for ordinary people, as historian Gyanendra
Pandey notes, could only be worked out "step-by-step in 1947–48 and
afterwards."[2] When violence between Hindus and Muslims forced people
to move across the new international border, "it was not always obvious to
them or to the new states that they would not go back."[3] A person displaced
by Partition told an interviewer many years later that she, like many others,
did not expect the division of territories to be forever.[4] The "very idea of
Pakistan was a kind of utopian notion in 1947," as a Bangladeshi literary
historian recalled those times, and in East Pakistan—the predecessor entity
of the state of Bangladesh—the dream eroded quite quickly.[5] Seen from
this perspective, it was perhaps inevitable that despite the insertion of an
international border and the introduction of an illegality regime, the flow
of people crossing into India would continue well beyond the immediate
years of Partition. That Partition generated a massive new flow of Hindus
into India is well known. What is less well-known—and contrary to the
expectations of the architects of Partition—is that it did not stop an old

pattern of migration from densely populated deltaic eastern Bengal into relatively sparsely populated Northeast India: that of poor Muslim peasants in search of land and livelihoods.

The legal status of migrants from across the border remains a controversial issue in India. "Repatriates? Infiltrators? Trafficked Humans?"—the title of an essay on population movement from across the Partition's eastern border into India captures the perennially contested nature of the issue.[6] The constitutional definition of Indian citizenship does "not confer political recognition by religious identity."[7] But many in India believe that the Indian state has a historical obligation to those left on the "wrong" side of the border.[8] Hindu Partition refugees do not generally occupy a minoritized space in most parts of India. It is relatively easy for them to integrate into local society. In neighboring West Bengal, for example, the refugee population provided the communist parties that dominated the state's politics for decades, many of its cadres, and some of its important leaders.[9] While the integration of Partition refugees may be incomplete, says one writer, "they have not been a minority after migration to West Bengal."[10] But in Northeast India, the challenge has played out very differently for two reasons. First, both migration from eastern Bengal and opposition to it in this settlement frontier began well before 1947. Second, there is the "forgotten story of India's Partition"—that of the district of Sylhet.[11] This region—a part of Bangladesh today—was a district of the province of Assam before it became a part of East Pakistan in 1947. The status of this Bengali-speaking region was a controversial issue in the politics of colonial Assam. Assamese Hindu political leaders of the Indian National Congress advocated its separation from Assam well before Partition. In some Sylheti Hindu Partition refugee narratives, they bear more responsibility for Sylhet becoming a part of Pakistan than even Muslim League politicians that fought for a separate Pakistan.[12] A significant segment of Northeast India's population bears the burden of the intergenerational trauma and memories of the partitioned geography of Sylhet. Not surprisingly, there is among them a very different view of this history—and its implications for post-Partition India—from that in the rest of Northeast India.

Siddharth Deb's *The Point of Return* is a fictional account of the fate of Hindu Bengali Partition refugees in an anonymous Northeast Indian hill state. The locals there view them as interlopers. The refugees left "their homes forever to try and find themselves within the nation." But here they realize that their journey is not quite over. "The hills that appeared beyond the horizon were only another mirage, their destination just another place that would reject them."[13] Deb's fictional account provides clues to the minoritized space that Partition refugees—like other ethnic nonlocals—occupy in what were once the excluded areas of the colonial frontier province. The indigene-migrant divide defines the politics of these areas. Some of the consequences will be discussed in Chapter 3. The experience of the "settled districts" of the erstwhile colonial frontier province, that is, present-day Assam, has been very different. The perception that unauthorized migrants from across the border—both Hindu and Muslim—enter India in large numbers and are allowed to vote and exercise a political voice has been a source of significant political disquiet. Since the citizen/foreigner binary is foundational to the contemporary global political imaginary—a part of "the national order of things"[14]—this is perhaps only to be expected. This chapter takes up that part of the story. In the last quarter of the twentieth century this unresolved question of nation and citizenship led to a bloody period of insurgency and counterinsurgency in Assam. That will be the focus of Chapter 5.

Political tensions around the issue of citizenship of post-Partition migrants have come to a head in Assam with the rise of the BJP—a political formation known both for its strong support of the cause of Partition refugees and for its advocacy of a firm line between Hindu and Muslim unauthorized immigrants. Any Hindu migrant from Pakistan or Bangladesh, irrespective of when s/he entered India, it believes, deserves refugee status and to be on the road to citizenship. But Muslims crossing the border into India are "illegal immigrants." The aborted Citizenship (Amendment) Bill of 2016 would have effectively introduced this distinction into Indian law. The nuances of the regional and local histories of Northeast India are of no interest to the political formations associated with Hindu majoritarianism. But in the face of widespread opposition to the bill in Assam and the rest of Northeast India, this effort to amend Indian citizenship laws had to be abandoned, at least for now. The bill was passed in the lower house of Parliament, but the government did not introduce it in the upper house. When the final session of Parliament under the previous Modi government came to a close in February of 2019, this bill was allowed to lapse.

## THROUGH COLONIAL EYES: ASSAM
## AS A SETTLEMENT FRONTIER

The story of the industrial production of tea in nineteenth-century Assam begins with vast tracts of "wastelands" being given away to European "tea planters." Settling Assam's so-called wastelands was an important priority for British colonial administrators. The population density of Assam—like that of many other frontier regions of Asia—was low, and the local peasantry was not attracted to wage labor in plantations.[15] Under these conditions it became possible to produce tea on an industrial scale only by recruiting workers from other parts of India. Already by 1921, tea workers and their descendants were a sixth of the population of the province.[16] Colonial administrators, however, had a far more expansive view of Assam's wastelands than just the lands where tea would grow. They saw the low-lying areas of the floodplains of the Brahmaputra—used in pre-colonial times for seasonal cultivation, not for year-round cultivation and settlement—also as a vast potential revenue-earner. Their reclamation had to wait until the early twentieth century, when the demand for raw jute went up in Bengal's jute industry; Muslim migrants from densely populated deltaic eastern Bengal were then encouraged to settle those lands. They began coming on their own once social networks connected the two regions. This flow of migrants gathered significant momentum in the 1930s and 1940s.[17]

Because of the intensity and size of this migration, Assam quickly became a part of the territorial imaginary of a future homeland for the Muslims of the subcontinent. The All-India Muslim League emerged as a significant political force in colonial Assam. It participated in a number of elected provincial governments. During those times, it "doubled up its efforts to prove that Assam was in reality a Muslim-majority province since the hill and the plains tribes along with the tea garden labour population could not be counted as Hindus."[18] Fewer than four months before the Partition of 1947, the leader of the Muslim League and the founder of Pakistan, Mohammed Ali Jinnah, wrote to Viceroy Lord Louis Mountbatten to reiterate his claim that the province of Assam had a plurality of Muslims.[19] But the Muslim League and its policies of unrestricted immigration to Assam faced stiff opposition both ideologically and politically from the Assam Provincial Congress and its regional allies. Unfortunately, India's "retrospectively constructed" official nationalism ignores and systematically delegitimizes "the multiple alternative strands of popular nationalism and communitarianism that lost out in the final battle for state power."[20]

People from many parts of the subcontinent—apart from the groups mentioned so far—migrated to Assam during the British colonial period.[21] Prominent among them were the large number of educated Hindu Bengalis who were drawn by the opportunities opened up by the extension of British colonial rule to this frontier region. Thanks to Bengal's longer experience of colonialism—and exposure to English—they had the skills to occupy many new middle-class positions in the colonial bureaucracy. Since Sylhet was a district of Assam, it further facilitated their recruitment to those positions. In the early twentieth century, more than half of the total number of literate persons—and those literate in English—in the entire province of Assam were from Sylhet.[22] Anindita Dasgupta, a scholar of the Partition of Sylhet, describes the position of Sylhetis in the provincial bureaucracy: "In the district headquarters of the colonial government of Assam, the Sylheti was . . . disproportionately employed in various provincial government offices and in the emerging professions of law, teaching and even trading and contract jobs. Bengali clerks, doctors and lawyers, most of them Sylhetis, with the advantage of their early initiation to English education and the British-Indian administrative system, monopolized government jobs and professions."[23]

The overrepresentation of Sylhetis in the provincial bureaucracy was even more evident at the headquarters of the colonial frontier province in Shillong. Its location close to Sylhet gave them a further advantage.[24] The net effect of this pattern of recruitment to the provincial bureaucracy was to give Assam's colonial experience a "demographic layering" with a political edge similar to that of countries across Northeast India's eastern border. Historian Mandy Sadan describes the experience of colonial rule in parts of Southeast Asia as one of "being governed from a western metropole but with the daily experience of the social, political and economic colonization . . . by people (predominantly men) of Asian origin, who were the agents of that colonization or else were seeking to take advantage of it." If for Burmese subjects of the British Empire the complex encounter with South Asian migrants was a "vital part of being colonized," in French colonial Indochina, particularly Cambodia and Laos, it was Vietnamese bureaucrats that were the "local face of French colonization."[25] These words could be easily rewritten to apply to Assam.

DEMOGRAPHIC TRANSFORMATION AND IDENTITY SHIFTS
In discussions of immigration from eastern Bengal to Assam, a passage from an eighty-year-old colonial document has become a staple in serious scholarship, as well as political pamphleteering. In that widely cited passage, C. S. Mullan, the British official responsible for the 1931 Census, noted:

> Probably the most important event in the province during the last twenty-five years—an event, moreover, which seems likely to alter permanently the whole future of Assam and to destroy more surely than the Burmese invaders of 1820 the whole structure of Assamese culture and civilization—has been the invasion of a vast horde of land-hungry Bengali immigrants, mostly Muslims, from the districts of Eastern Bengal and in particular from Mymensingh. . . . It is sad but by no means improbable that in another thirty years Sibsagar district will be the only part of Assam in which the Assamese will find himself at home.[26]

Mullan's words predate Partition by a decade and a half. Both eastern Bengal and Assam were then part of British India, and Sylhet was a part of Assam. During the brief period when eastern Bengal and Assam constituted a single province (1905–11), the migration flow "increased, with provincial support."[27] During the decade leading to Partition, the Muslim League was part of a number of provincial governments of Assam, and those popularly elected governments supported this migration. Yet as recently as 2014, an important ruling by the Indian Supreme Court looked for authority in the apprehensions voiced by Mullan. The ruling chided the Indian government for leaving Partition's eastern border porous.[28] Mullan's prediction about the demographic transformation of Assam proved prescient. But while he was right about the speed and scale of this transformation, he could not have anticipated its sociological and political consequences. Migration from eastern Bengal became a politically explosive issue only a few years after Mullan wrote those lines. The issue became mired in "the clamor for territories to be incorporated within Pakistan and India [that] made people either fear or hope that Assam would become a part of Pakistan."[29]

Mullan, of course, did not foresee Partition, nor could he have imagined that a majority of those migrating from eastern Bengal to Assam a generation later would be Hindus, not Muslims. Nor did he anticipate the extraordinary process of ethnic change that migrants and their descendants would go through. It could not have possibly crossed Mullan's mind that "the entire East Bengali Muslim peasant community" settled in the Brahmaputra Valley would one day adopt Assamese as their first language.[30] In this book, I will refer to this community as *Miya* or *Miya Musalman*—using the Assamese terms—or Miya Muslims instead of calling them Muslims of east Bengali descent, as I have done in previous writings. There is now a radical Miya poetry movement in Assam. These young poets seek to reappropriate the word *Miya*—traditionally used by the Assamese as a pejorative word for people of that ethnic background. These activist poets prefer the term *Miya* to alternatives such as *No-Axomiya* or *neo-Assamese* because of its assimilative assumptions, and to *Bengali-origin Muslims* because that designation fails to take into account that newer generations of that community—or even their parents—are not immigrants but were born in Assam.[31] M. S. Prabhakara once made a perceptive remark on the language switch by the Miya Muslim community. The real fears of the ethnic Assamese in the Brahmaputra Valley, he observed, are not what most observers understand them to be. It is not so much that they fear that Bengali speakers would eventually outnumber them or that immigration threatens the existence of Assamese language and culture; their actual fear is that the new generation of Assamese speakers would claim Assamese as their own language: "stealing away, as it were, a crucial cultural patrimony which defines the Assamese people."[32]

Miya Muslims are distinguished from ethnic Assamese Muslims or the *Muslim-Axomia* (also called *Tholua* or *Khilonjia*). But the ethnic Assamese Muslims are not a single ethnic community: distinctions are usually made among groups such as *Goriya, Moriya, Syed,* and *Deshi.*[33] There are a number of other Muslim communities such as *Bhotia* and up-country or *Juluha*—people who trace their descent from Uttar Pradesh and Bihar.[34] *Deshi Musalmans* have become politically more vocal and visible in recent years. Their forefathers, according to an activist of the Deshi Janagosthiyo Mancha (Deshi Peoples' Forum), were "Koch Rajbongshis in the erstwhile Goalpara district but later converted to Islam." This organization brings together "people from indigenous communities such as Koch, Rabha, Mech, Garo, Nath, Yogi and Kalita who embraced Islam following the footsteps of Ali Mech," who is believed to have converted to Islam in the thirteenth century. Deshi Musalmans consider him the founding father of their community. Their political self-assertion during the past few years is particularly significant in light of the escalating controversy over unauthorized migration and citizenship in Assam. The community has come together, explains this Deshi Janagosthiyo Mancha activist, because their concerns do not receive adequate attention from public officials because of their misrecognition as "Bangladeshis."[35]

The effects of migration from eastern Bengal on society, culture, and politics in Assam have been seismic. Yet it is hard to claim that Mullan's apprehension—that it would destroy "the whole structure of Assamese culture and civilization"—has come true. The percentage of Assamese speakers in the state's population rose from 31.4 percent to 56.7 percent between 1931 and 1951. This happened because the Miya Muslim community began to identify themselves as Assamese speakers in post-Partition Assam. Had they not done so in the 1951 Census, the claim of the Assamese language to being the official language of the state would have been significantly weaker. "It is not unlikely," speculated the superintendent of census operations in Assam in 1951, that "some amongst the persons who have returned their mother tongue as Assamese had done so from devious motives, even though their knowledge of Assamese may not amount to much."[36] Whatever may be the truth of this speculation, language identifications do "depend both upon perceived life chances offered by particular language choices and, equally important, and connected to the question of life chances, upon patterns of elite political competition for power."[37] In Assam, for a long time, there was, as political scientist Myron Weiner once phrased it, "an unspoken coalition between the Assamese and the Bengali Muslims against the Bengali Hindus."[38] Miya Muslims adopted Assamese as their first language—the language in which future generations would receive education—and supported ethnic Assamese candidates in elections. In return, the state government—dominated by Assamese speakers—would not try to "eject Bengali Muslims from lands on which they have settled in the Brahmaputra valley, though earlier Assamese leaders had claimed that much of the settlement had taken place illegally."[39] The political situation has changed dramatically since then. But the relative position of Assamese speakers in Assam in numerical terms remains important and a politically sensitive issue for the stability of this settlement frontier, though since the census of 1991 they form a plurality but not a majority.

One interesting effect of the language switch by Miya Muslims is that the word *Assamese* no longer functions as an unqualified ethnic identifier as it once did. It partly explains the emergence of a new term—*ethnic Assamese*—to refer to Assamese speakers who are not of east Bengali descent or of ethnic tribal descent but have "indigenous" roots.[40] When the president of the prestigious Asam Sahitya Sabha [Assam Literary Conference] expressed the view that Assamese should be the region's lingua franca because a majority understands it, a leader of a Bodo ethnic organization expressed outrage. The Asam Sahitya Sabha ("Asam" is the spelling used in the official name of this organization) is an influential body; it has a mass membership and a significant presence in the state's public life. Accepting Assamese as the lingua franca, said the Bodo leader, would hasten the process of Assam's "Bangladesh-ization" since "Bangladeshis" have "colonized" Assam by adopting the Assamese language. The Guwahati-based newspaper *The Sentinel* expressed apprehension that "a Bangladeshi" would one day preside over the prestigious Asam Sahitya Sabha.[41]

There is little doubt that the migration of Muslims from eastern Bengal has significantly changed Assam's religious demography. Given the modern history of the subcontinent, this can hardly be inconsequential. According to the census of 2011, Muslims constitute 34.2 percent of the population of Assam—the second highest among Indian states after Jammu and Kashmir. Between 2001 and 2011 the proportion of Muslims in the population grew at a higher rate in Assam than in the rest of India. In the country as a whole, it went up by less than 1 percent, from 13.4 percent to 14.2 percent. But in Assam, it went up by 3.3 percent, from 30.9 percent to 34.2 percent. An Assamese BJP politician has even asserted that Muslims in Assam are not a minority since they are a majority in nine of Assam's twenty-seven districts.[42] But minority status is not a function of numbers alone; it is a function of social power.[43] Moreover, a statement like this can obscure the fact that Assam's contemporary religious demography is the result of a migration flow that began more than a century ago. This bit of history gets short shrift in the shrill political rhetoric about "illegal Bangladeshi migrants." At the same time, it is true that this demographic trend—of the growth in the relative size of Assam's Muslim population—has persisted into the post-Partition years. That the growth rates of Muslims are higher "in the districts that share a border with, or lie close to the border with, Bangladesh" than in areas that make up "the heartland of the indigenous Assamese Muslims"—where the growth rate is close to that for the Hindu population—is usually cited as evidence to support the claim that continued migration from Bangladesh is a factor behind this demographic trend.[44]

Since India's "identification revolution"—the greatly enhanced ability of the modern state "to individually designate its own nationals so as to legally differentiate between citizens and aliens present on its territory"[45]—remains a work in progress; estimating the number of irregular migrants crossing the Partition border into Assam is a highly fraught exercise. I do not intend to enter this debate in this book. All available estimates are extrapolations from census figures and electoral rolls, and they are intensely contested. While no one disputes that there is a large number of "foreigners" or "Bangladeshis" in Assam, the implicit definitions and the estimated numbers vary enormously. Assam appears to belong to a category of places in the world where, as a scholar of comparative migration puts it, unauthorized cross-border migration is "invisible" only in the sense that "publicly, no one has systematic data, but if one digs deeper, the state has confidential estimates based on reports and surveys by intelligence or police agencies."[46]

## CROSSING PARTITION'S BORDER: SHADES OF GRAY

People in most societies hold a variety of positions on the phenomenon of unauthorized migration and the appropriate policy response to it.[47] It may be productive to distinguish among the different frames that shape the Indian view of the unauthorized migrant crossing the Partition's border. For many, migrants violate the territorial sanctity of Indian national space. For others, whether s/he is a Hindu or a Muslim is important: they see the former as an illegal alien—even an "infiltrator"—and the latter as a refugee. To yet others, the year when a person had crossed the border is crucial since that's how Indian citizenship laws have until now defined citizenship in post-Partition India. And many others see another set of values—the land rights of indigenous peoples—as trumping the claims of the cross-border migrant to citizenship and land rights. The competing frames align our mental maps with our inner moral geography.

India's citizenship laws until now have more or less embodied what could be called the Nehruvian frame. They had retained the spirit of the Nehru-Liaquat pact, which the leaders of India and Pakistan signed in 1950 amid fears of further outbreaks of violence against Muslims in India and against Hindus in Pakistan. The two leaders drew a time line and decided that after that date, the two countries would maintain the demographic status quo.[48] In the words of diplomatic historian Pallavi Raghavan, its goal was to reassure "minority populations of their security within the country and to discourage them from migrating."[49] Thus Indian law, at least until now, does not distinguish between Hindu and Muslim arrivals from Pakistan or Bangladesh. Both categories of migrants are foreigners. Legally speaking, they are like citizens of any other country, and if they wish to become Indian citizens, they must go through a process akin to naturalization. But, as should be apparent by now, Indian citizenship laws do not necessarily provide the most authoritative frame when it comes to the status of Hindu post-Partition migrants. Many Indians see their presence in India as technically illegal but licit. This can be called a soft Hindu nationalist frame—soft because while it is associated only with Hindu cultural nationalism, it has resonance well beyond this political circle, especially among Partition refugees. Former Indian foreign minister Jaswant Singh once said that continued migration of Hindus to India is "the compelling logic of the consequences of partition."[50] It is unlikely that he saw Muslim migrants as part of the same "compelling logic." Singh is one of Hindu nationalism's best-known moderate voices. But Hindu majoritarians are not as subtle. They would like to see Indian law treat Hindus as refugees and Muslims as "illegal immigrants" or even "infiltra-tors." The implicit definition of a "Bangladeshi" in the discourse of Hindu majoritarianism is a Muslim; it does not include Hindus.

A REGIONAL PATRIOTIC FRAME

In large parts of Assam—the Brahmaputra Valley, in particular—ir-regular migrants crossing the Partition border are viewed through the lens of a third frame, which I will call regional patriotism.[51] This frame has developed in the course of Assam's long and embattled history as a settlement frontier—a sparsely populated "periphery" into which agricul-turalists from the rest of the subcontinent were moving—and the demo-graphic layering of the colonial experience. Since British colonial times, Assam has stubbornly resisted being regarded by its rulers as a land with-out people—or, with very few people.[52] Settlement frontiers, after all, are not natural; they are constructed. It is unequal political power and often conquest that turns territories inhabited by some people into frontiers for other people. Once the modern politics of numbers was introduced, it was probably inevitable that the question "Whose land is it anyway?" would emerge as key in Assam's politics. Efforts to reclaim the land and the past, and to assert the historical presence of collectivities against the discourse of power, have been a theme in the politics of Assam for nearly a century. Well before Partition, local resistance had forced changes in the colonial-era settlement policy and even defined the battle lines.[53] In fact, political mobilization based on the regional patriotic frame had formed part of the anticolonial coalition built by the Indian National Congress in Assam. Like mobilizations in other parts of British colonial India that focused on concrete goals, it was a building block of the anticolonial politics of the Congress in Assam.

In Assam, as elsewhere, there were tensions between the regional patriotic frame that informed the politics of the provincial Congress and the pan-Indian frame of the Indian National Congress. These tensions came to the fore during Jawaharlal Nehru's visit in 1937 as president of the Congress amid a raging controversy over immigration from eastern Bengal. Nehru, in his public speeches, called on the people of Assam to prioritize India's major "national problems"—the twin goals of attaining independence and eradicating poverty—over "provincial problems." Among "provincial problems," he listed three issues on which Assamese public opinion was most exercised. All three issues related to immigration from eastern Bengal: the possible separation of Sylhet, the settlement of immigrants, and the Line System designed to restrict the areas open to settlement by new immigrants. The Assamese public intellectual Jnananath Bora criticized Nehru for failing to appreciate the local understanding of these issues. If the so-called provincial problems are a secondary priority, the best way to give them the priority they deserve is "to make Assam an independent nation, a *deś* [country] rather than a *prades* [region]." When the United Liberation Front of Assam (Ulfa) appeared on the scene in the 1980s, an independentist intellectual of a new generation, Parag Kumar Das, "categorically reclaimed the legacy of Jnananath Bora while making a case for secession of Assam from India."[54] This period will be the focus of Chapter 5.

At the time of Partition, no other issue separated the leadership of the Assam Congress from the all-India Congress more than the settlement of refugees. The Congress government of the state, led by Gopinath Bordoloi, tried to restrict the numbers to be settled in Assam on the ground that there was insufficient land available to accommodate them. A state government circular of May 1948 read, "In view of the emergency created by the influx of refugees into the province from East Pakistan territories and in order to preserve peace, tranquility and social equilibrium in towns and villages, the government reiterates its policy that settlement of land should be in no circumstances made with persons who are not indigenous to the province."[55]

Many organizations of Hindu Partition refugees complained about the state's administrative machinery's reluctance to include the names of Partition refugees in the electoral roll for the first election in independent India.[56] In a letter to the Assam chief minister, Prime Minister Nehru said that the state "was getting a bad name for its narrow-minded policy." The position that Assam did not have enough land to accommodate refugees, he said, was unacceptable: "It is patent that if land is not available in Assam, it is still less available in the rest of India." According to a careful historian of this controversy, Nehru treated the Assam chief minister's judgments "with little respect" and displayed "impatience and condescension."[57] In the Constituent Assembly, Assamese leaders proposed—unsuccessfully—a federation with strong autonomous states, which would have a say on the question of immigration. The hesitation of the Assam government officials about including the names of Partition refugees in the electoral rolls ran counter to the mainstream opinion in post-Partition India. Ornit Shani, who has studied how India's first set of electoral rolls based on adult franchise was generated, writes of the situation in Assam: "In the contestations over the refugees' place on the electoral roll, rivaling conceptions of membership in the nation surfaced. In Assam, for example, ethno-nationalist attitudes manifested particularly toward the non-Assamese 'floating population,' many of who were Hindus from East Pakistan. Local authorities expressed a view of membership in the state that was defined by a descent group and delimited to the 'children of the soil,' who were eligible to have full rights. Thus ethno-nationalist conceptions were not necessarily on the basis of religion."[58]

The leaders of the Assam Congress not only wanted fewer refugees to be resettled in Assam; they also asserted the state government's prerogatives on matters of citizenship and immigration. But the response of the national leaders was patronizing and dismissive. Jawaharlal Nehru, for instance, said sarcastically, "I suppose one of these days we might be asked for the independence for Assam." As the controversy over how many refugees were to be settled in Assam continued, Deputy Prime Minister Sardar Vallabhbhai Patel called Bordoloi's successor, Bisnuram Medhi, a narrow-minded parochial person.[59] The idea of Assam's independence did not remain a joke for long. Nor could the label of "parochialism" smother the desire for independence among a younger generation of Assamese three decades later.

These developments parallel those that occurred in the Pakistani province of Sindh over settling Muslim refugees migrating from the Indian side of the border. Like Assam's Bordoloi, the prime minister of Sindh, Muhammad Ayub Khuhro, had reservations about Sindh's ability to accommodate as many refugees as demanded by Pakistani leaders. Although more than four million refugees had resettled in West Punjab by December of 1947, only 244,000 refugees were resettled in Sindh. Pakistan's minister for refugees and rehabilitation, Raja Ghazanfar Ali, chastised Khuhro for his unwillingness to accommodate more refugees in Sindh. By complaining of the burden of refugees on his province, the Sindh prime minister, said Ali, was raising the "virus of provincialism." Indeed, partly because of his stance on refugee resettlement, Khuhro was later dismissed from his position. The episode "not only strengthened Sindhi sentiment against the center, but also encouraged the precedent of executive action against elected representatives, which boded ill for the future."[60] The same can be said of the Indian ruling establishment's reaction to the Assamese leaders' reservations about settling refugees and its effects on the relations between Assam and New Delhi in subsequent years.

## THE PARTITION OF SYLHET AND OTHER MEMORIES OF PARTITION

The regional patriotic frame—while powerfully embedded in Assamese historical memory—does not resonate in all parts of Assam. This is to be expected considering the political and demographic history of this frontier province. The effects of the partition of Sylhet are one of the important sources of a counternarrative that is more aligned with the currently dominant discourse in the rest of India. Except for a part of the Karimganj subdivision—the four police station areas of Patharkandi, Ratabari,

Badarpur, and a portion of Karimganj—the rest of Sylhet District is now part of Bangladesh. Because of Sylhet's historical and cultural affinity with Bengal, the separation of this district from Assam at Partition is sometimes referred to as Sylhet's return to Bengal. Sylhet was a part of Bengal until 1874, when it was merged with the newly constituted Chief Commissioner's Province of Assam. The Mountbatten Plan of June 3, 1947, which formed the basis of the Indian Independence Act, stipulated a referendum for Sylhet because of the district's perceived peculiarity: a "predominantly non-Muslim" province contiguous to a "predominantly Muslim" one.[61] The referendum produced an outcome consistent with the political polarization of the time. A majority of Sylhetis were Muslims, and they voted to join eastern Bengal, which became East Pakistan. But since the referendum was decided by a relatively narrow margin, it gave rise to various what-ifs in the minds of Hindu Bengalis displaced by it—reflecting their mistrust of the ethnic Assamese political leaders of Assam.[62] Many of them believed that the Sylhet referendum was rigged: the dishonest dealings by the Assam Congress Committee intent on separating Sylhet from Assam produced that outcome.[63]

"The outcome of the referendum was greeted with immense relief and hope by Assam,"[64] although Assam in this context can only mean certain parts of the province—mostly the Brahmaputra Valley—and not others. But the sense of relief was short-lived. Assamese political leaders failed to foresee the massive migration of Hindus from Sylhet and the rest of eastern Bengal that was about to start once Partition became reality.[65] "Over the next few years," as Anindita Dasgupta explains, "large numbers of Sylheti Hindus from the ceded parts of Sylhet district began to relocate to the Indian north-east, particularly to southern Assam, where they had established considerable economic and social networks in the period 1874–1947."[66] What she calls southern Assam was the district of Cachar of that time. The parts of the Karimganj subdivision of Sylhet that did not become part of Pakistan were attached to that district after Partition. In terms of the contemporary political map of Assam, southern Assam is the predominantly Bengali-speaking Barak Valley: the districts of Cachar, Karimganj, and Hailakandi.

As I have indicated, a fundamentally different set of memories of Partition prevails among Hindu Bengalis in that part of Assam. Many of them have been in Assam for generations. They are not Partition refugees. In political terms, the Barak Valley of Assam is similar to Tripura, where Hindu Bengalis became the state's numerical majority—and its dominant face—following the settlement of large numbers of Partition refugees there. Hindu Bengalis do not occupy a minoritized space in these areas. In this regard, the Barak Valley of Assam and the state of Tripura are like cities such as Delhi, where Hindu refugees have historically provided support for political parties and organizations sympathetic to them. On the Pakistani side, the politics of these areas are comparable to "cities like Lahore, Sialkot, Multan, and Gujranwal [that] cannot be understood without reference to the refugee dimension."[67]

## MANAGING THE AMBIGUITIES OF CITIZENSHIP

During the Assam movement of 1979 to 1985, the rest of India became familiar with the "foreigner" question in that "remote" state for the first time in India's postcolonial history. Developments in Assam received unprecedented coverage in the national press during this period. The leaders of the Assam Movement claimed that as many as 4.5 to 5 million people in Assam—that is, 31 to 34 percent of the population in 1971—were foreigners and that the state's electoral rolls included the names of hundreds and thousands of foreigners.

But how did Assam manage to put a lid on this issue for more than three decades before it blew up in 1979? After the tensions over refugee settlement in the immediate post-Partition years subsided, the ruling Congress Party in Assam settled on a creative way of managing the ambiguities of citizenship. They took a nondiscriminatory and open-to-all approach to the franchise. Inclusion in the electoral rolls in Assam became a part of the Congress Party's patronage system controlled by local political brokers. In the absence of unfalsifiable identity documents, it became possible for almost any adult in Assam to be included in the electoral roll. The exercise of franchise in India does not depend on formal certificates of citizenship. A variety of rudimentary documents such as a "ration card"—which gives access to subsidized food—can pass as proxy for citizenship papers. But the perceived political influence of "suffraged noncitizens"[68] gradually made the issue of unauthorized migration and citizenship extremely volatile. Hiroshi Sato draws attention to the "fault lines" between the normative definition of citizenship in Indian law and the actual exercise of franchise being based on rudimentary documents.[69] With the Assam Movement these fault lines became the epicenter of a veritable political explosion, and its strong aftershocks are felt to this day.

Ironically, what disrupted the apparently smooth process of managing the ambiguities of citizenship in post-Partition Assam was not an action or a statement by a radical Assamese nationalist. In 1978, no less a constitutional authority than India's chief electoral commissioner made an astounding series of statements. S. L. Shakdher spoke publicly of the "large-scale inclusions of foreign nationals in the electoral rolls." Seemingly unaware of the political firestorm he was about to set off, he warned that "a stage would be reached when the state may have to reckon with the foreign nationals who may in all probability constitute a sizeable percentage if not the majority of population."[70] The words became the lightning rod of the Assam Movement. While it mobilized enormous popular support, it also made many people quite anxious. The ideologues of the Assam Movement may have couched their argument in constitutional and legal language, but the labels that gained currency—*Bangladeshi*, *illegal immigrant*, and *foreigner*—sounded menacing to many, and the holding of elections became a highly contested affair. The parliamentary elections of 1979 could not be held in most parts of Assam because of organized opposition; they were held in only two of fourteen parliamentary constituencies. The exceptions, predictably, were the two constituencies in the Barak Valley. Supporters of the Assam Movement boycotted the elections to the State Assembly in 1983. The confrontations and violence that took place during those elections included the infamous Nellie massacre, in which more than two thousand people were killed. I will discuss this issue further in Chapter 5.

The Assam Accord, signed in August of 1985, ended the Assam Movement and made certain distinctions between cross-border migrants from East Pakistan/Bangladesh into India based on various cutoff dates of entry. A calendar date that has a crucial place in the Assam Accord and a subsequent amendment to Indian citizenship laws is March 25, 1971. Interestingly enough, the significance of that date lies in developments that occurred not in India but in neighboring East Pakistan. It was when the Pakistani military crackdown of the liberation struggle in East Pakistan began, initiating a massive exodus to India. The date became important because, according to a bilateral agreement signed with India in 1972, Bangladesh took responsibility for those who moved to India after that date. According to the Assam Accord, those who came after March 25, 1971, were to be detected, their names deleted from electoral rolls, and expelled. Those who came between January 1, 1966, and March 24, 1971, would be disenfranchised for ten years. But immigrants from East Pakistan who entered Assam before January 1, 1966, would become Indian citizens. In effect, all those who crossed the Partition border into Assam in the quarter century following Partition—irrespective of whether the person was a Hindu or a Muslim—were given Indian citizenship. This was formalized by the insertion in 1986 of Section 6A into the Citizenship Act of 1955. It "introduced a sixth category of citizenship in India, which was to apply exclusively and exceptionally to Assam."[71] A public interest petition is currently under consideration of the Indian Supreme Court that challenges the constitutional validity of this three-decades old amendment.

The Assam Accord ended the Assam Movement in 1985, and fresh elections were announced, cutting short the tenure of the state government that came to power in 1983 following the election best remembered for its violence and record low turnouts. A new political party, formed by the leaders of the movement, won a majority of seats and formed the new state government in December of 1985. But in 1983, the Indian Parliament—when most of Assam had no representation because of the Assam Movement's boycott of the parliamentary elections in 1979—passed the Illegal Migrants (Determination by Tribunal) Act (IMDT law), severely limiting the ability of any government agency to act against those who are legally "foreigners"—that is, those who came after March 25, 1971. The effect of the IMDT law was to insulate them from the application of India's ordinary citizenship laws. It guaranteed an unauthorized foreigner the protection of a judicial process. It made identification as a foreigner difficult if not impossible. Under the Foreigners Act of 1946, the burden of proving citizenship status was on the person concerned. But the IMDT law reversed the burden, spelling out an elaborate procedure for a third person registering a complaint about someone suspected of being an unauthorized immigrant. The person making a complaint had to reside within the jurisdiction of the same police station as the person alleged to be an undocumented immigrant. This was a fairly solid protection since the solidarities based on local residential and ethnic networks were likely to trump the legal distinction between citizens and foreigners.

AFTER THE IMDT LAW: NEW UNCERTAINTIES

In July of 2005, the Indian Supreme Court declared the IMDT law unconstitutional. The ruling went further than what even the law's strongest critics in Assam could have hoped. The Court agreed with much of what the leaders of the Assam Movement had been saying all along. The IMDT law, said the Supreme Court, encouraged massive illegal migration from Bangladesh to Assam, and it was the "main barrier" to identifying unauthorized immigrants. The Court had little choice vis-à-vis its basic argument. The law may have been a clever political adaptation to the reality of cross-border migration, but its legal basis was precarious. But the Supreme Court's ruling did more than simply find the law unconstitutional. There can be "no manner of doubt," said the ruling, that Assam is facing "external aggression and internal disturbance" because of large-scale illegal immigration from Bangladesh. This gratuitous reference to "external aggression and internal disturbance" points to an emerging political reality: that the term *illegal immigrants* was slowly acquiring a new meaning at variance with the legal one—it excluded Hindu cross-border migrants. Anupama Roy calls this "the dominant framework of nationalism which cast a web of suspicion around all Bengali-speaking Muslims in Assam and the rest of the country."[72] The Supreme Court's ruling on the IMDT law was undoubtedly embedded in this emerging new common sense.

Indian courts and Parliament, however, often engage in "an iterative game of action-response-rejoinder that can be played out any number of times."[73] Faced with the State Assembly elections in Assam in early 2006, where the ruling on the IMDT law became a serious liability for the Congress Party, the Congress-led government in New Delhi issued two notifications that brought back the provisions of the IMDT law through the back door. By the end of the year, however, the Supreme Court nullified those notifications as well. But that was enough time for the Congress to squeak by and win elections. Another significant judicial verdict came in July of 2008 from the Gauhati High Court. A "large number of Bangladeshis" in Assam, said the court, play "a major role in electing the representatives both to the Legislative Assembly and Parliament and consequently, in the decision-making process towards building the nation."[74] These pronouncements by authoritative institutions seriously threatened the legitimacy of elected governments in Assam. By now, high constitutional bodies such as the Election Commission, the Supreme Court, and the Gauhati High Court have all spoken in favor of a tougher illegality regime—drawing a firm line between citizens and noncitizens and putting a stop to the practice of voting by suffraged noncitizens.

## HARDENING THE BORDER: SHIFTING POLITICS

"India-Bangladesh: Restoring Sovereignty on Neglected Borders" is the title of an article that appeared in 2003 in *Faultlines*, the quarterly publication of India's premiere internal security research and monitoring organization. Its authors drew attention to India's "rapidly changing internal security environment" with examples such as Pakistan's complicity in acts of terrorism in India, safe havens for Indian insurgent groups in Bangladesh, transborder criminal syndicates, and Islamic religious schools or madrassas along the Indo-Bangladesh border—allegedly a breeding ground for Islamic absolutism. They called for an end to the "security and impunity with which our borders are violated" and a "radical reevaluation" of the country's border management regime. The authors proposed measures such as the disenfranchisement of unauthorized immigrants, a halt to irregular migration, and the "integration of border populations into the mainstream."[75] The phrases may seem uncontroversial, but they overlook the definitional ambiguities of these terms on the ground: the well-documented difficulties of separating the legal from the illegal, the citizen from the noncitizen. It is hard to avoid the impression that the authors rely on a Hindu nationalist interpretive frame rather than one that can be supported by prevailing Indian citizenship laws.

Indian public opinion has now swung decisively in favor of hardening the Indo-Bangladesh border and securitizing immigration and border control. The global discourse of "Islamic terrorism" and the growing political influence of Hindu cultural nationalism have reinforced this trend. The permissive border regime and the influx of "Bangladeshis" had long been a matter of concern for Hindu nationalist organizations—and as I have indicated, for Hindu majoritarians, the word *Bangladeshi* refers only to Muslims. These organizations now seized on the issue of "illegal Bangladeshi migrants," giving it a Hindu majoritarian twist. Thus, in the summer of 2012, when violence broke out between the Bodos and Miya Muslims in western Assam, Hindu majoritarian organizations unequivocally blamed the eruption on "illegal Bangladeshi migrants." In effect, the "undifferentiated Muslim masses inhabiting western Assam"—many of them descendants of the early twentieth-century settlers from eastern Bengal—became "Bangladeshis."[76] The RSS publication *Organiser* covered the Assam violence extensively. A front-page headline declared: "Bangla Muslim Infiltrators Attack Bodo Villages, Torch Houses, Hamlets." The "Assam riots," said one article, "were between Indian citizens and foreigners, not ethnic clashes."[77] A BJP member of Parliament, after visiting the area, blamed the Congress Party's "brazen vote bank politics"—that is, its reliance on the political support of Miya Muslims—for creating a climate of insecurity for Hindus.[78] The RSS chief Mohan Bhagwat blamed the violence on the "policy of appeasement of minorities for votes." He called on the government to "identify and delete the names of these Bangladeshi infiltrators from voters' lists and deport them to their country," explicitly warning against applying the same rules to Hindus. No Hindu, he declared, can be a "foreigner" in India.[79]

BORDER POLITICS: WHO IS A "BANGLADESHI"?

By then, Hindu nationalism had made significant inroads into Assam. The BJP did unexpectedly well in Assam in the parliamentary elections of 2014, which brought the BJP-led National Democratic Alliance to power in New Delhi. The promise of decisive action on the influx issue was a major theme in its election platform. "You can write it down," said star campaigner and future prime minister Narendra Modi, "after May 16 these Bangladeshis better be prepared with their bags packed." The reference was to the day when results of the elections were expected.[80] The issue featured even more prominently in the BJP's Vision Document in the elections to the Assam State Assembly in 2016. The party promised to "completely seal" the Indo-Bangladesh border and to stop "infiltration."[81] BJP president Amit Shah promised to "completely free Assam of Bangladeshis."[82] In their political rhetoric, there was no ambiguity about how these Hindu majoritarian politicians define a "Bangladeshi"; they do not include Hindus. But the fact remains that this is not how the law defines citizens and foreigners in India or in Bangladesh.

In the 2016 elections to the Assam state legislature, the BJP's electoral alliance with a number of regional parties, notably the Asom Gana Parishad—the party that grew out of the Assam Movement—spoke powerfully of its intention to act decisively on the issue of unauthorized cross-border migration. The BJP's projected chief ministerial candidate, Sarbananda Sonowal, was a veteran of the Assam Movement. His association with the successful lawsuit against the IMDT law in the Supreme Court—*Sarbananda Sonowal v. Union of India*—reinforced his reputation as an uncompromising warrior for that cause. The BJP-led alliance won the election, and Sonowal became the state's chief minister. The political rhetoric of the election campaign, however, hid important differences. There were fault lines within the alliance that occasionally came to the fore during the election campaign. While national-level BJP politicians spoke of the danger from "Bangladeshis," their local allies spoke more about protecting *khilonjia* interests. The Assamese term *khilonjia* means original inhabitant. The BJP and its allies promised a *Khilonjia Sarkar*, the implicit contrast being one that would be beholden to "immigrant" power. Seen through the lenses of Assam's regional patriotic frame, the political influence of those of eastern Bengali descent—Hindus and Muslims alike—represent "immigrant power." So to the BJP's traditional supporters in the Barak

Valley, the talk of a *Khilonjia Sarkar* was not exactly reassuring; they have long been supporters of the BJP precisely because it has historically sided with Partition refugees, which from the *khilonjia* perspective represents "immigrant power." When campaigning in those areas, BJP politicians promised that Hindu refugees would be on a citizenship track once the party was elected to power. It contradicted the promise it made in other parts of Assam to implement the "Assam Accord in letter and spirit."[83] The Assam Accord of 1985 limits citizenship to those who migrated to Assam from East Pakistan before 1971, when Bangladesh came into being, and it does not distinguish between Hindu and Muslim migrants crossing the Partition's border.

The aborted Citizenship (Amendment) Bill of 2016 was an attempt to make good on the promise the BJP made to its supporters in the Barak Valley. Its ostensible purpose was to shelter persecuted religious minorities from Afghanistan, Bangladesh, and Pakistan. Sikhs, Buddhists, Jains, Parsis, and Christians are groups that the proposed law identifies as religious minorities. Muslim groups like Ahmadis—certainly a persecuted religious minority in Pakistan—are conspicuously absent. It is hard not to see this move as one that would have effectively introduced into Indian citizenship law a distinction between non-Muslim and Muslim immigrants crossing the Partition's borders. In the eyes of Hindu majoritarians, this is an unfinished piece of Partition business. But critics of the proposed amendment in Assam argued that it would effectively extend a welcome mat to Hindus remaining in Bangladesh and could trigger a new influx.[84]

In the meantime the Indian Supreme Court, which has built a global reputation for its interventionist stance, has become highly critical of the government for its lax border enforcement and its tolerance of unauthorized migration across the Partition's eastern border. In 2014 it admitted three petitions on this question by three activist organizations of Assam. Clearly, even after *Sonowal v. Union of India*, the process of judicializing the political debate on foreigners and citizens in Assam has continued. It is not unusual, of course, for "matters of outright and utmost political significance that often define and divide whole polities" to become judicialized.[85] But it raises unusually high expectations. Courts cannot deliver political miracles.

A two-judge bench of the Supreme Court has since weighed in on various aspects of the unauthorized immigration and border enforcement issues. "We have been reliably informed," said one of its rulings, "that the entire western border with Pakistan being 3300 km long is not only properly fenced but properly manned as well and is not porous at any point." By contrast, "most parts of the border with West Bengal and other northeastern states are also porous and very easy to cross." The two judges apparently were "at a loss to understand why 67 years after independence, the eastern border is left porous." They directed the Indian government to complete the fencing of the border and to maintain "vigil along the riverine boundary . . . by continuous patrolling." In addition, they have asked that the government (a) speed up the process of identifying unauthorized immigrants by setting up more Foreigner Tribunals and making adequate resources available to them and (b) develop, in consultation with the government of Bangladesh, appropriate mechanisms and procedures for deporting those found to be undocumented immigrants.[86] The two-judge bench also stepped into a process known as the updating of the National Register of Citizens (NRC), initiating "one of the most ambitious judiciary-led bureaucratic exercises in the history of the country."[87] The goal is to have an authoritative list of genuine Indian citizens living in Assam. The Supreme Court has specified a time line for the completion of the process. Many in Assam believe that the updating of the NRC will finally settle Assam's tangled "foreigners" question. At the heart of the NRC process lies what is called "legacy data." To be included in the NRC, a person has to identify an ancestor whose name appears in certain select government sources, such as a pre-1971 electoral roll, and provide documentary evidence of connection to that person through family lineage. This has proven to be a daunting challenge for many, especially for poor people with limited literacy and for women, whose names usually don't make it into land records or even family trees. "Technical flaws in documentary endowment," writes Jacqueline Bhabha, a scholar of human rights and law, "are not randomly distributed across citizen populations. . . . Destitution, illiteracy, and pervasive stigma militate against the organizational and institutional clout needed to navigate intricate bureaucratic procedures."[88] This insight is key to understanding the limitations of the NRC process. The process, however, has not uniformly relied on documentary evidence. An administrative rule devised for this purpose allows local administrators to identify entire villages or communities as "original inhabitants," which could be grounds for being included in the NRC. The rationale for this category—its inclusions and exclusions—has not been satisfactorily explained. The attempt to amend India's citizenship laws in the middle of the NRC process added another layer of controversy. This was widely seen as an attempt to exempt Hindu unauthorized cross-border migrants from the consequences of noninclusion in the NRC. Despite pious hopes, it seems unlikely that the NRC will bring legal closure to Assam's decades-old citizenship controversy. Unwittingly, it may be setting in motion a dynamics of disenfranchisement: hundreds and thousands of people could be effectively declared noncitizens at the end of the process, bringing a new form of precarious citizenship into being. Public interest law scholar Mohsin Alam Bhat's observation could not be more timely. "The appearance of legal process and formality," he writes, "will not extricate NRC from its context and consequences. There is an urgent need, particularly on the part of the Supreme Court, to recognise this and offer a more humane and inclusive conclusion to a process that is inching towards a tragedy."[89]

## WALLED SOVEREIGNTY: THE IMPOSSIBLE DESIRE

The steps to put India's identification revolution on a fast track, to harden the Indo-Bangladesh border, and to securitize immigration and border control may or may not achieve their avowed goals. But their effects are likely to be significant and far-reaching. The fence on the Indo-Bangladesh border, writes historian Malini Sur, "effortlessly shapeshifts from a matrix of wires and metal pillars through which Indians and Bangladeshis enquire about divided families and gossip, into a site of closure and suffering."[90] Willem van Schendel once called it a "killer border" because of the number of unauthorized border crossers shot and killed by border guards.[91] The efforts to toughen the illegality regime governing the Partition border along with the trends toward a majoritarian bias in Indian citizenship laws do not bode well for the future. One reason why their effects can be especially pernicious in this frontier region is that many settlers and their descendants—and not just Miya Muslims—live in and cultivate "forest lands," "grazing lands," and various kinds of public lands. These land-use designations are no more than legal fictions in many parts of Assam. To assume that they are solid facts on the ground can further dispossess some of the world's most disenfranchised people. There have been media reports of a "spectre of eviction" haunting "Assam's Bengali Muslims."[92] In western Assam some people displaced by ethnic violence were unable to return to their homes even after the violence had subsided because their homes and fields are in areas officially designated as "reserve forests." Since no one can be a legal landholder in a "reserve forest," every person is technically an encroacher. If the settlement itself is unauthorized, a family displaced from a "reserve forest" has no legal right to return to it. Thus, what may initially appear to be a case of temporary displacement because of an outbreak of ethnic violence could turn into permanent dispossession. In Assam today the legal fiction of "forest lands" and the suspicion of being "encroachers" or "false nationals" are increasingly doing what literary theorist Rob Nixon calls the "imaginative work of expulsion" that can happen before the police, the bulldozers, and the elephants arrive to do the physical eviction.[93]

India's Border Security Force has proposed "Wagah-like shows" to promote "border tourism" in Northeast India.[94] Wagah is a town on the India-Pakistan border where Indian and Pakistani soldiers participate in a flag-lowering ceremony, where they ritually enact their hostility toward each other. The performance underscores—and exaggerates—the lines drawn by Partition.[95] There are no Wagah-like performances on the Partition's eastern border partly because the two borders are not alike. The more or less complete "exchange of population" that occurred in Punjab during Partition—and the extraordinary brutality that went with it—has no exact parallel in the East. Decisions on whether or not to move to the other side were not all made in 1947. The process has been open-ended. But the situation is now changing. The Border Security Force is not alone in seeking a rigorously policed Indo-Bangladesh border. Many in India would like to see the post-Partition Indian state become a "normal sovereign state" with normal borders and mandatory state-issued identity documents being required for entering the country and for exercising voting rights.[96] After all, the "wish for well-defined, fixed boundaries" that comes out of the nineteenth-century idea of "exclusive and uncontested territorial state power"[97] remains part of the dominant global political imaginary: the national order of things. Ernest Gellner had famously compared it with Amedeo Modigliani's paintings, where "neat flat surfaces are clearly separated from each other" and "there is little if any ambiguity or overlap." He contrasted it with the "riot of diverse points of colour" in the impressionist canvases of Oskar Kokoschka: his metaphor for the world before nations.[98] Today there is "an emerging repertoire of efforts to produce previously unrequired levels of certainty about social identity, values, survival, and identity."[99] This hunger for certainty is, to some extent, behind the cultural fundamentalisms that plague our world. If there is a desire to see a Kokoschka-to-Modigliani type of transformation of the Partition's eastern border, the managers of the Indian state can hardly afford to ignore it. But whether they can gratify it is another matter.[100]

The nation-state walls and fences being built today and the greater policing of international borders all across the world are symptoms of the crisis of the nation-state system. These "mundane arrangements, most of them unknown two-hundred or even one-hundred years ago," as political theorist Timothy Mitchell reminds us, "help manufacture an almost transcendental entity, the nation state."[101] The Indo-Bangladesh border fence, after all, is not meant to stand as a fortification against an invading army—India and Bangladesh are friendly countries—but to protect against nonstate transnational actors: cross-border migrants and "Jihadi terrorists."[102] The capacity of states to control the flow of goods and people across borders is eroding worldwide. In many parts of the world, states had never fully developed that capacity. If at least in some parts of the world the nation-state had once monopolized loyalty, "transnational mobile practices"[103] now point to the significant erosion of that capacity. And postcolonial states like India can only strive for that kind of monopoly; they have never actually enjoyed it—as reflected, among other things, in the lateness of the identification revolution fitfully taking place now. The impossible desire for walled sovereignty in the world today reflects the desire to become a "normal state" or to remain one. Dealing with this increasing "anxiety of incompleteness"[104] will be a major challenge for India in coming years.

CHAPTER 3

# DEVELOPMENT AND THE MAKING OF A POSTCOLONIAL RESOURCE FRONTIER

How do ordinary people get involved in destroying their environments, even their own home places?
—Anna Lowenhaupt Tsing, *Friction*

NORTHEAST INDIA HAS BEEN A FRONTIER in more than one sense. In addition to its history as a settlement frontier and the resultant group conflicts examined in the previous chapter, the region has long been a resource frontier. While insights from Borderland Studies have added significantly to our understanding of the region, the frontier themes—at least explicitly framed that way—have not received much attention. This is not surprising. The two words *frontier* and *border* share some common ground, but they are not alike. Borderland Studies explicitly excludes from its purview what two authors of a foundational article call "the classical themes of the frontier—that is, demographic, political, or economic expansion into 'empty' territories."[1] Nor does the "binomial focus" of the central trope of border theory and scholarship[2] encourage the exploration of connections between the frontiers of today and the geopolitics of capitalism or of national and global security.

Settlement frontiers are sometimes distinguished from extractive or resource frontiers—places where mineral extraction, timber harvesting, establishing plantation crops, or the generation of hydropower motivate incursions.[3] The distinction is not obvious. If migration into new lands is what makes a settlement frontier, land is "the ultimate natural resource."[4] But if one makes that distinction, a region can be both a settlement and a resource frontier. Northeast India may be the perfect example. This duality is key to why the idea of rightful shares—"allocations properly due to rightful owners,"[5] that is, those who consider themselves to be native to a territory—has become the favored mode of political claims-making in this region. The settling of frontiers in the manner of previous centuries is inconceivable today. This is largely because of the global imposition of the nation-form and "the modern partitioning of the global population into citizens of numerous discrete states."[6] Yet the frontier continues to advance in less spectacular ways. In many parts of the world landless and land-poor people push the frontiers of settlement in search of livelihood opportunities. Among these people may be those displaced by development projects, natural disasters, political and ethnic conflicts, or circumstances attributable to climate change. They move to sparsely populated lands and struggle to make a living from land instead of pursuing the more familiar path of rural to urban migration. In the Northeast Indian state of Assam, people displaced by floods and erosion often move to lands that are near or inside poorly demarcated reserve forests and wildlife sanctuaries. Settling in such disputed lands put them at loggerheads with political groups with an "anti-poor" strand of "urban environmentalism"[7] and those that suspect them of being false nationals. When state institutions take their side, the settlers—who may have already suffered through multiple displacements—become vulnerable to fresh eviction drives.[8] As should be evident from the discussion in the previous chapter, the exclusions built into the national order of things have particular political saliency in Northeast India. Large numbers of people occupy stigmatized social spaces and are suspected of being false nationals: foreigners, migrants, refugees, or undocumented aliens.[9] The plight of these "unimagined communities" underscores the deeply contradictory nature of the projects of postcolonial nationhood and development.[10]

Frontiers are rarely empty spaces without people. They may be places full of promise to some, but to those whose life-space is invaded, incursion comes as a shock, a disruption, and a trauma.[11] The frontier encounter is therefore a stubborn source of conflicts, even though it may take years—and sometimes decades—for them to surface. Locals may view migrants and their descendants as "ethnic others" for generations;[12] and in places where they are seen as not belonging, their lives can be perilous. They come into conflict with peoples living there from before or those who can make political claims based on indigeneity: of "being original or first settlers" or at least of "prior dwelling, of being there before."[13] But often it is hard to graft the easy binaries of indigenous/settler, insider/outsider, or tribal/nontribal on the "tangled thicket of tenure relations."[14] Politics entrapped in these binaries risk legitimizing new patterns of exploitation, dispossession, subordination, and subcitizenship. In principle the land issues, even when entangled in a web of claims and counterclaims, could be adjudicated and settled peacefully and justly, utilizing tools such as symbolic reparations, public apologies, and commemorations. It is possible to reimagine settlement frontiers as inclusive, diverse, and hybrid places.[15] But conditions—local, national, and global—do not always favor the pursuit of a politics of inclusion. In some situations ethnic activists feel emboldened to seek the restoration of the status quo ante, which creates risks of violence and forced expulsions. Thus, in the context of Indonesia, anthropologist Tania Murray Li writes of "migrants who are at least as vulnerable as indigenous people, and often more so," becoming victims of ethnic cleansing.[16]

Extensive settlement frontiers may be rare in our times, but resource frontiers are not. There have been far-reaching shifts in the geography of development and underdevelopment. The organization of manufacturing, and its spatial distribution in the world, has gone through profound changes. But economic development still needs "resources from both the expanse of geographical space and the depth of geological time."[17] The global scramble for resources such as minerals, oil, natural gas, timber, and land has new players. New resource frontiers have opened up, and the exploitation of resources in some old ones has intensified. But the landscapes being enclosed and mobilized into resource frontiers had often served as some people's subsistence commons before. Those groups do not always fit the label "indigenous people" used by international bodies.[18] But when subsistence commons become resource frontiers, large numbers of poor people—whether "indigenous" or not—lose their traditional ways of making a living. This is why development's "shiny side" continues to have "a dark side of displacement and dispossession"[19] and why successful "developing countries"—even booming "emerging economies"—now host growing megacities of the poor.[20]

## THE POLITICAL DYNAMICS OF FRONTIER MAKING

Environmental historian Ramchandra Guha once described Northeast India as one of metropolitan India's last remaining resource frontiers. He calls India "an ecological disaster zone marked by high rates of deforestation, species loss, land degradation, and air and water pollution."[21] In certain parts of Northeast India, this is evident even to the naked eye. Thus, in the state of Meghalaya, environmental anthropologist B. G. Karlsson found that "though there are places of great natural beauty, the general situation is rather dismal, largely at odds with the official rhetoric of the state's spectacular greenness." For Karlsson, what stood out about the hills of Meghalaya, where he did his field research, was the devastated landscape of the coal country: "the scarred hillocks denuded of vegetation, some literally shoveled away." He saw "boulders and soil . . . being loaded onto trucks, carried away . . . to be used as ground fill or for construction." Here is his graphic description of the devastation of a landscape as it was unfolding in front of him:

> As the machines cut into the hillsides of the northern slopes, the red soil is exposed, and with rain and wind it erodes and covers everything. During the rains, roads and tracks become almost impassable because of the red mud. Coal trucks ply all over the state, and in the places where coal is being mined, reloaded, and stored, everything is covered instead in black. Run-offs from the coal pits enter the water system, making the water acid and toxic with high levels of heavy metals, killing fishes and other organisms and making it extremely hard for people to access safe drinking water.[22]

"Primitive, hazardous and crude" is how Debojyoti Das describes the artisanal and small-scale coal mining practices that prevail. The commonly used method of "rat-hole mining" takes the following form: "land is first cleared by cutting and removing the ground vegetation. Pits ranging from 5 to 100 meters are dug to reach the coal seam. Thereafter, tunnels are cut into the seam sidewise to extract coal, which is first brought into the pit by using a conical basket or a wheelbarrow, and is then taken out and dumped."[23] The term *rat-hole* refers to the deep and narrow crevices used to extract coal. The "initiators of extraction" on these hills, significantly, are not "profit-driven outsiders" but "local and are members of communities often cast as victims of resource extraction."[24]

Anthropologist Anna Tsing's stark question introducing this chapter acquires particular poignancy in the hills of Northeast India. How, indeed, do ordinary people end up destroying their own home places and environments? Among people who have benefited handsomely from Meghalaya's coal boom are landowners of ethnic tribal descent legally considered indigenous to the state and nonowners who, through elite connections, are able to bring community lands with coal deposits under private control. The coal boom ended abruptly in April of 2014, when the National Green Tribunal (NGT) banned the mining and the transportation of coal in Meghalaya. The effectiveness of the ban, however, has come under a cloud of questions, especially after an incident in December of 2018, when an illegal coal mine in the state was flooded by water from a nearby river, trapping fifteen miners and killing them. The news was widely reported in the national and the international media. Rescue efforts were effectively abandoned after more than a month, and the miners were assumed dead.[25] While the NGT's ban had offered a ray of hope for Meghalaya, says a report authored by a group of social activists of Meghalaya, "through legal maneuvers, administrative and political tricks played on behalf of the mining lobby, the intent and purpose of this historic order has been bent beyond recognition."[26] Meghalaya's coal boom—and the significant writings on it—provides important insights into the political dynamics of the making of resource frontiers in the excluded areas of the old colonial frontier province.[27]

Customary laws specific to Scheduled Tribes considered indigenous to the state govern the ownership of lands and forests in Meghalaya. This is because the Indian Constitution's Sixth Schedule and the laws constituting a number of the new states have retained many of the protocols that governed the excluded areas during colonial times. Thus, unlike India's other mining regions, where mineral rights lie with the state—not with the landowner—in Meghalaya, the person who controls the surface land owns the mineral wealth.[28] Whatever else the word *tribe* may mean, what is relevant in this context is that tribes are corporate identities in the sense that they are group identities that are "officially recognized, sanctified, and legitimized by the state and its institutions."[29] Institutions of the postcolonial state in Northeast India recognize some tribes as indigenous to the territory of a state and not others. A person of ethnic tribal descent considered indigenous to Meghalaya would usually lease out land with coal deposits to a mining contractor—typically a person of nontribal ethnic descent—though some landholders directly engage in mining often with capital borrowed from a mining contractor with the promise of future coal delivery. The coal boom in Meghalaya has brought prosperity to significant numbers of people. The mineowners are sometimes persons of modest means, though always of indigenous ethnic tribal descent. "All you need is a small investment and a lot of luck," said one mineowner.[30] In the mining regions of Meghalaya, however, locals quickly learn to distinguish between the big mineowners and the small ones: "sports utility vehicles, usually shiny and black, are the conveyance of choice for 'malik,' as the big mine owners are known locally. The smaller mine owners usually drive white Maruti Gypsy."[31] A key role in the illegal trade and production of coal is played by the "coal mafia"—to use the local parlance. Land with valuable coal deposits sometimes changes hands through the use of coercion or threats of violence: "Once those men come and ask for your land, you have to give it for whatever price they offer," said a person in the mining area to a reporter.[32] Meghalaya's coal boom has left a trail of environmental destruction, and an itinerant poorly paid migrant workforce—many of them underage—face horrific working and living conditions. Moreover, the native communities living in the mining belt sometimes see the migrant workers as unwelcome outsiders and a threat to their cultural identity. This makes their already vulnerable situation even more perilous. Occasionally, the animosity against the migrant workers has even "exploded into violent outbursts."[33]

Resource frontiers are anything but natural. Before natural resources can be turned into corporate raw materials, nature has to be disengaged from local ecologies and livelihoods.[34] There are always particular contingent historical circumstances under which nature gets turned into a commodity.[35]

Thus, during the Cold War the militarization of what was then referred to as the Third World and the growth of transnational corporate power led to the emergence of new capitalist resource frontiers in various parts of the world. For example, the twenty-first century "wildness" of Indonesia's mountainous and forested region of southeast Kalimantan, as Anna Tsing has shown, was the creation of privatization programs of the 1990s that gave away large tracts of land to logging, mining, palm oil plantation, and pulp-and-paper companies. Indonesia's politically connected powerful families and military officers were among the stakeholders in the companies that acquired those lands.[36] The political dynamics behind the rise of Meghalaya as a coal frontier are very different. The process has perhaps been more "democratic" than Indonesia's but certainly no less exploitative and destructive in social and ecological terms. The decision made by the leaders of newly independent India to live with elements of the colonial indirect rule regime discussed in Chapter 1 has proven fateful. It shaped the particular resource extraction regime that emerged and the constellation of winners and losers.

This political dynamic will not surprise historically informed observers. The colonial architects of indirect rule in the excluded areas could not have imagined that the institutions they improvised out of necessity for purposes of political control would take on a new life in late twentieth-century India and that India's energy and resource demands—and the aggressive supply chains required to meet them—would reach those areas. Colonial ideas about civilizational hierarchies and a sense of racialized paternalism were at work in the creation of those institutions. The capacity to become full market subjects, it was assumed, is differentially distributed. Colonial administrators and ethnographers considered some ethnically defined groups to be culturally incapable of becoming full market subjects and decided that they needed protection.[37] As a result, those laws—still enforced today—prohibit the sale of land owned by a person of tribal ethnicity to a person who is not of ethnic tribal descent. But the same laws do not prohibit land alienation if the land transfer does not involve a person of nontribal ethnic descent or the unequal accumulation of land within ethnic tribal communities. Such laws misread mechanisms of dispossession and overestimate bonds of community.[38] Thus, in Meghalaya today the ownership of land, including mineral deposits, is supposed to be in the hands of the community. But those lands have largely been captured by ethnic tribal elites.[39] Unlike in India's other mining regions, Meghalaya's coal mines are "owned by private interests rather than the state" and are unregulated.[40] The state's political class became deeply implicated in the coal business. According to one newspaper report: "The truth is every aspect of life in Meghalaya, including politics, is linked to the coal trade. While declaring his assets ahead of the elections, Mukul Sangma, Meghalaya's chief minister, had mentioned owning several [plots of] non-agricultural lands including coal mine quarries in West Khasi Hills district, estimatedly [*sic*] worth upwards of Rs 2 crore. His wife and daughter too own several mines."[41]

Distinguished journalist and author Sanjoy Hazarika also writes of the coal-baron politicians of Meghalaya. Here is his portrait of one such figure: "Powerful barons like Vincent Pala, owe their provenance to coal. He rose from a petty government officer to a coalmine owner and then rose through the local Congress party to seize its parliamentary seat in Shillong. In the process, he became one of the wealthiest persons in the state, and was appointed a minister of state for water resources (rather ironic, considering that the massive exploitation of coal had so polluted water resources and streams in the Jaintia Hills that water turned lethally blue and undrinkable)."[42]

It is hardly surprising that during most of the boom period, the state government of Meghalaya barely touched mining practices except for expressing "moral anxieties about prostitution and drug use" in the mining areas.[43] In the name of not intervening in the constitutionally sanctioned customary rights of "the community" over land and forest, it avoided making policy affecting mining operations. Things began to change only after 2005.[44] The peculiar pattern of land ownership and the absence of mining regulations allowed mine operators to "employ reckless mining practices that devastate the environment and threaten workers' safety."[45] The partnership between tribal landholders of indigenous ethnic ancestry and contractors of nontribal ethnic descent produced a highly profitable business model that adapted creatively to the institutional legacies of indirect rule in the excluded areas. Most of the profits from coal were "divided between the mining contractors and the owner, with a handful of rupees trickling down to the labourers."[46]

The 2014 order of the NGT that banned coal mining and coal transportation was a response to a petition by civil society organizations of the neighboring Dima Hasao District in Assam. The petition complained of acid mine drainage running into streams and rivers that merge into the River Kopili, which flows through that district. It made the river's water toxic and unfit for agricultural use, as well as lethal for aquatic life.[47] Acid mine drainage had earlier led to the severe corrosion of the machinery of a hydroelectric power plant on that river, and the plant had to be shut down for a period.[48] By the time Meghalaya's coal-mining practices had come to the NGT's attention, civic organizations and the media had begun shedding light on the seamy side of the coal boom—the environmental damage and dangerous working conditions, as well as the use of child labor. Ethnic organizations that speak in the name of the state's indigenes also became increasingly vocal in their criticism of the mines for employing large numbers of migrants from neighboring states and from Bangladesh and Nepal.[49] But branding the migrant labor force illegal also became an easy way to achieve labor subordination and control. It made many workers dependent on their employers for protection against potential action by state agencies and even more vulnerable to extreme exploitation.[50]

The NGT, mandated to act only on environmental issues, found the overall situation alarming. "We are of the considered view," said its order, "that such illegal and unscientific method can never be allowed in the interest of maintaining ecological balance of the country and safety of the employees." Neither the government nor the people of the country benefit from "such illegal mining of coal." Even though the petition that the tribunal was acting on related to mining only in the Jaintia Hills area of Meghalaya, its order was comprehensive. It sought to put an end to the "illegal and unscientific operations of rat-hole mining" in the entire state of Meghalaya.[51] It is extremely unlikely that we have seen the end of the coal frontier in Meghalaya or of the making of new resource frontiers in Northeast India. Ironically, the coal ban is widely criticized in Meghalaya on grounds that it has destroyed the livelihoods of "indigenous peoples." The language is stunning. In the standard literature, the rise of capitalist resource frontiers is usually associated with posing a threat to indigenous people's livelihoods. This is because resource frontiers make claims on the resources of the latter's subsistence commons, and it eventually unmoors them from the commons. Yet according to one reporter, "nearly everyone" in Meghalaya's coal country was critical of the NGT's order and was in favor of coal mining. These were clearly not voices of an indigenous community still moored to its subsistence commons. A woman who rents out a patch of land to other mine owners for dumping extracted coal, and who owns a few mine quarries herself, said, "If the ban isn't lifted we won't have anything to eat. Everything here comes from coal."[52] Although some mining has continued despite the ban—as became abundantly clear from the fatal December 2018 mining disaster—the Meghalaya state government and other influential actors have begun to pursue a number of initiatives to revive and formalize mining operations in the state. The coal ban was a major issue in the elections to the Meghalaya State Assembly in February of 2018. According to one reporter, a wide range of people affected by the coal ban—"coal miners and traders, truck owners, motor parts shop owners, garages, small cha and ja (tea and rice) establishments"—were determined to "punish the Congress government for making no effort to fight the ban."[53] They supported the BJP—the ruling party in New Delhi—in the hope that it would lift the NGT's coal ban. The BJP won only two of the sixty seats in the Meghalaya State Assembly, but it maneuvered to become part of the coalition that now rules Meghalaya. The fate of the NGT's coal ban is still undecided.

Meghalaya is not unique. Similar political dynamics are at work in the other excluded areas of the old frontier province; they involve coal as well as other natural resources. Dolly Kikon writes about villages in the foothills of Nagaland where coal mining has "rapidly swallowed cultivable lands, choked natural springs and killed aquatic life." A tribal elite "directly profits from the coal trade, has the capital to amass large tracts of prospective sites for oil exploration, and disregards environmental and community rights." Ethnic Naga tribal elites bought large plots of land across coal-mining sites and proximate to oil wells abandoned during past political turmoil. "Coal mining and the prospects for a carbon future in Nagaland," she writes, "are rapidly transforming social relations among neighbours, kin and the state."[54] The extraction regime formed along similar lines in the state of Arunachal Pradesh when the timber trade boomed a couple of decades ago. Elites of state-recognized Arunachali ethnic tribal descent profited enormously from it. The timber trade was "by and large controlled by the large-scale business from outside the state." But its junior partner and facilitator was the local business class of Arunachali tribal descent. They "managed to corner a substantial share for themselves. Some of them invested the surplus in establishing sawmills, plywood factories and transportation businesses."[55] The state's emerging hydropower-extraction regime now follows the same pattern, though the earnings are larger than from timber or coal extraction.[56]

## DEVELOPMENT AND RESOURCE FRONTIERS

The official figure on coal production in Meghalaya—it went up from almost forty-three thousand tons in 1979 to slightly more than 5.5 million tons in 2014[57]—is likely to be an underestimate, but it gives the time line of the state's postcolonial coal boom. It followed the reorganization of the colonial frontier province, and it unfolded when developing the "backward areas" of Northeast India emerged as an important policy priority of the Indian government. If the experience of Meghalaya's coal boom was the product of postcolonial initiatives to develop these "backward areas," how should one approach the idea of development? The Citizens' Report put together by social activists provides a moving summary of the effects of coal mining and its meaning vis-à-vis the idea of development: "Over the years, we, the citizens of Meghalaya, have watched helplessly the large-scale destruction of our ecology through indiscriminate environmentally destructive mining and the grabbing of community land. For most of us indigenous tribal Meghalayans, this was not the development paradigm we had fought for. When the Constitution of India gave our tribal communitarian values protection under the Sixth Schedule, it did not foresee the misuse of such a protection by a small section of local tribal elite to defend their criminal appropriation of the commons and communitarian resources like land, water, forests and minerals."[58]

Development, I would suggest, is best seen not as a process of change destined to transform all societies—and promote human well-being—but as a powerful idea and a practice engaged in by developmental states and development agencies.[59] Their historically contingent priorities shape the particular trajectories of change. Development has been aptly called "a concept of monumental emptiness [that] can mean just about everything, from putting up skyscrapers to putting in latrines, from drilling for oil to drilling for water, from setting up software industries to setting up tree nurseries."[60] The concept has faced a crisis of confidence from time to time. But each time it has managed to reinvent itself as "new and improved," insisting on "being judged by a yet distant future, rather than a past that has been lived and experienced."[61] Once development recovers from one of its recurrent crises of confidence, a new forward-looking, inclusive, and optimistic vocabulary appears to take over, lending "the legitimacy that development actors need in order to justify their interventions."[62]

Meghalaya is hardly unique. Almost everywhere in the world the effects of development have been "messy, contradictory and multilayered."[63] Consider anthropologist Stacy Leigh Pigg's account of Nepal's encounter with development. In the indigenized version of the ideology of development in that country, social change came to be represented as social mobility. The promise—in terms of the imagery of development—was for "a life modelled on that of the most affluent Nepalis, yet in its implementation the increased access to resources that would foster true economic mobility is seldom made possible." Not surprisingly, few in rural Nepal want to be seen as a lowly "target" of development projects. Instead, they all aspire to become a higher-status agent of development—that is, a salaried government or an international NGO worker that implements development.[64] This is hardly unique to Nepal. If a structure of "permanent deferral" pervades all development agendas, the deficient subjects—that is, those portrayed as needing development[65]—reject the idea of developmental time.[66] Everyone wants a piece of the developmental action, and they want it now. All across the "developing world," the apparatus of development—the jobs in government, development agencies, and NGOs—and the public and private resources spent on development are a significant source of wealth, power, status, and social mobility.[67] If we understand the concept of development in this way, Meghalaya's coal boom, which has generated wealth—but at the expense of the environment, public health, and even the lives of workers—would seem unexceptional.

There is a lot to be said for treating development not as a category of analysis but as a category of practice[68] or as a native category.[69] One can think of development as an identity discourse in the manner that Mary Louise Pratt says modernity was "Europe's (or the white world's) identity discourse as it assumed global dominance." The idea of modernity, she writes, "was one of the chief tropes through which Europe constructed itself as a center, as *the* center, and the rest of the planet as a—its—periphery."[70] The material effects of development—roads; automobiles; changes in housing and clothing styles; the use of electricity; access to schools, colleges, and modern health care—have profound effects on the ways in which people make sense of themselves and the world. Development, says geographer and political ecologist Thomas Perreault, "forms a conceptual context that shapes meanings, aspirations, and social understandings. Identities of individuals, groups, and places are formed through the lens of, and in relationship to, the seductive promise of development."[71] The pursuit of development is intimately tied to the desire for recognition, equity, and justice.[72] Colonial-era anthropologists and some contemporary activists preoccupied with the authenticity of cultures and their preservation fail to recognize the signifi-cance of the emergence of development as a site of cultural politics and contestation. In Northeast India, Christian missionaries may have under-stood this better than anyone else—though not because they were interested in understanding the subtleties of cultural change among the people they were trying to convert. The desire for development grows out of the quest for equal dignity and for equal membership within a new world society.[73] Even some radical critics of the idea of development now grudgingly rec-ognize this. Thus, postdevelopment thinker Wolfgang Sachs laments that "across the world hopes for the future are fixed on the rich man's patterns of production and consumption." The world has seen political and economic decolonization, he writes, but not the decolonization of the imagination. And the consequences, from his perspective, are grim. "The longing for greater justice on the part of the South is one reason for the persistence of the development creed—even if, in this century, neither the planet nor the people of the world can any longer afford its predominance."[74]

When the province of eastern Bengal and Assam was created in 1905, historian Bodhisattva Kar tells us that if anxiety about being grouped together with the "savage Assamese" characterized the reaction of the Bengali *bhadralok*, the Assamese elite was utterly dismayed at being "relegated to the levels of Lushais and other hill tribes."[75] Since its very beginning, colonial modernity in this frontier province has relied on elites shifting the burden of primitiveness onto nonelites.[76] A hundred years ago the Assamese gentry, in the words of the historian Jayeeta Sharma, "morbidly conscious of their inclusion among the 'barbarous hordes' who inhabited British India's frontiers," drew on the linguistic and racial theories of the time to assert their "claims to modernity while simultaneously pushing the burden of primitiveness onto 'non Aryan' neighbors"—including migrant tea plantation workers.[77] Postcolonial modernity continues to reproduce this "improvement template,"[78] pushing the burden of primitiveness and backwardness to newer groups of people.

## THE ALLURE OF ETHNIC HOMELANDS

India's Northeast policy, as we saw in Chapter 1, has evolved via a process of muddling through, as Northeast India emerged as an official region of eight states.[79] The colonial-era protocols of protection and exclusion acquired a new lease on life as peace and order became the top priorities of a national security–minded governing elite in New Delhi. The excluded area protocols were now packaged as policies of positive discrimination or affirmative action. Most of the excluded areas are now states of the Indian Union. But they are states with a crucial difference: the elected state governments consist almost entirely of politicians belonging to the core ethnic groups—the Scheduled Tribes that the postcolonial state and its institutions sanctify and legitimize as indigenous to that state in accordance with the colonial ethnoterritorial frame. These core ethnic groups have near-exclusive access to public employment, business and trade licenses, rights to land ownership and exchange, and the right to seek elected office. They are, in other words, de facto ethnic homelands. The economist authors of an article on agrarian change in Arunachal Pradesh describe the state's polity and society as "ethnicized." Because citizenship in the state is "ethnicized," the ethnic tribal elites are able to maintain their hold as "representatives of the 'community.'"[80] Table 1 summarizes the data on the composition of the state legislatures of Northeast India in terms of the distribution of seats reserved for Scheduled Tribes and the nonreserved general seats.

In the legislative assemblies of Arunachal Pradesh, Mizoram, and Nagaland—Excluded Areas in colonial times—all but one seat are reserved for Scheduled Tribes. In Meghalaya, which was a Partially Excluded Area, fifty-five of the sixty seats are reserved. The law freezes the balance between

TABLE 1. *Reserved seats for Scheduled Tribes in state legislative assemblies in Northeast India*

| STATES | ST[†] as % of Population* | TOTAL Members | GENERAL Seats | RESERVED Seats (STs[†]) | RESERVED Seats (SCs[‡]) |
|---|---|---|---|---|---|
| ARUNACHAL | 68.8 | 60 | 1 | 59 | 0 |
| ASSAM | 12.5 | 126 | 102 | 16 | 8 |
| MANIPUR | 40.9 | 60 | 40 | 19 | 1 |
| MEGHALAYA | 86.2 | 60 | 5 | 55 | 0 |
| MIZORAM | 94.4 | 40 | 1 | 39 | 0 |
| NAGALAND | 86.5 | 60 | 1 | 59 | 0 |
| SIKKIM | 33.8 | 32 | 18 | 12 | 2 |
| TRIPURA | 31.8 | 60 | 30 | 20 | 10 |

*Calculated based on Census of 2011
†ST=Scheduled Tribe
‡SC=Scheduled Caste

reserved and unreserved seats, thus disallowing demographic changes—
and the required statutory delimitation of constituencies that follows—to
change this balance. In effect, the particular ethnic composition of the
political class of these states is legally guaranteed, at least for now.

India now can boast of a visible well-to-do Northeast Indian elite
of ethnic tribal descent. An important contributor to it, not often commented on, is that they successfully compete for positions reserved for STs
in the upper tiers of the Indian civil services. This is partly because of the
advantage of English proficiency that many Northeastern STs have over
communities listed as ST in mainland India. The former Indian diplomat
Lalthlamuong Keivom writes proudly of the fact that STs from Northeast
India, especially of the Chin-Kuki-Mizo group, have a significant presence
in India's elite civil services such as the Indian Foreign Service, the Indian
Administrative Service, and the Indian Police Service. "Today you will find
them," he writes, "in every Ministry in Delhi, including the President's Office and Parliament Secretariat." A number of them have been ambassadors
and high commissioners of India. The first Scheduled Tribe member of the
Indian Administrative Service is from the Biate community of the Chin-
Kuki-Mizo group spread across a number of states of Northeast India. He
entered the civil service as early as 1954.[81] The emergence of an elite of
ethnic tribal descent is to some extent the result of the exclusionary hold
that the core ethnic tribal elites now have over the local state apparatus of
the erstwhile excluded areas. The unregulated coal mining in Meghalaya
has been aptly described as a product of the "increasing capture of the state
apparatus by the mining barons and their administrative cohorts."[82] State
patronage and protection have also played a critical role in the emergence
of large agricultural estates in Arunachal Pradesh. Powerful politicians and
their relatives control almost all tea and large horticultural estates in that
state.[83] They benefit from substantial state support in the form of direct
subsidies, marketing assistance, and indirect subsidies such as the illicit
use of workers on the government's payroll in private estates. The state,
as Barbara Harris-White and her coauthors put it, "is deeply implicated
in the primary accumulation of the tribal elites."[84] The hill societies of
Northeast India, says Karlsson, are "increasingly becoming a class-divided

society in which some people have managed to take possession of huge tracts of land and control the lucrative extraction of timber, coal, and other resources, while the number of people whose access to land is insufficient or nonexistent access to land is increasing day by day."[85]

Not surprisingly, politicians and activists that belong to the core ethnic tribal groups of the ethnic homeland states are zealous defenders of these protocols. Even in the rest of Northeast India, the perceived advantages of the excluded area legacy have captured the imagination of ethnic activists. It would not be an exaggeration to say that the states of Northeast India that were once excluded areas now define the aspirations window for others; that is, their achievements are seen as attainable by others situated similarly in the region.[86] A potent new kind of political mobilization now flourishes in Northeast India. Borrowing from anthropologist James Ferguson, I have called it the claim to rightful shares: allocations properly due to rightful owners. Such a claim requires that the law recognize certain groups of people as insiders and others as outsiders within a territory. The statutory language that makes such a legal distinction possible is that of protective status on grounds of indigeneity, relative "backwardness," or perceived vulnerability vis-à-vis ethnically defined outsiders. The mobilization of groups seeking new preferences is, of course, a familiar theme in Indian politics. But in Northeast India such demands tend to take a territorial and exclusionary form, thanks to the institutional legacy of the colonial ethnoterritorial frame. Thus, groups without their homelands now aspire to being defined as the core ethnic tribal group in a territory recognized as their homeland, where they would benefit from these protocols. New groups demand recognition as Scheduled Tribes; those that already have Scheduled Tribe status seek the protection of the Constitution's Sixth Schedule (that can be traced back to the protocols governing the excluded areas in colonial times); and those that have Sixth Schedule status ask for full-fledged statehood. Two particular features of India's constitutional order have allowed this form of politics to flourish. First, the Constitution leaves the question of groups that are entitled to preferences—mainly the status of a Scheduled Tribe in the context of Northeast India—constitutionally and politically open.[87] Second, India's demos-enabling "federalism"[88] puts few constraints on the Parliament's power to make and break states. The Indian Parliament can create a new state by changing the political boundaries of an existing state, with minimal consultations with the elected legislature of the affected state. The ease with which states can be made and broken reinforces the idea that any demand for an ethnic homeland could be successful if backed by sufficient evidence of political support, including capacity for violence. Given the history of how the states of Northeast India came into being, even full statehood appears to be an eminently realistic political goal to ethnic activists in the region.

The demand for extending the Inner Line is now heard in parts of Northeast India that were not an excluded area under colonial rule, notably in Manipur and in the state of Meghalaya—a Partially Excluded Area in colonial times. To be sure, in Manipur the demand is for the "implementation of [an] Inner Line Permit System (ILPS) or a similar mechanism."[89] The appeal of the Inner Line lies in the fact that Indian citizens, as well as foreigners, require permits to enter these states. It becomes a legal way of excluding ethnic "outsiders"—whether Indian citizens or alleged foreign nationals—from political claim making. The claims by those who see themselves as rightful owners now command significant local political backing in the region. As a result, the hold of land or other resources by "outsiders"—that is, immigrants and successive generations of descendants—has become quite tenuous in some areas. This can happen even without state authorities formally conceding an ethnic homeland of some kind.

## CHANGING RELATIONS TO LAND

With the rise of resource frontiers, people's relations to land in Northeast India are changing dramatically. During Meghalaya's coal boom, land was valued not for its yield or the kind of crops it produced but for coal deposits. Even a plot of land that could be used only for dumping extracted coal because of its location could bring home an income.[90] In the hills of Meghalaya, agriculture is no longer the focus of the ambitions and dreams of young people, nor is it the focus of their parents' aspirations for them. Yet the political saliency of land claims looms as large as ever. This is primarily because of the value that land has acquired in the context of the mobilization of those landscapes into resource frontiers. Harris-White and her coauthors tell us that in the state of Arunachal Pradesh elites of Arunachali ethnic tribal descent try to "control as much land as possible" because restrictions on transactions in land markets put land values on a steep upward curve. The most highly valued land is in urban areas because it "attracts high sales values as well as high rent, when sold or rented out for non-agricultural and residential use." But newly enclosed lands are also turned into commercial agricultural estates producing tea, horticultural crops, or vegetables. Commercial agriculture, however, is only a tiny part of the state's economy. Most de facto landowners of the core ethnic groups that have managed to acquire substantial chunks of land lease it out to migrant tenants that have no legal residential or property rights in the state because of the Inner Line Permit regime in place.[91]

With the prospects of Arunachal Pradesh becoming a hydropower resource frontier, significant land-value premiums have become associated with proximity to hydropower project sites. In this twenty-first-century frontier economy, it is no longer a matter of governments paying compensation for land acquisition. Private companies are willing to pay unprecedented amounts of money for transferred land-use rights. Mibi Ete cites the example of an influential and politically connected family that was paid as much as Rs. 2,70,000 (approximately US$3,860 but equivalent to significantly more in local purchasing power) a month. The amount included "direct welfare" payments, as well as rent and lease payments for real estate and vehicles leased by the company from members of the family. The company in question is the Luxembourg-based hydropower developer Velcan Energy. Since the expatriate managers of the company tend to "think in Euros" she explains, they "were willing to spend money as long as the job was done." The area in Arunachal's West Siang District that she studied saw a significant rise in land disputes in anticipation of such potential windfalls. There are even examples of companies being pressured "to rearrange the layout of the project facilities" so that groups that can claim indigeneity in a particular location can gain from the transfer of land-use rights. Even the naming of a hydropower project has sometimes become controversial because of the signals it sends regarding the ethnic communities that might be able to demand compensation based on ancestral land claims. Ete found little opposition to hydropower projects in that part of Arunachal Pradesh; there were only distributional conflicts over gains. Moreover, "there was a broad consensus that 'If anything has to happen in this area, it can only be through the private companies. The government has had its chance and it failed.'"[92] The future of many of these projects, however, seems less certain now than it did a few years ago. Despite the memorandums of understanding signed in exchange for large amounts of money,[93] not many dams have entered the construction phase. A number of private companies are now trying to withdraw or enter into partnership with the public sector National Hydel Power Corporation.[94]

It is the income-earning opportunities from activities other than direct farming that explains why scholars of hydropower development in Arunachal Pradesh and Sikkim report the significant presence of "pro-development actors" at the grassroots.[95] In Northeast India today, the century-old improvement template and the theme of overcoming the burden of primitiveness and backwardness is fully alive and well, and they continue to be reproduced. Ete tells us of the Ramo people—a small group considered indigenous to the Sii valley of West Siang District. The reason they support the location of a hydropower project site in their ancestral lands is their self-perception "of marginality, powerlessness and backwardness vis-à-vis other tribes of the district and state." Their experiences in the district headquarters or the state capital, where numerically larger and hence politically more influential groups—perceived as being more advanced—look down upon them as backward and rustic, reinforce this self-perception. Ete attended a public meeting where a number of speakers lamented that the community has "produced only a handful of high-ranking government officials, a sure sign of lack of development."[96] They hope that investments by hydropower developers will enable them to become as "advanced" as their peers.

## THE NEW PROSPERITY, CHANGING LAND RELATIONS, AND MIGRATION

The following account of a village that benefited from coal mining illustrates the prosperity brought about by Meghalaya's rise as a coal frontier: "Shangpung is a small village in the heavily-mined coal belt of the West

Jaintia Hills. Almost everyone here owns a concrete house, beautifully constructed and painted in bright colours. It is difficult to miss the biggest building in the village that houses a church and a school. Maruti cars are ubiquitous and seem to be the preferred choice of personal transport. The money that the coal brought infused a new level of prosperity into the lives of locals."[97]

Of course, those who prosper from mining profits do not stay in those ecologically devastated mining areas for long. "Flush with success," notes a study published in 2007, "they've now relocated to Shillong, Meghalaya's capital city, and Jowai, the district headquarters of Jaintia Hills, buying up property and houses in rich suburbs."[98] This is the other part of the answer to the question raised by this chapter's epigraph. The profits from coal in Meghalaya have opened for some people new horizons and possibilities that were unimaginable a generation ago. One NGO activist told a journalist that this newly prosperous class now sends their children to be educated in Delhi or Bangalore, and "some even go to China and Russia to become doctors."[99]

In previous chapters, I have referred to emigration of Northeasterners to metropolitan India. Strangely enough, in Indian official thinking about the region, there is barely any recognition of the significance of this phenomenon.[100] But thanks to the work of scholars like Duncan McDuie-Ra, B. G. Karlsson, and Dolly Kikon, we now know a good deal about it. A theme that emerges from their work is what Karlsson and Kikon describe as the "stretched lifeworlds" of most Northeastern migrants.[101] While emigration was traditionally thought of as exiting one place and entering another, there is now a more fluid geography at work. People move back-and-forth, and Northeastern migrants are no exception. In the towns and villages of Northeast India, the number of remittance-receiving households is growing. Northeasterners living in Delhi may have become an important part of the city's economic life, but few hold stable jobs. This has led McDuie-Ra to wonder what an economic downturn—reduced investments in call centers, decline in retail jobs, or further challenges for the Indian airline industry— might mean for the migration flow and for the remittance economies back home. How would the returning migrants be reintegrated into the local economies?[102] Whether or not such a scenario is realistic, it is safe to say that while many a returning migrant may dream of becoming an independent entrepreneur in food, fashion, software, or the hospitality sectors, few are likely to think of his or her future in terms of agriculture. Yet for most of these people and their families, land is sure to remain an important source of income—perhaps even the most important one if remittances dry up. Such a scenario makes the politics of rightful shares more comprehensible, though not more excusable or fair. It is important therefore to ask who does the hard, physical labor in the fields?

While there is no general answer, the study of agrarian change in Arunachal Pradesh by Harris-White and her coauthors provides some important clues. They tell us of a pattern where land is controlled by ethnic tribal Arunachalis but is farmed by migrant sharecroppers who lack even the right to live in that state, thanks to a colonial era protocol: the Inner Line Permit regime. They find this "an increasingly visible form of production in the paddy-producing areas of the state." They find that most of the informal leasing arrangements are "neo-feudal" in character. Some even include "the imposition of private and arbitrary exactions in kind."[103] It is not clear how generalizable their finding is, but it is safe to say that many ethnic tribal Arunachalis now take advantage of opportunities for rental income from migrant tenants doing settled cultivation in lands that were traditionally either uncultivated or used for shifting cultivation. The pattern is likely to hold for some of the other old excluded area states as well, where, in the words of former senior Nagaland civil servant Alemtemshi Jamir, people who have land do not have the labor or capital to extend settled cultivation, and those with labor do not have access to land for permanent cultivation.[104]

The *Arunachal Pradesh Human Development Report 2005* provides a portrait of migrant tenants in the state that complements the study by Harris-White and her coauthors. The report makes the bullock-driven plow brought to the state by migrant sharecroppers the symbol of the state's "agricultural modernization," since settled cultivation has expanded in the state primarily through its use.[105] For illustrative purposes, the report includes the story of one Jamir Ali. He lived at that time in the Dikrong

River Valley and had moved to Arunachal from the adjacent Lakhimpur District of Assam in the foothills of Arunachal. He leased five acres of land on an informal sharecropping arrangement, and his family of seven lived in a thatched hut he built on that land. Apart from the share of the crop, earnings from seasonal labor, including the part of his wages as a rickshaw driver that he could keep—the other part he pays as rent to the rickshaw owner—are the family's sources of livelihood. Huts that belong to migrant sharecroppers "dot the entire valley," says the report, and "people like Jamir Ali are increasingly becoming common in the other valleys of Arunachal as well."[106] But just as the reader contemplates how this unconventional road to Arunachal's "agricultural modernization" might play itself out, we are reminded that access to land in Arunachal is the domain of customary law, and the Inner Line Permit regime severely restricts the rights of "outsiders." There are no official land records, and the land rental markets are entirely informal. The contracts to lease lands are always oral and have no legal sanction; they are "short-term and eviction may take place any time."[107]

There is no chance of Jamir Ali's sharecropping rights ever becoming secure nor of his terms of tenancy improving through political action, which is at least theoretically possible in any nonexcluded area. From the point of view of human development—the focus of this government report—we learn that "most sharecroppers have been able to improve their economic condition, but very few sharecroppers manage to send their children to school." Jamir Ali's great grandfather had migrated to Assam from My- mensingh District in eastern Bengal in the early part of the twentieth century.[108] So he is probably not surprised once in a while to be called a "Bangladeshi." But whether unauthorized immigrants or descendants of earlier immigrants, the Jamir Alis of Northeast India—often seen as false nationals and de facto second-class citizens—now play a key role in the economy of the region: as marginalized sharecroppers in Arunachal Pradesh, as disenfranchised workers in the coal mines of Meghalaya, and in many other subaltern roles. But there appears to be no place for them in Northeast India's economic future as imagined in official narratives.

Questioning the wisdom of making "nondominance" the primary con- sideration in deciding whether any particular group of people should be regarded as "indigenous,"[109] anthropologist John Bowen once asked if "a reversal in political fortunes could create newly 'indigenous' peoples out of formerly dominant ones"?[110] In Northeast India this is not a rhetorical question but an empirical one. A focus on this region as a resource frontier draws attention to new forms of exploitation, dispossession, subordination, and subcitizenship that have emerged under the postcolonial dispensation. Scholars and policy analysts have paid far less attention to these issues than to the questions of identity that have shaped the political dynamics of this postcolonial resource frontier.

## CHAPTER 4

# THE NAGA CONFLICT
## *Ceasefire Politics and Elusive Peace*

The conventional model of a peace process is drawn from
international negotiations in which there are two sides with
equal legal standing and roughly commensurate capabilities.
The format of the talks is a square table, with the parties
facing one another, and the mediator at the head of the table.
. . . What [they] wanted was not a square table in which the
government faced the rebels, but a round table in which all
stakeholders, armed and unarmed could represent themselves.
—Alex de Waal, "Violence and Peacemaking
in the Political Marketplace"

ON AUGUST 3, 2015, at a ceremony held in the Indian prime minister's official residence, the Indian government and the National Socialist
Council of Nagaland (IM)[1]—the NSCN-IM—announced the signing
of a "framework agreement." The NSCN-IM and the Indian government
had signed a ceasefire agreement in 1997, and the two sides have had
a series of negotiations since then.[2] But they gained fresh momentum
when the BJP-led government headed by Narendra Modi came to power
in 2014. The news of the agreement gave rise to great expectations that
Northeast India's oldest armed conflict might finally come to an end. At
the time of this writing (February 2019) the tenure of the Modi government is nearing completion. But the expectations of a negotiated end to
the Naga conflict have waned significantly. There are media reports of the
talks having reached a "dead-end."[3] Many fear that the fragile gains made
in the last few years may be lost if elections lead to significant political
realignments.[4] The influential Naga civil society organization Forum for
Naga Reconciliation has called for "re-imagining the Indo-Naga Peace

Process." The Indian official most directly connected to the negotiations, however, has denied that talks have reached a dead end. He says that they continue to yield results.[5]

The talks have been secretive. Officially no detail of the negotiations is made public. Yet there has been much speculation about the institutional arrangements being envisaged. The NSCN-IM has long maintained that two of its demands—Naga sovereignty and the integration of the Naga inhabited areas—are nonnegotiable. While its decision to talk with the Indian government is generally interpreted as a sign that it is now willing to settle for something less than full independent statehood, the NSCN-IM has not publicly acknowledged a change of stance. Any suggestion by Indian officials that it has agreed to give up its demand for sovereignty, or that the two sides are seeking a solution within the framework of the Indian Constitution, is immediately met with strong denials by the NSCN-IM. Nevertheless, the rebel organization's second "nonnegotiable" demand— Nagalim, or Greater Nagaland, as detractors call this irredentist territorial imaginary—has become the focus of growing public attention since the NSCN-IM began negotiating with the government. It is widely assumed that the final agreement would sketch out a new governmental structure addressing this issue.

Narratives of Naga nationalism have long been imbued with the idea that the Naga homeland includes contiguous areas in the Northeast Indian states of Arunachal Pradesh, Assam, and Manipur, as well as parts of Burma/Myanmar. This territorial imaginary has an interesting relationship to the uneven geography of power of this former imperial frontier. The district of Naga Hills of British colonial times was divided into administered, unadministered, and loosely administered segments. "Over the period of British intrusion," writes Andrew West, "the administered area boundary moved gradually eastwards from the plains continuing in the 1920s." The British conquest was incomplete at the end of Raj, and "the British handed over to India and Burma a tract of hill country with inhabitants that had never been administered and controlled by the imperial power."[6] This tract of unadministered land, however, was claimed as British territory. It was part of the "frontier of active protection" in Viceroy Curzon's conception of the threefold frontier of empire discussed in Chapter 1. In other words, the imagined Naga homeland of the Naga nationalists spans the spaces of governance located in all three of Curzon's threefold frontier: the administrative border, the frontier of active protection, and the outer or advanced strategic frontier.[7] Undoubtedly, there are some people living in these territories who desire to live in a future Naga homeland, though it is probably true of Nagas rather than non-Nagas. Significant sections of the latter have, in fact, expressed strong opposition to the Nagalim project. As a result, the prospect of secret negotiations yielding territorial concessions to the NSCN-IM has spurred hopes as well as fears in the region.[8] It has affected politics within the state of Nagaland as well, where there is now "an inchoate sons-of-soil movement," which is openly—though not rhetorically—critical of the Nagalim project and the NSCN-IM. The NSCN-IM's authority to speak for all Nagas now faces significant challenge.[9]

NAGA NATIONALISM: A BRIEF HISTORICAL OVERVIEW

The Naga National Council (NNC) under its leader, Angami Zapu Phizo, had declared the independence of the Nagas from the British on August 14, 1947—a day before India itself became independent: a fact of great significance in narratives of Naga nationhood. The NNC organized a plebiscite in 1951 and claimed that there was near-unanimous support among Nagas for independent statehood. It organized a successful boycott of India's first general election in 1952 and set up a parallel government. Independent India's first prime minister, Jawaharlal Nehru, believed that the idea of Naga independence was "absurd"; it didn't deserve even a moment's consideration.[10] After some initial effort at negotiations, his government responded to the Naga rebellion with brutal military force. The consequences of the decision are felt to this day. The experience of forced displacements during village regrouping, for example, "hugely increased the support for the insurgents, not necessarily ideologically, but as a matter of justice."[11] Drawing on conversations conducted many years later with Nagas who endured those counterinsurgency campaigns, social anthropologist Nandini Sundar concludes that while the Indian state expected to "commandeer political affiliations," the experience of

village regrouping had "only buried them underground." The entire population of Nagaland "became 'UG' (underground) or as they preferred to
call themselves, 'national workers,' fighting for the Naga nation."[12] Phizo
escaped to what was then East Pakistan (today's Bangladesh), and after
traveling incognito through a number of countries, he reached London
in June of 1960 and secured political asylum in the United Kingdom.
From his base in London, he campaigned for international support but
without much success. His physical absence from the scene began to affect the dynamics of Naga politics. This was, after all, long before the
telecommunications revolution of the late twentieth century that made
long-distance nationalism viable.[13] But even though Nehru was able to
secure the acquiescence of the international community to his repressive
measures,[14] he could not have possibly imagined that the conflict would
remain unresolved more than half a century later.

In 1957, the district of Nagaland and the Tuensang Frontier Division—a territory that was part of the North East Frontier Tracts (and
later the North East Frontier Agency) in colonial times—were merged
into a new administrative-territorial unit called the Naga Hills–Tuensang
Area. This became the state of Nagaland in 1963—formally, a full-fledged
state of the Indian Union. The NSCN-IM later coined the name *Nagalim*
to distinguish the geographical imaginary of the land of the Nagas from
the territory that makes up the state of Nagaland. But the Indian government's concerted efforts to mobilize support for its policies through
various means—including the transfer of significant resources to Naga
elites in the form of grants and subsidies to the state of Nagaland—began
yielding results. The state government of Nagaland depends almost entirely
on funds from the central government. Because Nagaland was "created
out of a political necessity," writes Alemtemshi Jamir—a former Naga
civil servant who was once the state's development commissioner—it was
not expected to be "economically viable for a long time." It has a "huge
overloaded governmental structure, the sustenance of which, occupies
almost all the energies and resources of the Government," which leaves
"very little resource for other activities including development."[15] In 1975
a group of Naga moderates signed the Shillong Accord with the Indian

government effectively accepting this political status quo, and soon Phizo and the NNC lost their position of preeminence in Naga politics. But a group of dissenters launched the National Socialist Council of Nagaland five years later. It declared the Shillong Accord a sellout and a betrayal of the Naga cause. The NSCN split in 1988, and the NSCN-IM became the dominant faction of the breakaway organization.[16] Led by Isaak Chishi Swu, who passed away in June of 2016, and Thuingaleng Muivah, this faction emerged as a serious political force and the standard-bearer of Naga nationalism.

Significantly, Muivah, now the sole surviving founding leader of the NSCN-IM, is a Tangkhul Naga from Manipur—a princely state in colonial times. Relative latecomers to the Naga fold, the Tangkhuls were not represented in the Naga Club that petitioned the Simon Commission in 1929—a foundational event in narratives of Naga national identity. Nor did the plebiscite organized by Phizo in 1951 extend to these areas. But the rebel organization has built significant support among the Tangkhuls. During their fieldwork in Muivah's home district of Ukhrul in Manipur in 2016, Shalaka Thakur and Rajesh Venugopal found the NSCN-IM's organizational presence in that area to be an "illustrative case of [a] parallel governance system at its most acute."[17] The state of affairs can be best described as actually existing shared sovereignty:[18] with institutions of the Indian government and those run by the NSCN-IM sharing attributes of statehood such as the capacity to wield coercive violence and extract revenue, as well as substantial levels of popular legitimacy and support.[19] In the course of the long history of the Indian state institutions' engagement with the Naga nationalist movement, a variety of ad hoc arrangements have emerged among state governments, armed political groups focused on battles over state power, and nonstate-armed actors focused on control over economic resources.[20] The ceasefire and the peace negotiations of the past two decades have given a further fillip to these practices. This has kept the question of effective sovereignty in abeyance, which now presents significant challenges to the Naga peace process. Even if a "final agreement" of some sort is signed in the near future, a durable settlement of the Naga conflict is likely to remain elusive.

## THE NAGAS, THE NAGA HILLS, AND THE NAGA NATION

In an essay published in 1922, John Henry Hutton, an early twentieth-century colonial official whose writings are an important part of the received wisdom about the Nagas, explained the category of Naga: "The expression 'Naga' is ... useful as an arbitrary term to denote the tribes living in certain parts of the Assam hills, which may be roughly defined as bounded by the Hokong valley in the north-east, the plain of the Brahmaputra Valley to the north-west, of Cachar to the south-west and of the Chindwin to east. ... The south of the Manipur Valley roughly marks the point of contact between the Naga tribes and the very much more closely interrelated group of Kuki tribes—Thado, Lushei, Chin, etc."[21]

Hutton's idea of the Naga people and their territory—despite the tentativeness of his formulations ("useful as an arbitrary term")—became central to the twentieth-century Naga political imagination.[22] Colonial writings of the previous century emphasized that the term *Naga* "is quite foreign to the people themselves" and that there was no evidence of the name ever being an endonym.[23] In fact, the British probably used the term initially only "to distinguish hill people from the plains people."[24] It is not surprising, therefore, that more than eighty years after the publication of Hutton's essay, the editors of a volume of essays titled *Naga Identities* found that "no one can say how many Naga tribes there actually are today."[25] There are anywhere between thirty and eighty tribes that belong to "the Naga group," and in some areas the situation is "fluid."[26] It should be remembered that *Naga* is not a linguistic label. The people described as Naga speak a variety of languages that belong to "at least two, and possibly several, completely distinct branches of Tibeto-Burman."[27]

The Nagas were pioneers among tribal communities of Northeast India to call themselves a nation—and, in effect, to reject the colonial designation tribe.[28] That there would be a move to find an alternative to *tribe* as a collective self-description is not surprising. The term *tribe* in British colonial usage in this part of the world referred to a particular "relationship of very unequal power. To be tribal meant to be subordinated to a superior power with a civilizing mission."[29] John Thomas, a scholar of the history of

the relationship between Christianity and Naga national identity, believes
that the Nagas preferred the word *nation* because it allowed them to avoid
being "dragged into a system of socio-religious hierarchy that structures
the Indian caste society.... They did not want to have anything to do with
such a society and wanted to be defined as a 'nation' in their own right."[30]
The NNC named its official publication *The Naga Nation* as far back as the
1940s. The Indian government later banned this publication.[31]

The idea of a Naga nation developed hand in hand with the process of
conversion to Baptist Christianity. A key force in fostering a "pan-Naga
identity" was the missionary network that brought hundreds of Naga youth
from different communities together.[32] Christian proselytization is a key
theme in the campaign for Naga nationhood. "Nagas for Christ" was once
used as a motto. The Council of Naga Baptist Churches (CNBC) was
formed to unite "the Naga tribes under the banner of 'Nagas for Christ'
and encouraging the Naga churches to play a constructive role in the Naga
national life."[33] At the same time, because some Nagas—albeit a minority—
continue to follow local religious traditions and practices, the conflation
between Christianity and Naga identity has also been a politically sensitive issue. But as far as the NSCN-IM is concerned, the Christian idea of
salvation is foundational to its worldview. It provides "an almost prophetic
vision of Nagalim," writes a Naga scholar of religious studies and theology,
"that combines an evangelical and soteriological theology, and providence
for the Naga nation through the Old Testament idea of 'chosenness.'"[34] In
fact, the NSCN-IM's flag features a rainbow in the blue sky—a reference to
the Genesis story of God's covenant with Noah after the Flood—and sig-
nifying the idea of God's covenant with the Nagas.[35] The Christian message
of salvation has facilitated both the incorporation of newer groups into the
Naga fold and the expansion of the political influence of the NSCN-IM
into these areas. Thus, the Tangkhuls of Manipur—the NSCN-IM leader
Muivah's community—are relative latecomers to the Naga fold. But their
early conversion to Baptist Christianity prepared the ground for their full
embrace of Naga nationhood. Significantly, Christianity among Nagas grew
much faster during the years of counterinsurgency and resistance. The sense
of being Naga intensified, taking the form of a "distinctly Christian national

identity . . . positioned against a dominant 'Hindu/Muslim' India."[36] The
Forum for Naga Reconciliation, the civil society organization I referred to
earlier, which has emerged as a major force in the peace process outside the
negotiating room, enjoys the support of important church organizations.
It is led by Wati Aier, a Christian public intellectual, who until recently
headed the Oriental Theological Seminary, an important Baptist educational institution in Nagaland.

Since the factional divisions of Naga politics often follow tribal lines—
that is, the lines of the officially recognized Naga subtribes such as Ao,
Angami, Lotha, Tangkhul, and so forth—some analysts consider those
identity categories to be more "real" than the Naga identity. This, however,
is a misunderstanding of the project of Naga nationhood. Naga nationalists aspire to Naga unity, and they view those tribal loyalties as residues
of a premodern past and an obstacle to Naga solidarity. The aspiration to
break away from the "backwardness and parochialism" of the tribal past
and become part of the "enlightened and modern" world of Christianity
is inseparable from the idea of the Naga nation. The NSCN-IM leader
Muivah once called "tribalism" a "malignant bacteria" that threatens the
solidarity of the Naga people.[37] That does not mean that the political divisions among Nagas are not substantial. For a number of years following
the ceasefire agreement of 1997 between the Indian government and the
NSCN-IM, fatalities as a result of interfactional warfare increased, whereas
violence between armed rebels and security personnel came down. The
killings were reduced only after a covenant for reconciliation was signed
between Naga factions in 2008.[38] This effort also led to the formation of
the FNR—the Forum for Naga Reconciliation. The role of the Christian
themes of covenant and reconciliation in this context is noteworthy.

The analytical problems of reifying groups and treating them "as if they
were internally homogeneous, externally bounded groups, even unitary
collective actors with common purposes," are now well recognized. As
Rogers Brubaker put it: "It is clear that organizations, not ethnic groups as
such, are the chief protagonists of ethnic conflict and ethnic violence and
that the relationship between organizations and the groups they claim to
represent is often deeply ambiguous."[39] Naga public intellectual Charles

Chasie blames factional conflicts on Nagas having acquired "a cause" before becoming a people. There was a time when the cause had helped Nagas become a people. But subsequently, the cause itself became the main thing, and it "preceded the process of our becoming a people." As a result, "the building of our nationhood got neglected and even began to slide backwards. What further accentuated this neglect was the explanation that our nationhood was already a fact and that our people would automatically unite and become one, cooperating with each other, once the Cause was achieved. The logical extension of such [a] thinking process is that only a few 'traitors' were standing in the way."[40] Chasie laments that unlike parts of the world where external mediation can facilitate political settlements, geopolitical dynamics dictate that Nagas must rely entirely on their internal resources to unite. Interestingly, he invokes "nation-building" to focus attention on the task involved: "you simply can't build a nation without massive and continuous nation-building works."[41]

### SHARED SOVEREIGNTY: FACTS ON THE GROUND

On August 14, 2015—a little more than a week after the signing of the framework agreement—Muivah surprised everyone by announcing that the Indian government and the Nagas would share "sovereign powers." Indian officials had clearly hoped that the content of the negotiations would be kept under wraps until a final settlement was reached. Following Muivah's speech, there was immediate speculation in the Indian media that "secession" remains the goal of the rebel organization, and it became a matter of some anxiety among government officials. Their response was to call it "a misreading of Muivah's position." The phrases "sharing sovereign powers" and "sovereignty lies with the people," they claimed—somewhat ingeniously—are concepts drawn from the Indian Constitution.[42] The effort clearly was to square Muivah's assertion with familiar Indian "cartographic anxieties" about representational practices.[43]

This is not the only time since the signing of the framework agreement that the status of the NSCN-IM's supposedly nonnegotiable sovereignty demand has caused controversy. When the governor of Nagaland, P. B. Acharya, said that the NSCN-IM has dropped the demand for a sovereign

Nagaland,[44] the organization issued a press statement denying it. The governor, it said, was "totally misinformed or ignorant" of the agreement: "The framework agreement says that according to the universal principle sovereignty lies with the people, not [the] government. Therefore, the sovereignty of India lies with the Indian people and the sovereignty of the Nagas lies with the Naga people. However, there will be [a] sharing of sovereign power for enduring peaceful co-existence of the two entities. The Nagas will never accept any agreement that betrays their principle."[45]

The distinction between constituted power and constituent power, and the notion that sovereignty belongs to the underlying constituency and not to a governmental apparatus, are, of course, important theoretical ideas. They can be of help in designing democratic transitions from armed conflicts. But without agreement on what shared sovereignty means in concrete institutional terms, they don't say much. Attempts to seek clarification, even from Ravindra Narayan Ravi—the Indian official representing the government in the negotiations with the NSCN-IM—were unsuccessful. Asked whether the final settlement would be within the framework of the Indian Constitution, he replied: "We don't talk of the Constitution. We are talking on the issues." But he added that "there is no question of Nagas giving up sovereignty."[46] In short, no one knows for sure what the NSCN-IM leaders are ready to give up and what they are holding on to.

Constructive ambiguity is, of course, a familiar technique in negotiations. Language "sufficiently elastic to allow it to be read differently by the opposing sides" took the Northern Ireland peace process forward.[47] Ambiguity can help by deferring difficult questions for later resolution. But it can also raise unrealistic expectations. In the context of this complex nondyadic conflict, it has inevitably stirred anxieties among stakeholders not represented at the negotiating table. In this chapter I take the phrase "shared sovereignty" as a category of practice and show how the phrase is being mobilized to serve certain political ends.[48] It provides useful clues to a hybrid political regime taking shape on the ground—a kind of "wartime political order."[49]

Shared sovereignty is the latest in a number of key phrases that have entered the public discussion about the likely terms of a final political settlement. In 2003, former prime minister Atal Bihari Vajpayee—significantly, also of the BJP—had said, "Nagaland has a unique history. We are sensitive to this historical fact."[50] He probably meant it as a subtle acknowledgment of the fact—important to Naga nationalists—that Naga protest against incorporation into India began before India's independence. It was seen as belated recognition by the Indian government that it is historically inaccurate to call the Naga movement a "separatist insurgency"—the crucial implication being that it is unlike the run-of-the-mill rebel groups of Northeast India. There is an expectation that this recognition would affect the scope of the final peace settlement: that its terms would be significantly more generous—both in symbolic and substantive terms—than the other peace accords that the Indian government has signed with armed groups in the region. Ever since Vajpayee's 2003 statement, India's official acknowledgment of the "unique history of the Nagas" has become a refrain among NSCN-IM leaders and their supporters.

Modern states like to maintain the fiction of Weberian sovereignty: the claim to "the monopoly of the legitimate use of force" within its territory.[51] Muivah's statements and the NSCN-IM's open display of the symbols of a state-in-waiting challenge this fiction.[52] Former Indian national security adviser M. K. Narayanan expressed dismay at the "play of words" referring to the use of the phrase "shared sovereignty." It could have far-reaching implications, he warned: "Accepting the Indian Constitution is an inalienable principle, and whether 'shared sovereignty' violates the basic principles of the Indian Constitution needs to be examined."[53] When it comes to Northeast India, however, New Delhi has been willing to live with modes of organizing political authority that would be unacceptable in other parts of India. There is a long history of significant structures of parallel government run by the NSCN-IM and other Naga rebel groups, which have had the acquiescence of Indian state institutions in the form of nonenforcement or reduced enforcement of laws. Arguably, the postcolonial state in Northeast India has long made significant compromises on its claim to a monopoly of violence and a monopoly of taxation.

Significantly, Muivah gave his shared sovereignty speech on August 14, 2015—a day traditionally celebrated by all factions of the Naga national movement as Naga Independence Day. He spoke at the NSCN-IM's headquarters: the biblically named Camp Hebron. Extremely adept at using the "languages of stateness,"[54] Muivah spoke as *Ato Kilonser* (prime minister) of the unrecognized Government of the People's Republic of Nagalim (GPRN). He unfurled the blue Nagalim flag and spoke from a bulletproof enclosure guarded by self-styled soldiers of the Naga Army—that is, armed NSCN-IM combatants. A local newspaper carried the report with the headline "Naga Sovereign Rights Affirmed."[55] Muivah's speech and the symbolism of a state-in-waiting surrounding the celebrations exemplify the long-standing efforts of the rebel group to create a compelling set of facts on the ground.

Numerous observers have commented on the collection of taxes and the dispensation of justice by the NSCN-IM and other Naga rebel factions.[56] Shalaka Thakur and Rajesh Venugopal found during their fieldwork in Muivah's home district of Ukhrul in Manipur in 2016 that the GPRN—controlled by the NSCN-IM—has an "extensive, and autonomous revenue collection system" in that area.[57] All armed political groups in Northeast India raise funds. They like to describe these funds as voluntary donations, but in less sympathetic circles they are called extortions. The NSCN-IM refers to them as the Naga national tax. Whether they are donations, taxes, or extortion is in the eye of the beholder. According to a senior official of the Nagaland state government, because the NSCN factions rely on public support, they did not target the average person prior to the ceasefire. But now there is evidence of significant levels of fund-raising affecting most people living in Naga areas. According to one report, poor households pay a house tax of one thousand rupees, and businessmen and government officials pay as much as a quarter of their income to each of the four rebel groups. People get receipts for their payments on official rebel stationery.[58] In 2015, a person living in Nagaland told an Indian journalist that he pays "an annual house tax" to various rebel factions. He said that it is "wrong" that "a family has to pay up to Rs. 10,000 a year to different factions in the name of the 'national cause.'" His main hope from a final peace agreement is that he would not have to make those payments.[59] In Manipur's Ukhrul District, Thakur and Venugopal found that the NSCN-IM-controlled

GPRN taxes "households, commerce, employees, and government contracts." Salaried employees pay 2 percent of their salaries as taxes to the
GPRN and most village households pay a flat tax of 250 rupees. There is a
5 percent tax on government-funded infrastructure projects. But in the case
of certain programs such as the National Rural Employment Guarantee
Scheme, as much as 20 percent of the total allocated funds could go to the
coffers of the GPRN in the form of taxes collected from various parties.
The GPRN maintains a transparent accounting system, and it provides
official receipts as evidence of payment.[60]

No tax collection regime can be free of coercion. The relationship
between the NSCN-IM and Naga citizens around the Camp Hebron
headquarters of the rebel organization, writes Dolly Kikon—an ethnographer knowledgeable of everyday life in that area—is "predominantly
militaristic." The ground realities that include surveillance mechanisms,
she writes, are at odds with the "homogenous Naga experience" projected
by Naga leaders. "Members of the Naga public have been subjected to
body searches, whipped, tortured, questioned and in some cases executed.
In the same manner, NSCN-IM cadres have been lynched, stoned, beaten
up and driven out of towns and villages by angry Naga mobs."[61] Although
the NSCN-IM enjoys significant support in Manipur's Ukhrul District,
there is resentment of the rebel organization's "culture of military authoritarianism." Tensions rise especially when people are intimidated into
paying more taxes.[62]

The role played by coercion and surveillance in the collection of taxes,
however, should not lead one to underplay the substantial legitimacy that the
Naga militant organizations enjoy among the Naga public. This legitimacy
and support is inseparable from the history of the Naga conflict, especially
the intense intersubjectivity and the relationships of cooperation that have
grown since the time when Nagas were on the receiving end of counterinsurgency. Those memories have been kept alive by two narratives—of
salvation through faith in Christ and of Naga nationalism. The conditions
on the ground are similar to what Charles Tilly called "multiple sovereignty,"
which he considered the key criterion for separating armed conflicts and
civil wars from ordinary crimes or riots. He defined it as the situation when

a population obeys more than one set of governmental institutions: "They pay taxes, provide men to its armies, feed its functionaries, honor its symbols, give time to its service, or yield other resources despite the prohibition of a still-existing government they formerly obeyed."[63]

According to India's leading internal security research organization, the administrative structure of the NSCN-IM's "parallel government" extends down to the town and village levels. The rebel organization also runs a government-in-exile that manages its interaction with the media and with formal and nonformal international organizations. It "sends emissaries abroad to garner support and raise funds." India's major security research and monitoring organization once estimated its annual budget to be between Rs. 200 million to Rs. 250 million funded by "parallel structures of 'taxation' (extortion)."[64] These figures are now dated. Former Indian intelligence official R. N. Ravi, before he took over his current position as the government of India's interlocutor to the Naga peace talks, described how NSCN-IM cadres "dressed in battle fatigues and armed with sophisticated combat weapons freely roam the streets of towns and villages" and had "set up multiple garrisons, almost in every district." He blamed the central government of that time for giving "the militia a free military run of the Naga inhabited areas" and for "the retreat of the state."[65] This is similar to the description of conditions on the ground by two academics who have done field research in Nagaland. "Indian security forces in Naga villages and towns," write Dolly Kikon and Duncan McDuie-Ra, "are often indistinguishable from the Naga insurgents on the streets." Both groups seek "to assert control over slices of territory, over sections of the formal and informal economies, and over the provision of services and infrastructure."[66]

While the term *Nagalim* is used only by the NSCN-IM and its supporters, the belief that the Naga conflict cannot be resolved without addressing the issue of Nagalim—that is, the integration of the Naga inhabited areas—is widely shared among Nagas, even though non-Nagas living in those areas may not be supportive. Even the Nagaland state legislature has endorsed the demand for the "integration of all Naga-inhabited contiguous areas under one administrative umbrella" as many as five times: the first time as far back as December of 1964, a year after the state of Nagaland was created, and most recently in July of 2015.[67] The public expression of support, however, hides serious differences. As I have indicated, there is a long history of rivalry among political factions into which the original NNC is now split. The movement speaking on behalf of the "Nagas of Nagaland," to which I referred earlier, is a coalition that has come together under the umbrella organization Naga National Political Groups (NNPGs). It includes a number of Naga political factions, including the parent organization—the NNC. It supports the aspirations of the "Nagas of Manipur" but opposes transplanting the "population from beyond the boundary into present Nagaland state"—a clear reference to the Tangkhul Nagas of Manipur. Negotiations that exclude political organizations of "mainland Nagaland," it argues, cannot solve the Naga question.[68]

But the elected state government of Nagaland has vigorously supported the negotiations between the NSCN-IM and the Indian government. This has been the case especially since 2003, when the Nagaland People's Front (NPF) fought and won elections on a platform of facilitating the "peace process." It would be hard to implement an agreement between the rebel organization and the Indian government without the elected state government of Nagaland being fully on board. The NPF's "stand of playing the role of active facilitator to the peace process," said the then chief minister of the state Neiphiu Rio, "was a paradigm shift away from the stand of the previous government and the scenario cleared all hurdles on the home front for the peace process."[69] Rio was drawing a contrast between his stance and that of the previous chief minister of the state, who was highly critical of the NSCN-IM. One implication of Rio's statement was that his government would, if necessary, resign in order to accommodate the NSNC-IM leaders in a new Nagaland state government. Such a scenario would parallel the successful accord signed between the government of India and the Mizo National Front (MNF) in 1986. Following the signing of that accord, Chief Minister Lalthanhawla had resigned and the MNF leader, Laldenga, became chief minister initially of an interim government and subsequently the elected chief minister of the state.

The NPF is no longer in power in Nagaland. But since 2018, Neiphiu Rio has returned as the state's chief minister. He resigned from the NPF when the party severed ties with the BJP. Rio believes that the break with the ruling party in New Delhi would hurt the chances of a final settlement. His new party, the Nationalist Democratic Progressive Party (NDPP) contested the 2018 election as an ally to the BJP. Chief Minister Rio maintains close ties with the NSCN-IM. The good working relations between elected Naga politicians and NSCN-IM leaders—with the blessings of the government in New Delhi—that have developed since the ceasefire are a textbook example of informal partnership between a state and a nonstate armed entity.

The NSCN-IM appears to regard the facts that it is able to create on the ground as some sort of a foundation for a future political dispensation. These facts provide an image of shared sovereignty, which, along the lines of Max Weber's switchmen metaphor, has encouraged the NSCN-IM (as well as its rivals) to stake claims and to turn this image into reality. "Not ideas, but material and ideal interests," wrote Weber, "directly govern men's conduct. Yet very frequently the 'world images' that have been created by 'ideas' have, like switchmen, determined the tracks along which action has been pushed by the dynamic of interest."[70] One of the goals of the NSCN-IM at the negotiations has been to acquire concessions that would effectively extend formal recognition to those facts. The negotiation over power, therefore, is taking place at multiple sites and not only around the negotiating table. This occurs against the backdrop of a history of willingness on the part of Indian state institutions to make concessions to armed groups in Northeast India—allowing them significant leeway in matters of "taxation" and the administration of justice, which can be thought of as provisional modes of organizing political authority.

CEASEFIRE POLITICS

The peace initiative toward Nagas is part of a significant policy shift on the part of the Indian government toward armed conflicts in Northeast India. A ceasefire and negotiations policy has been in place since the 1990s.[71] A Home Ministry document describes "a paradigm shift" in the government's "initiatives to fight insurgency and restore law and order."[72] According to this official template, following a ceasefire or a Suspension of Operations agreement, rebel groups are typically housed in what are called Designated Camps. They are in state-owned lands usually located in somewhat remote areas, and they all have a similar layout.[73] In 2012, Ravi, now the Indian government's interlocutor for the Naga peace talks, and then a recently retired Indian Intelligence official, gave the following rationale for these Designated Camps: "Dialogue takes time. The Government can't let the rebel groups roam free till talks conclude. So the Government introduced the idea of camps, where the cadres are kept isolated and under observation." Meant as a halfway house for rebel combatants, in theory, individuals are not supposed to leave the camps. They are allowed to retain their weapons supposedly for their self-protection, and the rules in some camps require that the weapons are securely stored. One state government official, however, calls the rule a farce.[74] But there are significant differences between camps meant for armed organizations that formally "surrender" and those meant for groups under ceasefire. The status of being an armed group under ceasefire allows the NSCN-IM to display its military prowess, as it does in Camp Hebron. This is the case with a number of other Naga rebel factions as well.[75] When reporters of *India Today* visited the headquarters of the Khole-Kitovi faction of the NSCN in Khehoi in 2012, they found about one hundred Naga fighters armed with AK-47s, M16s, rocket-propelled grenades, and light machine guns. Khehoi was then one of the sixty-three Designated Camps in the region managed by the Union Home Ministry and four state governments: Assam, Meghalaya, Manipur, and Nagaland.[76]

The Camp Hebron complex has grown out of a few old structures that once belonged to the government's forest department and were given to the NSCN-IM to accommodate its cadres following the ceasefire between the Indian government and the NSCN-IM in 1997. The growth and expansion of this complex underscores the gains that the organization made following the ceasefire. It refurbished the built structures, expanded into neighboring lands, and built a number of new structures. Camp Hebron, writes the Indian journalist Samudra Gupta Kashyap, "houses the three most important bodies of the NSCN-IM—the central headquarters, the general headquarters of its army, and the Tatar Hoho or parliament." In addition there are the residential quarters for "president Swu [who has since passed away], prime minister Thuingaleng Muivah, chief of army Lt Gen Phunting Shimrang, and many other top functionaries, besides barracks for soldiers and other workers."[77] According to another reporter, Ipsita Chakravarty, "neat cottages house the various departments of this government" such as the Finance Ministry, which manages the NSCN-IM's parallel taxation operations, and the Home Ministry, which supposedly oversees talks with the Indian government. Personnel of the Ministry of Information and Publicity guide visitors around the complex. Chakravarty found that it had "all the paraphernalia of government, paperwork, bureaucracy, protocol," and deep inside the camp were "the general headquarters of the Naga Army, where new recruits are still trained and armed."[78] The complex also includes an impressive Baptist church, perhaps "one of the more zealously protected churches in the world," with security checkpoints staffed by guards armed with AK-47s.[79] All this requires significant political clout, the indulgence of government authorities, and material resources. Camp Hebron is unmistakably about appearance: a familiar symbolic language of authority is deployed in order for it to be seen like a state: "permanent signs and rituals: buildings, monuments, letterheads, uniforms, road signs, fences."[80]

Such symbolic and substantive expressions of a state-in-waiting are not unique to Camp Hebron. In Muivah's home district of Ukhrul in Manipur the GPRN also has significant attributes of statehood.[81] And, significantly, it is able to achieve this despite the fact that non-Naga public opinion in Manipur is vehemently opposed to the NSCN-IM. The territorial imaginary of Nagalim involves claims over more than half of Manipur, and since the early days of the 1997 ceasefire, there has been powerful political mobilization in Manipur against possible territorial concessions to the rebel organization.[82] The dissonance between the two territorial imaginaries has an old history. Even some nineteenth-century colonial texts refer to "a long standing boundary dispute between Manipur and the Naga Hills."[83] Technically, the Naga ceasefire does not apply to Manipur, and the question of Designated Camps for NSCN-IM cadres is a matter of great political sensitivity. Yet Thakur and Venugopal observed in 2016 that the rebel organization in Ukhrul is able "to fluidly project coercive authority well beyond the bounds of its camps, often very openly and without challenge—although it is careful to calibrate that within a set of invisible red lines."[84]

In an article published in 2011, when the ceasefire with the NSCN-IM was on its fourteenth year, Åshild Kolås expressed doubts about whether the ceasefire was about creating conditions for peace at all. The benefits of ceasefires and endless negotiations, she observed, could easily outweigh the benefits of a final settlement. In 2007, the ceasefire with the NSCN-IM was extended indefinitely instead of being renewed annually. The very fact of its being in negotiation with the Indian government brought it prestige and clout—giving it substantial advantage over its rivals. It then appeared to Kolås that the NSCN-IM had fewer incentives to pursue a political settlement. "A seat at the negotiating table," as she put it, "empowers the actors who are invited to negotiate peace at the expense of those who are excluded." It enables them to "forge alliances with other 'overground' actors and stakeholders, including politicians, civil servants, and law enforcement agencies."[85] Indeed, in a 2012 book, the Indian journalist Sudeep Chakravarti claimed—perhaps with some exaggeration—that the "NSCN-IM has the clout to decide who wins and loses in a particular constituency in an election"; that it has an influence over bureaucratic appointments and its support for a chief minister "can maintain or break a coalition."[86] At least insofar as the politics of the state of Nagaland is concerned, there have been times since the 1997 ceasefire when there is no daylight between the ruling elite and a rebellious counterelite.

Although the NSCN-IM has derived substantial benefits from negotiating with the Indian government, Naga factions not in a similar relationship with the government risk confronting the full force of the hard state and of the law. The NSCN-K for instance, abrogated its ceasefire agreement with the government of India in March 2015—a few months before its rival faction signed the framework agreement with the government. It came to the conclusion that being in a ceasefire, but not being invited to the negotiations, was increasingly making it a marginal force in Naga politics. Since abandoning the ceasefire, this faction has faced the wrath of security forces and has been subjected to more rigorous law-enforcement. "For my friends, everything, for my enemies, the law"—this sentence attributed to a populist authoritarian former Brazilian president—is an apt description of the way the law is applied in the evolving system of actually existing shared sovereignty in the Naga areas. Consider an arrest in April of 2017 of three Nagaland government officials for "large-scale extortion and illegal tax collection" on behalf of the NSCN-K. The investigations that led to the arrests found that at least twelve state government departments made regular payments to "the NSCN-K and other militant organisations like the NSCN-IM and the Naga National Council." The charge against the arrested officials, however, applied only to providing "substantial amount to the NSCN-K by way of contributing government funds to the banned outfit, thereby supporting NSCN-K in furtherance of its unlawful activities."[87] Evidently, because the NSCN-IM is in negotiations with the government—and no longer a "banned outfit"—Indian state institutions look the other way when it comes to its collection of "a Naga national tax." Not surprisingly, the NSCN-IM has now emerged as a primus inter pares among the Naga rebel factions "nested within higher sovereignties."[88]

## POLITICAL ECONOMY OF THE INNER LINE: THEN AND NOW

In this section I will focus on a small part of the area included in the territorial imaginary of Nagalim: the disputed border region between Nagaland and Assam—a space of long-standing conflicts over control of land and other economic resources. These conflicts throw significant light on the nature of postcolonial sovereignty in this former imperial frontier. The disputed interstate borderline is also the Inner Line, which in colonial times separated the Naga Hills District—an "excluded" area—from the "settled" districts of Assam. The Inner Line has remained in effect in postcolonial Northeast India, and it regulates the entry of all nonresidents into Nagaland and into two other states: Arunachal Pradesh and Mizoram. First drawn in 1873, it was originally an attempt to fence off Assam's fledgling tea plantations, which were frequently attacked by "tribesmen" protesting their dispossession. Indeed, the decision in 1881 "to make the Naga Hills a British district," wrote a British colonial administrator and historian, was made because of the "necessity of protecting the borders of Nowgong and Sibsagar against raiding Nagas, which in the early days compelled us to penetrate in to the hills little by little."[89] The Inner Line, writes historian Bodhisattva Kar, was supposed to "demarcate 'the hills' from 'the plains,' the nomadic from the sedentary, the jungle from the arable—in short, 'the tribal areas' from 'Assam proper.'" But in reality it was not a fixed and rigid line; it was "a revisable, mobile and pliant boundary" that was repeatedly redrawn "in order to variously accommodate the expansive compulsions of plantation capital, the recognition of imperfection in survey maps, the security anxiety of the state and the adaptive practices of internally differentiated local communities."[90] In effect, land was repeatedly transferred "between administration and un-administration."[91]

Much of the land in this border region is now officially designated as Reserve Forests. But that is largely a legal fiction. Many families—cultivators and others—have settled in these areas. These settlements are especially ripe for contestation because of the difference between the land laws that prevail in the old settled districts of colonial Assam (i.e., present-day Assam) and the customary laws that govern landownership in Nagaland— an ethnic homeland state—where there are restrictions on land transfer to non-Nagas. "Decades of occupation and counteroccupation in pursuit of a favourable alignment," observe Ankush Agrawal and Vikas Kumar, "have transformed large parts of Assam's reserved forests into a patchwork of Assamese and Naga villages administered by the respective states."[92] According to one study, "under Golaghat District, along the disputed border," there are practically no traces of Reserve Forests left. There are only "huts and the land turned into cultivable fields yielding rich crops" with settlers who have come "from every corner of Assam, Nagaland and even nearby Bangladeshi nationals."[93] Significantly, parts of these foothills border tea plantations, and a segment of the population settled in these lands is from communities that identify themselves as *adivasi*. In Northeast India this word refers only to descendants of tea workers; it is not used as an equivalent of *indigenous people* as in other parts of India.[94] Evidently, the exploitative labor practices of nineteenth-century plantation capitalism have reverberated across successive generations of those who were once recruited as indentured workers. Their forefathers settled in what were once vast tracts of public lands after their contracts had expired. But few have formal legal titles since the lands are officially labeled Reserve Forests. Furthermore, no one can get fresh land titles today since an interim agreement obligates the state governments of Assam and Nagaland to maintain the status quo.[95] The location of Camp Hebron close to the Nagaland-Assam border has proved to be felicitous in this regard. It has given the NSCN-IM "an excellent base for engaging in cross-border operations outside the territorial limits of the ceasefire agreement and the jurisdiction of Nagaland state."[96] The presence of armed actors emboldened by the peace process has changed the de facto balance of power in these resource conflicts. Unless the final peace settlement protects the occupancy rights of these settlers, which is extremely unlikely, they risk dispossession. People without formal land titles, especially poor non-Naga cultivators, lack the political voice to make such a demand. Since the Naga conflict is framed exclusively as a bilateral one between Nagas and the Indian government, their interests are largely unrepresented in the Naga peace negotiations.

Significantly, this disputed border territory has valuable mineral resources, and because it is a legal gray zone in matters of land rights, control over mineral-rich lands has become a source of violent conflicts involving armed men. Hiren Gohain, a knowledgeable commentator on the subject, gave the following account of the economic motives underlying a spate of violence in the area in 2007: "The forest wealth, the rice (cultivated with the help of non-Naga migrant labour) in a food-deficit state, and above all mineral wealth like oil (of which there are proven large reserves in the area claimed from Assam) attract a new ruthless class of contractors and wheeler-dealers who would think nothing of killing off numbers of innocent people to lay their hands on these sources of wealth."[97] The state governments of Assam and Nagaland have agreed not to disturb the status quo until the border dispute is resolved. But while the NSCN-IM and the state government of Nagaland are on the same page on this issue, the NSCN-IM and other nonstate militias are not bound by the commitment made by the Nagaland government to maintain the status quo. This gives the rebel groups "a comparative advantage" in defending "Naga encroachments."[98]

Agrawal and Kumar provide an interesting account of an ingenious political use of cartography in this interstate border dispute—the postcolonial incarnation of the colonial-era conflicts over the Inner Line. They came across a number of mutually inconsistent maps of Nagaland in circulation that "differ from each other with respect to the border between Nagaland and Assam."[99] These are official maps in the sense that the publishers of the maps are all departments of the Nagaland state government. But the inaccurate maps, they claim, function to "formalise" claims over the area "encroached" on by Nagas. They enable the state government to avoid confrontation with the government of Assam or the government of India. If there is a pushback on an incorrect map, that particular map can always be withdrawn. Maps that are not objected to, however, can be used as evidence that Naga territorial claims have been acknowledged in practice, backing the facts on the ground.[100]

The discord over the border between Assam and Nagaland, as Hiren Gohain has perceptively observed, might "lie not in immemorial ethnic realities, but in the contemporary international economy."[101] Armed nonstate groups in informal partnership with state officials can be a more reliable provider of security for informal coal mining and other illegal but licit economic activities than a state with a monopoly of legitimate violence.[102] The political landscape of large parts of the contemporary world—especially in the Global South—is characterized by states that lack a monopoly of the legitimate use of violence and of taxing powers. Like the illegal coal mines of Meghalaya, this picture of the gray economy in the disputed Assam-Nagaland border fits well with an important trend in the political economy of the Global South. The economic transactions of the so-called informal economy require protection by its own kind of "armed forces"— more "an illicit world of violence and impunity" than the state monopoly of the legitimate means of violence.[103]

## FICTIONS OF SOVEREIGNTY AND THE CHALLENGES OF PEACEMAKING

In the contemporary world, it is misguided to look at armed conflicts as always being about a contest over the monopoly of the legitimate use of violence between armed groups and states.[104] The priorities of state officials trying to end armed conflicts are not necessarily the same as those of a peace activist or of an ordinary citizen. "Whatever be the system that comes out of the entire negotiation process," says Ravindra Narayan Ravi, India's interlocutor to the Naga talks, "one thing is very clear, that you cannot have a non-State militia, that is not acceptable. No society can have it."[105] But this is easier said than done. There is no evidence so far that dismantling the ad hoc arrangements that have sprung up between multiple state and nonstate actors has been on the agenda of India's peace negotiators. There is only a vague expectation that they would all wither away once a final peace settlement is signed. There are occasional media reports that the Indian government plans to recruit NSCN-IM cadres into its security forces. But under current circumstances, it would be unrealistic to expect serious initiatives in the area of disarming, demobilizing, and reintegrating "former" combatants. After all, the NSCN-IM can legitimately claim that "unless all other Naga groups are disarmed, they will need to retain their capacities to defend themselves."[106] The regime of actually existing shared sovereignty and the current state of "no war, no peace" could therefore become more than just a transitional arrangement.

In Manipur, as I have indicated, there are no NSCN-IM camps in a formal sense, and supposedly, the Naga ceasefire does not even extend to that state. Yet at least in Ukhrul District the realities are very different. And, significantly, legal fictions play a key role in maintaining political stability in this highly contested part of the imagined Naga homeland.[107] The elected chief minister of Manipur claims that the NSCN-IM does not have any "authorised designated camp" in Manipur, only "some mobile camps . . . and the camps go on shifting in the jungles."[108] But since there are bureaucratic protocols for monitoring these camps, Indian security officials have found an ingenious euphemism to describe these actually existing camps. They call them "Camps Taken Note Of."[109] Thus, managers of Indian state institutions can pretend that India controls and governs every inch of territory that belongs to India, and the NSCN-IM can claim that it already has "a state and self-governing territory which will eventually become sovereign."[110] It is likely that a similar state of affairs—a form of fluid, negotiated, or informal sovereignty—prevails in many other parts of "Nagalim" as well. These arrangements are likely to remain in place for the foreseeable future regardless of whether a final Naga peace agreement is signed. But for the Indian government to formally acknowledge this fundamental reality by conceding to the demand for a separate Naga flag to signify the idea of shared sovereignty is a wholly different matter. The flag issue has now emerged as a key sticking point in the negotiations. So far, Indian officials had comfortably assumed that acknowledging the "unique history" of the Nagas would have no real bearing on the substance of the negotiations. But a flag has become an important issue for the Forum for Naga Reconciliation, the organization that has called for reimagining "the Indo-Naga Peace Process." Significantly, the Forum is associated with a document called the "Declaration of the Naga Collective Spirit," which emphasizes "the historical fact that the Naga struggle started before India's independence" as the foundation of the moral authority of the Naga movement.[111] At the same time, in the prevailing political atmosphere, with heightened nationalist sentiment in the country—a product of the ruling party's own relentless ideological campaigns—the current government in New Delhi is hardly in a position to concede to this demand.[112] Bridging the gap between the facts on the ground and the fiction of the postcolonial state's unitary sovereign authority over territories that were once part of the imperial frontier is at the root of the current impasse in the Naga peace process.

Narratives of Naga nationalism typically begin with the petition presented by the Naga Club to the Simon Commission in 1929, and they highlight Phizo's declaration of Naga independence on August 14, 1947—one day before the Indian Independence Day. Thus, in chronological terms, the roots of Naga nationalism go back to a time when many anticolonial movements in many parts of the world were successfully asserting their right to national self-determination. Yet the Naga movement soon collided with the metrics of the possible[113] within the emerging postimperial world system of states. Lydia Walker captures the situation poignantly: "Phizo arrived in London during the summer of 1960, a moment when new nations became independent every week and the potential of a liberated post-colonial world seemed strongest. Yet a national claim from within a post-colonial state, especially India, the post-colonial state that served as the model for peaceful national liberation, tarnished the promise of national liberation, even then."[114]

Clearly, the global political circumstances proved unfavorable to the goal of Naga independence. But once we take this as a fact of history, what has become the principal structural hurdle to a political resolution of this conflict today is the design of the peace process. The leaders of the NSCN-IM like to say that they are not asking for someone else's land but only for the integration of areas where "the Nagas have been living since time immemorial."Their narrative blames external forces—first, the British colonial rulers, and subsequently, the Indian state—for dividing the land of the Nagas and creating a situation where "some Nagas are living in Manipur, some in Assam and some in Arunachal Pradesh."[115] Whatever the historical validity of this view, the format of the current negotiations—bilateral and secretive meetings between NSCN-IM leaders and the Indian government's interlocutor—is ill-equipped to resolve this complex conflict with multiple stakeholders. Yet at this stage of the conflict, it is beyond the capacity of the institutions of the Indian state to broaden the negotiations and bring in the other stakeholders—especially representatives of non-Naga groups. This chapter's epigraph draws attention to this predicament. The situation is similar to what Alex de Waal describes in another context as an attempt to find a square solution for a round problem.[116] The Naga conflict is now anything but a bilateral conflict that can be settled by two parties meeting at a square table. It requires discussions where all stakeholders—armed and unarmed, Naga and non-Naga—are seated at a round table. The challenge is rooted in the very nature of the Naga national project and its convoluted history. Unfortunately, path dependency makes it politically impossible for Indian state institutions to explore a different negotiating format that is more likely to produce a stable and just peace.

## CHAPTER 5

# DISCOURSE OF INSURGENCY AND THE
# PEDAGOGY OF STATE VIOLENCE

> In the case of the armed forces, the assertion of unbroken
> continuity was rather more paradoxical, so that even today
> one is forced to witness such unlovely ironies as regiments
> of the Indian Army displaying the trophies of colonial
> conquest and counterinsurgency in their barrack-rooms or the
> Presidential Guards celebrating their birth two hundred years
> ago under the governor-generalship of Lord Cornwallis!
> —Partha Chatterjee, "Development Planning and the Indian State"

THE HOUSE WITH A THOUSAND STORIES is a novel set against the
backdrop of the "secret killings" in Assam: death squads in the dead of
night forcing their way into people's homes, dragging out targeted individuals, and murdering them.[1] "For a brief, tumultuous period between
1996 and 2001," writes a sociologist and human rights campaigner, "urban
and rural Assam was awash with reports of dead bodies being recovered
in paddy fields, drains and even on the streets."[2] At least three hundred
men, women, and children were killed in this manner according to one
estimate.[3] Most victims had some ties with the United Liberation Front of
Assam (Ulfa)—though usually indirect ones. Some were siblings or parents
of members of the rebel organization.[4] Media coverage of those incidents
was usually framed within a narrative of factional warfare between Ulfa
militants and defectors. But few in Assam doubted that the counterinsurgency establishment was calling the tune with Ulfa defectors as willing or
reluctant accomplices. To borrow the words of two theorists of "sovereignty
in practice," no one knew for sure whether the "death squads operating
in the dark of the night, actually work on behalf of state institutions or
against their will." But that did not stop "ordinary people" from naming
"the state as being the actor behind such acts."[5]

A new state government elected to power in 2001 ordered judicial inquiries into the killings. But these inquiries came up against a wall of silence erected by police and law-enforcement agencies. In the face of formidable obstacles to gathering facts and evidence, the first two inquests made little headway. But thanks to the diligence and persistence of the third inquiry, headed by Khagendra Nath Saikia, a former judge of the Indian Supreme Court, we now know a good deal about this period of counterinsurgent terror in Assam.[6] Its findings did not lead to any prosecution. But it established beyond doubt that they were not the work of rogue security officials or of Ulfa defectors settling private scores. The inquiry managed to find enough details on a significant number of cases where the political motive was unmistakable: it was to induce defections from Ulfa. The report of the Saikia Commission zeroes in on thirty-five cases[7] and sums up the harrowing pattern: "The modus operandi was to visit the family and ask the members to persuade its ULFA members to surrender. If they failed in doing so, a team was sent to survey the location and the structure of the house. Then armed and masked men would visit the house, knock at the door, wake up the family members, drag them out, and shoot the targets dead. In some cases, they would take away the victim, secretly kill the person elsewhere and dump his body in a secluded place."[8] The use of this brutal tactic of counterinsurgency on the cheap paid off.[9] The death squad murders, says the former Ulfa leader Sashadhar Choudhury, led to a wave of defections from Ulfa. They struck terror inside the rebel organization, putting intense emotional and moral pressure on its cadres. The only way they could hope to spare their parents and siblings that terrible fate was to "surrender." Among those killed in this gruesome manner, Choudhury chillingly lists his own brother; the entire family of Ulfa's publicity secretary, Deepak Das, who went by the *nom de guerre* Mithinga Daimary; and a brother of the leader of the organization's military wing.[10]

There is now a rich body of Assamese fiction set against the backdrop of this grim chapter of Assam's postcolonial history.[11] Short stories and novels convey the terrorizing effect on everyday people "generated through a dialectic of visibility and invisibility, of public knowledge and unknowability."[12] Yet few Indians outside the Northeast have heard of the use of death squads as a tool of counterinsurgent terror in Assam. Three Assamese journalists wrote a book in English summarizing the Saikia Commission's findings. Each had written "thousands of words" in the local media on that subject, said the authors in the book's preface. But the rest of India "virtually has no clue about the magnitude of this extraordinary series of violence and how it changed the course of socio-political life of Assam forever."[13] Aruni Kashyap's *The House with a Thousand Stories* was well received in Indian literary circles. But it was read mostly as a stand-in for the broad, unnuanced media narratives about the region's political violence. The death squad murders did not receive special attention, nor did they cause particular indignation among Indian readers.

The rise of Ulfa and its brief flourish were unexpected. Until then, only the excluded areas of the erstwhile frontier province were known as sites for organized armed resistance against the postcolonial political dispensation. The Naga movement discussed in Chapter 4 is a quintessential case. After all, pan-Indian anticolonial political movements—both the Indian National Congress and the All India Muslim League—did well in the settled districts of Assam. With the important exception of the Partition of Sylhet, the borders of the colonial frontier province—especially those that separated the excluded areas from the settled districts—were largely unchanged during the first two decades after decolonization. In the eyes of many in the old excluded areas, the plains Assamese—and the state government they controlled—were the face of Indian misrule during that time. The Naga and Mizo rebellions were not only against the Indian state but also against policies of the state government of undivided Assam, which was often implicated in decisions to employ repressive tactics in the rebel areas. In debates in the state legislature of Assam, opposition politicians were critical of the government for those policies.[14] Ulfa was the first significant movement advocating armed resistance to emerge in the settled districts of the old frontier province. Its rise underscores the fluidity of relations on which national identities are founded,[15] as well as the neighborhood or spillover effects of armed conflicts. It also raises questions about the analytical use of the vocabulary of insurgency. Should any political opposition that proclaims a commitment to armed struggle—irrespective of its capabilities and political history—be labeled an insurgency? Or should the actual nature of the challenge it presents, and the political context of the emergence of this political tendency, be part of our consideration as well?

## INSURGENCY/COUNTERINSURGENCY
## AND CONTENTIOUS POLITICS

In November of 1990 a minority government precariously in power in New Delhi for seven brief months declared Assam a "disturbed area" under AFSPA and banned Ulfa. In effect, the rebel organization was effectively proclaimed an existential threat to the state.[16] Subsequently, a "military metaphysics"[17]—or a military definition of reality—took over, and it began to dominate the official narrative. It shaped the government's subsequent response to what was ultimately a political challenge. But there was nothing inevitable about this turn of events; a host of contingent factors—most importantly, the ready availability of AFSPA as a policy tool—were at play. It is important not to unreflectively buy into the vocabulary of insurgency and use the term as an analytical category: there is a military definition of political reality that comes with it. Counterinsurgency became the policy of choice vis-à-vis Ulfa only after the coming of the hard state to Assam in 1990, when state authorities began using its coercive powers in earnest, quickly displacing other viable options.

The quotation from Partha Chatterjee that opens this chapter refers to the irony of army regiments in contemporary India displaying trophies won in colonial battles of conquest and counterinsurgency. But it is not merely that these regiments display symbols of their imperial past to promote camaraderie and esprit de corps among the present generation of soldiers. India's postcolonial counterinsurgents routinely cite canonical texts of counterinsurgency warfare, which typically belong to the era of struggle between imperial powers and colonial subjects. They rely on those texts for their strategies and tactics as well. For example, like their imperial predecessors, they talk of their operations being "population-centric" and not "enemy-centric." To this day, winning hearts and minds—most famously associated with Field Marshall Gerald Templer's war against the communist insurgency in colonial Malaya—remains an important component of the Indian Army's counterinsurgency campaigns in Northeast India. Even at the time of this writing, the Indian Army continues to carry out hearts-and-minds campaigns in Assam and in other parts of the region—using the unfortunate acronym WHAM: Winning Hearts and Minds.[18]

Once a military metaphysics began to define Ulfa, the policy space shrank visibly; alternative policy choices began to be excluded from consideration. In principle, it is possible to use a country's criminal justice system to deal with—and effectively neutralize—a rebel group engaging in armed resistance. In a democracy, there are good reasons to pursue this course of action. Channeling politically motivated crimes through the criminal justice system can have important pedagogical benefits for society. But unfortunately, the existence of the AFSPA regime—and the ease with which the political executive could suddenly decide to treat Ulfa as if it was an existential threat to the state—led officials to choose the easy option. An executive notification declaring Assam a "disturbed area" and declaring Ulfa unlawful was all that was needed. It prepared the ground for the deployment of the Indian Army. The criminal justice system was avoided wherever possible after this shift. Even the government's approach to peace began to be significantly shaped by the army's counterinsurgency doctrine.

According to defense analyst Rajesh Rajagopalan, while the political nature of insurgencies is widely recognized, "the Indian Army has developed a doctrine that carries this theme farther than most other armies." Because military victory against "insurgencies" is impossible, "problems of insurgency have to be solved by political agreement with the insurgents." The role of the army is to "restore normalcy" to enable the parties to arrive at a "political solution."[19] There is ample evidence that measures designed to restore "normalcy" have caused serious, lasting damage to institutions of democracy in Northeast India. A former top Indian police official in the region, E. V. Rammohan, gives two examples of such dysfunctional outcomes. In the early 1990s, the then chief minister of Assam created what Rammohan describes as "a mafia" out of Ulfa defectors. They "were allowed to keep their weapons and operate as gangs under unofficial patronage" despite the fact that many of them were implicated in serious crimes, including murder. Their "victims were the very people who were to be won over to the government side and who were to be weaned away from the insurgents." The result was "an indignant populace, who were further alienated and a police force who had become terrorists themselves."[20] Police official Rammohan's second example is from Manipur, where a special force—the Commandos—that the state government created to carry out counterinsurgency operations "soon deteriorated into a state terrorist force." They took a leaf out of the book of the "insurgents" and began "extorting money from the business community." Rammohan spells out the consequences for the public: "Here were five to six underground groups extorting money from the traders and here was a special wing of the police force, set up to arrest the under ground [*sic*], who also demanded their share of the extortion pool. To whom could the people now turn?"[21]

What Rammohan calls a "mafia"—made up of Ulfa defectors—is popularly known in Assam as Sulfa (surrendered Ulfa). The first set of defections occurred immediately after the Indian Army's second counterinsurgency campaign against Ulfa, Operation Rhino, which took place in 1991. An amnesty program by state government—supposedly for the rehabilitation of former Ulfa cadres and their reintegration into society—led to a spate of defections. But, as Angshuman Choudhury points out, the policy in reality was one of "co-opting the surrendered militants into its elaborate security wheel as informants" against their former comrades. The death squad killings in Assam occurred at the height of the Sulfa phenomenon. The amnesty policy, writes Choudhury, "triggered a camouflaged form of lawlessness and political violence. SULFA became a 'running trophy' of sorts, getting passed down from the Congress to the AGP government as a ready-to-use counter-terrorist force.... They began operating like an organised crime gang or a drug cartel—non-ideological, utilitarian, and profit-making. In return for actionable intelligence, the state offered them a carte blanche to indulge in their independent money-making ventures like extortions, kidnappings, illegal businesses, and contraband smuggling. The government not just looked away from all of SULFA's wrongdoings, but also became an active stakeholder in their shadow businesses."[22]

Amnesty was made available to almost anyone who decided to "surrender"—no matter how opportunistically. Typically, they were de facto rather than de jure amnesties. There was no effort to explain these decisions to the public. The political executive in an exercise of prosecutorial discretion made the decision not to pursue legal charges or not to object to bail petitions of individual leaders—no matter how egregious their alleged crime. There was public criticism of this policy even at a time when Ulfa had enjoyed significant support in Assam. Many saw the amnesties as a violation of the basic norms of political, moral, and legal equality that rode roughshod over the victims' right to an effective legal remedy. Patricia Mukhim, a well-known public intellectual of the region, wrote powerfully against the practice. State institutions, she said, have "no right to grant a general amnesty to militants." Only victims of families can forgive killers of civilians if and when they "are reconciled to their loss." She was critical of the "surrender policy" because of its exclusion of "civil society" as a legitimate stakeholder in those decisions.[23] Mukhim's essay illustrates a kind of argument that one frequently encounters in Northeast India: support for a rights-based approach to the rule of law rather than one that places the state's perceived security interests above anything else.[24]

In my introduction I noted the analytical difficulties of applying the term *insurgency* to the armed conflicts of Northeast India. The idea of a mass-based insurgency—the focus of conventional counterinsurgency theory—bears almost no relation to Ulfa or most other armed groups of the region. The incoherence of state institutions and the imperfections in the rule of law create the political space for them. The so-called insurgent groups all have known ties with mainstream actors in politics, business, and the bureaucracy.[25] Ulfa's brand of "politics by other means" blended seamlessly with "official, prescribed politics."[26] It is analytically rewarding to view Ulfa through the theoretical lens of contentious politics: to focus attention not narrowly on Ulfa the organization but on the interactive dynamics between the rebels and their competitors, antagonists, the power-holders, and the relevant audiences.[27]

NOT A SOLO ACT: POLITICS OF NATION AND CITIZENSHIP

Ulfa was not "a solo act but a complex interactive process."[28] The phenomenon grew out of the contentious politics associated with the Assam Movement of 1979–85, which raised serious questions about the foundational assumptions of nation and citizenship in post-Partition India. Ulfa started as a radical fringe of the Assam Movement. The atmosphere of political turmoil provided a fertile environment for it to grow. It flourished during the tenure of the first government of the Asom Gana Parishad (AGP) from 1986 to 1990. The leaders of the Assam Movement formed this regional political party after they signed the Assam Accord in 1985. A number of influential AGP leaders close to Ulfa became ministers in the first AGP government of Assam (1985–89), and they felt obligated to extend patronage and protection to Ulfa. An authoritative book on Ulfa even argues that the first AGP government had for all intents and purposes built up the rebel organization.[29] "Democracy in India," writes Thomas Blom Hansen, "has produced a culture of politics that is incredibly fluid, situational and dynamic—where stable constituencies, alliances, equations and ideological principles are in constant flux and redefinition." It does not take much to create "a collective mood, or the illusion of a collectivity driven by a mood," and those who are able to do that can set political agendas for certain periods.[30] Ulfa's rise and brief flourish has affinity with the kind of ephemeral political phenomena to which Hansen draws attention.

The rebel organization's political fortunes began to turn in the final days of the first AGP government. Influential business groups such as the tea industry and traders forced to make ransom payments to Ulfa began complaining to the government in New Delhi about the security conditions in the state. Reflecting the normalization of the AFSPA regime in Northeast India, a contemporary news report described the prevailing situation: "There was a sense of inevitability about it all. That Assam was turbulent enough for the army to move in was a foregone conclusion."[31] In November of 1990, the governor of Assam reported to the central government that public officials in Assam had become "totally ineffective" and that "the statutory authorities" were in a state of panic and unable to discharge their functions.[32] The Indian minister of home affairs declared, rather dramatically, that almost the whole state government machinery was with Ulfa.[33] Superficial and sensationalist assessments such as these made it easy for the minority government in power in New Delhi to dismiss the AGP government and bring the state under President's Rule. The whole of Assam was declared a "disturbed area" under AFSPA; Ulfa was banned, and the Indian Army was ordered to launch a counterinsurgency campaign against it. This marks the coming of the hard state to Assam. But was this near-panic response by an insecure government in New Delhi the most effective way to meet the political challenge of Ulfa? Were policies such as the state's indulgence and patronage of Sulfa and the terror of death squads worth the long-term damage to the quality of Indian democracy?

Ulfa was founded in 1979 to establish a *Swadhin* or independent Assam. According to the Ulfa narrative, Assam lost its sovereignty in 1826 when it became part of British India, and it has been locked in a colonial relationship with New Delhi since decolonization. Ulfa texts blame the "arrogant and colonial" mind-set of India's power elite for choosing to name the region Northeast India. It described the decision as a forcible attempt "to impose Hindi culture on Assam and the region as a whole and to stifle the region's diverse and vibrant autonomous cultural life."[34] The issue of migration across the Partition's border and the enfranchisement of noncitizens did not feature directly on Ulfa's agenda. But its ideologues viewed Delhi's indifference to the serious consequences of unauthorized cross-border migration and enfranchisement of noncitizens as a symptom of the region's subordinate political status in the postcolonial Indian dispensation. In the debate on the subject then raging in the state, Ulfa represented an alternative voice. It appealed to all people living in Assam: *Axombaxi* rather than the Assamese people—transcending the narrowly ethnic appeal of the latter term. In one of its documents, Ulfa defined *Axombaxi* as anyone who, irrespective of his or her "prior identity, regards Assam as motherland, treats Assam's problems as his or her own, embraces Assam's culture and is prepared to fight for Assam's future."[35]

As we saw in Chapter 2, the issue of immigration from eastern Bengal had brought to the fore tensions between the pan-Indian and regionally specific forms of the emergent politics of the nation in Assam as far back as the 1930s.[36] There are affinities between the politics of Assam during the 1980s and the 1930s. Both periods—across a gap of fifty years and stretching across the colonial-postcolonial divide—saw powerful protests against immigration, and in both instances, pan-Indian politicians failed to engage with protests through "debate, clarification, and renegotiation typical of more egalitarian social relations."[37] A highly regarded Assamese public intellectual, Parag Kumar Das, who exerted significant influence on Ulfa's worldview and political goals, traced the intellectual lineage of the idea of an independent Assam to the intellectuals and activists who sparred with Nehru in the 1930s and 1940s on the same issue.[38] In 1996, at the height of the counterinsurgency campaign against Ulfa and of the Sulfa phenomenon, Das was killed by "unknown gunmen" in broad daylight in the middle of the city of Guwahati. The murder was never solved despite enormous public outcry. It was a forerunner of "secret killings" of the period.

It does not take a particularly astute observer to infer that securing an independent Assam through armed struggle was not a realistic political goal. Yet Ulfa had an astonishing hold on Assamese public opinion. Despite its many flaws, the rebel organization was widely seen as standing for "some legitimate and sound ideas of self-determination."[39] Few people approved of Ulfa's methods, but there was a great deal of respect and admiration for the sacrifice by its cadres in the cause of regional patriotism. Opinions about Ulfa varied widely in the Assamese public domain. But almost no one favored a military solution, which was openly advocated by many in the Indian national security establishment.[40] Even those unsympathetic to Ulfa in Assam—including state-level leaders of national political parties—viewed it as a legitimate opponent, perhaps misguided, but partisans of a just cause. To borrow from Carl Schmitt's categories, the most commonly held view of Ulfa in Assam was that of a *justus hostis*, a legitimate enemy or opponent with a just cause, while national security hard-liners viewed it as a perpetual or absolute enemy, a criminal force that should be subjected to punitive action.[41]

Whatever the value of state-centric realism as theoretical lens for conventional studies of international relations, it is not of much help for making sense of insurgent political cultures where members and supporters "interpret insurgency as justified by the injustice of existing social relations and state violence, and . . . interpret its costs, even the highest of them, as meaningful sacrifices."[42] Ulfa belongs to the kind of political phenomena that political anthropologist John D. Kelly says "should not be left for the realists of political science to assess and explain. We could use a different kind of realism."[43] Space limitations here do not allow for a review of Ulfa's entire three-decades-old history.[44] Suffice it to say that it was more powerful as an idea than its reality as a political and armed organization. This should not come as a surprise to students of social protest. As Charles Tilly has reminded us, "Hijacking, mutiny, machine breaking, charivaris, village fights, tax rebellions, foot riots, collective self-immolation, lynching, vendetta have all belonged to the standard collective action repertoire of some group at some time. . . . People have at some time recognized every one of them as a legitimate, feasible way of acting on an unsatisfied grievance or aspiration."[45] Since Ulfa is no longer a significant political force, some readers may react to the discussion in this chapter with a sense of weariness. "Insurgency" and counterinsurgency in Assam may indeed appear to be a thing of the past to some. It may even be argued that Assam is now on the path to joining the "national mainstream." For a while, such a narrative seemed unassailable after the electoral victory of the Hindu nationalist BJP in Assam. But has Assam really moved on? At the time of this writing it is hard to make that claim.

## ASSAM AFTER ULFA
The life and times of Ulfa formed the bloodiest period in the history of modern Assam. For more than three decades, its members—and groups that emerged as a result of Ulfa's demonstration effect—committed umpteen acts of violence against civilians and others they regarded as legitimate targets. The Indian Army, other paramilitary forces, and the state police committed numerous acts of abuse, including extrajudicial executions such as the death squad killings with which I began this chapter.

Thousands lost lives and limbs.[46] Surviving family members still try to cope with the trauma. In Assam's public life today, there are daily reminders of the conflicting memories and narratives of that period. Assamese literature constitutes a virtual public archive of the death squad killings and the violence of the days of Ulfa. It keeps the experience of the period alive in public memory. The Ulfa years left lasting marks on the system of power, especially when it comes to the use of state violence. The key issues of nation and citizenship that animated the politics of the period remain unresolved to this day. Elected governments in Assam, as the journalist Ipsita Chakravarty observed in 2016, continue to "rise and fall on the question of migration."[47] This became apparent once again in 2018 and early 2019, when the effort to amend India's citizenship laws—and effectively put Hindu unauthorized migrants from across the Partition's border on the citizenship track—stirred up a political storm, forcing New Delhi to abandon the effort.

"Being national," it has been said, remains "the condition of our times even as the national is buffeted by the subnational rise of local, regional, and ethnic claims" and transnational challenges of various kinds.[48] That may be true. But nationhood is ultimately a political claim—a "claim on people's loyalty, on their attention, on their solidarity."[49] Thus, being national is also a disciplining project, and its techniques, to paraphrase Partha Chatterjee, range between a pedagogy of violence and a pedagogy of culture. In retrospect, the counterinsurgency campaigns against Ulfa can be seen as state violence employed "to ensure the proper condition for cultural pedagogy"[50]—the coercive state apparatus put in service of the pan-Indian form of the politics of the nation. But the dynamics of the politics of nation and citizenship at the pan-Indian level has changed significantly since then because of the inroads made by more restrictive conceptions of the idea of India into the centers of political power.[51] For Hindu majoritarians, the relatively large size of Assam's Muslim population and its proximity to Muslim-majority Bangladesh are a potential source of danger to India's national unity.[52] They see the "infiltrator" from across the border as posing a serious threat to the nation. The current group of decision makers in Delhi take a hard-line Hindu majoritarian view on the question of unauthorized migrants crossing the Partition border. This view was behind the abortive attempt to change Indian citizenship laws through the Citizenship Amendment Bill of 2016. Yet in this region, where this issue has been the most contentious—and at the heart of successive episodes of ethnic and civil violence—there is no consensus in sight on who is an unauthorized cross-border migrant and who is not. The effort to redefine national citizenship to fit the Hindu majoritarian narrative threatens to destabilize a political settlement in Assam that has long been able to manage tensions around the question of migration from across the Partition border. I have indicated that a major reason why Assamese is the state's official language and Assamese the cultural face of the state is the fact that the large majority of Miya Muslims or Muslims of eastern Bengali descent are now Assamese speakers. Redefining national citizenship to suit the Hindu majoritarian narrative threatens to upset the state's fragile political balance. Although language is by and large no longer the center of group conflicts in India,[53] its return to that position in Assam cannot be ruled out.

## STRUCTURAL VIOLENCE AND SPECTACULAR VIOLENCE

Ulfa's political platform may have its ideological roots in a strand of regional patriotism with a long history, but its rapid coalescence into a significant political force in the 1980s follows a familiar pattern of "the repression of legitimate and deeply felt grievances," resulting in the escalation of support for radical militancy.[54] Such facts get lost in clumsy security narratives that begin and end with Ulfa's loudly proclaimed goals: its avowed commitment to armed resistance. But organizations like Ulfa are not born as "insurgencies." Ulfa's influence began to grow only after 1983. The shift cannot be understood without taking into account the structural violence in which relations between Northeast India and New Delhi are embedded. The elections to the Assam State Assembly in 1983 were the crucial turning point. Multiple rounds of negotiations between the central government and the leaders of the Assam Movement on the legal status of those crossing the Partition's border had failed to produce an agreement. But the campaign showed no sign of retreating. In this volatile situation, India's governing elites decided that it was time to force a resolution of the issue. A decision was made to hold elections in Assam, using the intensely contested electoral rolls at the heart of the political upheaval in the state. The claim that the electoral rolls were deeply flawed—that they included the names of hundreds and thousands of noncitizens—was the driving force of the Assam Movement. At that point, Indian government representatives were negotiating with the leaders of the campaign to find a middle ground for two long years. Clearly, they had effectively acknowledged the legitimacy of this claim, at least to some extent. But suddenly all that ceased to matter. In December of 1982, key political advisers to Prime Minister Indira Gandhi decided that it was an opportune time to hold elections in Assam since the Congress Party appeared to have a good chance of winning back power. Assam was then under President's Rule. Indira Gandhi's close political associate Rajesh Pilot was very pleased with the large crowds at her election rallies in neighboring Tripura.[55] Journalist Shekhar Gupta reports a conversation with Rajesh Pilot, who was then managing the Congress Party's election campaign in Tripura. "The next stop," he told Gupta, would be Guwahati, suggesting that the government had decided to hold elections in Assam in order to break the political impasse. "Are you serious?" asked Gupta.

> RP. Why not? People are fed up. They want elections. They want a po-
> litical government.
> SG. But who told [you] that? There will be bloodshed.

Gupta then asked why elections must be held at that point.

> RP. Because the agitators must be finished politically. This is the way to
> do it.
> SG. It will be impossible. . . .
> RP. How can you say that? If you put 5,000 of them in jail for the elec-
> tion period the problem is solved. It is only the mischief-mongers
> you have to tackle. The rest of the people will heave a sigh of relief.
> You don't know how powerful the government can be.[56]

The arrogance of power does not adequately describe the manner and timing of this decision. It was a textbook case of the way structural violence plays out. Highly unequal relations of power, as anthropologist David Graeber points out, are characterized by "norms sanctioned by the threat of physical harm in endless subtle and not-so-subtle ways."[57] The very essence of such relations is the reliance on the fear of force. A statement like "cross this line and I will shoot you" exemplifies relations of unequal power. It captures the ability of the stronger party to use violence and make "arbitrary decisions, and thus to avoid the kind of debate, clarification, and renegotiation typical of more egalitarian social relations." In lopsided power relations, the more powerful side is "not obliged to engage in a lot of interpretative labor."[58] To almost no one's surprise, the leaders of the Assam Movement called for a boycott of the elections—labeling them Assam's "final fight for survival." It radicalized the Assamese public sphere, and the elections turned into a battle of wills between the supporters of the Assam Movement and the institutions of the Indian state. There were violent confrontations between those who favored the decision to hold the elections—and participated in them—and those opposed. This dangerous situation, created by the decision to hold an election that nearly everyone expected to be boycotted by a majority of the state's population, was the context of the notorious Nellie massacre.[59] A contemporary account in the magazine *India Today* called the violence a "Hobbesian war of all against all."[60] Though unlike the Hobbesian state of nature, one should add, this was "the effect of sovereign coercive power," not its precondition.[61] The voter turnout hit record lows in areas where the boycott call was widely heeded, such as ethnic Assamese strongholds. The Congress Party won the election, but because of the historically low turnout, the newly elected state government lacked any semblance of legitimacy.

Sunil Nath, an important former Ulfa leader (who was then known by the nom de guerre Siddhartha Phukan), recalls how the attempt to defeat a largely peaceful popular movement by force led to a dramatic expansion of support for Ulfa. The "bulldozing through of elections to the State Legislative Assembly by the then Prime Minister Indira Gandhi," he wrote, caused support for Ulfa to grow. As "brute state power" was unleashed to hold the election, "the mature segments of Assamese society became vehemently anti-Congress," and "the youth rejected Indian-ness altogether."[62] Even though the Assam Movement ended with the signing of the Assam Accord in 1985, it soon became a commonly held view in Assam that despite the extraordinary popular support for the Assam Movement, it failed to achieve its primary goal.[63] This helped Ulfa make its case that the only sure path to Assam's future well-being was the pursuit of extraconstitutional methods. Ulfa's message found a ready constituency among the disappointed and disillusioned supporters of the Assam Movement.

The violent elections of 1983 foreshadowed another important development in Assam's subsequent political history. As I have indicated, violence broke out when supporters of the elections clashed with those who opposed them—that is, backers of the Assam Movement. This violence testified "not so much to 'communalism' as to the total breakdown of governance," in the words of the report in *India Today*.[64] The spectacular violence of Nellie, where more than two thousand Muslims were killed, has rightly drawn the most attention.[65] But framing the violence exclusively within the Indian discourse of "communalism"—the bureaucratic euphemism for Hindu-Muslim conflicts—obscures the crucial fact that there were incidents where the victims were Hindu Partition refugees and their descendants. Furthermore, there was no election boycott in the Barak Valley districts of Assam—the heartland of Bengali Hindu Partition refugees, where elections took place almost normally. The response to the elections of 1983 and the pattern of violence that unfolded brought into sharp relief the dissonance between the regional patriotic vision of nation and citizenship that animated the Assam Movement and the Hindu majoritarian framing of it. Shekhar Gupta's account of an episode that week anticipates the contestation over the politics of citizenship that would develop in Assam over the next three decades: "A few days after the killings, K. Sudershen, the Bauddhik Pramukh (intellectual chief) of the RSS, along with four of his key functionaries in Assam, sat in my hotel room in Gauhati [Guwahati] in a mournful mood and bitterly criticized the Assamese for refusing to make a distinction between 'Muslim infiltrators and Hindu refugees.' He was particularly upset about the killings in Khoirabari, near Goreswar in Kamrup district, and around Silapathar in North Lakhimpur district. The constant refrain was *'Hindu to arakshit hai'* (the poor Hindus are not protected)."[66]

The violence against Partition refugees and their offspring became the last straw for Hindu nationalist organizations from the Indian heartland. It made them more determined than ever to make an aggressive effort to force their particular ideas of national inclusion and exclusion—and on who should be a citizen and who should not—on Assam and the Northeast. A quarter century later, those efforts appeared to have paid off when a BJP-led coalition won elections in Assam in 2016.[67] But the intense opposition to the Citizenship Amendment Bill of 2016 in Assam and the rest of Northeast India, which forced the ruling party to abandon the effort, suggests that BJP's election victory did not mark an ideological triumph.

## MILITARY METAPHYSICS AND THE PEDAGOGY OF STATE VIOLENCE

Since counterinsurgency campaigns of the colonial era were inherently antinationalist, writes the legal historian Nasser Hussain, "along with issues of feasibility, their modern-day equivalents face a serious problem of legitimacy."[68] These words were written with the US operations in Iraq and Afghanistan in mind. The US and its allies highlight the lead role of the "host nation" in order to overcome the antinationalist bias inherent in these counterinsurgency campaigns. But "host nation" is, to say the least, a rather awkward choice of words; it implies that the "invading forces are guests."[69] But how do "internal" counterinsurgents address the same legitimacy challenge?[70] How does a postcolonial counterinsurgent state go about persuading its citizens that counterinsurgency operations at home are legitimate—especially when a circle of supporters and sympathizers share the insurgents' collective sense of injustice, deprivation, and humiliation and the belief that nonviolent channels to redress grievances are unavailable or ineffective? It may not be difficult to convince citizens of the Indian heartland about the legitimacy of counterinsurgency operations in areas outside the affective boundaries of the nation—or where the nation is seen as being in danger. But persuading citizens at the site of an "insurgency"—the civilian constituency of a rebel group—is an altogether different matter. A counterinsurgency campaign in such a situation can easily spiral into a crisis of national unity. It is not surprising that counterinsurgents and their propagandists try to portray "insurgents" as criminals and externally sponsored terrorists. As a report of a United Nations Policy Group once put it, "a time-tested technique to de-legitimize and demonize . . . opponents or adversaries" is to "label them as terrorists."[71] Indeed, Indian Army texts incorporate these elements into the very definition of an insurgency. In the category "Low Intensity Conflict," they include proxy war, terrorism, and insurgencies and border skirmishes. The subcategory insurgency is then defined as "an organised armed struggle by a section of the local population against the State, usually with foreign support."[72] Convincing the people of Assam that Ulfa was no more than a band of criminals backed by foreign powers—and thus beyond the pale of civil society—was no minor challenge for the Indian security establishment. But when Ulfa cadres were forced to take shelter in Bangladesh, the rebel organization's relationship with significant sections of mainstream Assamese opinion—the political constituency of the Assam Movement—did become somewhat strained. Many people came to believe that the need for sanctuary in Bangladesh might have forced Ulfa to make compromises on its stance on the question of unauthorized cross-border migration.

In a speech to a security think tank in New Delhi in June of 2001, S. K. Sinha, a former military general who was made the governor of Assam, gave the following account of his arrival in Assam as governor: "The feeling in Assam at that time was, here is a General coming, so there will be President's rule or military rule in Assam. It was, however, my very considered decision to work with a popular government in power and, as far as was possible, not to allow President's rule in Assam. Introduction of President's rule creates a direct confrontation between Delhi and the State, and any solution found under such circumstances would only be temporary, since the people would have a feeling that it was imposed upon them."[73] This is similar to the familiar "host nation" formula. The counterinsurgency campaign against Ulfa took the most comprehensive form during General Sinha's governorship, and all through that period "a popular government"—the second AGP government (1996–2001)—was in power in Assam. But the "operational control over all forces, including central paramilitary and State police employed on counter-insurgency duties," was with a Unified Command headed by the top Indian Army officer in the region.[74] "We couldn't have the kind of unity of command that General Sir Gerald Templer established in Malaya," lamented General Sinha, "but Unified Command was the closest we could achieve, and it worked."[75] The imperial nostalgia is unmistakable. General Sinha spoke proudly of his long military career, which began when he served as an officer in the British Indian Army. He did not feel constrained to talk publicly on how his military background and his hands-on experience with counterinsurgency were proving useful for performing his job as the constitutional head of a state government under a democratic dispensation. "The army was widely deployed," he said, "and my biggest asset was that, having been in the army for nearly 40 years, most of the officers there had worked under me and knew me. I could not possibly expect a more loyal and enthusiastic response than I received in Assam."[76] During General Sinha's governorship, the counterinsurgency campaign against Ulfa even incorporated a strategy of psychological warfare. The death squad killings with which I began this chapter also happened during this period. One of the ironies of this phase of counterinsurgency was the collaboration between Governor Sinha and the onetime leader of the Assam Movement, and now the state's chief minister, Prafulla Kumar Mahanta. Governor Sinha's public position on the question of immigration from across the Partition's border facilitated this collaboration. But more than ideological common ground sustained the alliance. The governor befriended the chief minister, and in public forums he sometimes addressed the young chief minister as "Prafulla Kumar, my son."[77] In his 2001 speech to security professionals in Delhi, General Sinha spoke of "a very difficult decision" he faced as governor. The Central Bureau of Investigation (CBI) had sought the governor's permission, required by statutes, to prosecute the state's elected chief minister for his involvement in a serious corruption case. The former general rejected the proposal, he said, at least partly because "political instability was the last thing Assam needed at that time." The allusion is clear: it was useful to have a "popular"—that is, formally elected—state government during the harsh counterinsurgency operations in the state. It is hard to miss echoes of the "host nation" formula. Protecting the chief minister from prosecution on charges of corruption appears to be a quid pro quo. But General Sinha maintains that he also had made the judgment, based on the documents that were made available to him, that there was no prima facie evidence against Chief Minister Mahanta.[78]

## PSYCHOLOGICAL WARFARE

In comparative terms, postcolonial India's comfort level with the discourse of insurgency and counterinsurgency is exceptional. Psychological warfare—getting a certain superficial handle on a people's culture and using it to manipulate them[79]—was a matter of great sensitivity in the context of British policy in Northern Ireland. There was significant resistance to the use of psychological operations against "our own people"— that is, "the citizens of Northern Ireland"—which included the Irish Republic Army.[80] But Indian officials are not only comfortable with the vocabulary of insurgency and counterinsurgency; they show no compunction about using psychological warfare against fellow Indians. In his June 2001 speech, Governor Sinha freely elaborated on the "psychological initiatives" that "took shape within a few weeks" of his arrival in Assam. The goal, he explained, was to use history as "a weapon to fight militancy." Since Ulfa "had talked in terms of Assam never being a part of India," he said, "the response would be to prove precisely how wrong they were."[81] He came to Assam rather well prepared to play this hand in his new job as governor. Even at his swearing-in ceremony in 1997, he spoke of the revered Assamese Vaishnava saint Srimanta Sankardev as a "national hero of India."[82] Sankardev was one of the three "inspirational figures" that he later identified in his campaign to make "the people of Assam . . . feel proud of their past, and the rest of India . . . feel proud of Assam." To his Delhi audience of security experts, General Sinha spoke proudly of this work he was doing in Assam as governor. With unmistakable arrogance he said, "I installed a painting of Shreeman [*sic*] Shankar Dev and had the Chief Minister of Assam sworn in under that picture, telling him that he was the first in Assam to take the oath under a picture of the Assamese reformer, though I hoped he would not be the last."[83] Soon after he arrived in the state, the general got a chance to try his hand as a revisionist historian of Assam. The following is his account of his contribution to a meeting of professional historians: "Top historians from all over the country were present, and in my opening address, I underlined the fact that historians had neglected Assam, but that history had not neglected it. . . . While textbooks wrote of the Indus Valley Civilisation, the Gangetic Valley Civilisation, etc., you hardly read anything about Brahmaputra Valley Civilisation. Rana Pratap and Shivaji are national military heroes, but there was a military hero of Assam in the same mould— Lachit Barphukan [*sic*]; his name is not known outside Assam."[84]

It is not surprising that Lachit Borphukon was the "inspirational figure" from Assam history that appealed to General Sinha the most.[85] Borphukon had been the Ahom official in charge of its territories in lower Assam. In 1671 he commanded the Ahom forces that defeated the vastly superior Mughal army led by Raja Ram Singh of Ajmer in the battle of Saraighat. The Ahom chronicles known as *Buranjis* refer only briefly to Borphukon's narrow victory in a naval battle against Ram Singh's forces. Yet this victory later "served as [the] basis for the proud claim by modern Assamese that Assam was one of the few regions to stave off 'alien' rule."[86] The *Buranjis*, however, refer to "these would-be conquerors from the Indian heartland" not as Mughals or Muslims but as *Bangals* or *Yavanas*.[87] Lachit Borphukon is a powerful symbol of Assam's autonomous past for many in Assam. He was an inspiring historical figure for Ulfa. An influential book published in 1980 was titled *Moidamor Pora Moi Lachite Koiso* (This is Lachit speaking from my moidam [burial tomb]), by Suresh Phukon.[88] It circulated widely during the early days of Ulfa and was a powerful influence on a whole generation of Ulfa members and sympathizers. The dramatic text imagines Borphukon as emerging from his tomb and commenting on Assam's past glory and present decay. Borphukon, the narrator, admonishes Assam's political class for betraying the interests of the people and pursuing their narrow and selfish interests. This imagined Borphukon identifies a number of well-known Assamese politicians of the past by name for creating Assam's crisis of unauthorized immigration and noncitizen enfranchisement. The narrator then praises a number of politicians and thought-leaders who are seen as standing up to Delhi and working for the greater good of Assam. The imagined Borphukon, speaking in the first person, declares that his death was ordained by destiny. But at that critical juncture in Assam's history, moved by the conviction, patriotism, and determination of a new generation of Assamese youth willing to sacrifice their lives for the future of their "country," he and his associates had returned.[89] The book was banned during the counterinsurgency campaign against Ulfa, and in 1991 the book's author, Suresh Phukon, died—reportedly from injuries he suffered while in detention.

In the early part of the twentieth century the celebration of *Lachit Dibox* or Lachit Day was a very low-key affair limited to a few localities of Upper Assam.[90] The publication in 1947 of S. K. Bhuyan's *Lachit Barphukan and His Times* was an important moment in the mythologization of this historical figure. This book is part of a genre of writing that historian Bodhisattva Kar calls a statist history of pre-British Assam that tries to retrieve "the lost sovereignty of Assamese history."[91] In 1962 the first bridge built on the River Brahmaputra near Guwahati was named Saraighat Bridge, noting its proximity to the legendary site of the battle. This was the first major move in the public memorializing of Borphukon. His statue was erected on the south bank of the river in the 1990s, "presumably to jog those 'historical' memories which a mention of Saraighat alone could not manage."[92] Under General Sinha's governorship, the celebration of *Lachit Dibox* in Assam saw a dramatic departure from past practices. In 2000, ministers of the central government attended the main celebration along with Governor Sinha. State ministers took ceremonial oaths to carry on Borphukon's legacy.[93] Among Governor Sinha's initiatives to memorialize Borphukon was an annual lecture in his memory at Gauhati University. The first Lachit Borphukon Memorial Lecture, in November of 1998, was given by no less a person than A. P. J. Abdul Kalam, who four years later became the president of India. Thanks to General Sinha's efforts, a statue of Borphukon was installed even at India's National Defence Academy, where officers of the Indian Armed Forces are educated. The academy also instituted the Lachit Borphukan [*sic*] Gold Medal awarded to the best cadet every year. Thus Borphukon, in the words of historian

Jayeeta Sharma, marched "out of historical liminality into the clamour of a fin-de-siècle public sphere," first as an icon for youthful Ulfa members and sympathizers, but then as an icon "of the state apparatus attempting to contain them." By the time Sharma's essay was published, in 2004, the efforts to "raise Lachit to prominence" were no longer led by Ulfa but by "the representatives of the establishment . . . within a general agenda of right-wing militaristic jingoism."[94]

Perhaps nothing helped Governor Sinha win the battle of public opinion in Assam more than his much-publicized *Report on Illegal Immigration into Assam*, submitted to the president of India in November of 1998. He could have easily listed it as part of his list of achievements in the area of psychological warfare. "Illegal migration" from Bangladesh to Assam, said the governor's report, was "the core issue" behind the state's recent political turmoil and "the prime contributory factor behind the outbreak of insurgency." The report won him accolades from many supporters of the Assam Movement. "The unabated influx of illegal migrants," said the report, threatened to reduce "the Assamese people to a minority in their own State, as happened in Tripura and Sikkim." The words could easily have been written by an ideologue of the Assam Movement. But the governor, a retired military general, couched the issue in national security terms, and he dwelt on the possible long-term consequences of this migration. The problem of "illegal immigration," he said, does not only affect Assam. It undermines Indian national security. Because of this "silent and invidious demographic invasion," said this report, Muslims had become a majority in a number of districts in Lower Assam. The report even raised the false specter of a demand for the merger of those districts with Bangladesh. The "rapid growth of international Islamic fundamentalism" and the fact that Bangladesh had "long discarded secularism" (a plausible position in 1998), said the report, "may provide the driving force for this demand." The "loss of Lower Assam will sever the entire land mass of the North East" and "will have disastrous strategic and economic consequences. No misconceived and mistaken notions of secularism should . . . blind us to these realities."[95] General Sinha, as governor of Assam, not only presided over the defeat of Ulfa; he prepared the ground for a militarized border security agenda and for the appropriation of the issue of unauthorized immigration and disenfranchisement of noncitizens by Hindu majoritarians—breaking the tight hold of the regional patriotic forces on the issue.

## AFTER ULFA: THE CHALLENGE OF
## REBUILDING LEGITIMACY

Defeating Ulfa militarily was not much of a challenge for the Indian Army. Ulfa had a significant political constituency, but it was little more than a small band of armed rebels. They were defeated quickly and decisively. For instance, the first military operation against Ulfa that took place in November and December of 1990, says a news report of the time, "turned out to be something of a dampener."[96] The Indian Army faced almost no resistance, raising doubts about Ulfa's actual strength; many even dismissed the organization as little more than a media creation. But it became amply evident quite soon that there would be a price to be paid for employing crude military methods for ending a political conflict that was fundamentally about a collision of national imaginaries. The rebel organization, to be sure, had enough influence in bureaucratic circles to have access to classified information. As a result, its top leaders "seemed to know the date on which the army would move in" and were able to escape before it arrived.[97]

In post-Ulfa Assam, rebuilding the legitimacy of state institutions has become a major concern for successive Indian governments. This becomes evident in a number of areas. For instance, in February of 2011, after Ulfa's political appeal, membership strength, and public image took a severe beating, a delegation of the still-outlawed group was received by high officials in the Ministry of Home Affairs in New Delhi. Ulfa's chairman, Rajib Rajkonwar—better known by his *nom de guerre*, Arabinda Rajkhowa—led the seven-member group. Just a few months before, he and a number of his colleagues were ensconced in safe havens in Bangladesh to avoid reprisals by Indian security forces. Yet their visit to the nation's capital even included a meeting with the then prime minister, Manmohan Singh. The delegation presented proposals to Home Ministry officials to serve as a basis for negotiations for an "honorable, meaningful and peaceful resolution of . . . issues between Assam and India."[98] It is unlikely that many people in Assam thought of Ulfa at that time as a political force that had the authority to negotiate "issues between Assam and India." It is equally doubtful that the Indian security establishment was pleased with media images of India's highest-ranking elected officials exchanging pleasantries with leaders of a defeated and outlawed armed group. Why give the rebel group visibility and recognition at a time when sustained counterinsurgency operations had broken its back? Ulfa leaders, national security bureaucrats could argue, were being given an opportunity to regain some of their lost luster. In their interaction with the press, Ulfa leaders spoke of constitutional safeguards for protecting the rights and the identity of the people of Assam. But there was no political appetite in New Delhi for discussing issues of such grand political scope. Yet Indian Home Ministry officials did not seem overly concerned with the substance of those proposals. They were more concerned about organizing the Ulfa leaders' visit to the national capital in a manner that would show the unmistakable signs of a reconciliation event: a "state performance par excellence in which the state needs to be resymbolized and restaged as a meaningful horizon in the aftermath of open violence and schism."[99]

A statement by the then home minister, Palaniappan Chidambaram, made around the same time, throws some light on what led to the decision to hold those high-level meetings with Ulfa leaders. He contrasted India's approach to armed conflicts with its neighbor Sri Lanka's; the allusion was to the Tamil insurgency in that country and its brutal end. For ethical and electoral reasons, he said, India would not take the Sri Lankan approach. Governments, he explained, "have to survive and also get re-elected and policymakers have to factor in all these before deciding on issues." Insurgency in Northeast India is "by and large . . . a problem that we can contain, control and resolve."[100] This was an important clue. When the meetings with Ulfa leaders took place in February of 2011, the elections in Assam were only two months away. To voters in Assam, they signaled the Congress Party's intention to pursue an honorable peace with Ulfa. It appears that the party's strategists had figured out that such a signal to the electorate in Assam could give it an edge over its rivals. To show that the ruling party was working toward such an outcome could shift enough votes to decide the outcome of the election. The political bet paid off; the Congress Party–led alliance won the election. In an election year that did not favor incumbent politicians, the Tarun Gogoi–led Congress Party defied the odds and was elected to power for a third consecutive term.

This was not the only time that Ulfa's militant politics connected seamlessly with mainstream electoral politics. Again in 2016, a few months before the elections in Assam, the BJP—now the country's ruling party—sensed a similar political opportunity. In November of 2015, the Bangladesh government transferred to Indian custody Ulfa's founding member and general secretary, Golap Barua—best known by his *nom de guerre*, Anup Chetia. Prime Minister Modi personally intervened to ensure the handover of this last major Ulfa leader still in Bangladesh.[101] Once in India, he did not remain in custody for long. Undoubtedly, the Assam elections, only a few months away, were part of the BJP's calculations.

In post-Ulfa Assam, the effort to reinvent Borphukon as an Indian national military hero, a campaign that began as a technique of psychological warfare, has continued vigorously. The official ceremonies and public monuments to commemorate Borphukon have multiplied, and the trend has now reached fever pitch. If war is the continuation of politics by other means, "preservation is also politics continued by other means."[102] Acts of commemoration are among those "other means." In 2006 the Assam state government built the Saraighat War Memorial Park near Guwahati with statues of Borphukon and Ahom soldiers in battle formation. On November 24, 2015, even Prime Minister Narendra Modi posted a message on Twitter saluting Lachit Borphukon "on his birth anniversary." Referring to him as "India's pride," Modi said that Borphukon's "valour during [the] Saraighat war can never be forgotten."[103] In 2016, a striking thirty-five-foot bronze statue of Lachit Borphukon, sword in hand and attended by the eighteen-foot statues of eight armed soldiers, was installed in the middle of the Brahmaputra River in Guwahati. A war memorial at the center of Guwahati, inaugurated the same year, features a panel portraying Borphukon and the battle of Saraighat, along with statues and panels honoring other Indian wars and war heroes—both historical and post-1947. In December of 2016, the Assam state government announced that portraits of Lachit Borphukon would now hang in all state government offices, including educational institutions. In June of 2017, a bronze statue of Borphukon was installed at the Headquarters of two Mountain Divisions of the Indian Army in Dinjan in Upper Assam. Speaking at the inauguration of the statue, Assam Chief Minister Sonowal "applauded the initiative of the Indian Army for paying tribute to the great warrior and highlighted the contribution of [the] Indian Army in development of Assam." The army general heading the Dinjan base "thanked the people of Assam for their trust and constant support to Armed Forces during the challenging times."[104] There is, however, no evidence thus far that the framing of Borphukon as an Indian military hero has successfully displaced his regional patriotic framing as a symbol of Assam's autonomous past.

In 2015, only months before the Congress Party's election defeat, Assam's former chief minister Tarun Gogoi inaugurated the Lachit Borphukon statue on the River Brahmaputra. "Many now want to project Lachit as a Hindu warrior," said this veteran Assamese politician, "but he was a warrior of Assam and with associates like Bagh Hazarika, he fought for protecting his motherland. We all have a responsibility towards the country and the State and this sculpture would always remind us of the same."[105] *Gogoi's description of Borphukon as "a* warrior of Assam," fighting for "protecting his motherland," is surely the familiar framing of Borphukon before his memory became a tool of Indian counterinsurgency. The name of the Assamese Muslim nobleman Bagh Hazarika always appears in the Assamese telling of the Borphukon story. "Bagh Hazarika is with me" is how Lachit Borphukon announces his imagined reemergence in the publication Moi Lachite Koiso that I referred to earlier. That Hindu majoritarians would try to erase the name of Borphukon's celebrated Muslim associate is not surprising. But the fact that his name features in both former chief minister Gogoi's speech and in a text associated with the rise of Ulfa is not accidental. Clearly, we have not heard the last word on the politics of memory around Lachit Borphukon.

WHAT LIES AHEAD?

Hindu majoritarians would like to believe that they are finally getting close to settling the question of national citizenship in post-Partition India in their preferred mode—by reining in a stubborn source of opposition in a part of the country where the issue has been most contested and divisive. But such a conclusion would be premature. The intense political debates in Assam on the Citizenship (Amendment) Bill of 2016 suggest that the ideological gap between the regional patriotic framing of the question and the Hindu majoritarian framing of it remains as wide as ever.

In the "contentious politics" perspective on Ulfa presented in this chapter, the twists and turns in the politics of Assam since 1979—the starting point of both the Assam Movement and Ulfa—deserve careful analytical attention. The beginnings of the Assam Movement resembled those of a social movement. Without the particular threats and opportunities it faced, the movement may have maintained that character. Neither the Nellie massacre nor the spectacular rise of Ulfa was inevitable. Seen through comparative lenses, the differences between regimes in two areas—"governmental capacity and extent (or lack) of democracy"—are quite significant in determining what happens to contentious politics over time.[106] While "low-capacity undemocratic regimes host most of the world's civil wars" and "low-capacity democratic regimes gather more than their share of military coups and struggles among linguistic, religious, or ethnic groups," social movements—and those that remain as that—occur mostly in high-capacity democracies. The differences are explained by "the dramatic variation in the sorts of threats and opportunities faced by potential claim makers in different regime environments."[107] Whatever else one can say about the conditions in post-Ulfa Assam, no one can claim that a higher capacity democracy is in place today than in the 1980s. The one continuous thread in the political life of Assam since the arrival of the hard state in 1990 is the Armed Forces Special Powers Act. During the past quarter century, the state has consolidated significant coercive powers in its hands. Despite the easy military victory against Ulfa, and the electoral victories of Hindu nationalists, the persistence of the AFSPA regime points to a persistent sense of unease and uncertainty among India's ruling elites about the political future of Assam. It is significant that in August of 2018, when the "disturbed area" designation under AFSPA was extended to the whole of Assam by six more months, the ostensible ground was the growing controversies surrounding the process of updating the National Register of Citizens (NRC).[108] No one really knows when or how the next significant episode of sustained social protests in Assam will unfold. But the institutions of Indian democracy are in no better position today to contain and channel them than they were four decades ago.

In an important ruling in 2016, the Indian Supreme Court reminded the executive branch that the practice of deploying the armed forces to assist civil power is premised on the assumption that "normalcy would be restored within a reasonable period." If the civil administration and the armed forces fail to achieve this, that "cannot be a fig leaf for prolonged, permanent or indefinite deployment of the armed forces." That would be a mockery of "our democratic process" and "a travesty" of the constitutional distribution of powers between the center and the states, which provides the legal foundation for the practice.[109] If the Indian government chooses to pay serious attention to this warning, it could produce a more creative approach to contentious politics in Northeast India. It is still possible to secure a more stable, secure, and democratic future for Assam if a democratic political will in the country were to consolidate.

CHAPTER 6

# THE STRANGE CAREER OF THE
# ARMED FORCES SPECIAL POWERS ACT

Conventional, simple-minded democratic views of the Sovereign
People are blind to the ways in which democracy can degenerate
into mere rule of a majority that considers itself the sole judge of
good and evil, so setting democracy on the road to totalitarian rule.
—John Keane, "Humble Democracy?"

IN AUGUST OF 2016, the Gandhian-inspired Manipuri activist Irom
Sharmila ended her much-publicized hunger strike protesting the Armed
Forces Special Powers Act (AFSPA).[1] Indian state authorities steadfastly
refused to recognize her action as a form of political resistance. They were
determined not to allow her physical suffering—and the threat of mar-
tyrdom—to become a site of contestation of the AFSPA regime or of the
authority of the Indian state. She was arrested on the charge of attempting
suicide—a punishable offense under Indian law at that time—and placed
in police custody. She was confined to a hospital room designated as a
"subjail" for this purpose and kept alive by force-feeding. She was released
at the end of each year so that the legal temporal limit on detention without
trial would not be exceeded, but then she would be rearrested a few days
later. For sixteen long years, Sharmila engaged in this remarkable form of
antipolitical politics against an unyielding state.[2] By all accounts, she ended
her protest on having reached the conclusion—surely a difficult one for
her—that no government in New Delhi will end the AFSPA regime in
the foreseeable future.[3]

Indian state authorities will surely claim that conditions in Assam and
Nagaland are slowly returning to "normal." Yet revoking AFSPA is no-
where on their agenda. Evidently, it is not regarded as part of normalcy in

Northeast India. Or perhaps the prevailing peace is not regarded as robust and sustainable enough to merit the revocation of this law. Rather remarkably, AFSPA remains in effect even in Mizoram—a state often showcased as the quintessential example of successful counterinsurgency—albeit only as a "sleeping act."[4] In May of 2015 the government of Tripura announced with much fanfare the "withdrawal" of AFSPA from the state. The withdrawal of a law is, of course, not quite the same as repealing it. In any case, Tripura's circumstances are unique. It is the only Northeastern state where Hindu Bengalis—their numbers much augmented by the arrival of successive waves of Partition refugees from East Pakistan/Bangladesh—are now an ethnic majority. Kuldeep Kumar, a former top police official of Tripura, is full of praise for the state's successful counterinsurgency campaign against armed rebels. But at the same time, he underscores the state's continued vulnerability. Its "tribal people," writes Kumar, "appear to be almost reconciled to their minority status." They realize that Tripura's post-Partition ethnic demography is there to stay. But the tribal population has also been the political constituency of armed rebellions in the state. Given the "harsh reality of electoral politics," writes Kumar, the state's tribal leaders have come to accept that there is no alternative to working with nontribal political leaders. But "the issues of marginalization of their ethnic identity, culture, development-induced displacement, poor education, and social and economic disempowerment continue to agitate tribals."[5] A more radically inclined scholar of Tripura, R. K. Debbarma, says that if that state has peace, it is the peace of the graveyard: "crushing the might of armed groups merely subdues the symptoms." Tripura's capital city, Agartala, according to Debbarma, has the appearance of "a settler colony." He believes that future challenges to the "institutionalized subordination" of this key segment of the state's population are quite likely.[6] His prognostication appears to be on the mark. During the controversy over the Citizenship Amendment Bill that erupted in the region in 2018–19, Tripura was frequently cited as a negative example of what continuing migration of Hindus from Bangladesh could do to the ethnic demography and political equilibrium of Northeast India. The state saw significant protests against the bill by organizations representing the tribal population. Those protests, according to a security and intelligence researcher, had "the potential to derail the sustained improvement in the security scenario over the past decade."[7] Thus, the Tripura government's decision in 2015 to withdraw AFSPA is unlikely to have much bearing on the long-term fate of this law in the region.[8]

AFSPA, in Irom Sharmila's view, is an act of war on society; it suspends normal everyday life. The Indian Supreme Court may have pronounced this law to be legal and constitutional, but as G. K. Pillai, a former Indian civil servant who once headed India's Home Ministry, points out sardonically, it did not change the perception in the AFSPA states that it gives carte blanche to the armed forces to commit human rights violations with impunity.[9] But the Supreme Court's 1997 ruling that declared AFSPA constitutional, it should be pointed out, also made a number of important recommendations. These have had little practical effect, however, on changing things on the ground. For instance, the ruling stipulated that a "disturbed area" proclamation be subjected to review every six months. This has been done but only in the most perfunctory way possible. For example, as a result of successive six-month extensions, the state of Assam has been a disturbed area under AFSPA since November of 1990—for more than a quarter of a century. The August 2018 official announcement of the routine six-monthly extension of AFSPA offered a rather curious explanation. The head of the Assam Police said, "The situation is peaceful, but we will not take a decision on withdrawing AFSPA till the NRC exercise is over."[10] But since then, there has been some talk of the "withdrawal" of AFSPA from Assam following the Tripura example. Manipur has been a disturbed area for a decade longer than Assam—since 1980. From 2004, the politically sensitive Municipal Area of Imphal has been exempted. But this has made little difference on the ground. A Supreme Court–appointed commission investigating the "fake encounters" in the state found that the exemption was routinely circumvented in practice. Because AFSPA applies only to the armed forces, the Imphal exemption restricts the Assam Rifles but not the Manipur Police. Many of the fake encounters investigated by the commission occurred during joint operations of the Assam Rifles and a special state police force called the Commandos (CDOs).[11] This arrangement allowed the security forces to ignore the Imphal exemption and operate in all parts of Manipur. It effectively gave the Commandos of the Manipur Police the same "protection" against prosecution as the Assam Rifles.[12]

Sharmila believes that no self-respecting democracy should make its citizens live under the indignity and cruelty of such a repressive law—a conviction that grew out of seeing its operation on the ground. Sociologist and political thinker Shiv Viswanathan aptly compares her stance to that of social philosopher and French Resistance activist Simone Weil. Sharmila was, in effect, saying like Weil: "I have no right to enjoy life when that normalcy, that dream of walking and living without constraint or fear is not available to my people."[13] Her fellow citizens in Manipur had no trouble relating to her message. But it did not resonate in the rest of India. The dominant perception of Manipur in the Indian heartland is of a faraway region where the nation faces grave danger from domestic and foreign enemies.[14] There was significant interest in Sharmila's hunger strike in the Indian media. But it was mostly talked about as the world's longest hunger strike; her cause—the effects of AFSPA on the everyday life of ordinary civilians—did not get much attention or support. In 2006, Sharmila managed to briefly take her protest to the Jantar Mantar in New Delhi—until recently the national capital's most recognizable site for public protests. She was quickly arrested and kept at a major hospital. The nurse attending her, reports journalist Anubha Bhonsle, "never understood why this woman who was quite capable of feeding herself, had to be fed through a tube." None of the nurses knew anything about Sharmila or her cause. Bhonsle reports the following conversation:

> "She's from Assam side," said one.
> "She is protesting about something there."
> "Arrey, dimag kharab hai, pagal hai." [Something wrong with her head, she is mad.][15]

But it is not only the national media or the Indian public that had limited interest in Sharmila's cause. The state government of Manipur worked hard to silence her and to keep her hunger strike out of public view. When two judges of the National Human Rights Commission (NHRC) visited her in Imphal in 2013, they found that while other prisoners were able to meet visitors and family members, a meeting with Sharmila required the chief minister's special permission. The state government, said the judges, was keeping Sharmila alive because "her death would create problems." But it was also "trying to break her spirit through . . . enforced isolation, for which there is no judicial mandate."[16] But even though Sharmila's unique form of protest was not recognized as an act of political resistance, for sixteen years she was able to ensure that the enforcement of AFSPA in Manipur would require the everyday performance of the violence of sovereignty on her body. This extraordinary act of protest may have resonated in an India of another era, but it failed to do so in twenty-first-century India.

## ON THE RECEIVING END OF AFSPA

Seven of the eight states of Northeast India—the exception being Sikkim—have been on the receiving end of AFSPA. In the 1950s and 1960s, AFSPA provided legal cover for some of the most repressive methods available in the repertoire of counterinsurgency used against Nagas and Mizos, including village regrouping: the forced relocation of the population in camps under close surveillance. The district of Mizo Hills—now the state of Mizoram—went through a period of "wholesale militarization, massive forced resettlement and war-like conditions." The following is Joy L. K. Pachuau and Willem van Schendel's account of the Indian response to the Mizo revolt in 1968:

> Fighter planes were sent to Aizawl and they strafed the town and adjacent villages. They also dropped incendiary bombs, setting the towns and villages ablaze and killing many. . . . The insurgents were appalled: "We never quite imagined that the government would do such a thing. . . . It occurred to us that the people we were fighting against were not normal human beings but evil spirits that were inhabiting the earth." This attack, the trauma of which established itself as a critical event in Mizo visions of India, remains the only time that the Government of India resorted to air strikes in its own territory.[17]

Anthropologist Nandini Sundar tells us that Mizos describe the days of village regrouping as *Khokhom*: being driven helter-skelter, "a term that sums up a world of terror, like the Palestinian *Nakbah* or catastrophe to refer to the forcible evacuations of 1948." In Nagaland, people mark time in terms of memories of regrouping with expressions like "the year we came back from the jungle."[18] Sanitized accounts of the postcolonial history of counterinsurgency in India, which takes the vantage point of the Indian state, claim that the campaign against the Mizos was a "success." It is common to hear in official circles that India has not "lost" any domestic counterinsurgency campaign. But this view from the nation's capital—the bureaucratic calculus of the "success" or "failure" of counterinsurgency—Sundar reminds us, says little about the experience of civilians in those areas. For Naga and Mizo survivors of village regrouping, "there was no 'success,' only hardship."[19] Even decades later, they remember the "search operations, the starvation, the regime of curfews and the reduction of identity to a roll call and a piece of paper," not the so-called campaigns for "hearts and minds." Indeed, the intense intersubjectivity and the relationships of cooperation and trust that Nagas and Mizos developed as victims of counterinsurgency warfare contributed significantly to the crystallization of their identities. For instance, Mizo youth culture, which Indians often think of as "Western," is a product of the time of counterinsurgency. All Mizos, including those unsympathetic to the revolt, saw the Indian Army as "invaders" with no respect for the people of Mizoram. During that time "Indian cultural practices lost the limited appeal. . . . Hindi songs were cold-shouldered and 'Indian' ideas of fashion and decorum were rejected."[20]

It is often said that the Indian state's counterinsurgency capacity has matured over time. But one can hardly claim that the death squads of Assam in the 1990s, or the "fake encounters" in Manipur of recent years, were any less nightmarish than the forced relocation of Naga and Mizo villagers in the 1950s and 1960s. In 2012, the Extra Judicial Execution Victim Families Association of Manipur (EEVFAM) petitioned the Supreme Court to investigate as many as 1,528 cases of fake encounters that allegedly occurred in the state between 1979 and 2012.[21] It is significant that the petitioning organization's locally used acronym, EEVFAM, matches an emotively powerful word in the local Meitei language, which evokes the pain and trauma of broken connections with loved ones.[22] A coalition of civil society groups managed to meet with and submit a memorandum to the United Nations Human Rights Council's Special Rapporteur on Extrajudicial, Summary and Arbitrary Execution with documentation of the 1,528 cases included in the EEVFAM petition.[23] Special Rapporteur Christof Heyns explained in his report on his Mission to India the Indian practice of fake encounter for the benefit of the rest of the world: "Where they occur, 'fake encounters' entail that suspected criminals or persons alleged to be terrorists or insurgents, and in some cases individuals for whose apprehension an award is granted, are fatally shot by the security officers. A 'shootout scene' is staged afterwards. The scene portrays those killed as the aggressors who had first opened fire. The security officers allege in this regard that they returned fire in self-defence."[24]

The Supreme Court appointed a three-member commission to inquire into the first six of the 1,528 cases in the EEVFAM petition so that it could be "fully satisfied about the truth of the allegations."[25] Not a single one of the small sample of six cases was found to be an actual "encounter." It would seem, said the commission in its report, "the security forces believed a priori that the suspects involved in the encounters had to be eliminated and the forces acted accordingly."[26] Drawing on these findings, the Supreme Court bench decided that the allegations could not "be summarily rubbished." Its interim judgment of July 2016 said that "there is some truth in the allegations, calling for a deeper probe." Since then, it has been trying to find out "the whole truth." Inquiries continue. After all, the EEVFAM petition includes information on more than fifteen hundred cases of fake encounters. But the petition has already produced an important ruling on the practice of deploying the armed forces to assist civil powers: reminding the government that the practice is premised on "normalcy" being restored within a reasonable period.[27]

## INDIAN DEMOCRACY AND THE DEBATE ON AFSPA

It is not accidental that Sharmila ended her hunger strike in 2016. Until then, civil protests and criticism by rights groups were able to move the needle of Indian public opinion on AFSPA—albeit very slightly. But the ideological climate shifted swiftly with the rise of the BJP to power. With a form of state-led ultranationalist majoritarianism coming to the helm, an iron curtain appears to have descended on any talk of reforming the AFSPA regime. But one should not overestimate the accomplishments of the debate on AFSPA during the previous political dispensation. In 2009, the then Congress government's home minister strongly defended this law before the UN High Commissioner for Human Rights. P. Chidambaram refused to give the UN official any assurance of reforming AFSPA. When she asked about the law's misuse, according to a senior Indian Home Ministry official, "she was politely but firmly told that the AFSPA is not applicable throughout the country. It is only effective in areas where terrorists operate."[28]

It has been said that the security state likes to offer a bargain to its citizens. In exchange for protection, it wants citizens to unquestioningly accept its decisions—no matter how arbitrary—and let "the ideals of democratic equality and accountability go by the wayside."[29] Those inspired by the idea of democratic citizenship, says political theorist Iris Marion Young, reject this bargain. Democratic citizenship is inconsistent with an idea of protection that reduces citizens to the status of dependents who would entrust their lives to state officials—and not question their decisions on what will keep them safe.[30] One example of the publicly articulated preference for democratic citizenship over securitized citizenship in Northeast India is the critique of amnesties to leaders of armed groups.[31] Such criticisms are heard even during times when the armed group in question has enjoyed significant public support.[32] In 2004, the abduction, suspected rape, and murder of a young woman, Thangjam Manorama, sparked powerful protests in Manipur. An act of exceptional courage and eloquence marked those protests. About a dozen middle-aged Manipuri women, standing naked in front of the Indian Army's base in Manipur's capital city, Imphal, held a banner that read, "Indian Army Rape Us." Through their nakedness and the bland and declarative banners, observes political theorist Ananya Vajpeyi, "the Manipuri women announced to the world: 'the raping of us Manipuri women is what the Indian Army does. We stand here to say this out loud and clear: this is the way it is. We embody resentment.'" Citizens may not be able "to resist the power of the

Indian State," but "resent it they can." The political emotion of resentment, she writes, drawing on an essay by Jean Améry, "counter-acts the process of the social acceptance of historical wrongs."[33]

In response to the emotionally wrenching and powerful anti-AFSPA protests in Manipur, the Manmohan Singh–led first United Progressive Alliance government appointed a committee headed by former Supreme Court Judge B. P. Jeevan Reddy to review AFSPA—the most significant move to date toward changing the status quo on AFSPA. The committee was asked to consider whether to amend the law—and bring it in line with the government's human rights obligations and commitments—or to replace it with "a more humane" law. Human Rights Watch called the decision one of the positive achievements of the first Manmohan Singh government.[34] The Reddy Committee visited various parts of Northeast India, meeting representatives of groups as well as individuals. The dominant view they encountered in the region's civil society circles was that AFSPA is "undemocratic, harsh and discriminatory." Since the law is specific to Northeast India, it "discriminates against the people of the region."[35] Clearly, the aspiration to enjoy the freedoms associated with a normal democracy animates the resistance to AFSPA in Northeast India. The Reddy Committee recommended the repeal of AFSPA and the incorporation of some of its key provisions into the Unlawful Activities Prevention Act. It proposed significant reforms, such as the creation of grievance cells in districts where the army operates to "ensure public confidence in the process of detention and arrest" since "there have been a large number of cases where those taken away without warrants have 'disappeared,' or ended up dead or badly injured."[36] But the government in New Delhi sat on the report for a long time, probably because of a strong push from the security establishment to reject its recommendations. Indeed, the report may not have seen the light of day had it not been leaked to a newspaper that posted it on its website. In retrospect, it appears to some analysts that the committee was formed only to contain the powerful protests against AFSPA in Manipur, and once this goal was served, interest in reforming the security regime began to wane.[37]

During the same decade, widespread anti-AFSPA protests occurred in Jammu and Kashmir as well.[38] There, too, reports of "fake encounters" precipitated public anger. The then chief minister, Omar Abdullah, prom-ised that AFSPA would be revoked or amended when the situation in the state improves. Kashmiri commentator Anuradha Bhasin Jamwal, however, asked rhetorically: "since when does he or any establishment in Jammu and Kashmir have the autonomy to deal with something that Centre imposes"?[39] Military generals and BJP politicians—then in opposition—were sharply critical of Abdullah. The people who talk of the dilution or withdrawal of AFSPA said the then army chief, V. K. Singh—now a BJP minister—do it for political gains.[40] The BJP leader, L. K. Advani, said that even to consider amending AFSPA or to withdraw troops from Jammu and Kashmir—the two, for him belonged together—is to surrender to Islamabad's "strategy of breaking India's unity."[41] It is not surprising that in the face of such strong and emotive nationalist political opposition, the talk of repealing—or even amending AFSPA—did not go very far.

In May of 2016 the weekly newspaper of the RSS published a tenden-tious and scurrilous article defending AFSPA—invoking the nation-in-danger rhetoric. Sharmila ended her hunger strike within three months of the publication of that article. Its author is a leading apparatchik of the RSS in Northeast India. AFSPA's goal, says the article, is to "flush out the terrorists in J&K [Jammu and Kashmir], Nagaland, Manipur and other disturbed areas of [the] North-East Region." It criticized the "uproar in Parliament to remove AFSPA." Critics of AFSPA "defame [the] Army and coronate militants." It accused "pseudo-human rightists" of being in league with "terrorists." The article describes Irom Sharmila as "a God-given stooge in the hands of terrorists and secessionist forces." When the "army is in action, the terrorists run for their life," which is why "pseudo-human rightists" become most active when "insurgencies" are at their peak. If the "debate on AFSPA is at its peak in Manipur," it is "because terrorism is at its peak there." The article credits the Framework Agreement of 2015 and the "active support and will-power" of the Nagaland government for creating a situation where "the issue of AFSPA is no more in Nagaland because Army operation is no more required and people enjoy peace and tranquility."[42] Of course, AFSPA is as firmly in place in Nagaland as ever. But since media attention on AFSPA is a source of embarrassment to Indian elites craving international recognition, the author of the article takes satisfaction in the fact that the talk of repealing or reforming AFSPA has ceased to make newspaper headlines ("the issue of AFSPA is no more"). What he would like to see happen, it seems, is that Northeasterners simply learn to live with AFSPA as a necessary part of life in democratic India. For only because of AFSPA has it been possible to achieve what he describes, quite remarkably, as a condition of "peace and tranquility" in the region.

It is said that political tolerance is "an essential endorphin of a democratic body politic." And tolerance, one must remember, is not about ideas one approves. "Political tolerance is forbearance; it is the restraint of the urge to repress one's political enemies."[43] The kind of rhetoric used in this article in support of AFSPA in a politically influential publication in mainland India attests to the validity of political theorist John Keane's warning quoted at the opening of this chapter: that democratic values such as respect for human dignity are not safe if elected majorities are able to impose their view of political conflicts as contests between good and evil. To prevent the erosion of democracy and the slide toward democratic authoritarianism, there must be robust countermajoritarian institutions that can limit majority sovereignty "in favour of a 'common democratic charter' that privileges . . . faith in the possibility of human progress, the inviolability of human dignity and the conviction that human suffering and injustice can be overcome through 'political work.'"[44]

To be sure, in the life of a democracy, there may be situations when rights may have to bow to security.[45] All democratic constitutions have emergency provisions for dealing with such contingencies. They typically define an emergency and lay out governmental powers and restraints during emergencies. But since a commitment to dignity is a foundational value of a democracy, the use of coercion should always be morally problematic. To deal with this conundrum, political thinker and commentator Michael Ignatieff once proposed a number of "lesser evil" tests for laws that enable coercive measures in a democracy. The first test that such a law must pass is the dignity test: does it preclude cruel and unusual punishment, torture, extrajudicial execution, and so forth? The second is the conservative test: is the proposed departure from due process standards really necessary? Third is the effectiveness test:

would the coercive measures under consideration make citizens more secure or less? Fourth is the last resort test to ensure that new coercive measures are adopted only after less coercive measures have been tried and failed. Finally, all such measures would have to pass the test of open adversarial review by legislative and judicial bodies.[46] It is hard to argue that AFSPA—and the murky counterinsurgency methods it countenances—even remotely meets any of Ignatieff's lesser-evil tests.

The AFSPA regime has become normalized largely because it is not based in the Indian Constitution's Emergency Provisions (Part 18, Articles 352–60)—the legal basis for the nationwide Emergency of 1975–77 and the institution of President's Rule. Even though fundamental freedoms are effectively suspended in a "disturbed area," it is not subject to the restraints of a constitutional emergency because it occurs under the authority of an ordinary law—not an emergency law. The temporal limits governing constitutional emergencies do not apply to AFSPA. Thus, certain parts of Northeast India have been "disturbed" under AFSPA for decades on end. President's Rule and a disturbed area proclamation under AFSPA were made simultaneously in Assam in 1990. President's Rule came to an end the following year. But AFSPA remains in place to this day.

According to Indian administrative discourse and practice, AFSPA belongs to the realm of ordinary public order policing: the "use of armed forces in aid of the civil powers"—a doctrine that is by no means unique to India. AFSPA is a textbook case of an undeclared emergency that international human rights treaties seek to prevent. The idea of derogation requires that legislatures "act and deliberate before extraordinary powers are exercised" so that unelected executive branch officials do not act as sovereigns and decide "when an emergency exists and what actions are required to respond to the emergency." A formally announced derogation of rights is intended to ensure that a suspension of rights is temporary: it is expected to trigger "international engagement and scrutiny of actions taken at the domestic level."[47] India has signed and ratified the International Covenant on Civil and Political Rights (ICCPR). State parties to the ICCPR commit themselves to the restraints prescribed in it in responding to a "public emergency" that "threatens the life of the nation." They may, in such situations, "take measures derogating from their obligations under the present Covenant to the extent strictly required by the exigencies of the situation." But the right to life and the norms regarding the prohibition of torture, slavery, and servitude are considered nonderogable. A state "availing itself of the right of derogation" is asked to "immediately inform the other State Parties" through the intermediary of the UN secretary general about "the provisions from which it has derogated and of the reasons by which it was actuated." The assumption made is that such measures must be exceptional and temporary. Governments are therefore supposed to communicate when such derogation is terminated.[48] As far back as 1997, the United Nations Human Rights Committee, which oversees the implementation of the ICCPR, had expressed dismay that "some parts of India have remained subject to declaration as disturbed areas over many years." In effect, said its report, India uses emergency powers for extended periods without following procedures spelled out in a covenant to which it is a signatory.[49] More recently, a senior representative of the UN Human Rights Council made the same point after a visit to India in 2013.[50]

India has steadfastly resisted efforts of UN human rights bodies to monitor AFSPA. But Indian officials and those representing the UN mostly talk past each other. The Indian position is that AFSPA does not invoke the Constitution's emergency powers and that the armed forces only assist—and do not supplant—civil powers. As a result, AFSPA does not come under the jurisdiction of the ICCPR. Indian officials have never tried to argue that the actual challenges faced in AFSPA states meet the test of a "public emergency" threatening "the life of the nation."[51] Instead, they make a circular argument: AFSPA and the legal immunities are necessary because India confronts public order situations that require the armed forces to assist civil powers. Once, an Indian Army chief even expressed the view that AFSPA is "misunderstood" by the public in the states where it is in effect. For him, the issue is remarkably simple: "soldiers . . . need legal protection to ensure that they perform their tasks efficiently."[52] Ajai Sahni, the head of a Delhi-based security think tank, believes that the debate on AFSPA has been "emotionally charged" and "extraordinarily muddied." After all, for the Indian Army to function in a "situation of widespread internal disorder," it is essential to have AFSPA or a comparable legislation that "confers necessary powers of search, seizure, arrest and engagement." Without such an "enabling" law, the army cannot do counterinsurgency operations. As long as there are counterinsurgency operations, AFSPA or a similar law is "indispensable."[53]

## THE LONG SHADOW OF IMPERIAL POLICING

In Chapter 1, I referred to the late Nari Rustomji of the Indian Civil Service blaming the terrible turn of events in the Naga areas in the 1950s on "the tradition of decision-making by precedent inherent in the administrative processes and inherited from the predecessor government."[54] The institutional inertia he was alluding to is quite telling. During British colonial rule, occasional military expeditions to teach the tribesmen a lesson were the standard tool of maintaining order in some parts of the excluded areas, including the Naga Hills. This terrible history was behind the disastrous decision to respond to the Naga rebellion with full military force. Institutional inertia marked many aspects of Indian decision making in matters related to the colonial frontier province during the early years after decolonization. The decision to adopt AFSPA was among them. When introduced in 1958 to deal with the Naga rebellion, it was not a newly designed law to meet "the exigencies of the situation" (to borrow the phrase used in the ICCPR). Instead, national security bureaucrats of the new republic—yet to be socialized into the imperatives of decolonization and political democracy—simply recycled a colonial-era ordinance—ironically, one that was used to quell the Quit India Movement of 1942 that Viceroy Lord Linlithgow described as "by far the most serious rebellion since that of 1857."[55]

The postcolonial Indian state has what political theorist Sudipta Kaviraj calls a "double, and in some ways, contradictory inheritance." It is a "successor to both the British colonial state and the movement of Indian nationalism."[56] As a coercive law with roots in the colonial era, AFSPA is not unique. India's "legal institutions and coercive apparatuses of the state remained similar to the last stage of colonial rule, to the disappointment of those who expected a radical overhaul of the state." But at the same time, "the ideological discourse of nationalism" created "vast popular expectations" that the postcolonial state would act differently once it was taken over by anticolonial nationalists.[57] When laws like AFSPA were first adopted, the generation of Indian politicians who fought colonial rule, wrote the Constitution, and held key positions in the government of independent India were aware of this double inheritance. Indeed, they actively debated its meaning and implications. This becomes apparent, for instance, in the debate in Parliament in 1951 on the Constitution's First Amendment Bill. This amendment, adopted even before the Constitution had completed its first full year, expanded the government's powers to restrict press freedom on grounds of state security. Accused by the opposition of trying to hold on to colonial practices of press censorship, Prime Minister Nehru turned the argument on its head. To mistrust the intentions of the Parliament of independent India, he said, is to be suspicious of democracy itself. He accused his critics of lacking "faith in ourselves, in our Parliament or our Assemblies."[58] In another context, Nehru defended the security forces this way: "We have our armed forces. They have fired upon Indians under British rule. But now they are a national army and so we treat them as our brave young comrades. The police should also be a nationalist force."[59] Vallabhbhai Patel, another important leader of the nationalist generation, told a gathering of police officials: "You have served the previous regime under different conditions. The people then had a different attitude to you, but the reasons for that attitude have now vanished. Now the time has come when you can secure the affection and regard of the people."[60] If Nehru's critics accused the government of defending laws that were once instruments of colonial repression, Nehru defended them on precisely the same grounds. "They were merely instruments of such repression," as Arudra Burra paraphrases Nehru's argument; "it is not laws but governments that repress."[61]

But is the issue that simple? What about the continuities of rules and protocols from the colonial past to the postcolonial present and their effects on lawmaking and law enforcement? Built into the institutional practices of the postcolonial Indian state are traces of the logic of colonial sovereignty. "Colonial forms of sovereignty," as Thomas Blom Hansen and Finn Stepputat remind us, "were more reliant on spectacles and ceremony, and demonstrative and excessive violence, than the forms of sovereign power that had emerged in Europe after several centuries of centralizing efforts." In the colonies, "the emphasis was rarely on forging consent and the creation of a nation-people, and almost exclusively on securing subjection, order, and obedience through performance of paramount sovereign power and suppression of competing authorities."[62] If Britain as a colonial power was more "successful" in its counterinsurgency operations—as a revisionist view of the history of late British imperialism sees it—those operations were conducted under highly "favorable" circumstances. As an imperial power, Britain controlled the legal machinery of the colony, enabling it to proclaim emergency laws, which gave the security forces the powers they considered necessary. As a result, as one historian wryly puts it, the cardinal principle of counterinsurgency that "the government must function in accordance with law is much easier to follow when the government can adapt that law to meet the needs of an emergency."[63] India's AFSPA regime bears traces of this history. It has been said that when the United States engages in counterinsurgency operations in faraway lands, it is inevitably faced with the question: "how feasible is a counterinsurgency strategy without the support of colonial institutions and practices"?[64] The question lies at the heart of AFSPA or of matters related to so-called internal counterinsurgencies in general.[65]

The roots of AFSPA and of the doctrine of the army coming to the aid of civil power lie in the history of imperial policing. The army and the police in British colonial India were "complementary rather than alternative agencies of control."[66] Internal security took up as much as one-third of the resources and manpower of the army.[67] "In all countries," observed the Simon Commission in 1929, "the soldier when in barracks may be regarded as available in the last resort to deal with domestic disturbances with which the policeman cannot cope." But the Indian case was entirely different, said its report. "Troops are employed many times a year to prevent internal disorder and, if necessary, to quell it."[68] In a classic text of the era, *Imperial Policing* (published in 1934), Maj. Gen. Sir Charles Gwynne divided "the police duties of the army" into three categories: (1) small wars with definite military objectives but ultimately aimed at establishing civil control; (2) situations where "normal civil control" breaks down, and the army becomes "the main agent" for maintaining or restoring order, including martial law when military authority temporarily supersedes civil authority; and (3) situations where the police forces under the control of civil authorities are inadequate for the challenges at hand and the army is called in to help. The three types of interventions differ in terms of the kinds of authority exercised by the military: the army exercises full authority in the first type of intervention and different levels of shared authority with the civil officials in the latter two types of intervention. Situations where such interventions occur, however, are fluid: an incident "may pass from one category to the other."[69]

The doctrine of the use of the armed forces in aid of civil powers is by no means unique to India. Canada and the United Kingdom, among other countries, have some versions of it. But custom and common law put more limits on it than in India. Moreover, postcolonial India resorts to it far more often than the other two countries. Most interventions are during "communal riots." Because the state police forces are often seen as partisan, there is wide acceptance of the idea among both officials and citizens that the army and the security forces under the central government's control may have to step into such situations. The practice is so well established that a commission inquiring into the Bombay riots of 1992–93 warned against delaying decisions to call on the armed forces if a situation demands it. "The top officers and the State Administration," advised the Justice B. N. Srikrishna Commission, "should not treat the calling out of the army or any other force as . . . a blow to their pride. In a contingency where it is required, after honest and self-searching appraisement, the army authorities should at once be moved for operational duties for dispersal of unlawful assemblies."[70] To those acquainted with the Indian official arguments defending AFSPA, the relevant sections of the British Defence Doctrine would seem quite familiar. At the core of the "legal doctrine governing the domestic use of military personnel" in the UK is "the absolute primacy of civil authorities; when Armed Forces personnel are used on domestic tasks they are only employed in support of relevant and legally responsible civil authorities."[71] In the United States, the Posse Comitatus Act prohibits the use of the military in operations such as "arrest; seizures of evidence; search

of persons; search of a building; investigation of a crime; interviewing witnesses; pursuit of an escaped prisoner; search of an area for a suspect and
other like activities." But it does not preclude "the military from providing
logistical support, technical advice, facilities, training, and other forms of
assistance to civilian law enforcement agencies."[72]

Most interventions by the Indian Army in matters of internal security
are quick "in-and-out" operations."[73] But in terms of Indian policing practices, those operations and the ones enabled by AFSPA are subtypes of the
same kind of public-order policing. They both involve the army's aid to civil
powers. As a result, in their arguments in support of AFSPA, Indian officials
do not feel the need to provide any details of the nature of the security challenges presented by particular "insurgencies." That the powers available to the
army for controlling a riot are inadequate is seen as enough of an argument
in favor of AFSPA. Even the discussion in the Reddy Committee's report
took this form. The relevant sections of India's Criminal Procedure Code, the
report points out, are "meant to meet situations where an unlawful assembly
endangers the public security," which happens during a communal riot. But
in these situations, the authority of the state is not challenged. This, however,
is not the case with situations that the army faces in Northeast India. But as
I have argued in previous chapters, this is not an empirically tenable position in the case of most so-called insurgences in Northeast India. If they
present a challenge to the might of the Indian state, in the vast majority of
cases the challenge is more rhetorical than substantive. Developing a more
responsive political process and strengthening state capacity—especially the
criminal justice infrastructure—could be a plausible and more democratic
way of addressing the underlying issues. Yet from the Reddy Committee's
perspective, the very fact that the two sets of circumstances are not alike
makes the case for AFSPA seem self-evident. The report spells out the difference between the two types of situations:

> Such situations must be distinguished from those arising in the North Eastern
> States like Manipur, Nagaland or Assam where the militants not only chal-
> lenge the authority of the State but by their composition, strength, aims and
> objectives present a problem which is spread over a large geographical area and
> is long term in nature. In situations of the latter kind, the provisions of the

Criminal Procedure Code would not be adequate. A permanent legal provision would be required which permits the army and the other Central forces to operate over an extended area and time period—of course, consistent with the rights and interests of the citizens and the security of the State.[74]

Thus, even for the Reddy Committee, which proposed significant reforms of the AFSPA regime, the mere fact that an armed conflict is not the same as a riot—and that the powers meant for the purpose of controlling a riot are not designed to deal with armed conflicts—was enough to justify "a permanent legal provision" permitting "the army and the other Central forces to operate over an extended area and time period." But the argument is unlikely to convince anyone who does not buy into the Indian official common sense about public order policing—the essential role of the armed forces in this activity and the legal immunity they consider necessary to operate in such situations. For India's military, AFSPA provides the legal protection that soldiers absolutely need to do their job. They seem to believe that the army's internal mechanisms, code of honor, and track record are good enough safeguards against human rights violations, despite all the evidence to the contrary available in countless reports by local, national, and international human rights bodies.

The most controversial part of AFSPA, its de facto immunity provision—the requirement of the central government's previous sanction for legal proceedings against actions by security personnel—is not unique to AFSPA. Many Indian statutes have some version of it. Its roots lie in the common law doctrine of sovereign immunity and the idea that public officials are entitled to the presumption of good faith vis-à-vis acts performed in the course of their official duties. What is distinctive about India, however, is the pervasiveness of this immunity provision across a variety of laws. Indeed, even India's Code of Criminal Procedure says that no court can take cognizance of an offense allegedly committed by a public servant in the discharge of his or her official duties except with the previous sanction of the government.[75] Ironically, the immunity provision stands in the way not only of the prosecution of security officials for human rights abuses; it is also an obstacle to prosecuting public officials for corruption. Even though most administrative traditions give some form of immunity to public officials, the pervasiveness of the immunity provision in Indian law surely has its roots in colonial sovereignty. The contrast with the immunity currently available to public officials in the United States is instructive. Public officials in the US are entitled to "qualified immunity." The US Supreme Court has fashioned a "constitutional theory of a reasonable public servant" to draw the line between acts that qualify for immunity and those that do not. The standard is "whether the official has (or has not) violated clearly established rights that a reasonable person in his or her position would have known." Thus, the notion of "qualified immunity" along with the notion of a reasonable public servant provides a shield to public officials from "the threat of civil lawsuits for money damages or legal harassment; . . . the power of the shield disappears, however, when they stray from the constitutional command, for example, by misusing power under the badge of the authority."[76]

Given the pervasive nature of the immunity provision in Indian law, the call for removal of the immunity clause from AFSPA appears to be a tall order even to some critics of AFSPA. Indian military officers react to the idea with utter incomprehension. Thus, the Indian commentator Siddharth Varadarajan believes that "given the balance of political and institutional forces in India today," getting rid of the immunity clause from AFSPA is "utopian." He therefore proposes that the immunity clause in AFSPA be amended to read: "No prosecution . . . shall be instituted against any person in respect of anything done or purported to be done in exercise of the powers conferred by this Act where the Central government provides reasons in writing and the competent court upholds the legal validity of these reasons." With such a clause, he explains, "the government would still have the right to intervene on behalf of a soldier who has committed an illegal act. But this would require a Minister to take personal responsibility for a decision."[77] Even this modest proposal met with little sympathy in Indian official circles. There has been no serious move to amend AFSPA on these lines.

## THE FUTURE OF AFSPA: THE ROAD
## TO DEMOCRATIC CITIZENSHIP

When it comes to the AFSPA regime in Northeast India, there has been remarkable continuity of policy from Jawaharlal Nehru to Narendra Modi. The beginnings of AFSPA were in the Nehru era, which many see as the golden era of Indian democracy. By the time Irom Sharmila came to the conclusion that no government in New Delhi will repeal AFSPA, Narendra Modi was India's prime minister. Official accounts of the history of AFSPA-enabled counterinsurgency operations are typically framed within a narrative of the gradual maturation of the government's counterinsurgency capacity. The following account by a retired Indian military brigadier is illustrative: "From the earlier 'jungle bashing,' routine searches, which produced little results . . . , the abysmal ignorance of the tribal culture, looking at the Mongoloid [*sic*] faces with a sense of bewilderment to more focussed operations against insurgents, refinement of basic infantry tactics, which resulted in the opening of the Counter-Insurgency and Jungle Warfare School, realisation of the centrality of winning the hearts and minds of the people, and yet, ensuring ascendancy over the hostile population, for it is in [the] nature of things to align with the winning side—the army has travelled a long way in its fight against insurgents."[78]

For Brigadier Sinha, while "winning the hearts and minds of the people" may be important, what is ultimately decisive is "ensuring ascendancy over the hostile population." The reason why military "ascendancy" over civilians works, he says, is quite simple: "for it is in [the] nature of things to align with the winning side." It is impossible to distinguish this view from the faith of British colonial officials in what they called the "beneficial" or the "moral" effect of "frequent displays of armed might."[79] When the Human Rights Committee of the ICCPR had discussed AFSPA in 1991, Rosalyn Higgins, a member of the committee, made a simple observation. Noting that the Indian attorney general said to the committee that the AFSPA provisions on the use of firearms "were very rarely used," she asked, "if they are very rarely used, they can't be 'strictly required by the exigencies of the situation' and it would be better to get rid of them."[80] But this view assumes "a closed economy of transgression and punishment, disturbance and the restoration of order."[81] If the capacity for excessive violence was built into the very logic of colonial sovereignty, the knowledge and experience that grew out of those habits remain inscribed in the institutional practices of the postcolonial Indian state to this day. The AFSPA regime is only one reminder of that legacy.

One cannot break away from the institutions and practices of colonial rule without the political will and the imagination to find ways to reanchor the institutions of the democratic postcolonial state in a radically different set of assumptions. The state's monopoly of legitimate violence in a democracy is "an ambiguous fiction, or rather it is never as 'real' as when it remains a non-actualized potentiality." It can effectively maintain order "only to the extent that it makes itself both unnecessary and yet somehow present."[82]

The ability to imagine a more democratic future for India enabled Irom Sharmila to engage in her remarkable act of citizenship.[83] Unlike ordinary practices of citizenship, such as voting or paying taxes, such acts of citizenship have historically expanded the horizons of citizenship all over the world. I will expand on this theme in my conclusion.

# CONCLUSION

The history of the world can be best observed from the frontier.

—Pierre Vilar

## A TALE OF TWO NARRATIVES

A curious fact about democracy in India is that a region that officials routinely describe as being troubled by insurgencies has among the country's highest voter turnout rates. One study finds that of the forty-two general elections to state legislatures with more than 80 percent voter turnout, thirty-one were in Northeast India. Of the sixty-one elections in which turnout exceeded 70 percent, fifty-two were in a state of Northeast India.[1] In 2012 Manipur's robust voter turnout numbers found their way into an unlikely document: an affidavit filed in support of the government in a public interest litigation lawsuit that charged security forces of hundreds of extrajudicial killings.[2] The country's highest court is convinced that there is some truth to the allegations and is now engaged in "a deeper probe." But because the number of incidents is large—many of them decades old and the resources available to the Supreme Court relatively limited—the progress in the investigations has been slow.[3] The Court has also had to contend with some pushback from India's security establishment.[4] Manipur's high levels of electoral participation are cited in this affidavit as evidence of a state of normalcy. It tries to show that people carry on with their daily lives despite "an insurgency problem." Counterinsurgency does not affect the "common man," and democratic institutions function better than normally.[5] It is hard to think of a more compelling example of representative democracy's "postcolonial neo-life," as John and Jean Comaroff once put it. It has been reduced to "a very 'thin' distillation of the concept: a minimalist, procedural version that . . . equates freedom with the occasional exercise of choice among competing, often indistinguishable alternatives."[6] The attorney general of an established postcolonial democracy cites evidence of high voter turnout as part of his legal defense of a government accused of hundreds of extrajudicial killings allegedly committed by its security forces. And this is done without any apparent sense of irony or contradiction—as if it could absolve the government from responsibility.

The legal affidavit spelling out the government's position can be read as official sociology of Northeast India's armed conflicts. It portrays the 2.3 million citizens of Manipur as being held in ransom by five thousand militants. There is no explanation of how the estimated number of militants was arrived at. The "root cause of militancy," says the affidavit, is "extortion" by armed groups whose leaders live luxuriously in "foreign countries."[7] The resources needed to support the lifestyles of leaders, it implies, are the very raison d'être of rebel groups that embrace the discourse of armed resistance. The rationale for AFSPA is the "legal and logistic protection" of Indian security forces: to enable them to operate in a "hostile environment" with "the required thrust and drive."[8] But if armed groups are no more than small cultlike formations—and the average citizen their victims—why would security forces find the environment for fighting them "hostile"? Shouldn't ordinary civilians welcome the forces of legitimate violence with garlands and open arms? It is sobering to contrast this official view with Manipuri civil disobedience campaigner Irom Sharmila's very different perception of the same law. She views AFSPA as tantamount to a declaration of war on normal life. This visceral conviction inspired her remarkable sixteen-year-long struggle of Gandhian-style "communicative suffering."[9]

It should be evident to the reader at this point that the assumption of a hard line separating institutional politics from politics through other means does not correspond to the realities of political life in Northeast India.[10] It is instructive to compare the legal affidavit's narrative with that of an essay by the distinguished Manipuri intellectual and theater director Lokendra Arambam, which asks the same question about "the root cause" of the "Manipur insurgencies"—to use his phraseology. Arambam seeks an answer in a very different realm: the "recovery of identity and dignity." Key events in Manipuri history such as the Anglo-Manipur War of 1891— the scars left by the trauma of defeat—and the dubious circumstances of the Princely State's merger with India in 1949 feature prominently in his account. Following the conquest of the ancient kingdom of Manipur in 1891, writes Arambam, British colonial forces occupied "the sacred capital of Kangla" and destroyed "all symbols of native authority and pride of the vanquished nation." Even after British colonial rule ended in 1947, the Kangla Palace—a hallowed symbol of Manipuri glory and pride—remained under the occupation of Indian security forces for nearly five decades. It was turned over to the Manipur government only in 2004, at a time when a wave of anger against the security forces had spilled into the streets in an unprecedented manner. Arambam recounts key episodes in the history of Manipur's "internal awakening" and resistance. The stories of struggle, pain, and sacrifice—told and retold in the oral traditions of ballads and folklore and inscribed in popular memory—he believes, are what explain the appeal of the idea of armed resistance to young Manipuris. But since academics writing about armed conflicts tend to take "the international state system" and the Indian state as givens of political life, they fail to understand the historical grievances that fuel Manipur's unrest. These intellectual habits and mind-sets, Arambam suggests, are serious obstacles to the understanding of Manipur's postcolonial predicament.[11]

The disconnect between this narrative and that of the Indian attorney general's affidavit—the different geographical imaginations, historical memories, and political sensibilities on which they draw—illustrates the analytical risks of denying or underplaying India's foundational diversity in any national unity discourse of a "casteless, raceless" India.[12] It is a powerful reminder that frontiers and borderlands are productive sites from which to think about the world of territorially circumscribed nation-states in which we live. This echoes the observation by French historian Pierre Vilar, whom I cite in this conclusion's epigraph.[13] "Whatever the mainstream culture of India is taken to be by those who are persuaded by the adequacy of this metaphor," says Mrinal Miri, a distinguished philosopher with roots in Northeast India, "there are cultures—many of our tribal cultures, for example,—which by even a very large stretch of imagination cannot be taken to be either sub streams or tributaries of this culture." Miri believes that "the metaphor of the mainstream is a powerful hindrance to the understanding of India."[14]

BEYOND STATE-CENTRIC THINKING

In October of 2018, reporters from the Indian national and regional media visited a small town in Assam where soldiers of the Indian Army's Eighteenth Punjab Regiment had killed five innocent civilians in 1994, falsely claiming them to be members of Ulfa, which was then a banned organization. The five men, now honored locally as the "Five Martyrs of Dangori Village," were picked up on suspicion of being involved in a politically motivated murder of the manager of a nearby tea estate. A court-martial in 2018 found the accused soldiers guilty of multiple murder. The verdict was widely reported in the media in Assam. The reports recounted the quarter-century-old macabre incident in terrifying and heart-wrenching details of the torture that the five men reportedly endured while in army custody before being shot at close range.[15] A leading Delhi-based online newspaper made a note of a plaque memorializing the victims at the place where their bodies were cremated. It read: "We, Prabin, Akhil, Pradip, Debojit and Bhaben, five innocent and unarmed young men, rest here as witnesses of the Indian state's heartless atrocities. . . . When you go back from here, tell everyone about the barbarianism of the Indian Army."[16]

As we saw in Chapter 5, there was nothing fated about Ulfa being officially treated as an "insurgency" or as an existential threat to the state—hardly an empirically tenable position. Under normal democratic conditions, such a profoundly impactful decision could not have been made without any public debate and with only the most superficial consideration of ground realities. Only the ready availability of AFSPA as a policy tool made this possible: a disturbed area proclamation by executive order is all it took. Let us now consider a counterfactual perspective that I briefly suggested in Chapter 5. Had Indian policies toward Ulfa been grounded not in a military metaphysics but in the criminal justice system instead, how would this have changed the trajectory of politics in Assam? The emergence of Ulfa triggered a serious debate in the Assamese public sphere on the limits and possibilities of Indian federalism.[17] Those lively discussions came to a screeching halt with the coming of the hard state, which promptly mobilized the state's coercive powers to suppress and silence those voices. Had criminal justice—and not military metaphysics—been the core of the Indian state's response to Ulfa, it is quite likely that those lively and productive debates would have continued. One can even imagine the debates shifting to open courtrooms and citizens accused of political crimes defending their positions in full view of the public. The exchanges could have produced positive learning effects for the Indian political system. Viewed from this perspective, the Ulfa chapter in Assam's postcolonial history would seem to be a tragic example of lost opportunity. Consider the popular writings of the late Parag Kumar Das, an influential Assamese newspaper editor and public intellectual known to be sympathetic to Ulfa.[18] The titles of some of his widely read books are self-explanatory: *Swadhinatar Prostab* (Proposal for independence), *Mok Swadhinata Lage* (I want freedom), *Swadhin Axomor Arthaniti* (Economy of independent Assam), and *Sanglat Fenla* (Call for independence).[19] Das's writings are powerful examples of the hopes expressed in the language of self-determination during a period when Assamese society was radically reassessing its present and its past. Unfortunately, because of the banal and uncritical use of the term *insurgency*—a black box that few analysts dare open—the politics of ideas that form part of such profound political-cultural moments in the life of a society do not receive the attention they deserve. This is also partly because scholars with a state-security orientation often lack the cultural competence and related skills to engage with the vernacular intellectual life in the societies of Northeast India.[20]

In his memoir, published in 2007, the Nigerian playwright and poet Wole Soyinka reflects on the ill-fated Biafran war for independence of the 1960s. "I was against secession," he wrote, "but only for practical considerations: I doubted Biafra's ability to survive the inevitable onslaught from the federal side. Not for one moment did I consider the secessionist movement itself an act of moral or political felony—it was simply politically and militarily unwise."[21] Something of the same sort can be said about the movements inspired by the idea of self-determination in Northeast India and their "unrealistic" goals. The "beautiful word 'reality' has been damned by the too many crimes committed in its name," observes the French philosopher Bruno Latour.[22] The point is powerfully brought home by the damage inflicted by the regrouping of villages during counterinsurgency operations in Mizoram and Nagaland in the 1950s and 1960s, the death squads of Assam in the 1990s—or some of the news stories from post-Ulfa Assam[23]—and the fake encounters of Manipur of recent years. Such violent abuses not only have their immediate costs: "our current payments in terms of everyday bitterness at the spoliation of society and human degradation"—to borrow the words that Václav Havel used in another context.[24] But even more consequential are the long-term damages: "the heavy tax we shall have to pay in the shape of [the] long-lasting spiritual and moral decline of society," as well as "the scarcely calculable surcharge which may be imposed on us when the moment next arrives for life and history to demand their due."[25] They highlight the tragic failure of political imagination in state-centric thinking and analysis.

## THIS IS WHAT DEMOCRACY LOOKS LIKE

As we have seen, leaders of Northeast India's armed groups actively engage in electoral politics.[26] Many of them maintain informal ties with mainstream politicians and bureaucrats; some mobilize electoral support for their favored candidates and manage to corner substantial amounts of government funds earmarked for "development." Generally, these armed groups have no reason to intervene in the peaceful conduct of elections. Their direct or indirect participation in elections may not explain why Northeast India has higher than average voting turnouts. But Jelle J. P. Wouters's ethnographic work throws some light on one major contributor in one Northeastern state, Nagaland: the phenomenon of proxy voting. The heads of households in Nagaland often cast ballots of all adult household members—using "proxy ballots." Wouters reports the following interesting exchange on an election day between armed guards posted at a polling station and voters waiting to cast their ballots: "'Why are you carrying so many voting slips?' the commandant snapped at a village elder. . . . 'One man, one vote. That's the rule!' The commandant scaled up his voice, seeing that nearly all voters had multiple slips in hand. His interference was met with loud disapproval. 'This is our village,' one villager known for his fortitude, stepped out of the queue and protested. 'Don't tell us how to play democracy!'"[27]

The locals in Nagaland see proxy voting as not only legitimate but as morally justifiable since it is "a man's duty to represent his family in the political sphere." They consider it an efficient way to exercise their franchise. Among the perceived benefits of proxy voting is that queues at polling stations are short. Proxy votes include those cast on behalf of family members who no longer live in the area—including young people studying or working in faraway cities. The practice is sure to account for a significant part of Nagaland's impressive voting turnout numbers. During the exchange at the polling station, the commander of the armed guards stuck to his position for a while, "drumming up electoral principles to his defense." But the atmosphere soon became tense, and he had to give in. The local way of "playing democracy" then took over, and "household voting was allowed to resume and bogus votes polled."[28]

At least in recent years, proxy voting has become a matter of concern to officials responsible for conducting elections in Nagaland. Thus, before the February 2018 elections, the state's chief electoral officer warned individuals and village councils against proxy voting. The warning, published in local newspapers, emphasized the importance of the "one man, one vote" principle, advising that "neither the head of the family nor the village council will be allowed to vote for others." People were warned that votes cast at polling stations where there was evidence of proxy voting would be nullified and the responsible officials disciplined.[29] The turnout in the 2018 election in Nagaland was significantly lower than in the previous election in 2013, and "strict vetting" appears to have played a role.[30] At the same time, there were reports of proxy voting at many polling stations.[31] But Wouters strikes an important cautionary note against the temptation to view proxy voting only through the lens of "the good little democrat's handbook"—simply as a flaw in the electoral process that undermines electoral legitimacy.[32] Turning an ethnographic eye to how democratic ideas and practices get "vernacularized and territorialized," he finds that in that part of Nagaland, "preexisting divisions and struggles over local standing and dominance etch themselves at the very center of democratic imagination."[33] Proxy voting plays a role in this process.

Following on the insight that democratic ideas and practices can be vernacularized in all manner of ways, let me now reflect on a single electoral outcome: the spectacular defeat in Manipur in 2017 of the iconic anti-AFSPA protester Irom Sharmila.[34] The episode may hold important lessons for our understanding of the question of legitimacy of democratic representative institutions in Northeast India. When ending her hunger strike in 2016, Sharmila announced that she would continue her struggle against AFSPA through other means, including contesting elections. She spoke of her goal to become the state's chief minister.[35] Her electoral debut a few months later attracted significant media attention. Sharmila started a new political party and took on Manipur's powerful chief minister in his home constituency. Five candidates contended for that seat. That the chief minister won by an overwhelming margin—more than ten thousand votes—did not surprise anyone. What was astonishing, however, was that Sharmila was not only not the runner-up; she received a meager ninety votes. Some in the Indian media described her defeat as "humiliating." Her struggle, said one mainland newspaper, "has probably reached a dead end. Where does she go from here? She fasted for 16 years, and then she lost an election badly. Both paths, of agitation and of electoral politics, seem to be closed to her now."[36]

But why did Manipuri voters choose to overwhelmingly reject a woman who personifies the state's popular opposition to AFSPA? It is clear that voters made a distinction between Sharmila the tireless anti-AFSPA campaigner—and a champion of civil disobedience—and Sharmila the aspirant for elected office. The basis of her appeal in that familiar first role was her visceral disapproval of AFSPA. Her censure grew out of her experience of seeing the law's actual enforcement in Manipur and its devastating effects on the lives of her people. Her fellow citizens could easily relate to her politics of situated knowledge and to her situated democratic imagination. This Sharmila spoke truth to power. But Sharmila, the candidate for elected office—with the AFSPA regime still intact in Manipur—was a wholly different matter. Voters' repudiation of her move to join electoral politics could not have been more severe. They interpreted her candidacy as a sign of her willingness to compromise with the political status quo. Manipuri historian Yengkhom Jilangamba argues that those who constitute Manipur's state government may be elected politicians, but people who elect them don't necessarily see them as their representatives. They see them as representing the political and financial power of New Delhi. The word *representative* in this context, he writes, should be understood to mean "agent, courier, or envoy, rather than someone representing the people." The meaning of democracy in Northeast India has for so long been reduced to the ritual of periodic elections that elected state governments are seen as doing the bidding only of the central government, not of the people who elect them. The benevolence of the powers that be in New Delhi is a key factor determining the political survival of elected state governments and even the careers of individual politicians. Not surprisingly, the people who elect them don't see the politicians in charge of the state government as having any meaningful authority.[37] The history of President's Rule in Manipur supports Jilangamba's claims. It is consistent with the argument I posed in Chapter 1 that a decisive voice for the country's national security establishment—embodied in the place-name given to the region—is built into Northeast India's governance structure. New Delhi can bend state-level democracy to its will in the name of national security. Sharmila may have thought that she would be able to bring about meaningful change by becoming the state's chief minister. But actually existing democracy in Northeast India has been so hollowed out that those who enthusiastically supported her struggle against AFSPA were highly skeptical: a few good individuals cannot change this hopelessly corrupt, compromised and well-guarded system.[38] Viewed from this perspective, Sharmila's electoral defeat can be read as a symptom of a crisis of legitimacy of India's representative institutions. There is, of course, more than one way to interpret Sharmila's electoral debacle. Yet it is safe to say that there is no evidence that the vast majority of voters in Manipur—or in Nagaland or anywhere else in Northeast India—"cast their ballots as a ritual act of patriotic fervor to the idea of India."[39]

## After Nation-Building and Development

In the middle of the last century, the political idea that all peoples have the right to self-determination had emerged as a high-order principle in the global arena. It was no longer just a political ideal; it became an international legal norm.[40] But its meaning was circumscribed by a number of contingent factors. The crisis of colonial empires and "a world newly ordered by American power" significantly influenced the unfolding of decolonization all across the globe.[41] The idea that all people have the right to self-determination seemed quite promising at the outset,[42] but it was expressly made applicable only to what the United Nations Charter came to describe as non-self-governing territories—defined and interpreted restrictively to mean "non-self-governing colonies."[43] As a result, self-determination became little more than the collective right of all the people that live in a particular colonial territory to "determine themselves into a modern western state form."[44] Not all territories that were "non-self-governing" by this narrow definition transitioned into independent statehood. Some, considered nonviable as potential independent states, for example, were given only the choice of merger with either of two neighboring larger colonial territories.[45] It thus became commonplace for leaders of postcolonial governments to be "both constrained and induced," as political theorist James Tully put it, "to modernise their ethnically diverse peoples and their hinterland" and "to define sharp boundaries of territory and unified nationhood where none existed."[46] Even democratic "multinational states"[47] that proclaimed "unity in diversity" as their foundational principle found it difficult to resist these imperatives of the time.

Cartographic anxiety is said to be the defining feature of the territorially circumscribed postcolony, and in the case of India—the child of Partition—it is "inscribed into its very genetic code."[48] Thus, until quite recently, all visitors entering India had to complete a Customs Declaration Form certifying that they were not importing into the country forbidden items, including "maps and literature where Indian external boundaries have been shown incorrectly." Another major Asian country—also an heir to a great civilization—took to publishing "national humiliation maps of 'lost territories'" or "aspirational maps" that normatively inscribe territories it does not actually control as a part of the nation.[49] It was perhaps inevitable that such banal nationalist identity practices would generate discontent in borderland regions and disputes with neighboring states. The imperative felt by national elites to make nations out of "social, cultural, geographical entities . . . with different pasts and presents" turned out to be their Achilles' heel.[50] Nation-building, quite predictably, became a conflict-prone exercise; it turned to demonizing enemies both within and without. This tendency became especially pronounced in situations where a majoritarian view began to assert "ownership" of a polity in the name of a "core" ethnoculturally defined "nation" and then tried to redefine the state as one that belonged exclusively to that "core" group.[51] This tactic turned minority populations, especially those with cross-border kin-groups, into false nationals.

It is significant that the idea of nation-building has gone through a fundamental change of meaning in the West since the time of decolonization. There was a time when the reference was to efforts to create a sense of national unity transcending regional, ethnic, linguistic, or religious loyalties. Active historical agency was then firmly lodged in the national elites of recently decolonized countries. This premise is a useful reminder of the time of decolonization as a "moment of possibility."[52] Nation-building then appeared as a blueprint for national futures, along with theories such as development and modernization.[53] These narratives, for all their shortcomings, were marked by "their refusal of racism, their conception of the possibility of a modernization open to all."[54] For Naga elites of Northeast India, nation-building came to mean something very specific: the project of building a new united Naga nation that could rise above tribal and factional loyalties.

The new iteration of nation-building that emerged in the West at the beginning of this century could not have been more different. It is a mandate claimed by the "coalitions of the willing" that the United States assembles from time to time to respond to imagined and real threats to its national security from developments occurring inside particular postcolonial states now judged to be "failed states." This new meaning of nation-building has disturbing affinity with imperial practices. Thus, the publication *Nation-Building and Counterinsurgency After Iraq* defines it as something that the United States military does abroad. When the US invaded Iraq in 2003, says James Dobbins, "no military in the world had more nation-building experience." He defines *nation-building* as "the use of armed force in the aftermath of a conflict to promote enduring peace and establish a representative government."[55]

Internally driven nation-building, as we know from the history of the world since decolonization, has faced some of the most formidable challenges in what were once the frontier regions of European colonial empires.[56] The layered and uneven nature of imperial sovereignty and power was particularly pronounced in these regions.[57] It is not surprising that the emergence of self-determination as a high-order principle inspired a multiplicity of movements of self-determination in many frontier regions of empire, including some seeking independence through armed resistance. They inevitably found themselves on a collision course with the metrics of the possible within the world system of states. Once the *uti possidetis* principle—the inviolability of the borders—was made applicable to the territories of postcolonial states and it became a binding norm of international law, the idea that "the full complement of states is already represented" became a foundational assumption of the post-imperial global order.[58] Yet despite the odds stacked against them, there has been no shortage of groups in the old frontier regions of empire that fashion themselves as "states-in-waiting,"[59] enjoying varying levels of local support and legitimacy. This is amply illustrated in the postcolonial history of Northeast India: in the examples from Assam, Manipur, and the Naga territories.

From the center of political power of the postcolonial state, Northeast India appears as a periphery located in a prior stage of developmental temporality, carrying the added burden of the national security vulnerabilities associated with a borderland. This worldview frames Indian policy: Northeast India "catching up" with the rest of the country and joining the "national mainstream" are key themes.[60] Since the region is the target of development and the central government does the developing,[61] keeping the region under New Delhi's tutelage appears to be the most normal thing to do. The region from this vantage point also needs protection from domestic and foreign enemies, since their actions put India's national security in peril. Northeast India's present, in this view of things, will always remain in transition; it will be left behind only when the region moves forward in developmental and nation-building time.[62] This governing philosophy must take most of the blame for the region's long-standing democracy deficits and the deeply flawed development trajectory that generates wealth for a few, barely subsistence-level employment for some, and impoverishment for many. Even the few success stories—those who lead a modern affluent lifestyle—are seen by locals not as "early examples of a soon-to-be generalized societal destination" but as beneficiaries of good fortune, official corruption, crime, or sheer ruthlessness.[63]

Yet the imaginaries of development inhabit not just the institutions of the Indian state; elected politicians, radical regionalists, and identity activists all seek "development." The aspiration to "close the development gap" or to "catch up" with "developed" places in India and elsewhere in the world has been a major theme in the postcolonial politics of the region. This has made it easy to co-opt political leaders of this intermittently rebellious region and their political platforms—though not without periodic waves of repression. The politics of recognition and the politics of managing spatial inequalities have coexisted more or less comfortably in Northeast India.[64] The region's peculiar governance structure has helped this state of affairs. Its small states have limited political weight, fiscal autonomy, and bargaining power at the national centers of power. Moreover, a number of these states, as I pointed out in Chapter 3, are de facto ethnic homelands, with the core ethnic groups having a near-exclusionary hold over the local state apparatus. The elites of dominant descent-based groups in these states have powerful incentives to ignore the emerging forms of exploitation, dispossession, subordination, and subcitizenship of ethnically "othered" groups. Development thinking may have lost its way in many parts of the world,[65] but in Northeast India, it has emerged as an ideology of convenience that suits both local and national elites.

Despite the developmental imaginary's iron grip across the ideological spectrum, when it comes to questions of free and equal dignity and rights, the mode of historicity associated with developmental time—"the syndrome of the 'not yet'"[66]—has few takers. Similar to development's deficient subjects that reject the idea of developmental time, people in Northeast India reject the notion of nation-building time used to justify limits on citizenship in the name of the national security: "truncated or low intensity citizenship" now,[67] full citizenship later. The insistence on democracy now manifests itself in multiple ways. This is consistent with what we know about democracy as a dominant belief in the contemporary world: as the default mode of political legitimacy.[68] Unfortunately, the study of democracy in mainstream political science has been seriously constrained by the national order of things. For a long time, it took the sovereign nation-state as unit of analysis—reflecting the "whole nation bias" of comparative political analysis that Stein Rokkan drew attention to decades ago.[69] Moreover, attention was limited to the procedural aspects of democracy—on democracy as a regime type in the minimalist procedural sense—rather than on the substance of actually existing democracies.[70] There is growing interest among political scientists in issues pertaining to the quality of democracy and in hybrid regimes that combine democratic and authoritarian traits.[71] The word *democracy* itself is now modified by an increasing number of adjectives. But if the democratic idea has commanded extraordinary moral force in the recent history of the world, it is not because of the appeal of democracy as a regime type but of democracy as a political ideal—"the best human weapon ever invented for humbling power."[72] Democracy in that sense cannot be a closed system; it is necessarily an unfinished project.[73] By definition this holds true of nondemocracies as well as democracies. The social struggle that democracy entails is an unfinished business in all democracies, whether "consolidated," "good," "transitional," "defective," or "failed."[74]

## Acts of Citizenship

In Chapter 6, I called Irom Sharmila's sustained protest against AFSPA an act of citizenship.[75] The concept makes a useful distinction between citizens whose conduct follows an existing script—the performance of traditional obligations of citizenship such as voting, obeying the law, and paying taxes—and the activist citizen who "engage[s] in writing scripts." Acts of citizenship challenge "already defined orders, practices and statuses."[76] There is a well-known paradox in the idea of the rights-bearing citizen: the idea is revolutionary and inclusionary, on the one hand, and conservative and exclusionary, on the other.[77] The traditional definition of citizenship as formal membership in a state misses its dynamic aspect: the evolution and transformation of citizenship over time. One can think of acts of citizenship as a force that fuels this dynamic. It is only to be expected that acts of citizenship would "often call the law into question and, sometimes, break it."[78] Could we, then, consider social movements in the region that have morphed into armed resistance acts of citizenship? Such a claim may seem paradoxical if one chooses to foreground their connection to political violence. But to assume that acts of citizenship must by definition exclude political violence would be inconsistent with the idea that the meaning of citizenship incorporates the "conflictive and disjunctive processes of change."[79] If acts of citizenship include "practices through which individuals engage in [the] making and re-making of the nation-state,"[80] sustained campaigns for greater autonomy—including armed resistance—are surely examples of such political practice.[81] As we have seen, the political constituents of Ulfa and of Naga rebel organizations and that of similar organizations in Manipur see them as standing for legitimate aspirations of self-determination. Regionally specific forms of the politics of the nation have grown and existed along with and in tension with pan-Indian forms ever since the beginnings of modern politics in the subcontinent.

To argue that the political interventions of rebel organizations deserve to be taken seriously and that acts of citizenship can be a useful analytic through which to approach them is not to endorse the normative claims for redemptive violence that some of these groups might make.[82] There is no clean moral line separating the violence of the oppressor from the violence of the oppressed. African social theorist Mahmood Mamdani had made an important observation regarding the influential Subaltern Studies project after his pathbreaking work on the Rwandan genocide. The greatest contribution of this group of scholars, he says, is "to rescue the subaltern from the status of being a victim in world history" and to shed light on it as an agent of history. But the fact that subaltern agency is "undergirded by specific institutions" did not receive the attention it deserved. If untransformed, "subaltern identity is likely to generate no more than an aspiration for trading places, for hegemonic aspirations."[83] As a result, yesterday's victims of violence can become perpetrators of violence today. Some of Mamdani's arguments are directly relevant to conditions in Northeast India. Political minorities have proliferated in this region not because of preexisting ethnocultural diversity but because of "a particular form of the state, the indirect rule state, whose genesis lies in the colonial period."[84]

In justifying their claims to rightful shares, ethnic activists of the region often reference precolonial kingdoms and territories. But the territorial *imaginaires* shaping their political projects are firmly grounded in the colonial ethnoterritorial frame discussed in previous chapters. The exclusionary group identities "sanctified, and legitimized by the [postcolonial] state and its institutions,"[85] cannot be the basis for rights and entitlements in the region forever. Northeast India urgently needs a politics of citizenship based not on memories of a real or imagined past but on a vision of a common future for the people who live in the region today.[86] Unfortunately, we are unlikely to see an expansion of the political imagination in the near future. India's prevailing governing philosophy is not conducive to fostering a climate of political innovation in the region. In the current scheme of things, it is hard to imagine the political space opening up for alternatives to the exclusionary politics of rightful shares to emerge in those parts of Northeast India where it has become the dominant form of claims-making.

There was a time not long ago when India was regarded as "an anomaly in a world of nation states" because of its diversity and plurality in languages, religions, cultures, and ethnicities. But many people now see non-nation-state rule as "exemplars for what is possible."[87] However, one thing that emerges clearly from Northeast India's troubled postcolonial history is that the era of nation-building has not been conducive to the growth and flourishing of non-nation-state political forms. There is little evidence that India may be heading toward becoming—as some people had once hoped—an exemplary "civilization state" that accommodates its foundational diversity rather than a conventional nation-state aspiring to the impossible goal of achieving internal homogeneity.[88] According to one reading of Indian history, the pattern of rule in the long durée has alternated between subcontinental empires and a network of regional kingdoms. The imperial form characterized by a strong center vis-à-vis subnational formations has won out for now, but it was not inevitable; and the equilibrium may still shift.[89] Whether it changes in the direction of more centralization or of regional autonomy will be important for future relations between India and its Northeast. But one essential condition for extending autonomy to Northeast India will be the advent of a more confident vision of India. The nation and its officialdom will have to find a way of seeing the Northeast as a true part of it and not as a latecomer to the nation and to development in perpetual need of protection, patronage, and tutelage. Until that happens, the peoples of Northeast India—like others excluded from "the circle of citizens"—will continue their struggles for the realization of a more robust form of democratic citizenship.[90]

# NOTES

## PREFACE

1. For a longer account of the history of my intellectual engagement with the region, see the preface of my *India Against Itself: Assam and the Politics of Nationality* (Philadelphia: University of Pennsylvania Press, 1999), xii–xxii.

2. E. J. Hobsbawm, *The Age of Empire: 1875–1914* (New York: Vintage, 1989), 3.

## INTRODUCTION

1. H. D. Harootunian, "Postcoloniality's Unconscious/Area Studies' Desire," *Postcolonial Studies* 2, no. 2 (July 1999): 128.

2. In this book I will use the phrase Northeast India or the Northeast. There is no standard way of writing the name of the region. The 1971 law that created the region as an official entity uses the form "North-Eastern Areas." The division of the Indian Ministry of Home Affairs dealing with the region is called the North East Division, and the central government ministry in charge of the region's development refers to it as the North Eastern Region.

3. See Peter Sahlins, "Response Paper," American Council of Learned Societies (ACLS) Project on "Official and Vernacular Identifications in the Making of the Modern World," 2003, http://archives.acls.org/programs/crn/network/meetings_nyc_sahlins.htm.

4. I paraphrase a statement by literary critic Magda al-Nowaihi made in another context. See Wail S. Hassan, *Immigrant Narratives: Orientalism and Cultural Translation in Arab American and Arab British Literature* (Oxford: Oxford University Press, 2011), 225.

5. Deepshikha Ghosh, "Even *Vaastu Shastra* Says Northeast Is Important, Says PM Modi," ndtv.com, March 3, 2018, www.ndtv.com/india-news/even-vastu-shastra-says-northeast-is-important-says-pm-modi-1819264 (emphasis mine).

6. I will treat Northeast India as a region in a "process geographical" sense, not in the sense of "trait geography," to use the distinction that Arjun Appadurai makes in "Grassroots Globalization and the Research Imagination," *Public Culture* 12, no. 1 (Winter 2000): 6–7. Northeast India is not a permanent geographical fact: an area with a "relatively immobile" set of traits in matters of material and cultural practices. It is an area determined by shifting forces "of action, interaction and motion." My focus is on some of those forces.

7. George Nathaniel Curzon [Lord Curzon of Kedleston], *Frontiers* (Romanes Lecture), 1907 (Oxford: Clarendon, 1907).

8. Thomas Blom Hansen and Finn Stepputat, introduction to *Sovereign Bodies: Citizens, Migrants, and States in the Postcolonial World*, ed. Thomas Blom Hansen and Finn Stepputat (Princeton, NJ: Princeton University Press, 2005), 3.

9. Sikkim's history is different. Unlike the rest of the region, it does not have a history of armed conflicts.

10. Christian Olsson, "'Legitimate Violence' in the Prose of Counterinsurgency: An Impossible Necessity?" *Alternatives: Global, Local, Political* 38, no. 2 (May 2013): 165.

11. Bethany Lacina, "Does Counterinsurgency Theory Apply in Northeast India?" *India Review* 6, no. 3 (2007): 165–83.

12. Lawrence E. Cline, "The Insurgency Environment in Northeast India," *Small Wars & Insurgencies* 17, no. 2 (June 2006): 128.

13. Quoted in Cline, "The Insurgency Environment," 128.

14. Lacina, "Does Counterinsurgency Theory Apply?" 165.

15. Sanjoy Hazarika, *Strangers No More: New Narratives from India's Northeast* (New Delhi: Aleph, 2018), 119.

16. See Sanjib Baruah, "Generals as Governors: The Parallel Political Systems of Northeast India," *Himal Southasian*, June 2001, 10–20; and Sanjib Baruah, "Nationalizing Space: Cosmetic Federalism and the Politics of Development in Northeast India," *Development and Change* 34, no. 5 (Nov. 2003): 915–39. These articles also appear as chapters 2 and 3 of my *Durable Disorder: Understanding the Politics of Northeast India* (New Delhi: Oxford University Press, 2005).

17. Two other laws with the same name were enacted later: one in 1983 to apply to Punjab and Chandigarh, the other for Jammu and Kashmir in 1990.

18. Government of India, "The Armed Forces (Special Powers) Act, 1958," www.satp.org /satporgtp/countries/india/document/actandordinances/armed_forces_special_power _act_1958.htm.

19. UN General Assembly, *Report of the Special Rapporteur on Extrajudicial, Summary or Arbitrary Executions, Addendum: Mission to India*, Human Rights Council, 23rd Sess., item 3, April 26, 2013, UN Doc. A/HRC/23/47/Add.1, 7, www.refworld.org/docid /51b98e624.html.

20. The annual report of India's Home Ministry for 2008–9, for example, lists the areas of the region that were declared "disturbed" under the rubric "Steps Taken by Government to Deal with the Situation in the North Eastern Region." The summary of the security situation that precedes that discussion merely states that "a number of States in the region have been witnessing various forms of insurgency, together with ethnic and communal violence/tensions in some cases." Among the "disturbed areas" listed, some are located in states that the same report describes as having had either "no violence" or "very limited violence." Government of India, *Annual Report 2008–09 of the Union Ministry of Home Affairs, Government of India* (New Delhi: Ministry of Home Affairs, 2009), 10–13, www.satp.org/satporgtp/countries/india/document/papers/annualreport _2008-09.htm.

21. Bibhu Prasad Routray, "China's New Game in India's Northeast," Mantraya.org, July 4, 2017, http://mantraya.org/analysis-chinas-new-game-in-indias-northeast.

22. Ajai Sahni, "Unexpected Calm," *South Asia Intelligence Review* 14, no. 43, April 25, 2016, http://old.satp.org/satporgtp/sair/Archives/sair14/14_43.htm.

23. South Asia Terrorism Portal, "India—Terrorist, Insurgent and Extremist Groups," 2017, www.satp.org/satporgtp/countries/india/terroristoutfits/index.html.

24. Khelen Thokchom, "Biren Mulls Rebel Policy," *The Telegraph*, Feb. 14, 2018.

25. Interview with T. R. Zeliang, Chief Minister of Nagaland, *The Telegraph*, June 15, 2015.

26. Shalaka Thakur and Rajesh Venugopal, "Parallel Governance and Political Order in Contested Territory: Evidence from the Indo-Naga Ceasefire," *Asian Security*, April 18, 2018, 1, https://doi.org/10.1080/14799855.2018.1455185.

27. Pankaj Sarma, "Assam Tops All States in Violent Crime," *The Telegraph*, July 22, 2018.

28. See Baruah, *Durable Disorder*.

29. See the discussion of this policy in Chapter 4.

30. See Ujjwal Kumar Singh, *The State, Democracy and Anti-terror Laws in India* (New Delhi: Sage, 2007), 16–18.

31. Thangkhanlal Ngaihte, "Painting a Wide Canvas with a Broad Brush," review of Sanjoy Hazarika, *Strangers No More: New Narratives from India's Northeast, Hindustan Times*, March 10, 2018.

32. Anil Kalhan et al., "Colonial Continuities: Human Rights, Terrorism, and Security Laws in India," *Columbia Journal of Asian Law* 2, no. 1 (2006): 105–6.

33. See Monirul Hussain, *Interrogating Development: State, Displacement and Popular Resistance in North East India* (New Delhi: Sage, 2008), 62.

34. Evidently, this occurred after the Public Accounts Committee (PAC) of the Indian Parliament in 2013 criticized the practice of installing golf courses on land appropriated for defense purposes. Golfing, it said, "could not be considered military activity." See "Civilians to Lose Playing Privileges on Army Golf Courses," *Indian Express*, July 26, 2015.

35. Ajai Kumar Singh, "Note by Dr. Ajai Kumar Singh, Member," in *Report of the Supreme Court Appointed Commission*, by N. Santosh Hegde, J. M. Lyngdoh, and Ajai Kumar Singh, vol. 1, pt. 6, 110, March 30, 2013, New Delhi.

36. Paul Staniland, "States, Insurgents, and Wartime Political Orders," *Perspectives on Politics* 10, no. 2 (2012): 245.

37. Robert H. Jackson, *Quasi-States: Sovereignty, International Relations and the Third World* (Cambridge: Cambridge University Press, 1990).

38. Staniland, "States, Insurgents, and Wartime," 246.

39. For example, the peace accords signed to resolve the Bodo conflict in Assam follows this logic. In February of 2003, the government of India, the state government of Assam, and the Bodo Liberation Tigers signed a Memorandum of Settlement that provided for creating the Bodoland Territorial Council. M. S. Prabhakara noted in an article published that year that given the "ethnic mix" of the area that came under the jurisdiction of the new body, a number of ethnic communities had reasons "to be apprehensive of the political and economic consequences of a formal acknowledgement of Bodo hegemony in areas

which they view, equally, as their home." Following this settlement, there have been multiple episodes of ethnic violence in the area that followed the lines anticipated in this article. M. S. Prabhakara, "Territories of Fear," *Frontline* 20, no. 24 (Nov. 22, 2003): www.frontline .in/static/html/fl2024/stories/20031205003103900.htm.

40. M. A. Athul, "Northeast: Criminal Nexus," *South Asia Intelligence Review* 17, no. 12 (Sept. 17, 2018): www.satp.org/south-asia-intelligence-review-Volume-17-No-12# assessment1.

41. Dolly Kikon, "The Predicament of Justice: Fifty Years of Armed Forces Special Powers Act in India," *Contemporary South Asia* 17, no. 3 (Sept. 2009): 276–78.

42. Justin Rowlatt, "Kaziranga: The Park That Shoots People to Protect Rhinos," BBC News, Feb. 10, 2017, www.bbc.com/news/world-south-asia-38909512.

43. Cited in North East Network, Guwahati, India, "Written Submission to Committee on Elimination of All Forms of Discrimination Against Women [CEDAW]: CEDAW General Discussion on 'Women in Conflict and Post-Conflict Situations,'" CEDAW, 37th Sess., Jan. 15–Feb. 2, 2007, www.ohchr.org/documents/HRBodies/CEDAW/Women conflictsituations/NorthEastNetwork.pdf.

44. Amitav Ghosh, "The Global Reservation: Notes Toward an Ethnography of International Peacekeeping," *Cultural Anthropology* 9, no. 3 (August 1994): 421.

45. UN General Assembly, *Report of the Special Rapporteur*, 7.

46. "Bruised Manipur Takes Centrestage," *The Telegraph*, Dec. 10, 2015.

47. Gerald L. Neuman, "Anomalous Zones," *Stanford Law Review* 48, no. 5 (May 1996): 1201.

48. Wajahat Habibullah, "Armed Forces Special Powers Act, Jammu & Kashmir," in *The Armed Forces Special Powers Act: The Debate*, ed. Vivek Chadha (New Delhi: Institute for Defence Studies and Analysis and Lancer's Books, 2013), 22.

49. Ananya Vajpeyi, "Resenting the Indian State: For a New Political Practice in the Northeast," in *Beyond Counterinsurgency: Breaking the Impasse in Northeast India*, ed. Sanjib Baruah (New Delhi: Oxford University Press, 2009), 36.

50. Guillermo O'Donnell, "Why the Rule of Law Matters," *Journal of Democracy* 15, no. 4 (Oct. 2004): 33–39.

51. I will discuss voter turnout in greater detail in my conclusion.

52. Jelle J. P. Wouters, "Polythetic Democracy: Tribal Elections, Bogus Votes, and Political Imagination in the Naga Uplands of Northeast India," *HAU: Journal of Ethnographic Theory* 5, no. 2 (Autumn 2015): 129.

53. Christian Lund, "Twilight Institutions: An Introduction," *Development and Change* 37, no. 4 (2006): 678.

54. Unlike many other parts of the world where the word *tribe* is considered problematic, its use in India is relatively uncontroversial. The reference is usually to communities recognized as "Scheduled Tribes" for purposes of protective discrimination or affirmative action programs. This is much like the practice in the United States, where access to services and resources meant for Native Americans require official recognition as members of an American Indian nation. In Northeast India, communities recognized as Scheduled Tribes proudly describe themselves as "tribal." In fact, they prefer

the terms *tribe* and *tribal* to the equivalent Indian term *adivasi*, which is popular in many other parts of India and, increasingly, among academics as well. In Northeast India, the only community that calls itself "adivasi," ironically, is one that is not officially recognized as a Scheduled Tribe. They are the descendants of tea workers brought as indentured laborers to Assam in the nineteenth and early twentieth centuries. Many of them trace their roots to Munda, Oraon, Santhal, and other people of the Jharkhand. Since their ethnic kin in their places of origin are recognized as Scheduled Tribes, activists from the community seek "tribal status" in Assam. I will use the term *tribe* freely in the rest of the book.

55. Duncan McDuie-Ra, *Civil Society, Democratization and the Search for Human Security* (New York: Nova Science, 2009), 37–38.

56. Joy L. K. Pachuau and Willem van Schendel, *The Camera as Witness: A Social History of Mizoram, Northeast India* (Delhi: Cambridge University Press, 2015), 272–73.

57. Mrinal Miri, "North-East: A Point of View," *Dialogue* 3, no. 2 (Oct.–Dec. 2001).

58. Dalel Benbabaali, "Questioning the Role of the Indian Administrative Service in National Integration," *South Asia Multidisciplinary Academic Journal* 5 (Sept. 2008): http://samaj.revues.org/633.

59. Sanjay Barbora, "Introduction: Remembrance, Recounting and Resistance," in *Garrisoned Minds: Women and Armed Conflict in South Asia*, ed. Laxmi Murthy and Mitu Varma (New Delhi: Speaking Tiger, 2016), 224.

60. The phrase "mainland India" has remarkable currency in Northeast India. There is, of course, no body of water separating the region from the "mainland." The practice appears to acknowledge a psychological gap between the region and the nation.

61. Barbora, "Introduction," 224–25.

62. Barbora, 225.

63. Anil Yadav, *Is That Even a Country, Sir! Journeys in Northeast India by Train, Bus and Tractor*, transl. from the Hindi by Anurag Basnet (New Delhi: Speaking Tiger, 2017), 8–9.

64. Yadav, 10.

65. Aditya Nigam, "Empire, Nation and Minority Cultures: The Postnational Moment." *Economic and Political Weekly* 44, no. 10 (March 7, 2009): 61.

66. A. Z. Phizo, "Phizo's Plebiscite Speech," delivered in Kohima, Nagaland, May 16, 1951, www.neuenhofer.de/guenter/nagaland/phizo.html.

67. B. G. Karlsson, *Contested Belonging: An Indigenous People's Struggle for Forest and Identity in Sub-Himalayan Bengal* (Richmond, UK: Curzon, 2000), 177–79.

68. See Diane L. Eck, *India: A Sacred Geography* (New York: Harmony, 2012), 4–5.

69. See Peter van der Veer, "Hindu Nationalism and the Discourse of Modernity: The Vishva Hindu Parishad," in Accounting for Fundamentalisms: The Dynamic Character of Movements, ed. Martin E. Marty and R. Scott Appleby (Chicago: University of Chicago Press, 1994), 656–60.

70. James C. Scott, *The Art of Not Being Governed: An Anarchist History of Upland Southeast Asia* (New Haven, CT: Yale University Press, 2009), 319. The regional focus of Scott's book "upland Southeast Asia" includes Northeast India.

71. Samudra Gupta Kashyap, "Behind the BJP's Spectacular Success in Northeast, Years of Silent Work by Sangh," *Indian Express*, March 27, 2017.

72. Robert F. Worth, "The Billionaire Yogi Behind Modi's Rise," *New York Times Magazine*, July 26, 2018, www.nytimes.com/2018/07/26/magazine/the-billionaire-yogi-behind-modis-rise.html.

73. Cf. Ravi Khangai, "The 'Other' Women in the Mahabharata," www.academia.edu/2614172/the_other_women_in_the_mahabharata.

74. Bhagwat spoke to a group of Assamese academics and newspaper editors. He said that "Rukmini was from Arunachal, Babhruvahana [son of Arjuna through Manipuri princess Chitrangada] was from Manipur, Bhim's wife Hidimba was from Nagaland" (quoted in Prasanta Rajguru, "Sanskrit Manoxicotar Xondhanot" [Toward understanding the orientation to Sanskrit], *Amar Axom*, March 5, 2017). I learned from an email correspondence with Prasanta Rajguru, editor of the Assamese daily *Amar Axom*, who attended the meeting, that Bhagwat spoke in Hindi, though the questions were in English. I have not translated the word *Dharma* since the word has multiple meanings.

75. Jacob Copeman and Aya Ikegame, "The Multifarious Guru: An Introduction," in *The Guru in South Asia: New Interdisciplinary Perspectives*, ed. Jacob Copeman and Aya Ikegame (New York: Routledge, 2012), 10–11.

76. Government of India, *Report of the Committee Under the Chairmanship of Shri M.P. Bezbaruah to Look into the Concerns of the People of the Northeast Living in Other Parts of the Country* (New Delhi: Ministry of Home Affairs, 2014), https://archive.nyu.edu/handle/2451/37861.

77. For an earlier formulation of this argument, see Sanjib Baruah, "A New Politics of Race: India and Its Northeast," *India International Centre Quarterly* 32, nos. 2 & 3 (Monsoon-Winter 2005): 165–76; repr. in *The Other Side of Terror: An Anthology of Writings on Terrorism in South Asia*, edited by Nivedita Majumdar, 223–35 (New Delhi: Oxford University Press, 2012); and Sanjib Baruah, "The *Mongolian Fringe*," *Himal Southasian* 26, no. 1 (Jan. 14, 2013): 82–86.

78. Jelle J. P. Wouters and Tanka B. Subba, "The 'Indian Face,' India's Northeast, and 'The Idea of India,'" *Asian Anthropology* 12, no. 2 (2013): 127.

79. According to the racial taxonomy that Blumenbach proposed in 1795, there are five biologically based races. He named them by associating physical traits with geographical location. These ideas of race have long been discredited and debunked.

80. Olaf Kirkpatrick Caroe, "India and the Mongolian Fringe"; repr. in *The North-Eastern Frontier: A Documentary Study of the Internecine Rivalry Between India, Tibet and China*, vol. 2, *1914–54*, ed. Parshotam Mehra (Delhi: Oxford University Press, 1980), 111–24.

81. The outer ring included Tibet, which was then expected to remain a buffer.

82. Caroe used the phrase "Assam tribal areas." Caroe, "India and the Mongolian Fringe," 112–17. Alastair Lamb, however, in his discussion of the Caroe text, uses the phrase "northern Assam." Alastair Lamb, *Tibet, China & India, 1914–1950: A History of Imperial Diplomacy* (Hertingfordbury, UK: Roxford, 1989), 289.

83. Lamb, *Tibet, China & India*, 458.

84. Bérénice Guyot-Réchard, *Shadow States: India, China and the Himalayas, 1910–1962* (Cambridge: Cambridge University Press, 2017), 19–20.

85. Caroe, "India and the Mongolian Fringe," 118.

86. Caroe, 117–18.

87. Robert Neil Reid, "A Note on the Future of the Present Excluded, Partially Excluded and Tribal Areas of Assam," in *On the Edge of Empire: Four British Plans for North East India, 1941–1947,* ed. David R. Syiemlieh (New Delhi: Sage, 2014), 80.

88. Vallabhbhai Patel, "Sardar Patel's Letter to Jawaharlal Nehru, 7 November 1950," repr. as Appendix 2 in Durga Das, *India from Curzon to Nehru and After* (New York: John Day, 1970), 460.

89. For a discussion of how race defines the experience of Northeastern migrants in Delhi, and their encounter with the racial slur "Chinki," see Duncan McDuie-Ra, *Northeast Migrants in Delhi: Race, Refuge and Retail* (Amsterdam: Amsterdam University Press, 2012), 87–117.

90. Wouters and Subba, "The 'Indian Face,'" 127.

91. McDuie-Ra, *Northeast Migrants in Delhi,* 44.

92. Bengt G. Karlsson and Dolly Kikon, "Wayfinding: Indigenous Migrants in the Service Sector of Metropolitan India," *South Asia* 40, no. 3 (2017): 448.

93. McDuie-Ra, *Northeast Migrants in Delhi,* 74–76, 184.

94. Karlsson and Kikon, "Wayfinding," 454–55.

95. Bhanu Joshi, Ashish Ranjan, and Neelanjan Sircar, "Understanding the Election in Assam (Part 1)," Working Papers, Centre for Policy Research, New Delhi, April 19, 2016, 2.

96. This estimate is by the Centre for North Eastern Studies and Policy Research, Jamia Millia Islamia, Delhi. Cited in Government of India, *Report of the Committee Under the Chairmanship of M. P. Bezbaruah,* 6.

97. Sumir Karmakar, "NE Girls to Tackle Delhi Road Romeos," *The Telegraph,* Nov. 21, 2016; and "North-Eastern People in Delhi Get Electoral Card," *Business Standard,* Feb. 7, 2017.

98. Government of India, *Report of the Committee Under the Chairmanship of M. P. Bezbaruah,* 2, 6.

99. Duncan McDuie-Ra, "The 'North-East' Map of Delhi," *Economic and Political Weekly* 47, no. 30 (July 28, 2012): 70–71. The phrase "live abroad in India" is from a study of consumerism in Delhi by Christiane Brosius. She takes the phrase from the advertising slogan "Get Ready to Live abroad in India" used by an Indian real estate developer. See Christiane Brosius, *India's Middle Class: New Forms of Urban Leisure, Consumption and Prosperity* (New Delhi: Routledge India, 2010), 69.

100. I borrow this phrase from Michel S. Laguerre. In his study of the minority question in the United States, Laguerre uses the expression to draw attention to the fact that minority status is not a matter of numbers but a function of social power. Dominant discursive practices legitimize and naturalize a hierarchical order, which places certain groups "in an inferior position . . . and undermines the equality factor that citizenship implies."

Michel S. Laguerre, *Minoritized Space: An Inquiry into the Spatial Order of Things* (Berkeley, CA: Institute of Governmental Studies Press, 1999), 3, 120.

101.  McDuie-Ra, *Northeast Migrants in Delhi*, 30.

102.  I borrow this expression from Joseph Pugliese, "Asymmetries of Terror: Visual Regimes of Racial Profiling and the Shooting of Jean Charles de Menezes in the Context of the War in Iraq," *Borderlands* 5, no. 1 (2006): www.borderlands.net.au/vol5no1_2006/pugliese .htm.

103.  Sunita Akoijam, "Feeling Nepali: A Manipuri in Kathmandu," *Himal Southasian* 24, no. 8 (August 2011): 57.

104.  Lakshmi Chaudhry, "Mystery of the NE Exodus: Why Bangalore?" *Firstpost* (Mumbai), August 16, 2012, www.firstpost.com/india/mystery-of-the-ne-exodus-why-bangalore -419876.html.

105.  Faraz Ahmed, "Social Media Is Lying to You About Burma's Muslim 'Cleansing,'" Pak-Alert Press, July 19, 2012, https://blogs.tribune.com.pk/story/12867/social-media-is-lying -to-you-about-burmas-muslim-cleansing.

106.  Chaudhry, "Mystery of the NE Exodus."

107.  Lawrence Liang, "Strangers in a Place They Call Home," *The Hindu*, August 18, 2012.

108.  Hazarika, *Strangers No More*, 279.

109.  Government of India, *Report of the Committee Under the Chairmanship of M. P. Bezbaruah*, 13–14.

110.  Rudraneil Sengupta, "When Racism Is 'Normal Fun,'" *Livemint* (New Delhi), Feb. 15, 2014. www.livemint.com/Leisure/joEOGauGv9nRm8kyJ3UlSJ/When-racism-is -normal-fun.html.

111.  "SC Directs Security & Inclusion of NE People," *The Telegraph*, Dec. 15, 2016.

112.  Hazarika, *Strangers No More*, 282.

113.  B. K. Nehru, *Nice Guys Finish Second: Memoirs* (Delhi: Penguin India, 2000), 477.

114.  The expression is borrowed from Pugliese, "Asymmetries of Terror."

CHAPTER 1

1.  The term *colony* in General Sinha's statement refers to residential neighborhoods like Delhi's Defence Colony. His figure on Nagaland's population is not quite accurate. What he may have had in mind is the population at the time when the state was created. Nagaland's population, according to the most recent census (2011), is 1.9 million.

2.  Anssi Paasi, "Region and Place: Regional Identity in Question," *Progress in Human Geography* 27, no. 4 (2003): 477, 480. Some parts of this chapter appeared earlier in Sanjib Baruah, "Territoriality, Indigeneity and Rights in the North-East India," *Economic and Political Weekly* 43, nos. 12 & 13 (March 22, 2008): 15–19; and Sanjib Baruah, "Politics of Territoriality: Indigeneity, Itinerancy and Rights in Northeast India," in *Territorial Changes and Territorial Restructurings in the Himalayas*, ed. Joëlle Smadja (Delhi: Adroit, 2013), 69–83.

3.  James Onley, "The Raj Reconsidered: British India's Informal Empire and Spheres of Influence in Asia and Africa," *Asian Affairs* 40, no. 1 (March 2009): 44–62.

4. B. P. Singh, *The Problem of Change: A Study of North-East India* (New Delhi: Oxford University Press, 1997), 8, 117.

5. For an earlier assessment of this process see my article "Nationalizing Space: Cosmetic Federalism and the Politics of Development in Northeast India," *Development and Change* 34, no. 5 (Nov. 2003): 915–39; repr. in my *Durable Disorder: Understanding the Politics of Northeast India* (New Delhi: Oxford University Press, 2005), 33–58.

6. Government of India, States Census 2011, https://www.census2011.co.in/states .php.

7. The settled districts also included the district of Sylhet, which is now a part of Pakistan/Bangladesh.

8. Government of India, Census, 1931, *Assam Part I: Report* (by C. S. Mullan) (Shillong: Assam Government Press, 1932; repr. Delhi: Manohar, 1992), 3.

9. See Chapter 6.

10. The Constitution does not use the term *federal*; India is officially a Union of States.

11. Robert Neil Reid, "The Excluded Areas of Assam," *Geographical Journal* 103, no. 1/2 (1944): 19.

12. Reid, 19–21.

13. Arjun Appadurai, *"Putting Hierarchy in Its Place," Cultural Anthropology 3, no. 1 (1988): 36–37.*

14. Paul Gilroy, *"There Ain't No Black in the Union Jack": The Cultural Politics of Race and Nation* (London: Hutchinson, 1987), 39.

15. James Johnstone, *My Experiences in Manipur and the Naga Hills* (London: S. Low, Marston, 1896), 17.

16. For discussion of this issue see Matthew Rich, "Hill and Plains in the Colonial Imaginary of India's Northeast: Khasi Citizens and Tribal Subjects" (master's thesis, University of Chicago, 2006). I owe this point to Rich.

17. David Ludden, "Investing in Nature Around Sylhet: An Excursion into Geographical History," *Economic and Political Weekly* 38, no. 48 (Nov. 29, 2003): 5084.

18. Reid, "Excluded Areas of Assam," 27–28.

19. Andrew G. Clow, "The Future Government of the Assam Tribal Peoples," in *On the Edge of Empire: Four British Plans for North East India, 1941–1947*, ed. David R. Syiemlieh (New Delhi: Sage, 2014), 188–89.

20. David Scott, "Norms of Self-Determination: Thinking Sovereignty Through," *Middle East Law and Governance* 4, nos. 2 & 3 (2012): 201.

21. In an earlier article I described this political arrangement as cosmetic federalism. See note 5 above.

22. Lauren Benton, *A Search for Sovereignty: Law and Geography in European Empires, 1400–1900* (Cambridge: Cambridge University Press, 2009), 2.

23. George Nathaniel Curzon, *Frontiers* (The Romanes Lecture) (Oxford: Clarendon, 1907), 41.

24. Bodhisattva Kar, "When Was the Postcolonial? A History of Policing Impossible Lines," in *Beyond Counterinsurgency: Breaking the Impasse in Northeast India*, ed. Sanjib Baruah (New Delhi: Oxford University Press, 2009), 55.

25. Bert Suykens, "State-Making and the Suspension of Law in India's Northeast: The Place of Exception in the Assam-Nagaland Border Dispute," in *Violence on the Margins: States, Conflict, and Borderlands*, ed. Benedikt Korf and Timothy Raeymaekers (New York: Palgrave Macmillan, 2013), 173.

26. Benton, *A Search for Sovereignty*, 8.

27. Robert Neil Reid, "A Note on the Future of the Present Excluded, Partially Excluded and Tribal Areas of Assam," in *On the Edge of Empire: Four British Plans for North East India, 1941–1947*, ed. David R. Syiemlieh (New Delhi: Sage, 2014), 42–43.

28. Bérénice Guyot-Réchard, *Shadow States: India, China and the Himalayas, 1910–1962* (Cambridge: Cambridge University Press, 2017), 4.

29. Mahmood Mamdani, "Making Sense of Political Violence in Postcolonial Africa," in *Fighting Identities: Race, Religion and Ethno-nationalism*, ed. Leo Panitch and Colin Leys (London: Merlin, 2003), 137.

30. Mamdani, 137.

31. Joy L. K. Pachuau and Willem van Schendel, *The Camera as Witness: A Social History of Mizoram, Northeast India* (Delhi: Cambridge University Press, 2015), 50–52.

32. Julian Jacobs, with Alan Macfarlane, Sarah Harrison, and Anita Herle, *The Nagas: Hill Peoples of Northeast India: Society, Culture, and the Colonial Encounter* (1990; London: Thames and Hudson, 2012), 153.

33. James Philip Mills, *The Ao Nagas* (1926; Bombay: Oxford University Press, 1973), 421.

34. See James Ferguson, "Of Mimicry and Membership: Africans and the 'New World Society,'" *Cultural Anthropology* 17, no. 4 (2002): 551–69.

35. This formulation is borrowed from anthropologist Godfrey Wilson (cited in Ferguson, "Of Mimicry and Membership," 555). Wilson had said this in the context of northern Rhodesia in a paper published in 1941.

36. Mahmood Mamdani, "What Is a Tribe?" *London Review of Books* 34, no. 17 (Sept. 13, 2012): 20–22.

37. For an example see my discussion of a controversy over the succession rules among the Khasis in Meghalaya in Baruah, *Durable Disorder*, 183–87.

38. This was the effect of creating the Bodoland Territorial Council in Assam in 2003 following a Memorandum of Settlement signed with the Bodo Liberation Tigers. The formation of this council involved an amendment of the Constitution's Sixth Schedule. It extended certain provisions of the Sixth Schedule for the first time to an area that was not an excluded area in colonial times. See also note 39 of my introduction.

39. Prabhu P. Mohapatra, "Assam and the West Indies, 1860–1920: Immobilizing Plantation Labor," in *Masters, Servants, and Magistrates in Britain and the Empire, 1562–1955*, ed. Douglas Hay and Paul Craven (Chapel Hill: University of North Carolina Press, 2004), 475.

40. Mohapatra, 479–80.

41. George M. Barker, *Tea Planter's Life in Assam* (Calcutta: Thacker, Spink, 1884), 87.

42. Amalendu Guha, *Planter Raj to Swaraj: Freedom Struggle and Electoral Politics in Assam* (New Delhi: People's Publishing House, 1977), 335.

43.  Z. A. Ahmad, *Excluded Areas Under the New Constitution*, Congress Political and Economic Studies, no. 4 (Allahabad, India: Political and Economic Department of the All-India Congress Committee, 1937), https://archive.org/stream/excludedar easo35320mbp/excludedareaso35320mbp_djvu.txt.

44.  Adnan Naseemullah and Paul Staniland, "Indirect Rule and Varieties of Governance," *Governance* 29, no. 1 (Jan. 2016): 16.

45.  I borrow the phrase *cordon sanitaire* from Onley, "The Raj Reconsidered," 44, though Onley uses it in a somewhat broader context.

46.  Olaf Kirkpatrick Caroe, "India and the Mongolian Fringe" (1940); repr. in *The North-Eastern Frontier: A Documentary Study of the Internecine Rivalry Between India, Tibet and China*, vol. 2, *1914–54*, ed. Parshotam Mehra (Delhi: Oxford University Press, 1980), 111.

47.  Michael Hutt, *Unbecoming Citizens: Culture, Nationhood, and the Flight of Refugees from Bhutan* (New Delhi: Oxford University Press, 2005), 22.

48.  I borrow this expression from Juan M. Amaya-Castro, "Illegality Regimes and the Ongoing Transformation of Contemporary Citizenship," *European Journal of Legal Studies* 4, no. 2 (2011): 137–61. Most countries have a certain number of people who are in the country illegally. But the means by which states enforce immigration laws "range between the very lax and the very strict." Amaya-Castro proposes the phrase "illegality regime" as a way to distinguish between the kinds of immigration laws that states adopt and the means of their enforcement to govern irregular migrants.

49.  This is not the case with Africa. See, e.g., Mahmood Mamdani, "The Social Basis of Constitutionalism in Africa," *Journal of Modern African Studies* 28, no. 3 (Sept. 1990): 359–74.

50.  Mona Chettri, "Choosing the Gorkha: At the Crossroads of Class and Ethnicity in the Darjeeling Hills," *Asian Ethnicity* 14, no. 3 (June 2013): 302.

51.  For an elaboration on this argument, see Arambam Noni, *1949: The Story of India's Takeover of Manipur* (Imphal, Manipur: Centre for Alternative Discourse, 2018), 39–44.

52.  John Parratt and Arambam Saroj Nalini Parratt, "Integration or Annexation? Manipur's Relations with India, 1947–1949," in *Self-Determination Movement in Manipur*, ed. Aheibam Koireng Singh, Shukhdeba Sharma Hanjabam, and Homen Thangjam (New Delhi: Concept, 2015), 56.

53.  Lokendra Arambam, "Narratives of Self-Determination Struggles in Manipur," in *Self-Determination Movement in Manipur*, ed. Aheibam Koireng Singh, Shukhdeba Sharma Hanjabam, and Homen Thangjam (New Delhi: Concept, 2015), 93–94.

54.  This argument was made by legal scholar Naorem Sanajaoba in his "Problem of 1949 Annexation of Manipur," trans. Aheibam Koireng Singh, *Imphal Times*, Oct. 19, 2017. The words *duress* and *coercion* used by Sanajaoba are from the Vienna Convention on the Law of Treaties, which invalidates treaties concluded under certain kinds of duress and coercion. For a brief discussion of the circumstances under which the Maharaja of Manipur signed the agreement fully merging the princely state of Manipur with India, see my *Durable Disorder*, 59–60.

55.  M. S. Prabhakara, "Burdens of the Past," *Frontline* 21, no. 18 (August 28, 2004): www.frontline.in/static/html/fl2118/stories/20040910006101200.htm.

56. Arambam, "Narratives of Self-Determination Struggles," 93–94.

57. This continuity with the colonial era arrangements is not unique to the Sixth Schedule. The Indian Constitution of 1950 "owed the majority of its provisions to Westminster: some 250 out of its 395 articles were taken word for word from the Government of India Act passed by the Baldwin cabinet in 1935." Perry Anderson, *The Indian Ideology*, 2nd enl. ed. (Gurgaon, Haryana: Three Essays Collective, 2015), 107.

58. Vallabhbhai Patel, "Sardar Patel's Letter to Jawaharlal Nehru, 7 November 1950"; repr. as Appendix 2 in Durga Das, *India from Curzon to Nehru and After* (New York: John Day, 1970), 460.

59. Cf. Steffen Jensen, "Battlefield and the Prize: The ANC's Bid to Reform the South African State," in *States of Imagination: Ethnographic Explorations of the Postcolonial State*, ed. Thomas Blom Hansen and Finn Stepputat (Durham, NC: Duke University Press, 2001), 107.

60. Nari Rustomji, *Imperilled Frontiers: India's North-Eastern Borderlands* (New Delhi: Oxford University Press, 1983), 31–32.

61. "Elephants, Exploration and Engineering," *Middle East Reservoir Review*, no. 1 (Jan. 1, 2000): www.slb.com//media/Files/resources/mearr/num1/exploration.pdf.

62. Quoted in Nani Gopal Mahanta, *Confronting the State: ULFA's Quest for Sovereignty* (Delhi: Sage India, 2013), 27.

63. Jawaharlal Nehru, "Note, Shillong, 19 October 1952," in *Documents on North-East India*, vol. 4, *Assam (1936–1957)*, ed. S. K. Sharma and Usha Sharma (New Delhi: Mittal, 2006), 288.

64. Pachuau and Schendel, *The Camera as Witness*, 142.

65. Nehru, "Note, Shillong, 19 October 1952," 288–89.

66. Tania Murray Li, *The Will to Improve: Governmentality, Development, and the Practice of Politics* (Durham, NC: Duke University Press, 2007), 14–15.

67. Bérénice Guyot-Réchard, "Nation-Building or State-Making? India's North-East Frontier and the Ambiguities of Nehruvian Developmentalism, 1950–1959," *Contemporary South Asia* 21, no. 1 (2013): 31–32.

68. The *Oxford English Dictionary* defines *pacification* as "a process or operation (usually a military operation) designed to secure the peaceful cooperation of a population or an area where one's enemies are thought to be active." To pacify is "to reduce to peaceful submission."

69. Rajeev Bhargava, "The Crisis of Border States in India," in *Multination States in Asia: Accommodation or Resistance*, ed. Jacques Bertrand and André Laliberté (Cambridge: Cambridge University Press, 2010), 77.

70. Bhargava, 77–78.

71. Singh, *The Problem of Change*, 117.

72. Sanjib Baruah, "Generals as Governors: The Parallel Political Systems of Northeast India," *Himal Southasian*, June 2001, 10–20. A revised version of this article appears as chapter 3 of Baruah, *Durable Disorder*, 59–80.

73. Guha, *Planter Raj to Swaraj*, 73. Guha's comment was directed at an editorial by Padmanath Gohain-Barua published in the newspaper *Asam Banti* on July 10, 1905.

74.  See James Ferguson, *Global Shadows: Africa in the Neoliberal World Order* (Durham, NC: Duke University Press, 2006), 178.

75.  Government of India, Ministry of Development of North Eastern Region, http://mdoner.gov.in.

76.  Government of India, "North East Division," Ministry of Home Affairs, http://mha.nic.in/northeast_new (site discontinued).

CHAPTER 2

1.  I borrow the title for this chapter from the lecture series "Partition: The Long Shadow," organized by Urvashi Butalia and published under that title by Zubaan Books, Delhi, in 2015. I am grateful to her for inviting me to speak in that series, which proved to be the beginning of a long and rewarding intellectual journey for this author.

2.  Gyanendra Pandey, *Remembering Partition: Violence, Nationalism, and History in India* (Cambridge: Cambridge University Press, 2001), 39–40.

3.  Cabeiri Debergh Robinson, "Too Much Nationality: Kashmiri Refugees, the South Asian Refugee Regime, and a Refugee State, 1947–1974," *Journal of Refugee Studies* 25, no. 3 (Sept. 2012): 351.

4.  Krishnaa Dutta, quoted in Anindita Dasgupta, "Denial and Resistance, Sylheti Partition 'Refugees' in Assam," *Contemporary South Asia* 10, no 3 (2001): 355.

5.  Anisuzzaman, quoted in Ananya Jahanara Kabir, "Utopias Eroded and Recalled: Intellectual Legacies of East Pakistan," *South Asia* 41, no. 4 (Nov. 2018): 1.

6.  Willem van Schendel, "Repatriates? Infiltrators? Trafficked Humans?" *South Asia Refugee Watch* 2, no. 2 (Dec. 2000): 30–63.

7.  Robinson, "Too Much Nationality," 351.

8.  See, e.g., O. P. Gupta, "Rights of Hindu Refugees in India," *Organiser*, Oct. 27, 2012. This is a publication of the RSS. Gupta argues that "India was created as a homeland for all Hindus of undivided India so Hindus from neighbouring countries have moral, social and political claim for right of residence in present day India, and in any case better claim over Bharat than any other refugee."

9.  Manas Ray, "Growing Up Refugee," *History Workshop Journal* 53, no. 1 (March 2002): 151.

10.  Tetsuya Nakatani, "Partition Refugees on Borders: Assimilation in West Bengal," in *Minorities and the State: Changing Social and Political Landscape of Bengal*, ed. Abhijit Dasgupta, Masahiko Togawa, and Abul Barkat (New Delhi: Sage India, 2011), 66.

11.  Anindita Dasgupta, "Remembering Sylhet: A Forgotten Story of India's 1947 Partition," *Economic and Political Weekly* 43, no. 31 (August 2, 2008), 18–22.

12.  Dasgupta, "Denial and Resistance," 345, 350–51.

13.  Siddhartha Deb, *The Point of Return* (New York: HarperCollins, 2004), 292, 295.

14.  Liisa Malkki, "National Geographic: The Rooting of Peoples and the Territorialization of National Identity Among Scholars and Refugees," *Cultural Anthropology* 7, no. 1 (Feb. 1992): 26. In the rest of the book I will use Malkki's phrase "the national order of things" without quotation marks.

15. Sunil Amrith, "Struggles for Citizenship Around the Bay of Bengal," in *The Postcolonial Moment in South and Southeast Asia*, ed. Gyan Prakash, Michael Laffan, and Nikhil Menon (London: Bloomsbury, 2018), 109.

16. Myron Weiner, *Sons of the Soil: Migration and Ethnic Conflict in India* (Princeton, NJ: Princeton University Press. 1978), 90.

17. Amalendu Guha, *Planter Raj to Swaraj: Freedom Struggle and Electoral Politics in Assam, 1826–1947* (New Delhi: People's Publishing House, 1977), 281–86.

18. Udayon Misra, *Burden of History: Assam and the Partition—Unresolved Issues* (New Delhi: Oxford University Press, 2017), 74.

19. Misra, 92.

20. Ayesha Jalal, "South Asia," in *Encyclopedia of Nationalism: Fundamental Themes*, vol. 1, ed. Alexander J. Motyl (San Diego, CA: Academic Press, 2001), 741.

21. See my discussion of the migrant communities of Assam in Sanjib Baruah, *India Against Itself: Assam and the Politics of Nationality* (Philadelphia: University of Pennsylvania Press, 1999), 52–64.

22. Moushumi Dutta Pathak, *You Do Not Belong Here: Partition Diaspora in the Brahmaputra Valley* (Chennai: Notion, 2017), 45.

23. Dasgupta, "Denial and Resistance," 346.

24. Dutta Pathak, *You Do Not Belong Here*, 45.

25. Mandy Sadan, "Contested Meanings of Postcolonialism and Independence in Burma," in *The Postcolonial Moment in South and Southeast Asia*, ed. Gyan Prakash, Michael Laffan, and Nikhil Menon (London: Bloomsbury, 2018), 51–52.

26. Government of India, Census, 1931, *Assam Part I: Report* (by C. S. Mullan) (Shillong: Assam Government Press, 1932; repr. Delhi: Manohar, 1992), 49–52.

27. David Ludden, "Spatial Inequity and National Territory: Remapping 1905 in Bengal and Assam," *Modern Asian Studies* 46, no. 3 (May 2012): 508–9.

28. Supreme Court of India, *Assam Sanmilita Mahasangha & Others v Union of India & Others*, Dec. 17, 2014, https://indiankanoon.org/doc/50798357. This ruling set off the process of updating the National Register of Citizens, currently under way in Assam.

29. Malini Sur, "Battles for the Golden Grain: Paddy Soldiers and the Making of the Northeast India–East Pakistan Border, 1930–1970," *Comparative Studies in Society and History* 58, no. 3 (July 2016): 812.

30. Monirul Hussain, *The Assam Movement: Class, Ideology and Identity* (Delhi: Manak, 1983), 207.

31. Shalim M. Hussain, "Changing the Narrative: 'I Beg to State I Am Not a Bangladeshi, I Am An Assamese Asomiya!'" *The Citizen* (Delhi), May 2, 2016.

32. M. S. Prabhakara, "Of State and Nationalism," *Frontline* (Chennai) 16, no. 21 (Oct. 9–22, 1999): https://frontline.thehindu.com/static/html/fl1621/16210680.htm.

33. I am grateful to Raihana Azmeera Sultana for sharing her work on Assamese Muslims with me. She has recently completed her doctoral thesis, "Region, Religion and Identities: A Study of Goriya Muslims of Assam," at the Jamia Millia Islamia in Delhi.

34. Yasmin Saikia, "Who Are the Muslims of Assam?" *Outlook* (New Delhi), April 22, 2016.

35.  Sumir Karmakar, "Deshi Muslims Seek OBC Tag," *The Telegraph*, Jan. 8, 2018. See also Richard M. Eaton, *The Rise of Islam and the Bengal Frontier, 1204–1760* (Berkeley: University of California Press, 1996).

36.  Cited in Sujit Chaudhuri, "'A God-Sent' Opportunity?" *Seminar*, no. 510 (Feb. 2002): www.india-seminar.com/2002/510/510%20sujit%20chaudhuri.htm.

37.  Paul R. Brass, "Elite Interests, Popular Passions, and Social Power in the Language Politics of India," in *Ethnonationalism in India: A Reader*, ed. Sanjib Baruah (Delhi: Oxford University Press, 2010), 81.

38.  Weiner, *Sons of the Soil*, 124.

39.  Weiner, 124.

40.  Baruah, *India Against Itself*, xvi–xvii.

41.  "Of Bangladesh-ization," editorial, *The Sentinel* (Guwahati), Dec. 28, 2009. The name of the state Assam is transliterated into English as "Asam" or "Axom" as well.

42.  "Nine Districts in Assam Muslim-Majority: Himanta," *The Sentinel*, March 1, 2017. There are now thirty-three districts in Assam. The number of districts was twenty-seven in 2011, when the last census took place.

43.  The phrase "minoritized space" is intended to emphasize this.

44.  Wasbir Hussain, "Assam: Demographic Jitters," *South Asia Intelligence Review* 3, no. 10 (Sept. 20, 2004): www.satp.org/satporgtp/sair/archives/3_10.htm. This article was published in 2004, and the comments relate to the 2001 census data.

45.  The phrase "identification revolution" is associated with French historian Gérard Noiriel. The quoted parts are from Claire Beaugrand's summary of Noiriel's definition in "Deconstructing Minorities/Majorities in Parliamentary Gulf States (Kuwait and Bahrain)," *British Journal of Middle Eastern Studies* 43, no. 2 (2016): 239n21.

46.  Kamal Sadiq, *Paper Citizens: How Illegal Immigrants Acquire Citizenship in Developing Countries* (New York: Oxford University Press, 2009), 37.

47.  Earlier versions of the discussion in this section appeared in Sanjib Baruah, "Partition and the Politics of Citizenship in Assam," in *Partition: The Long Shadow*, ed. Urvashi Butalia (Delhi: Zubaan, 2015), 75–98; Sanjib Baruah, "Partition's Long Shadow: The Ambiguities of Citizenship in Assam, India," *Citizenship Studies* 13, no. 6 (Dec. 2009): 593–606; and Sanjib Baruah, "Assam: Confronting a Failed Partition," *Seminar*, no. 591 (Nov. 2008): www.india-seminar.com/2008/591/591_sanjib_baruah.htm. Reproduced with the permission of the copyright holders and the publisher.

48.  Jaswant Singh, "Assam's Crisis of Citizenship: An Examination of Political Errors," *Asian Survey* 24, no. 10 (Oct. 1984): 1059.

49.  Pallavi Raghavan, "The Making of the India-Pakistan Dynamic: Nehru, Liaquat, and the No War Pact Correspondence of 1950," *Modern Asian Studies* 50, no. 5 (2016): 1666.

50.  Singh, "Assam's Crisis of Citizenship," 1059.

51.  I use the term *regional patriotism* following what Ayesha Jalal refers to as "regionally specific patriotisms" that predate undivided India's encounter with colonial rule. See Jalal, "South Asia," 739.

52.  An earlier version of this discussion appears in my *Postfrontier Blues: Toward a*

*New Policy Framework for Northeast India* (Washington, DC: East-West Center, 2007), 26–27. Reprinted with permission.

53. See Misra, *Burden of History*.

54. Bodhisattva Kar, "Can the Postcolonial Begin? Deprovincializing Assam," in *Handbook of Modernity in South Asia: Modern Makeovers*, ed. Saurabh Dube (New Delhi: Oxford University Press, 2011), 54n45.

55. Quoted in Sujit Chaudhuri, "'A God-Sent' Opportunity?"

56. See Ornit Shani, "Making Universal Franchise and Democratic Citizenship in the Postcolonial Moment," in *The Postcolonial Moment in South and Southeast Asia*, ed. Gyan Prakash, Michael Laffan, and Nikhil Menon (London: Bloomsbury, 2018), 167–74.

57. Nirode K. Barooah, *Gopinath Bardoloi, Indian Constitution, and Centre-Assam Relations, 1940–1950* (Guwahati: Publication Board Assam, 1990), 29–30.

58. Shani, "Making Universal Franchise," 172.

59. Quoted in Barooah, *Gopinath Bardoloi*, 33, 26.

60. Ian Talbot, "India and Pakistan," in *Routledge Handbook of South Asian Politics*, ed. Paul R. Brass (New York: Routledge, 2010), 36.

61. Quoted in Bidyut Chakrabarty, *The Partition of Bengal and Assam, 1932–1947* (London: RoutledgeCurzon, 2004), 176.

62. Dasgupta, "Denial and Resistance," 351.

63. Dutta Pathak, *You Do Not Belong Here*, 44.

64. Nabanipa Bhattacharjee, "'We Are with Culture but Without Geography': Locating Sylheti Identity in Contemporary India," *South Asian History and Culture* 3, no. 2 (April 2012): 218.

65. Bhattacharjee, 218–19.

66. Dasgupta, "Remembering Sylhet," 19.

67. Talbot, "India and Pakistan," 36.

68. I borrow this expression from Sadiq, *Paper Citizens*, 142.

69. Hiroshi Sato, "Normative Space of the Politics of Citizenship in Eastern India," in *Elusive Borders: Changing Sub-regional Relations in Eastern India*, ed. Kyoko Inoue, Etsuyo Arai, and Mayumi Murayama (Tokyo: Institute of Development Economics, 2005), 103–4.

70. Quoted in Ajit Kumar Sharma and Others to Prime Minister Indira Gandhi, "Indian Citizens Versus Foreign Nationals," memorandum (Guwahati: Asom Jagriti, 1980), 12.

71. Anupama Roy, *Mapping Citizenship in India* (New Delhi: Oxford University Press, 2010), 96.

72. Roy, 98.

73. Pratap Bhanu Mehta, "The Rise of Judicial Sovereignty," *Journal of Democracy* 18, no. 2 (April 2007): 74–75.

74. Quoted in "Bangladeshis in Assam Have Become Kingmakers: Court," *The Hindu*, June 29, 2008.

75. Kanchan Lakshman and Sanjay K. Jha Lakshman, "India-Bangladesh: Restoring Sovereignty on Neglected Borders," *Faultlines* 14 (July 2003): 124–25, 157.

76. Banajit Hussain, "The Bodoland Violence and the Politics of Explanation," *Seminar*, no. 640 (Dec. 2010): www.india-seminar.com/2012/640/640_banajit_hussain.htm.

77. Shyam Khosla, "Assam Riots Were Between Indian Citizens and Foreigners, Not Ethnic Clashes," *Organiser*, August 26, 2012.

78. Tarun Vijay, "Assam: The Agony of Being a Hindu," *Organiser*, August 19, 2012.

79. Mohan Bhagawat, "Don't Neglect Hindu Sentiments: It's the Foundation of India's Culture—Mohan Bhagawat," *Organiser*, Nov. 4, 2012.

80. Deepshikha Ghosh, "Mr Modi, Bangla-speaking Does Not Mean Bangladeshi: Mamata Banerjee," ndtv.com, April 28, 2014, www.ndtv.com/elections-news/mr-modi -bangla-speaking-does-not-mean-bangladeshi-mamata-banerjee-559255.

81. "BJP's Assam Vision Document Promises Crackdown on Infiltration," *Times of India*, March 25, 2016.

82. Samudra Gupta Kashyap, "BJP Will Rid Assam of Bangladeshis: Amit Shah," *Indian Express*, April 10, 2016, https://indianexpress.com/article/elections-2016/india /india-news-india/bjp-will-make-assam-completely-free-of-bangladeshis-amit-shah.

83. Kashyap.

84. This apprehension is not without some foundation. This bill is similar to a US law on refugees of the Cold War era. From 1952 to 1980, the very definition of a refugee in US law was shaped by the Cold War. A refugee was defined as a person fleeing "from a Communist-dominated country or area." See Michael S. Teitelbaum, "Immigration, Refugees, and Foreign Policy," *International Organization* 38, no. 3 (Summer 1984): 430. Cubans became the biggest beneficiaries of this policy because of the island nation's proximity to the US. Not unlike India's citizenship amendment bill, Cuban immigrants could no longer be regarded as illegal in the US after the Cuban Adjustment Act of 1966. They qualified for US residency within a year of residence in the US and were eligible for citizenship five years later, no matter how they entered the country. Since they were admitted to the US for humanitarian reasons—allegedly for fleeing communist oppression—Cubans quickly became a significant immigrant group in the US. The Cuban population in the US grew by sixfold within a decade after the Cuban Revolution of 1959. Had the proposed citizenship amendment bill become law in India, it could have stimulated a similar wave of emigration of Hindus from Bangladesh and to a lesser extent from Pakistan and Afghanistan as well. To be sure, the aborted amendment would have limited refugee status and a road to citizenship to those already in India. But the US experience of Cuban migration to the United States during the Cold War suggests that refugee policy can have an important signaling function in encouraging or discouraging migration flows.

85. Ran Hirschl, "The Judicialization of Mega-politics and the Rise of Political Courts," *Annual Review of Political Science* 11 (2008): 93.

86. Supreme Court of India, *Assam Sanmilita Mahasangha & Others v. Union of India & Others*, 51–59.

87. Mohsin Alam Bhat, "On the NRC, Even the Supreme Court Is Helpless," *The Wire*, Jan. 7, 2019, https://thewire.in/law/nrc-supreme-court-crisis.

88. Jacqueline Bhabha, "The Politics of Evidence: Roma Citizenship Deficits in Eu-

rope," in *Citizenship in Question: Evidentiary Birthright and Statelessness*, ed. Benjamin N. Lawrence and Jacqueline Stevens (Durham, NC: Duke University Press, 2017), 45–46.

89. Bhat, "On the NRC."

90. Malini Sur, "Spectacles of Militarization," *IIAS Newsletter* [International Institute for Asian Studies, Leiden, The Netherlands], no. 71 (Summer 2015): 28.

91. Cited in Sur, 28.

92. Suvojit Bagchi, "The Spectre of Eviction That Haunts Assam's Bengali Muslims," *The Hindu*, March 25, 2017.

93. Rob Nixon, "Unimagined Communities: Developmental Refugees, Megadams and Monumental Modernity," *New Formations*, no. 69 (Summer 2010): 62.

94. "BSF Proposes Wagah-Like Shows in Two Border Out Posts in Meghalaya," *Indian Express*, Feb. 24, 2017. In October of 2018, an official of the Border Security Force said, however, that despite the "enthusiasm" and "demand" for a "Wagah-type" event on the Indo-Bangladesh border in Meghalaya, organizing it would require more time, planning, and resources. Inspector General L. Mohanti of the BSF said, "What we are talking about is not a road-show. It's a massive parade. If 7,000 odd people turn up every day to see the parade, where is the infrastructure? We need gallery [*sic*] for so many people and also other basic amenities like restaurants and hotels for these people." See "Wagah-Type Parade at Dawki to Take Time," *Assam Tribune*, Oct. 29, 2018.

95. Gurharpal Singh, "Beyond Punjabi Romanticism," *Seminar*, no. 567 (Nov. 2006): www.india-seminar.com/2006/567/567_gurharpal_singh.htm.

96. "To become a normal sovereign state with normal citizens," write Thomas Blom Hansen and Finn Stepputat, "continues to be a powerful ideal, releasing considerable creative energy, and even more repressive force, precisely because its realization presupposed the disciplining and subordination of other forms of authority." Thomas Blom Hansen and Finn Stepputat, introduction to *Sovereign Bodies: Citizens, Migrants, and States in the Postcolonial World*, ed. Thomas Blom Hansen and Finn Stepputat (Princeton, NJ: Princeton University Press, 2005), 3.

97. Michiel Baud and Willem van Schendel. "Toward a Comparative History of Borderlands," *Journal of World History* 8, no. 2 (Fall 1997): 216–17.

98. Ernest Gellner, *Nations and Nationalism* (Ithaca, NY: Cornell University Press, 1983), 139–40.

99. Arjun Appadurai, *Fear of Small Numbers: An Essay on the Geography of Anger* (Durham, NC: Duke University Press, 2006), 7.

100. Cf. Wendy Brown, *Walled States, Waning Sovereignty* (New York: Zone, 2010), 109, 133.

101. Timothy Mitchell, "The Limits of the State: Beyond Statist Approaches and Their Critics," *American Political Science Review* 85, no. 1 (March 1991): 94.

102. Cf. Brown, *Walled States, Waning Sovereignty*, 21.

103. Barak Kalir, Malini Sur, and Willem van Schendel, "Introduction: Mobile Practices and Regimes of Permissiveness," in *Transnational Flows and Permissive Polities: Ethnographies of Human Mobilities in Asia*, ed. Barak Kalir and Malini Sur (Amsterdam: University of Amsterdam Press, 2012).

104. Appadurai, *Fear of Small Numbers*, 8.

CHAPTER 3

1. Michiel Baud and Willem van Schendel, "Toward a Comparative History of Borderlands," *Journal of World History* 8, no. 2 (1997): 214.

2. María Josefina Saldaña-Portillo, "From the Borderlands to the Transnational? Critiquing Empire in the Twenty-First Century," in *A Companion to Latina/o Studies*, ed. Juan Flores and Renato Rosaldo (Malden, MA: Blackwell, 2007), 505–6.

3. John Friedman, "Borders, Margins, and Frontiers: Myths and Metaphor," in *Frontiers in Regional Development*, ed. Yehuda Gradus and Harvey Lithwick (Lanham, MD: Rowman and Littlefield, 1996), 1–2.

4. Lynton Keith Caldwell and Kristin Shrader-Frechette, *Policy for Land: Law and Ethics* (Lanham, MD: Rowman and Littlefield, 1993), 6.

5. The phrase is from James Ferguson, *Give a Man a Fish: Reflections on the New Politics of Distribution* (Durham, NC: Duke University Press, 2015), 178.

6. Barry Hindess, "Divide and Rule: The International Character of Modern Citizenship," *European Journal of Social Theory* 1, no. 1 (1998): 63.

7. The formulation is historian Arupjyoti Saikia's; cited in Arunabh Saikia, "In Assam, a Massive Eviction Drive Throws New Light on Old Pressures on Land," Scroll.in, Dec. 1, 2017, https://scroll.in/article/859806/in-assam-a-massive-anti-encroachment-drive-throws-new-light-on-old-pressures-on-land.

8. See, e.g., Saikia.

9. Liisa Malkki, "Citizens of Humanity: Internationalism and the Imagined Community of Nations," *Diaspora* 3, no. 1 (Spring 1994): 57. Malkki borrows the phrase "false nationals" from Etienne Balibar.

10. See Rob Nixon, "Unimagined Communities: Developmental Refugees, Megadams and Monumental Modernity," *New Formations*, no. 69 (Summer 2010): 62.

11. Anna Lowenhaupt Tsing, *Friction: An Ethnography of Global Connection* (Princeton, NJ: Princeton University Press, 2004), 28–29.

12. Tania Murray Li, "Beyond 'The State' and Failed Schemes," *American Anthropologist* 107, no. 3 (2005): 391.

13. Bengt G. Karlsson, "Anthropology and the 'Indigenous Slot': Claims to and Debates About Indigenous Peoples' Status in India," *Critique of Anthropology* 23, no. 4 (Dec. 2003): 416–17.

14. Li, "Beyond 'The State,'" 392.

15. Willem van Schendel, "The Dangers of Belonging: Tribes, Indigenous Peoples and Homelands in South Asia," in *The Politics of Belonging in India: Becoming Adivasi*, ed. D. J. Rycroft and S. Dasgupta (London: Routledge, 2011), 38.

16. *Tania Murray Li, "Ethnic Cleansing*, Recursive Knowledge, and the Dilemmas of *Sedentarism*," *International Journal of Social Science* 54, no. 173 (Sept. 2002): 361.

17. Wolfgang Sachs, "Preface to the New Edition," in *The Development Dictionary: A Guide to Knowledge as Power*, ed. Wolfgang Sachs, 2nd ed. (London: Zed, 2010), xi.

18. See Benedict Kingsbury, "'Indigenous Peoples' in International Law: A Constructivist Approach to the Asian Controversy," *American Journal of International Law* 92, no. 3 (July 1998): 414–57.

19. Sachs, "Preface," x.

20. Aditya Nigam, "Empire, Nation and Minority Cultures: The Postnational Moment," *Economic and Political Weekly* 44, no. 10 (March 7, 2009): 58.

21. Ramachandra Guha, *How Much Should a Person Consume? Environmentalism in India and the United States* (Berkeley: University of California Press, 2006), 232.

22. Bengt G. Karlsson, *Unruly Hills: A Political Ecology of India's Northeast* (New York: Berghahn, 2011), 11–12.

23. Debojyoti Das, "Border Mining: State Politics, Migrant *Labour and Land Relations Along the India–Bangladesh Borderlands*," in *The Coal Nation: Histories, Ecologies and Politics of Coal in India*, ed. Kuntala Lahiri-Dutt (Burlington, VT: Ashgate, 2014), 91.

24. Duncan McDuie-Ra and Dolly Kikon, "Tribal Communities and Coal in Northeast India: The Politics of Imposing and Resisting Mining Bans," *Energy Policy* 99 (Dec. 2016): 261.

25. "Operations for Rescue of Trapped Miners in Meghalaya Not Abandoned, Centre Tells SC," *Business Standard*, Jan. 21, 2019, www.business-standard.com/article/news-ians /operations-for-rescue-of-trapped-miners-in-meghalaya-not-abandoned-centre-tells-sc -119012101103_1.html.

26. *Curse of Unregulated Coal Mining in Meghalaya: A Citizens' Report from Meghalaya*, 2 vols. (Shillong: N.p., Jan. 2019), 2:5. The report does not give the names of its authors, but according to a newspaper report, social activists Agnes Kharshing, Amita Sangma, Angela Rangad, and Michael N. Syiem were among those who released the report in the state capital of Shillong. See "Citizens' Report Urges Halt on Coal Mining in Meghalaya," *Times of India*, Jan. 15, 2019.

27. Meghalaya was a Partially Excluded Area (see Chapter 1) in colonial times, partly because Shillong—now the capital of Meghalaya—was the capital of the colonial frontier province of Assam. As I explained in Chapter 1, I use the term "excluded areas" (in lowercase) to include what in colonial times were the Excluded Areas, the Partially Excluded Areas, and the Tribal Areas of Assam.

28. This legal situation is changing. See "Ownership of Mineral Rights Vests with Landowners, Says Supreme Court," *Times of India*, July 16, 2013.

29. Seyla Benhabib, "Strange Multiplicities: The Politics of Identity and Difference in a Global Context," *Macalester International* 4, article 8 (Spring 1997): 37.

30. Quoted in Furquan Ameen Siddiqui, "Curse of the Black Gold: How Meghalaya Depends on Coal," *Hindustan Times*, March 2, 2015.

31. Arunabh Saikia, "Livelihood or Fear: What Really Drives Illegal Coal Mining in Meghalaya?" Scroll.in, Jan. 12, 2019, https://scroll.in/article/908515/livelihood-or-fear-what -really-drives-illegal-coal-mining-in-meghalaya.

32. Saikia.

33. Debojyoti Das, *Cultural Politics, Identity Crisis and Private Capitalism in Coal Mines of Meghalaya, Northeast India*, Case study no. 16, Artisanal and Small-Scale Mining in Asia-Pacific Case Study Series (Canberra: Australian National University [Crawford School of Public Policy], 2007), 12.

34. Tsing, *Friction*, 28–29, 33.

35. Anna Tsing, "Contingent Commodities: Mobilizing Labor in and Beyond Southeast Asian Forests," *in Taking Southeast Asia to Market: Commodities, Nature, and People in the Neoliberal Age*, ed. Joseph Nevins and Nancy Lee Peluso (Ithaca, NY: Cornell University Press, 2008), 27.

36. Tsing, *Friction*, 28–29, 33.

37. Tania Murray Li, "Indigeneity, Capitalism, and the Management of Dispossession," *Current Anthropology* 51, no. 3 (June 2010): 387–88.

38. Li, 387–88.

39. See Karlsson, *Unruly Hills*, 126–72.

40. Das, *Cultural Politics*, 13.

41. Siddiqui, "Curse of the Black Gold." NB: Mukul Sangma is no longer the state's chief minister.

42. Sanjoy Hazarika, *Strangers No More: New Narratives from India's Northeast* (New Delhi: Aleph, 2018), 243.

43. McDuie-Ra and Kikon, "Tribal Communities and Coal," 265.

44. McDuie-Ra and Kikon, 265.

45. Das, *Cultural Politics*, 13.

46. Das, 12.

47. Siddiqui, "Curse of the Black Gold."

48. "Two Kopili Power Units Shut Down: Mining in Jaintia Hills Affects Machines," *The Telegraph*, June 20, 2013.

49. McDuie-Ra and Kikon, "Tribal Communities and Coal," 265.

50. Das, "Border Mining," 85.

51. National Green Tribunal at Principal Bench, New Delhi, *All Dimasa Students Union Dima Hasao Dist. Committee v. State of Meghalaya & Others*, April 17, 2014.

52. Quoted in Siddiqui, "Curse of the Black Gold."

53. Arunabh Saikia, "'Phaltu sarkar': In Meghalaya, the Ban on Coal Mining Could Cost the Congress Heavily (Part 1)," Scroll.in, Feb. 13, 2018, https://blogs.lse.ac.uk/southasia/2018/02/17/phaltu-sarkar-in-meghalaya-the-ban-on-coal-mining-could-cost-the-congress-heavily-part-1.

54. Dolly Kikon, "Coal Fuels Dreams of Naga Prosperity," Asian Studies Association of Australia, *Asian Currents*, Sept. 9, 2016, http://asaa.asn.au/coal-fuels-dreams-of-naga-prosperity/#.

55. Barbara Harris-White, Deepak K. Mishra, and Vandana Upadhyay, "Institutional Diversity and Capitalist Transition: The Political Economy of Agrarian Change in Arunachal Pradesh, India," *Journal of Agrarian Change* 9, no. 4 (Oct. 2009): 537.

56. For a general background to the building of hydropower dams in Arunachal Pradesh, see Sanjib Baruah, "Whose River Is It Anyway? The Political Economy of Hydropower in the Eastern Himalayas," *Economic and Political Weekly* 47, no. 29 (July 21, 2012): 41–52.

57. McDuie-Ra and Kikon, "Tribal Communities and Coal," 261.

58. *Curse of Unregulated Coal Mining*, 2:4.

59. See Alan Thomas, "Development as Practice in a Liberal Capitalist World," *Journal of International Development* 12, no. 6 (August 2000): 773–87.

60. Sachs, "Preface," xi.

61. Mark Duffield, "Development, Territories, and People: Consolidating the External Sovereign Frontier," *Alternatives* 32, no. 2 (April–June 2007): 227. Duffield discusses an article by William Easterly, "The Cartel of Good Intentions: The Problem of Bureaucracy in Foreign Aid Work," *Journal of Economic Policy Reform* 5, no. 4 (2002): 223–50. The phrase "new and improved" is Easterly's.

62. Andrea Cornwall and Karen Brock, "Beyond Buzzwords: 'Poverty Reduction,' 'Participation' and 'Empowerment' in Development Policy," Programme Paper no. 10, Geneva, Switzerland, United Nations Research Institute for Social Development, 2005, 9.

63. Li, "Beyond 'The State,'" 383.

64. Stacy Leigh Pigg, "Inventing Social Categories Through Place: Social Representations and Development in Nepal," *Comparative Studies in Society and History* 34, no. 3 (July 1992): 501n22, 511.

65. Tania Murray Li, *The Will to Improve: Governmentality, Development, and the Practice of Politics* (Durham, NC: Duke University Press, 2007), 15.

66. James Ferguson, "Decomposing Modernity: History and Hierarchy After Development," in *Global Shadows: Africa in the Neoliberal World Order* (Durham, NC: Duke University Press, 2006), 178.

67. Pigg, "Inventing Social Categories," 511.

68. Rogers Brubaker and Frederick Cooper, "Beyond 'Identity,'" *Theory and Society* 29, no. 1 (Feb. 2000): 4–6.

69. This parallels James Ferguson's treatment of modernity, not as "an analytic term to be defined and applied" but as a native category in the sense in which anthropologists use the term. See Ferguson, "Decomposing Modernity," 177.

70. Mary Louise Pratt, "Modernity and Periphery: Towards a Global and Relational Analysis," in *Beyond Dichotomies: Histories, Identities, Cultures, and the Challenge of Globalization*, ed. Elisabeth Mudimbe-Boyi (Albany: State University of New York Press, 2002), 27–29.

71. Thomas Perreault, "'A People with Our Own Identity': Toward a Cultural Politics of Development in Ecuadorian Amazonia," *Environment and Planning D: Society and Space* 21, no. 5 (2003): 585.

72. Sachs, "Preface," vii–ix.

73. James Ferguson, "Of Mimicry and Membership: Africans and the 'New World Society,'" *Cultural Anthropology* 17, no. 4 (2002): 555.

74. Sachs, "Preface," x.

75. Bodhisattva Kar, "Can the Postcolonial Begin? Deprovincializing Assam," in *Handbook of Modernity in South Asia: Modern Makeovers*, ed. Saurabh Dube (New Delhi: Oxford University Press, 2011), 51.

76. Jayeeta Sharma, *Empire's Garden: Assam and the Making of India* (Durham, NC: Duke University Press, 2011), 203–4.

77. Sharma, 9, 196.

78. Kar, "Can the Postcolonial Begin?" 50.

79. Earlier versions of this section appear in Sanjib Baruah, "Territoriality, Indigeneity and Rights in the North-East India," *Economic and Political Weekly* 43, nos. 12 & 13

(March 22, 2008): 15–19; and Sanjib Baruah, "Politics of Territoriality: Indigeneity, Itinerancy and Rights in North-East India," in *Territorial Changes and Territorial Restructurings in the Himalayas*, ed. Joëlle Smadja (Delhi: Adroit, 2013), 69–83.

80. Harris-White, Mishra, and Upadhyay, "Institutional Diversity," 533, 535.

81. Lalthlamuong Keivom, "Ethnic Churning CHIKUMI Style," in *Our Common Crisis: What Are We to Do?* Arambam Somorendra Memorial Lectures, ed. Lokendra Arambam, Homen Thangjam, and Shukhdeba Sharma Hanjabam (Imphal, Manipur: Ashangba Communication, 2016), 182–83.

82. *Curse of Unregulated Coal Mining*, 2:5.

83. In strict legal terms no one could privately own land in Arunachal Pradesh before 2018, when a new land law—the Arunachal Pradesh (Land Settlement and Records) (Amendment) Act, 2018—was adopted. But state-issued land-possession certificates have long allowed individuals to exercise de facto property rights over some land.

84. Harris-White, Mishra, and Upadhyay, "Institutional Diversity," 536–37.

85. Karlsson, *Unruly Hills*, 66.

86. Debraj Ray, "Aspirations, Poverty, and Economic Change," in *Understanding Poverty*, ed. Abhijit Vinayak Banerjee, Roland Bénabou, and Dilip Mookherjee (Oxford: Oxford University Press, 2006), 410.

87. Myron Weiner, "The Political Consequences of Preferential Policies: A Comparative Perspective," *Comparative Politics* 16, no. 1 (1983): 46.

88. Alfred Stepan, *Arguing Comparative Politics* (New York: Oxford University Press, 2001), 338–39.

89. "Imphal Rallies for Implementation of ILP," *Morung Express*, Sept. 4, 2017.

90. Siddiqui, "Curse of the Black Gold."

91. Harris-White, Mishra, and Upadhyay, "Institutional Diversity," 535–36.

92. Mibi Ete, "Hydro-Dollar Dreams: Emergent Local Politics of Large Dams and Small Communities," in *Geographies of Difference: Explorations in Northeast Indian Studies*, ed. Mélanie Vandenhelsken, Meenaxi Barkataki-Ruscheweyh, and Bengt G. Karlsson (London: Routledge, 2018), 118–19.

93. Baruah, "Whose River Is It Anyway? 45.

94. Azera Parveen Rahman, "Private Dam Builders Back Out of Brahmaputra Dams," *The Third Pole*, Feb. 25, 2016, www.thethirdpole.net/2016/02/25/private-dam-builders-back-out-of-brahmaputra-dams.

95. Ete, "Hydro-Dollar Dreams," 109–27; and Duncan McDuie-Ra, "The Dilemmas of Pro-development Actors: Viewing State-Ethnic Minority Relations and Intra-ethnic Dynamics Through Contentious Development Projects," *Asian Ethnicity* 12, no. 1 (2011): 77–100.

96. Ete, "Hydro-Dollar Dreams," 117.

97. Siddiqui, "Curse of the Black Gold."

98. Das, *Cultural Politics*, 14.

99. Siddiqui, "Curse of the Black Gold."

100. Duncan McDuie-Ra points out that the Indian government's nearly six-hundred-page policy document *Vision 2020*, published in 2008, "is replete with references to

creating employment and building economic capacity in the region but contains virtually no mention of the impacts of out-migration on human capital." Duncan McDuie-Ra, *Northeast Migrants in Delhi: Race, Refuge and Retail* (Amsterdam: Amsterdam University Press, 2012), 83.

101. The idea of stretched lifeworlds is developed by Fiona Samuels. Karlsson and Kikon use it in their study of Northeastern migrants. See Bengt G. Karlsson and Dolly Kikon, "Wayfinding: Indigenous Migrants in the Service Sector of Metropolitan India," *South Asia* 40, no. 3 (2017): 459.

102. McDuie-Ra, *Northeast Migrants in Delhi*, 85, 98.

103. Harris-White, Mishra, and Upadhyay, "Institutional Diversity," 536.

104. Alemtemshi Jamir, "Keynote Address," in *Dimensions of Development in Nagaland*, ed. C. Joshua Thomas and Gurudas Das (New Delhi: Regency, 2002), 7.

105. *Arunachal Pradesh Human Development Report 2005* (Itanagar: Department of Planning, Government of Arunachal Pradesh, 2006). I have previously discussed this part of this report in Sanjib Baruah, *Postfrontier Blues: Toward a New Policy Framework for Northeast India* (Washington, DC: East-West Center, 2007), 27–30. Reprinted portions are used here with permission from the East-West Center.

106. *Arunachal Pradesh Human Development Report 2005*, 64–65.

107. *Arunachal Pradesh Human Development Report 2005*, 28.

108. *Arunachal Pradesh Human Development Report 2005*, 64.

109. Among scholars writing on Northeast India, anthropologist B. G. Karlsson has explicitly argued this position. Championing the collective rights of an indigenous people, he writes, cannot be "conflated with the type of indigeneity politics enacted in the Rwanda genocide. Power is a central aspect to be considered. Claims to indigenousness by dominant, majority groups are an altogether different story." He adds, however, that it "would be naive to assume that indigenous subjects are somehow less prone to intolerance and, at times, hatred against those perceived as intruders or outsiders." Karlsson, "Anthropology," 417.

110. John R. Bowen, "Should We Have a Universal Concept of 'Indigenous Peoples' Rights'? Ethnicity and Essentialism in the Twenty-First Century," *Anthropology Today* 16, no. 4 (August 2000): 13.

CHAPTER 4

1. NSCN-IM is a faction of what began as the National Socialist Council of Nagaland or NSCN. IM stands for the initials of the names of the two leaders, Isaak Chishi Swu and Thuingaleng Muivah. The other NSCN factions to which I refer in this chapter, NSCN-K and NSCN-KK, are also named after the initials of the leaders' names.

2. For a discussion of this peace process during an earlier phase, see my "Confronting Constructionism: Ending India's Naga War," *Journal of Peace Research* 40, no. 3 (May 2003): 321–38.

3. Sushant Singh, "Peace Talks: Key Naga Group Says No Headway," *Indian Express*, Jan. 15, 2019.

4. Sushant Singh, "Clock Ticking, Naga Talks Stuck for Long over Issue of Symbols," *Indian Express*, Jan. 7, 2019.

5. Singh, "Peace Talks."

6. Andrew West, "Writing the Nagas: A British Officers' [*sic*] Ethnographic Tradition," *History and Anthropology* 8, no. 1–4 (1994): 62.

7. George Nathaniel Curzon, *Frontiers* (The Romanes Lecture) (Oxford: Clarendon, 1907), 41.

8. See Baruah, "Confronting Constructionism."

9. Ankush Agrawal and Vikas Kumar, "Cartographic Conflicts Within a Union: Finding Land for Nagaland in India," *Political Geography* 61 (Nov. 2017): 141.

10. Quoted in Bertil Lintner, *Great Game East* (New Haven, CT: Yale University Press, 2015), 70.

11. Nandini Sundar, "Interning Insurgent Populations: The Buried Histories of Indian Democracy," *Economic and Political Weekly* 46, no. 6 (2011): 49.

12. Sundar, 49.

13. Benedict Anderson, "The New World Disorder," *New Left Review*, no. 193 (May–June 1992): 12–13.

14. Thanks to the acceptance of the *uti possidetis* rule—the borders of postcolonial states being regarded as inviolable—by the postimperial state system.

15. Alemtemshi Jamir, "Keynote Address," in *Dimensions of Development in Nagaland*, ed. C. Joshua Thomas and Gurudas Das (New Delhi: Regency, 2002), 3–4.

16. I deal with the splits in the Naga nationalist movement conceptually in Baruah, "Confronting Constructionism." For a historical account of these splits, see R[eisang] Vashum, *Nagas' Rights to Self Determination: An Anthropological-Historical Perspective* (New Delhi: Mittal, 2000), 77–110.

17. Shalaka Thakur and Rajesh Venugopal, "Parallel Governance and Political Order in Contested Territory: Evidence from the Indo-Naga Ceasefire," *Asian Security* (2018): 7, https://doi.org/10.1080/14799855.2018.1455185.

18. As I will explain below, I take the phrase "shared sovereignty" as a category of practice, not as a category of analysis.

19. Thakur and Venugopal, "Parallel Governance," 16.

20. For a conceptual discussion of this phenomenon see Diane E. Davis, "Non-state Armed Actors, New Imagined Communities, and Shifting Patterns of Sovereignty and Insecurity in the Modern World," *Contemporary Security Policy* 30, no. 2 (2009): 240.

21. J. H. Hutton, introduction to *The Lhota Nagas*, by James Philip Mills (London: Macmillan, 1922), xvi.

22. Hutton was known in colonial circles as the foremost authority on the Nagas. He was intimately involved in Naga affairs at a crucial period of their history. He was the deputy commissioner of the Naga Hills District—the most important colonial official on the ground—for an extended period, including when the Indian Statutory Commission (the Simon Commission) visited the Naga Hills in 1929. Hutton wrote the Assam government's official memorandum submitted to the commission, which recommended the exclusion of the hill districts from the proposed constitutional reforms. As deputy commissioner, he was the official who received the historic Naga Club petition addressed to the commission. Earlier, he had "explained to his staff and the *Dubashis* (interpreters) the

proposed reforms." The last surviving member of the delegation, who died in 1985, told administrator and author Murkot Ramunny that he was the person who drafted the Naga Club's petition and that Hutton "only corrected one word." Murkot Ramunny, *The World of Nagas* (New Delhi: Northern Book Centre, 1988), 24–25.

23. J. Butler, quoted in West, "Writing the Nagas," 64.

24. West, 64.

25. Michael Oppitz, Thomas Kaiser, Alban von Stockhausen, and Marion Wettstein, "The Nagas: An Introduction," in *Naga Identities: Changing Local Cultures in the Northeast of India*, edited by Michael Oppitz, Thomas Kaiser, Alban von Stockhausen, and Marion Wettstein (Gent, Belgium: Snoeck, 2008), 16.

26. Oppitz, et al., 16.

27. Robbins Burling, "The Tibeto-Burman Languages of Northeastern India," in *The Sino-Tibetan Languages*, ed. Graham Thurgood and Randy J. LaPolla (New York: Routledge, 2003), 172.

28. John Thomas, *Evangelising the Nation: Religion and the Formation of Naga Political Identity* (Delhi: Routledge India, 2015), 194–95.

29. Willem van Schendel, "The Dangers of Belonging: Tribes, Indigenous Peoples and Homelands in South Asia," in *The Politics of Belonging in India: Becoming Adivasi*, ed. D. J. Rycroft and S. Dasgupta (London: Routledge, 2011), 21.

30. Thomas, *Evangelising the Nation*, 194–95.

31. Thomas, 102, 111.

32. Julian Jacobs, with Alan Macfarlane, Sarah Harrison, and Anita Herle, *The Nagas: Hill Peoples of Northeast India: Society, Culture, and the Colonial Encounter* (1990; London: Thames and Hudson, 2012), 156.

33. Thomas, *Evangelising the Nation*, 197.

34. Arkotong Longkumer, "Moral Geographies: The Problem of Sovereignty and Indigeneity Amongst the Nagas," in *Rethinking Social Exclusion in India: Castes, Communities and the State*, ed. Minoru Mio and Abhijit Dasgupta (New York: Routledge, 2018), 154–55.

35. Rukmini Callimachi, "'Passage from India': Rebels Fight for Christian Nation in Nagaland," *Daily Herald* (Arlington Heights, IL), Nov. 3, 2017 (originally published in 2003), www.dailyherald.com/article/20170311/news/170319735.

36. Arkotong Longkumer, "*Exploring the Diversity of Religion: The Geo-political Dimensions of Fieldwork and Identity in the North East of India*," Fieldwork in Religion 4, no. 1 (2009): 54.

37. Quoted in Longkumer, "Moral Geographies," 155.

38. Vasundhara Sirnate Drennan, "The Naga Conflict: Can an Accord End an Insurgency?" Hindu Centre for Politics and Public Policy, August 7, 2015, www.thehinducentre.com /the-arena/current-issues/article7511878.ece.

39. Rogers Brubaker, *Ethnicity Without Groups* (Cambridge, MA: Harvard University Press, 2004), 16.

40. Quoted in Madhumita Das, "The Territorial Question in the Naga National Movement," *South Asian Survey* 20, no. 1 (March 2013): 36.

41. Das, 36.

42. Quoted in Praveen Swami, "Meetings to Seal Naga Deal," *Indian Express*, Oct. 2, 2015.

43. Sankaran Krishna, "Cartographic Anxiety: Mapping the Body Politic in India," *Alternatives* 19, no. 4 (Fall 1994): 507–21.

44. "Centre to Absorb Some NSCN (IM) Cadres into SF: Acharya," *Nagaland Post*, Sept. 10, 2015.

45. NSCN-IM, "Rejoinder to the Press Statement of P. B. Acharya, Governor of Nagaland and Assam," Nagalimvoice, Sept. 11, 2015, www.nagalimvoice.com/rejoinder /rejoinder-to-the-press-statement-of-p-b-acharya-governor-of-nagaland-and-assam.

46. H. Chishi, "Unity Key to Naga Peace Process: Ravi," *The Telegraph*, Dec. 9, 2015.

47. Feargal Cochrane, *Northern Ireland: The Reluctant Peace* (New Haven, CT: Yale University Press, 2013), 184.

48. See Rogers Brubaker and Frederick Cooper, "Beyond 'Identity,'" *Theory and Society* 29, no. 1 (Feb. 2000): 4–6.

49. Paul Staniland, "States, Insurgents, and Wartime Political Orders," *Perspectives on Politics* 10, no. 2 (2012): 243–64.

50. Samudra Gupta Kashyap, "How Atal Bihari Vajpayee Won Naga Hearts," *Indian Express*, August 4, 2015.

51. Max Weber, "Politics as a Vocation," in *From Max Weber: Essays in Sociology*, ed. H. H. Gerth and C. Wright Mills (New York: Oxford University Press, 1958), 78.

52. Lydia Walker, "States-in-Waiting: Nationalism, Internationalism, Decolonization" (PhD diss., Harvard University, 2018).

53. M. K. Narayanan, "The Devil Is in the Details," *The Hindu*, Sept. 11, 2015.

54. Thomas Blom Hansen and Finn Stepputat, "Introduction: States of Imagination," in *States of Imagination: Ethnographic Explorations of the Postcolonial State*, ed. Thomas Blom Hansen and Finn Stepputat (Durham, NC: Duke University Press, 2001), 5–10.

55. "Naga Sovereign Rights Affirmed," *Morung Express*, August 15, 2015, http://morung express.com/naga-sovereign-rights-affirmed.

56. See, e.g., M. S. Prabhakara, "Going Round the Mulberry Bush," *The Hindu*, March 20, 2010.

57. Thakur and Venugopal "Parallel Governance," 11.

58. Sandeep Unnithan and Kaushik Deka, "North-East Rebel Groups Freely Brandish Arms, Extort Protection Money from Locals and Run Parallel Governments," *India Today*, Oct. 5, 2012, www.indiatoday.in/magazine/special-report/story/20121015-north-east -rebel-groups-freely-brandish-arms-extort-protection-money-from-locals-760072-1999 -11-30.

59. Samudra Gupta Kashyap, "Beyond the 'Separate Naga Identity' Lie Similar Aspirations," *Indian Express*, August 9, 2015.

60. Thakur and Venugopal, "Parallel Governance," 11–14.

61. Dolly Kikon, "What Is Unique About Naga History?" *Economic and Political Weekly* 50, no. 35 (August 29, 2015): 10.

62. Thakur and Venugopal, "Parallel Governance," 10–11.

63. Charles Tilly, quoted in Roy Licklider, "How Civil Wars End: Questions and Methods," in *Stopping the Killing: How Civil Wars End*, ed. Roy Licklider (New York: New York University Press, 1995), 9.

64. South Asia Terrorism Portal, "National Socialist Council of Nagaland-Isak-Muivah," www.satp.org/satporgtp/countries/india/states/nagaland/terrorist_outfits /nscn_im.htm.

65. R. N. Ravi, "Nagaland: Descent into Chaos," *The Hindu*, Jan. 23, 2014.

66. Dolly Kikon and Duncan McDuie-Ra, "English-Language Documents and Old Trucks: Creating Infrastructure in Nagaland's Coal Mining Villages," *South Asia* 40, no. 4 (2017): 778.

67. See Kashyap, "Beyond the 'Separate Naga Identity.'" The three other endorsements were in August of 1970, September of 1994, and December of 2003.

68. "Decision of Nagas of Mainland Nagaland Clear: NNPGS," *Eastern Mirror*, March 9, 2017, www.easternmirrornagaland.com/decision-of-nagas-of-mainland -nagaland-clear-nnpgs.

69. Neiphiu Rio, "Speech at Consultative Meeting, Niathu Resort, Chumukedima, Dimapur, Nagaland, 25th August 2015," *Eastern Mirror*, Oct. 8, 2015.

70. Max Weber, "The Social Psychology of the World Religions," in *From Max Weber: Essays in Sociology*, ed. H. H. Gerth and C. Wright Mills (New York: Oxford University Press, 1958), 280.

71. Åshild Kolås, "Naga Militancy and Violent Politics in the Shadow of Ceasefire," *Journal of Peace Research* 48, no. 6 (Nov. 2011): 790.

72. Government of India, "Innovative Methods in Fighting Insurgency," https://mafiadoc .com/innovative-methods-in-fighting-insurgency-in-north-east-india-_59d2c6921723 dd036915d52f.html.

73. Unnithan and Deka, "North-East Rebel Groups."

74. Unnithan and Deka. The quotation from R. N. Ravi also appears in this report.

75. For example, the NSCN-K (Khaplang) and NSCN-KK (Khole-Kitovi) factions.

76. Unnithan and Deka, "North-East Rebel Groups."

77. Kashyap, "Beyond the 'Separate Naga Identity.'"

78. Ipsita Chakravarty, "At Camp Hebron, an Ambitious Project Is Under Way: A Peace Accord to Settle the Naga Question," Scroll.in, Dec. 4, 2015, http://scroll.in/article /769840/at-camp-hebron-an-ambitious-project-is-under-way-a-peace-accord-to-settle -the-naga-question.

79. Brook Larmer, "Can India's Land of Former Headhunters Make Peace?" *National Geographic*, August 26, 2015, https://news.nationalgeographic.com/2015/08 /150826-nagaland-india-myanmar-headhunters-baptists.

80. Hansen and Stepputat, "Introduction," 7–8.

81. Thakur and Venugopal, "Parallel Governance."

82. For a discussion of these protests, see Baruah, "Confronting Constructionism," 332–34.

83. James Johnstone, *My Experiences in Manipur and the Naga Hills* (London: S. Low, Marston, 1896), 93.

84. Thakur and Venugopal, "Parallel Governance," 8.

85. Kolås, "Naga Militancy," 791.

86. Sudeep Chakravarti, *Highway 39: Journeys Through a Fractured Land (New Delhi: Fourth Estate, 2012), 39, 46–47.*

87. See "NSCN-K Tax Racket Busted," *The Telegraph*, April 27, 2017. The report attributes these words to a senior National Investigation Agency official.

88. The phrase is Caroline Humphrey's, quoted in Thomas Blom Hansen and Finn Stepputat, "Sovereignty Revisited," *Annual Review of Anthropology* 35 (Oct. 2006): 306.

89. Robert Neil Reid, *History of the Frontier Areas Bordering on Assam: From 1883–1941* (Shillong: Assam Government Press, 1942), 99–100.

90. Bodhisattva Kar, "When Was the Postcolonial? A History of Policing Impossible Lines," in *Beyond Counterinsurgency: Breaking the Impasse in Northeast India*, ed. Sanjib Baruah (New Delhi: Oxford University Press, 2009), 52–55.

91. Bert Suykens, "State-Making and the Suspension of Law in India's Northeast: The Place of Exception in the Assam-Nagaland Border Dispute," in *Violence on the Margins: States, Conflict, and Borderlands*, ed. Benedikt Korf and Timothy Raeymaekers (New York: Palgrave Macmillan, 2013), 173.

92. Agrawal and Kumar, "Cartographic Conflicts," 129.

93. Constantine Kindo and Daniel Minj, "Territorial Dispute in the District of Golaghat, Assam," in *Conflict Mapping and Peace Processes in North East India*, edited by Lazar Jeyaseelan (Guwahati: North Eastern Social Research Centre, 2008), 14.

94. van Schendel, "The Dangers of Belonging," 27.

95. Suykens, "State-Making," 168.

96. Kolås, "Naga Militancy," 790.

97. Hiren Gohain, "Violent Borders: Killings in Nagaland-Assam," *Economic and Political Weekly* 42, no. 32 (August 11, 2007): 3283.

98. Suykens, "State-Making," 168, 181.

99. Agrawal and Kumar, "Cartographic Conflicts," 124.

100. Agrawal and Kumar, 146.

101. Gohain, "Violent Borders," 3283.

102. See Davis, "Non-state Armed Actors."

103. Diane E. Davis, "Violence and Insecurity: The Challenge in the Global South," MIT Center for International Studies, Audits of the Conventional Wisdom, Nov. 1, 2006, 3, https://cis.mit.edu/sites/default/files/documents/Davis1106Audit.pdf.

104. Staniland, "States, Insurgents, and Wartime," 246.

105. Saisuresh Sivaswamy, "Exclusive! How the Naga Accord Was Reached," an interview with Ravindra Narayan Ravi, Rediff.com, August 12, 2015, www.rediff.com/news/interview /exclusive-how-the-naga-accord-was-reached/20150812.htm.

106. Ajai Sahni, "Nagaland: Tentative Accord," *South Asia Intelligence Review* 14, no. 6 (August 10, 2015): www.satp.org/satporgtp/sair/Archives/sair14/14_6.htm#assessment1.

107. See Thakur and Venugopal "Parallel Governance."

108. "Manipur Iterates Border Resolution," *The Telegraph*, July 22, 2017.

109. Sushil Kumar Sharma, "The Naga Peace Accord: Manipur Connections," Institute for Defense Studies and Analyses, Dec. 18, 2015, https://idsa.in/policybrief/the-naga-peace-accord-manipur-connections_sksharma_181215.

110. Thakur and Venugopal "Parallel Governance," 17.

111. Singh, "Clock Ticking."

112. "Keep Talking," editorial, *Indian Express*, Jan. 16, 2019.

113. I borrow this expression from Arjun Appadurai, "Hope and Democracy," *Public Culture* 19, no. 1 (Winter 2007): 30.

114. Walker, "States-in-Waiting," 84.

115. T. Muivah, quoted in Kalyan Chaudhuri, "Territory Tussles," *Frontline* 20, no. 4 (Feb. 15, 2003): www.frontline.in/static/html/fl2004/stories/20030228002504500.htm.

116. Alex de Waal, "Violence and Peacemaking in the Political Marketplace," *Accord: An International Review of Peace Initiatives*, no. 25 (London: Conciliation Resources, 2014): 17, www.c-r.org/accord/legitimacy-and-peace-processes/violence-and-peacemaking-political-marketplace.

## CHAPTER 5

1. Aruni Kashyap, *The House with a Thousand Stories* (New Delhi: Viking, 2013).

2. Sanjay Barbora, "Road to Resentment: Impunity and Its Impacts on Notions of Community in Assam," in *Landscapes of Fear: Understanding Impunity in India*, ed. Patrick Hoenig and Navsharan Singh (New Delhi: Zubaan, 2014), 114.

3. Sanjoy Hazarika, *Strangers No More: New Narratives from India's Northeast* (New Delhi: Aleph, 2018), 141. This estimate is for the years between 1998 and 2001.

4. Not all extrajudicial killings in Assam during this period were politically motivated. There were opportunistic killings of innocent civilians by security personnel motivated by misaligned incentives of counterinsurgency: awards and citations that were supposed to honor valor but were based on body counts of the number of insurgents killed. See Kishalay Bhattacharjee, *Blood on My Hands: Confessions of Staged Encounters* (New Delhi: Harper Collins India, 2015).

5. Thomas Blom Hansen and Finn Stepputat, introduction to *Sovereign Bodies: Citizens, Migrants, and States in the Postcolonial World*, ed. Thomas Blom Hansen and Finn Stepputat (Princeton, NJ: Princeton University Press, 2005), 29.

6. In September of 2018, the Gauhati High Court declared the constitution of the Saikia Commission to be illegal because of certain technicalities. The legal challenge was brought forward by Prafulla Kumar Mahanta, who was both the chief minister and home minister of Assam at the time of the secret killings. The report had cast aspersions on his role in those killings. See "HC Quashes KN Saikia Report on Secret Killings," *Assam Tribune*, Sept. 4, 2018.

7. "Panel Opens Can of Worms," *The Telegraph*, Nov. 17, 2007.

8. Mrinal Talukdar, Utpal Borpujari, and Kaushik Deka, *Secret Killings of Assam* (Guwahati: Nanda Talukdar Foundation and Bhabani Books, 2008), 12.

9. Alex de Waal, "Counter-Insurgency on the Cheap," *London Review of Books* 26, no. 15 (August 5, 2004): 25–27.

10. Sashadhar Choudhury, "An Annotated Interview with Sashadhar Choudhury, Foreign Secretary, United Liberation Front of Asom [Assam]," by Rajeev Bhattacharyya and Nikhil Raymond Puri, *Perspectives on Terrorism* 7, no. 2 (2013): www.terrorismanalysts .com/pt/index.php/pot/article/view/257/html.

11. For an excellent literary-critical analysis of some of these writings, see Amit R. Baishya, *Contemporary Literature from Northeast India: Deathworlds, Terror and Survival* (New York: Routledge, 2019).

12. Banu Bargu, "Sovereignty as Erasure: Rethinking Enforced Disappearances," *Qui Parle* 23, no. 1 (Fall/Winter 2014): 44.

13. Talukdar, Borpujari, and Deka, *Secret Killings of Assam*, xi.

14. For the debate in the Assam Assembly on the counterinsurgency campaign against the Mizo National Front, see Hazarika, *Strangers No More*, 102–4.

15. Prasenjit Duara, "Historicizing National Identity, or Who Imagines What and When," in *Becoming National: A Reader*, ed. Geoff Eley and Ronald Grigor Suny (New York: Oxford University Press, 1999), 151.

16. *Securitization* is the term that theorists of the Copenhagen School of security studies use for the process that frames an issue as "an existential threat" to a state. Securitization legitimizes the use of extraordinary measures—including coercion—that are outside the norms and routines of everyday political practice. It opens "the way for the state to mobilize, or to take special powers, to handle existential threats." See Barry Buzan, Ole Wæver, and Jaap de Wilde, *Security: A New Framework for Analysis* (Boulder, CO: Lynne Tienner, 1998), 21. When it comes to Northeast India, the Armed Forces Special Powers Act makes securitization a much easier process. All that is needed is an executive notification declaring a state or a part of a state where the targeted group operates to be a "disturbed area" and to declare the group or faction unlawful. Such an executive order enables the deployment of the armed forces against that group.

17. This expression is derived from "the military metaphysics—the cast of mind that defines international reality as basically military." C. Wright Mills, *The Power Elite* (New York: Oxford University Press, 1956), 222.

18. Lawrence E. Cline, "The Insurgency Environment in Northeast India," *Small Wars & Insurgencies* 17, no. 2 (June 2006): 143.

19. Rajesh Rajagopalan, "'Restoring Normalcy': The Evolution of the Indian Army's Counterinsurgency Doctrine," *Small Wars & Insurgencies* 11, no. 1 (2000): 44, 58.

20. E. N. Rammohan, "Manipur: Blue Print for Counterinsurgency," *Faultlines* 12 (May 2002): 16.

21. Rammohan, 16.

22. Angshuman Choudhury, "Justice: Contours of the Assamese Insurgency," Hardnewsmedia.com, July 19, 2016, www.hardnewsmedia.com/2016/07/justice-contours -assamese-insurgency.

23. Patricia Mukhim, "Surrender Policy: Bad in Law," *The Telegraph*, April 8, 2013.

24. On the tensions between a democratic and a securitized citizenship, see Xavier Guillaume and Jef Huysmans, "Introduction: Citizenship and Security," in *Citizenship and Security: The Constitution of Political Being*, ed. Xavier Guillaume and Jef Huysmans (London: Routledge, 2013), 1–17.

25. Bethany Lacina, "Does Counterinsurgency Theory Apply in Northeast India?" *India Review* 6, no. 3 (2007): 165–83.

26. Doug McAdam, Sidney Tarrow, and Charles Tilly, *Dynamics of Contention* (Cambridge: Cambridge University Press, 2001), 6.

27. McAdam, Tarrow, and Tilly, 6.

28. Charles Tilly and Sidney Tarrow, *Contentious Politics*, 2nd ed. (New York: Oxford University Press, 2015), 171. Earlier versions of the discussion in this section appear in my "The State and Separatist Militancy in Assam: Winning a Battle and Losing the War?" *Asian Survey* 34, no. 10 (Oct. 1994): 863–77; "Separatist Militants and Contentious Politics in Assam: The Limits of Counter-Insurgency," *Asian Survey* 49, no. 6 (Nov.-Dec. 2009): 951–74; "Upending ULFA," *Himal Southasian* 24, no. 10–11 (Oct.-Nov. 2011): 18–20; and "Rise and Decline of a Separatist Insurgency: Contentious Politics in Assam, India," in *Autonomy and Ethnic Conflict in South and South-East Asia*, ed. Rajat Ganguly (London: Routledge, 2012), 27–45. Reproduced with the permission of the copyright holders and the publishers.

29. Nani Gopal Mahanta, *Confronting the State: ULFA's Quest for Sovereignty* (New Delhi: Sage India, 2013), 86.

30. Thomas Blom Hansen, "Politics as Permanent Performance: The Production of Political Authority in the Locality," in *The Politics of Cultural Mobilization in India*, ed. John Zavos, Andrew Wyatt, and Vernon Hewitt (New Delhi: Oxford University Press, 2004), 21.

31. Uttam Sengupta, "Even as Army Takes on Banned ULFA, Assam Faces Prolonged Stretch of Instability," *India Today*, Dec. 31, 1990, www.indiatoday.in/magazine/special-report /story/19901231-even-as-army-takes-on-banned-ulfa-assam-faces-prolonged-stretch-of -instability-813451-1990-12-31.

32. D. D. Thakur, "Governor's Report to the President," reproduced in judgment delivered by Chief Justice A. Raghuvir of the Guwahati High Court in *Nibaron Borah and Others v. Union of India*, March 20, 1991. Repr. in *News of North East: A Monthly Compilation of Clippings* (Guwahati: Eastern Press Service, May 1991), 22.

33. Subodh Kant Sahay, cited in Sanjoy Hazarika, *Strangers of the Mist: Tales of War and Peace from India's Northeast* (New Delhi: Penguin India, 1994), 190.

34. Xomyukta Mukti Bahini Axom (United Liberation Front of Assam). *Xomyukta Mukti Bahini Axomar Doxom Protistha Dibox, Bixex Procar Potro* [Tenth foundation day of Ulfa, special publicity pamphlet], April 7, 1979; repr. in Manoj Kumar Nath, *Ulfa: Xeujia Xopon, Tejronga Itihax* (Guwahati: Aak-Baak, 2013), 28, 38.

35. United Liberation Front of Assam (Xomyukta Mukti Bahini Axom), *Xodosya Toka Bohi* (Cadre Handbook) (N.p.: United Liberation Front of Assam, n.d.), 15, 19. I have also discussed this pamphlet in Sanjib Baruah, *India Against Itself: Assam and the Politics of Nationality* (Philadelphia: University of Pennsylvania Press, 1999), 148.

36. I use the term *regional patriotism* following historians of South Asia who talk about "regionally specific patriotisms" that predate the encounter with colonial rule. See Ayesha Jalal, "South Asia," *Encyclopedia of Nationalism: Fundamental Themes*, vol. 1, ed. Alexander J. Motyl (San Diego, CA: Academic Press, 2001), 739. Partha Chatterjee writes on a similar note: "In the days when the nation was being produced imaginatively without the actual shape of a state, many possibilities of communities that colonial knowledge would have declared as radically distinct came together into large political solidarities." Partha Chatterjee, *The Nation and Its Fragments: Colonial and Postcolonial Histories* (Princeton, NJ: Princeton University Press, 1993), 225.

37. David Graeber, "*Dead Zones of the Imagination: On Violence, Bureaucracy, and Interpretive Labor*," *HAU: Journal of Ethnographic Theory* 2, no. 2 (2006): 115.

38. For a discussion of Das's political ideas see my conclusion.

39. Hiren Gohain, "Chronicles of Violence and Terror: Rise of the United Liberation Front of Assam," *Economic and Political Weekly* 42, no. 12 (March 24, 2007): 1012.

40. See for e.g., "Assam Governor for Strong Military Operation Against ULFA," *The Hindu*, Jan. 26, 2006. This report quotes General Ajai Singh, then the governor of Assam and a veteran of the Indian Army's counterinsurgency in the region: "What is (there) to talk [with Ulfa]? They should surrender and seek rehabilitation. Otherwise they should be crushed because such talks only help the militants."

41. Carl Schmitt, *The* Nomos *of the Earth in the International Law of the* Jus Publicum Europaeum, trans. G. L. Ulmen (New York: Telos, 2003), 120–22.

42. Elisabeth Jean Wood, *Insurgent Collective Action and Civil War in El Salvador* (New York: Cambridge University Press, 2003), 25.

43. John D. Kelly, "U.S. Power, After 9/11 and Before It: If Not an Empire, Then What?" *Public Culture* 15, no. 2 (Spring 2003): 348.

44. For a comprehensive historical account of Ulfa, see Mahanta, *Confronting the State*. For my essays on Ulfa during various phases of its history, see chapters 6, 7, and 8 of my *Durable Disorder: Understanding the Politics of Northeast India* (New Delhi: Oxford University Press, 2005); and sources cited in note 28 above.

45. Charles Tilly, *Collective Violence, Contentious Politics, and Social Change: A Charles Tilly Reader*, ed. Ernesto Castañeda and Cathy Lisa Schneider (New York: Routledge, 2017).

46. According to one estimate about twelve thousand of its members and eighteen thousand others had died. Hiren Gohain, cited in Nath, *Ulfa*, 161.

47. Ipsita Chakravarty, "How the Fear of Migrants Became the Driving Force of Politics in Assam." Scroll.in, Feb. 19, 2016, https://scroll.in/article/802983 /from-votebank-to-spectre-how-political-parties-imagine-the-outsider-in-assam.

48. Geoff Eley and Ronald Grigor Suny, "Introduction: From the Moment of Social History to the Work of Cultural Representation," in *Becoming National: A Reader*, ed. Geoff Eley and Ronald Grigor Suny (New York: Oxford University Press, 1999), 32.

49. Rogers Brubaker, "In the Name of the Nation: Reflections on Nationalism and Patriotism," *Citizenship Studies* 8, no. 2 (2004): 116.

50. Partha Chatterjee, "Legacy of Bandung," in *Bandung, Global History, and International Law: Critical Pasts and Pending Futures*, ed. Luis Eslava, Michael Fakhri, and Vasuki Nesiah (Cambridge: Cambridge University Press, 2017), 658.

51. Sunil Khilnani, *The Idea of India* (New York: Farrar Straus Giroux, 1997), xiii–xiv.

52. According to the 2011 census, Muslims constitute 34.22 percent of the total population of Assam. The percentage of Muslims in India as a whole is 14.23 percent. Religion Census 2011, www.census2011.co.in/religion.php.

53. Paul R. Brass, "Elite Interests, Popular Passions, and Social Power in the Language Politics of India," in *Ethnonationalism in India: A Reader*, ed. Sanjib Baruah (Delhi: Oxford University Press, 2010), 89.

54. Sidney Tarrow, "Inside Insurgencies: Politics and Violence in an Age of Civil War," *Perspectives on Politics* 5, no. 3 (Sept. 2007): 593.

55. When it comes to the issue of cross-border migration and the citizenship controversy, Tripura's circumstances are somewhat unique. But pan-Indian parties often have an undifferentiated view of Northeast Indian politics.

56. Shekhar Gupta, *Assam: A Valley Divided* (Delhi: Vikas, 1984), 29. I discussed this exchange between Pilot and Gupta in an earlier book as well. See Sanjib Baruah, *India Against Itself: Assam and the Politics of Nationality* (Philadelphia: University of Pennsylvania Press, 1999), 130–31.

57. Graeber, "Dead Zones," 117.

58. Graeber, 115–16. I use the phrase "structural violence" in the sense that Graeber does, which is somewhat different from the standard usage.

59. Makiko Kimura, *The Nellie Massacre of 1983: Agency of Rioters* (New Delhi: Sage, 2013).

60. Arun Shourie, "Assam Elections: Can Democracy Survive Them?" *India Today*, May 31, 1983, 57.

61. Marshall Sahlins, "Iraq: The State of Nature Effect," *Anthropology Today* 27, no. 3 (June 2011): 26.

62. Sunil Nath, "Assam: The Secessionist Insurgency and the Freedom of Minds," *Faultlines* 13 (Nov. 2002): 29, 38–39. Sunil Nath, under the *nom de guerre* Siddhartha Phukan, was Ulfa's publicity secretary until his defection in 2002.

63. This is largely because of the Illegal Migrants (Determination by Tribunal) Act (IMDT law) that the Indian Parliament adopted in 1983. In 2005 the Indian Supreme Court found this law to be unconstitutional. See Chapter 2.

64. Shourie, "Assam Elections," 57.

65. Kimura, *The Nellie Massacre of 1983*.

66. Gupta, *Assam*, 121–22.

67. The BJP also did well in Assam in the parliamentary election of 2014, which elected Narendra Modi prime minister. The president of the party, Amit Shah, in a speech in September of 2015, "heaped lavish praise" on the RSS for "its effort to integrate North East with the rest of India." He said that "more than 272 fulltime RSS pracharaks" had worked in the region and that "there are many institutions, which got inspiration from the RSS." "BJP Flays UPA for Making DoNER 'Dormant,'" *Assam Tribune*, Sept. 15, 2015.

68. Nasser Hussain, "Counterinsurgency's Comeback: Can a Colonialist Strategy Be Reinvented?" *Boston Review*, Jan./Feb. 2010, http://bostonreview.net/world/counterinsurgency%E2%80%99s-comeback.

69. Hussain.

70. David P. Fidler points out that despite many similarities between the US and India counterinsurgency doctrines, there are substantive differences because whereas Indian counterinsurgency operations have been mostly "internal," US counterinsurgency operations, at least in the twentieth century, have all been overseas. India's only experience of conducting counterinsurgency overseas was in Sri Lanka. By contrast, the US engagement with internal counterinsurgency ended in the nineteenth century "with the conclusion of the Civil War and the destruction of Native American opposition to Manifest Destiny." David P. Fidler, "The Indian Doctrine for Sub-conventional Operations: Reflections from a U.S. Counterinsurgency Perspective," in *India and Counterinsurgency: Lessons Learned*, ed. Sumit Ganguly and David P. Fidler (New York: Routledge, 2009), 208, 214. The crude distinction made between internal and external counterinsurgency implies that postcolonial India's counterinsurgency operations and those that the US conducted against Native Americans are analogous since they all fit the category "internal." I doubt that the Indian counterinsurgency establishment and its supporters would take kindly to the implied equivalence. It certainly does not help with the chronic legitimacy deficit of India's postcolonial counterinsurgency operations in Northeast India.

71. UN General Assembly, *Report of the Policy Working Group on the United Nations and Terrorism*, 57th Sess., item 162, Provisional Agenda, Measures to Eliminate International Terrorism (August 6, 2002), 6. UN Doc. A/57/273-S/2002/875.

72. Government of India, *Indian Army Doctrine*, pt. 1 (Shimla: Headquarters Army Training Command, 2004), 16.

73. S. K. Sinha, "Violence and Hope in India's Northeast," lecture at the Institute for Conflict Management, New Delhi, June 2001. In *Faultlines* 10 (Jan. 2002): 17.

74. Government of India, Ministry of Home Affairs Order, Jan. 4, 1997. Cited in Wasbir Hussain, "Multi-force Operations in Counter Terrorism: A View from the Assam Theatre," *Faultlines* 9 (July 2001): 44.

75. Sinha, "Violence and Hope," 18.

76. Sinha, 17.

77. Anil Yadav, *Is That Even a Country, Sir! Journeys in Northeast India by Train, Bus and Tractor*, trans. from the Hindi by Anurag Basnet (New Delhi: Speaking Tiger, 2017), 32.

78. Sinha, "Violence and Hope," 17.

79. Marshall Sahlins, "Preface," in *The Counter-Counterinsurgency Manual: Or, Notes on Demilitarizing American Society*, ed. Network of Concerned Anthropologists (Chicago: Prickly Paradigm, 2009), iii.

80. David Miller, "Sociology, Propaganda and Psychological Operations," in *Stretching the Sociological Imagination: Essays in Honour of John Eldridge*, ed. Andrew Smith, Matt Dawson, Bridget Fowler, and David Miller (New York: Palgrave Macmillan, 2015), 163–88. The quotes are from an intelligence agent's deposition before a public inquiry on the events in Derry, Northern Ireland, on January 30, 1972, known as Bloody Sunday.

81. Sinha, "Violence and Hope," 18.

82. Arshiya Sethi, "An Overlay of the Political: The Recognition of Sattriya," *Seminar*, no. 676 (Dec. 2015): www.india-seminar.com/2015/676/676_arshiya_sethi.htm.

83. Sinha, "Violence and Hope," 19. The honorific "Srimanta," attached to the name of Sankardev in Assam, is used exclusively to refer to this highly venerated figure. Governor Sinha confuses it with "Shreeman," a widely used Indian honorific before the name of a male individual. No Assamese would ever confuse *Shreeman* with *Srimanta*.

84. Sinha, 18–19.

85. The last name *Borphukon* is sometimes spelled *Borphukan* or *Barphukan*. I have used *Borphukon*, which is closer to the Assamese pronunciation of the name, except when it is spelled differently in a cited work or a quotation.

86. Jayeeta Sharma, "Heroes for Our Times: Assam's Lachit, India's Missile Man," in *The Politics of Cultural Mobilization in India*, ed. John Zavos, Andrew Wyatt, and Vernon Hewitt (New Delhi: Oxford University Press, 2004), 176. My discussion of the politics of memory around Lachit Borphukon relies significantly on this essay.

87. J. Sharma, 176.

88. Suresh Phukon, *Moidamor Pora Moi Lachite Koiso* (Sibsagar, Assam: Rupam Prakashan, 1980). Moidams are Ahom burial grounds for royals and nobles.

89. For a discussion of *Moidamor Pora Moi Lachite Koiso* and its significance, see Mahanta, *Confronting the State*, 43–46.

90. J. Sharma, "Heroes for Our Times," 179.

91. Bodhisattva Kar, "The Tragedy of Suryya Bhuyan: An Essay," *Biblio* (New Delhi) 13, nos. 5 & 6 (May-June 2008): 27.

92. J. Sharma, "Heroes for Our Times," 187.

93. J. Sharma, 188.

94. J. Sharma, 190–91.

95. "Report on Illegal Migration into Assam Submitted to the President of India by the Governor of Assam," November 8, 1998, www.satp.org/satporgtp/countries/india/states/assam/documents/papers/illegal_migration_in_assam.htm.

96. Sengupta, "Even as Army Takes on Banned ULFA."

97. Sengupta.

98. Cited in Sushanta Talukdar, "Peace Talks Last Opportunity, Says ULFA Chairman," *The Hindu*, August 8, 2011.

99. Sharika Thiranagama, "Claiming the State: Postwar Reconciliation in Sri Lanka," *Humanity* 4, no. 1 (Spring 2013): 102–3.

100. "Electoral Consideration Can't Be Ignored: PC on Naxalism," *Hindustan Times*, May 11, 2010, www.hindustantimes.com/delhi-news/electoral-consideration-can-t-be-ignored-pc-on-naxalism/story-ei19qddd2PeGpn3G2t3uRI.html

101. "ULFA Leader Anup Chetia Handed Over to India," *Indian Express*, Nov. 12, 2015.

102. Diane Barthel, *Historic Preservation: Collective Memory and Historical Identity* (New Brunswick, NJ: Rutgers University Press, 1996), 80.

103. Narendra Modi, "PM Salutes Lachit Borphukan, on His Birth Anniversary," Nov. 24, 2015, www.narendramodi.in/pm-salutes-lachit-borphukan-on-his-birth-anniversary-377261.

104. "Army Installs Lachit Borphukon's Statue at Dinjan Base," *Northeast Today*, June 6, 2017, www.northeasttoday.in/army-installs-lachit-borphukans-statue-at-dinjan-base.

105. "Bir Lachit Borphukan Statue Unveiled in the Heart of Brahmaputra," *Northeast Today*, Feb. 1, 2016, www.northeasttoday.in/bir-lachit-borphukan-statue-unveiled-in-the -heart-of-brahmaputra.

106. Tilly and Tarrow, *Contentious Politics*, 57.

107. Tilly and Tarrow, 58–59.

108. Prabin Kalita, "Assam Declares Entire State 'Disturbed,' Extends AFSPA by 6 Months for Smooth NRC Exercise," *Times of India*, August 30, 2018.

109. Supreme Court of India, *Extra Judicial Execution Victim Families v. Union of India & Another*, Writ Petition (Criminal) no. 129 of 2012, July 13, 2016, https://indiankanoon .org/doc/83144198. This lawsuit is discussed further in Chapter 6.

## CHAPTER 6

1. An earlier version of this chapter was published as Sanjib Baruah, "Routine Emergencies: India's Armed Forces Special Powers Act," in *Civil Wars in South Asia: State, Sovereignty, Development*, ed. Aparna Sundar and Nandini Sundar (New Delhi: Sage India, 2014), 189–211, © Aparna Sundar and Nandini Sundar, all rights reserved. Reproduced with the permission of the copyright holders and the publisher.

2. See Václav Havel, "Politics and Conscience," in *Václav Havel or Living in Truth*, ed. Jan Vladislav (London: Faber and Faber, 1989), 156–57.

3. Her public position, however, was that she would continue her opposition to AFSPA through other means.

4. In response to the committee that reviewed AFSPA in 2004–5, the home secretary of Mizoram said that AFSPA was "a sleeping Act" in that state in the sense that no area in Mizoram was declared "disturbed" under AFSPA since the Mizo Peace Accord was signed, which ended the Mizo rebellion in 1986. Government of India, *Report of the Committee to Review the Armed Forces (Special Powers) Act, 1958* (New Delhi: Ministry of Home Affairs, 2005), 144.

5. Kuldeep Kumar, *Police and Counterinsurgency: The Untold Story of Tripura's COIN Campaign* (New Delhi: Sage, 2016), 241.

6. R. K. Debbarma, "Where to Be Left Is No Longer Dissidence: A Reading of Left Politics in Tripura," *Economic and Political Weekly* 52, no. 21 (May 27, 2017): 21.

7. M. A. Athul, "Tripura: Destabilizing Gambit," *South Asia Intelligence Review* 17, no. 32 (Feb. 4, 2019): www.satp.org/south-asia-intelligence-review-Volume-17-No-32.

8. Anubha Bhonsle, "Why Tripura's AFSPA Withdrawal May Have Little Bearing for Rest of 'AFSPA States'"? *News18*, May 28, 2015, www.news18.com/news/india/why -tripuras-afspa-withdrawal-may-have-little-bearing-for-rest-of-afspa-states-998247.html.

9. G. K. Pillai, preface to *The Armed Forces Special Powers Act: The Debate*, ed. Vivek Chadha (New Delhi: Institute for Defence Studies and Analysis and Lancer's Books, 2013), vii.

10. Prabin Kalita, "Assam Declares Entire State 'Disturbed,' Extends AFSPA by 6 Months for Smooth NRC Exercise," *Times of India*, August 30, 2018, https://time sofindia.indiatimes.com/india/assam-declares-entire-state-disturbed-extends-afspa -by-6-months-for-smooth-nrc-exercise/articleshow/65600577.cms?utm_source=content

ofinterest&utm_medium=text&utm_campaign=cppst. For a discussion of the NRC exercise, see Chapter 2.

11. For the beginnings of this police force see Chapter 5.

12. N. Santosh Hegde, J. M. Lyngdoh, and Ajai Kumar Singh, *Report of the Supreme Court Appointed Commission*, New Delhi, vol. 1, March 30, 2013, 87. E. V. Rammohan, a former top police official in the region, described the Commandos as "a state terrorist force" (see my discussion in Chap. 5).

13. Shiv Visvanathan, "Manipur Needs Its Life Back," *India Today*, Sept. 1, 2014.

14. There are, of course, important voices from that mainland who have been critical of AFSPA. "Irom Sharmila, like the dead Thangjam Manorama," said Karnataka-born M. S. Prabhakara in a speech in Manipur, "shames the nation-state, that is India, my and your India." M. S. Prabhakara, "Sovereignty Struggles in Northeast India: Where Are They Going?" in *Our Common Crisis: What Are We to Do?* Arambam Somorendra Memorial Lectures, ed. Lokendra Arambam, Homen Thangjam, and Shukhdeba Sharma Hanjabam (Imphal, Manipur: Ashangba Communication, 2016), 112–13.

15. Anubha Bhonsle, *Mother, Where's My Country? Looking for Light in the Darkness of Manipur* (Delhi: Speaking Tiger, 2016), 52–53 (translation mine). By "Assam side," the nurse means Northeast India. Even in the nation's capital, it seems that the term *Northeast* has not caught on among all sections of society. Contrary to the expectation of Indian policy makers, it has not replaced "the hitherto more familiar unit of public imagination, Assam," though the racialized regime of visuality is obviously at work.

16. Esha Roy, "Irom Sharmila Detention: Human Rights Panel Sends Notice to Manipur Govt," *Indian Express*, Nov. 4, 2013.

17. Joy L. K. Pachuau and Willem van Schendel, *The Camera as Witness: A Social History of Mizoram, Northeast India* (Delhi: Cambridge University Press, 2015), 305.

18. Nandini Sundar, "Interning Insurgent Populations: The Buried Histories of Indian Democracy," *Economic and Political Weekly* 46, no. 6 (2011): 48.

19. Sundar, 48.

20. Pachuau and van Schendel, *The Camera as Witness*, 409.

21. Supreme Court of India, *Extra Judicial Execution Victim Families v. Union of India & Another*, Writ Petition (Criminal) no. 129 of 2012, July 13, 2016, https://indiankanoon.org/doc/83144198.

22. I first learned this from human rights activist Babloo Loitongbam. My conversations with poet and sociologist Soibam Haripriya helped me understand the meaning better. I am deeply grateful to them for explaining this to me. In the Meitei language *ee* (blood) is a part of kinship terminology, and the word *pham* refers to place. EEVFAM in Meitei, says Haripriya, evokes "a lost connection of kin in the midst of missing bodies, missing bodies leading to incomplete funerary rites, a connection that one cannot go back to, a connection of blood destroyed by spilt blood" (personal email, Nov. 4, 2018).

23. Civil Society Coalition on Human Rights in Manipur and the UN, "Manipur: A Memorandum on Extrajudicial, Arbitrary or Summary Executions submitted to Christof Heyns, Special Rapporteur on Extrajudicial, Arbitrary or Summary Executions," March 28, 2012, Guwahati, India.

24. UN General Assembly, *Report of the Special Rapporteur on Extrajudicial, Summary or Arbitrary Executions, Addendum: Mission to India*, Human Rights Council, 23rd Sess., item 3, April 26, 2013, UN Doc. A/HRC/23/47/Add.1, 5, www.refworld.org/docid /51b98e624.html.

25. Hegde, Lyngdoh, and Singh, *Report*, 1–3.

26. Hegde, Lyngdoh, and Singh, 82–85.

27. See my discussion of the implications of this part of the ruling in the concluding paragraph of Chapter 5.

28. "Govt. Snubs UN Official on AFSPA," *Indian Express*, March 24, 2009.

29. Iris Marion Young, "The Logic of Masculinist Protection: Reflections on the Current Security State," *Signs* 29, no.1 (Autumn 2003): 3.

30. Young, 13.

31. See Xavier Guillaume and Jef Huysmans, "Introduction: Citizenship and Security," in *Citizenship and Security: The Constitution of Political Being*, ed. Xavier Guillaume and Jef Huysmans (London: Routledge, 2013), 1–17.

32. Along with my discussion of this issue in Chapter 5, see Patricia Mukhim, "Surrender Policy: Bad in Law," *The Telegraph* (Guwahati), April 8, 2013.

33. Ananya Vajpeyi, "Resenting the Indian State: For a New Political Practice in the Northeast," in *Beyond Counterinsurgency: Breaking the Impasse in Northeast India*, ed. Sanjib Baruah (New Delhi: Oxford University Press, 2009), 28, 48.

34. Human Rights Watch, "Human Rights Overview, 2005," http://hrw.org/english /docs/2006/01/18/india12272.htm.

35. Government of India, *Report of the Committee to Review*, 42–43.

36. Government of India, *Report of the Committee to Review*, 79.

37. Subir Bhaumik, "Repeal AFSPA in India," Southasian Monitor.com, May 8, 2017. https://southasianmonitor.com/2017/05/08.

38. As I have indicated, AFSPA has been enacted to apply to two other states outside of Northeast India. While the focus of this chapter is on AFSPA in Northeast India, the experience of Jammu and Kashmir—the only states outside the Northeast where the law is currently in effect—becomes relevant in this context.

39. Anuradha Bhasin Jamwal, "Politics of Human Rights Abuses," *Kashmir Times* (Srinagar), April 26, 2009.

40. "Demand for Changes in AFSPA for Political Gains," *Indian Express*, June 26, 2010.

41. "J&K Administration Has Collapsed, Says Advani," *Times of India*, Sept. 15, 2010.

42. Jagdamba Mall, "Must Remain Armed with AFSPA," *Organiser*, May 21, 2016, 17.

43. James L. Gibson, "Enigmas of Intolerance: Fifty Years After Stouffer's *Communism, Conformity, and Civil Liberties*," *Perspectives on Politics* 4, no. 1 (March 2006): 21–22.

44. John Keane, "Humble Democracy? On the Need for New Thinking About an Aging Ideal," in *Iraq, Democracy and the Future of the Muslim World*, ed. Ali Paya and John L. Esposito (New York: Routledge, 2011), 87.

45. Michael Ignatieff, *The Lesser Evil: Political Ethics in an Age of Terror* (Princeton, NJ: Princeton University Press, 2004). An earlier version of the discussion in this

paragraph appears in my *Postfrontier Blues: Toward a New Policy Framework for Northeast India* (Washington, DC: East-West Center, 2007), 14–15, www.eastwestcenter.org/publications/postfrontier-blues-toward-new-policy-framework-northeast-india.

46. Ignatieff, *The Lesser Evil*, 23–24.

47. Kent Roach, "Ordinary Laws for Emergencies and Democratic Derogations from Rights," in *Emergencies and the Limits of Legality*, ed. Victor Ramraj (Cambridge: Cambridge University Press, 2008), 234–45.

48. UN General Assembly, "International Covenant on Civil and Political Rights," Dec. 16, 1966, www.ohchr.org/en/professionalinterest/pages/ccpr.aspx.

49. United Nations, "Appendix F: Human Rights Committee Concluding Observations on Caste," August 4, 1997, par. 19, www.hrw.org/reports/1999/india/India994-21.htm.

50. UN General Assembly, *Report of the Special Rapporteur* (see note 24 above).

51. UN General Assembly, "International Covenant on Civil and Political Rights."

52. "Demand for Changes in AFSPA for Political Gains," *Indian Express*, June 26, 2010.

53. Ajai Sahni, "By the Law, for Law and Order," *Tehelka* (New Delhi), June 24, 2006.

54. Nari Rustomji, *Imperilled Frontiers: India's North-Eastern Borderlands* (New Delhi, Oxford University Press, 1983), 31–32.

55. Quoted in "Growth of a Demon: Genesis of the Armed Forces (Special Powers) Act, 1958," *Manipur Update* 1, no. 1 (Dec. 1999): www.geocities.ws/manipurupdate/december_feature_1.htm.

56. Sudipta Kaviraj, "The Post-Colonial State: The Special Case of India," *Critical Encounters*, Jan. 19, 2009, http://criticalencounters.wordpress.com/2009/01/19/the-post-colonial-state-sudipta-kaviraj.

57. Kaviraj.

58. Quoted in Arudra Burra, "The Cobwebs of Imperial Rule," *Seminar*, no. 615, Nov. 2010, 81.

59. Quoted in Dipesh Chakrabarty, "'In the Name of Politics': Democracy and the Power of the Multitude in India," *Public Culture* 19, no. 1 (2007): 55.

60. Quoted in Government of India Second Administrative Reforms Commission, *Fifth Report: Public Order*, June 2007, ii.

61. Burra, "Cobwebs of Imperial Rule," 83.

62. Thomas Blom Hansen and Finn Stepputat, "Introduction: States of Imagination," in *States of Imagination: Ethnographic Explorations of the Postcolonial State*, ed. Thomas Blom Hansen and Finn Stepputat (Durham, NC: Duke University Press, 2001), 4.

63. Thomas R. Mockaitis, "Low-Intensity Conflict: The British Experience," *Conflict Quarterly* 13, no. 1 (1993): 9.

64. Nasser Hussain, "Counterinsurgency's Comeback: Can a Colonialist Strategy Be Reinvented?" *Boston Review*, Jan./Feb. 2010, http://bostonreview.net/world/counterinsurgency's-comeback.

65. David P. Fidler, "The Indian Doctrine for Sub-conventional Operations: Reflections from a U.S. Counterinsurgency Perspective," in *India and Counterinsurgency: Lessons Learned*, ed. Sumit Ganguly and David P. Fidler (New York: Routledge, 2009), 208, 214.

See my discussion of this distinction between internal and external counterinsurgency in Chapter 5n70 above.

66. David Arnold, quoted in Gyanesh Kudaisya, "'In Aid of Civil Power': The Colonial Army in Northern India, *c.* 1919–42," *Journal of Imperial and Commonwealth History* 32, no. 1 (2004): 45.

67. Kudaisya, 42.

68. Quoted in Kudaisya, 43.

69. Charles W. Gwynn, *Imperial Policing* (London: Macmillan, 1934), 3–5.

70. Quoted in Government of India, *Fifth Report: Public Order*, Second Administrative Reforms Commission, June 2007, 144.

71. "British Defence Doctrine," quoted in Jonathan Stevenson, "The Role of the Armed Forces of the United Kingdom in Securing the State Against Terrorism," *Connections* 4, no. 3 (2005): 125.

72. Jeffrey D. Brake, "Terrorism and the Military's Role in Domestic Crisis Management: Background and Issues for Congress," *CRS Report for Congress* (Washington, DC: Congressional Research Service, April 19, 2001), 12.

73. Kuldeep Mathur, "The State and the Use of Coercive Power in India," *Asian Survey* 32, no. 4 (1992): 346.

74. Government of India, *Report of the Committee to Review*, 41.

75. "Central Government Act: Section 197 in the Code of Criminal Procedure, 1973," https://indiankanoon.org/doc/12704.

76. Yong S. Lee, *A Reasonable Public Servant: Constitutional Foundations of Administrative Conduct in the United States* (Armonk, NY: M. E. Sharpe, 2005), xv.

77. Siddharth Varadarajan, "A Modest Proposal on AFSPA," *The Hindu*, Sept. 6, 2010, www.thehindu.com/opinion/columns/siddharth-varadarajan/A-modest-proposal-on-AFSPA/article15905357.ece.

78. S. P. Sinha, "CI Operations in the Northeast," *Indian Defence Review* 21, no. 2 (April–June 2006): www.indiandefencereview.com/spotlights/c-i-operations-in-the-northeast/2.

79. Arnold, quoted in Kudaisya, "'In Aid of Civil Power,'" 44.

80. UN Human Rights Committee, "India: Examination of Second Periodic Report by Human Rights Committee, Recommendations to Bring Indian Laws and Practices in Line with International Human Rights Standards," 41st Session, March 26–27, 1991, New York, www.amnesty.org/en/documents/asa20/005/1993/en.

81. Nasser Hussain, *The Jurisprudence of Emergency: Colonialism and the Rule of Law* (Ann Arbor: University of Michigan Press, 2003), 129.

82. Christian Olsson, "'Legitimate Violence' in the Prose of Counterinsurgency: An Impossible Necessity?" *Alternatives* 38, no. 2 (May 2013): 158.

83. Engin F. Isin, "Theorizing Acts of Citizenship," in *Acts of Citizenship*, ed. Engin F. Isin and Greg M. Nielsen (London: Zed, 2008), 15–43.

## CONCLUSION

1. Samarth Bansal, "North-Eastern Flourish at the Ballot," *The Hindu*, April 14,

2016. This is the case with six states of Northeast India's eight states: Manipur, Meghalaya, Mizoram Nagaland, Tripura, and Sikkim.

2. Supreme Court of India, *Extra Judicial Execution Victim Families v. Union of India & Another*, Writ Petition (Criminal) no. 129 of 2012, July 13, 2016, 27, https://indiankanoon.org/doc/83144198.

3. Of the 1,528 cases of "fake encounter" killings detailed in the petition, the Supreme Court has ordered India's Central Bureau of Investigation (CBI) to investigate ninety-eight cases. As of August 2018, the CBI had registered forty-three First Information Reports—a document prepared by police officers on the first receipt of information of a cognizable offense. Only in two cases have charges been filed in a court of law. In one of these cases an Indian Army major was arrested on the charge of murdering a high school student in "an encounter killing" that occurred nine years earlier. See Imran Ahmed Siddiqui and Pankaj Sarma, "Army Officer Booked in 'Fake Killing,'" *The Telegraph*, August 3, 2018. A month earlier, the Supreme Court bench summoned the CBI's head and reproached him for the "unduly long time" that his agency has taken to complete investigations. "Manipur Encounters: Expedite Probe, Issue Involves Life & Death, Says SC," *Outlook*, July 30, 2018, www.outlookindia.com/newsscroll/manipur-encounters-expedite-probe-issue-involves-life—death-says-sc-eds-updating-with-more-details/1360221.

4. Around seven hundred officers and soldiers of the Indian Army petitioned the Supreme Court to protest the investigations and prosecutions. Army personnel, according to one of the petitions, were "being persecuted and prosecuted for carrying out their bona fide duties." It charged that the protection provided by AFSPA against prosecution is being "diluted" by the Court's action. See "Over 380 Army Personnel Move Supreme Court on AFSPA," *Indian Express*, Sept. 1, 2018. This kind of independent legal action by military officers is unprecedented; arguably, it is a breach of military discipline. Yet the central government supported the army personnel in court on the grounds that the orders had a demoralizing effect on the security forces. The Court, however, dismissed the petitions, saying that it was forced to order the investigations and prosecutions only because the government has failed to investigate the extrajudicial killings and act against the offending security personnel. Shruti Mahajan, "'If There Is Loss of Life, Shouldn't There Be an Inquiry?' SC Dismisses Plea Against CBI Probe in Manipur Killings," *Bar & Bench*, Nov. 30, 2018, https://barandbench.com/if-there-is-loss-of-life-shouldnt-there-be-an-inquiry-sc-dismisses-plea-against-cbi-probe-into-manipur-killings.

5. Quoted in Supreme Court of India, *Extra Judicial Execution Victim Families*, 8.

6. John L. Comaroff and Jean Comaroff, "Law and Disorder in the Postcolony: An Introduction," in *Law and Order in the Postcolony*, ed. Jean Comaroff and John L. Comaroff (Chicago: University of Chicago Press, 2006), 3.

7. "Foreign support" is built into the Indian Army's official definition of an insurgency. See the discussion in Chapter 5 and note 70 of that chapter.

8. Quoted in Supreme Court of India, *Extra Judicial Execution Victim Families*, 8.

9. Michael Biggs, "When Costs Are Beneficial: Protest as Communicative Suffering," *Sociology Working Papers*, no. 2003–4 (Oxford: University of Oxford, Dept. of Sociology, 2003).

10. See Doug McAdam, Sidney Tarrow, and Charles Tilly, *Dynamics of Contention* (Cambridge: Cambridge University Press, 2001), 6.

11. Lokendra Arambam, "Narratives of Self-Determination Struggles in Manipur," in *Self-Determination Movement in Manipur*, ed. Aheibam Koireng Singh, Shukhdeba Sharma Hanjabam, and Homen Thangjam (New Delhi: Concept, 2015), 90–95, 119–23.

12. Purba Das, "Casteless, Raceless India: Constitutive Discourses of National Integration," *Journal of International and Intercultural Communication* 6, no. 3 (August 2013): 221–40.

13. Vilar is quoted in Peter Sahlins, "State Formation and National Identity in the Catalan Borderland During the Eighteenth and Nineteenth Centuries," in *Border Identities: Nation and State at International Frontiers*, ed. Thomas M. Wilson and Hastings Donnan (Cambridge: Cambridge University Press, 1998), 31. Vilar said this with Catalonia and Spain in mind.

14. Mrinal Miri, "Nation, Diversity and Education," *Man and Society* 7 (Winter 2010): 3–4.

15. See, e.g., Atul Kumar Burman, "Biyar Emahor Dinai Xenai Karhisil Pradipor Soku: Dongorir Xopto Swahid Kandor Bisar" (The army gouged out Pradip's eyes exactly a month after his wedding day: Legal probe into the killings of the Five Martyrs of Dangori), *Amar Axom*, Oct. 16, 2018.

16. Arunabh Saikia, "This Assam Town Hasn't Forgotten How the Army Took Away Five Civilians and Killed Them in 1994," Scroll.in, Oct. 19, 2018, https://scroll.in/article/898739/this-assam-town-hasnt-forgotten-how-the-army-took-away-five-civilians-and-killed-them-in-1994.

17. These discussions took place in a number of Assamese newspapers, notably the weekly *Budhbar*, edited by Parag Kumar Das.

18. See my brief discussion of Das in Chapter 5.

19. For an analysis of some of his ideas, see "Parag Das: The Ideologue," in Nani Gopal Mahanta, *Confronting the State: ULFA's Quest for Sovereignty* (New Delhi: Sage India, 2013), 110–39; and Rakhee Kalita, "Writing Terror: Men of Rebellion and Contemporary Assamese Literature," in *Beyond Counterinsurgency: Breaking the Impasse in Northeast India*, ed. Sanjib Baruah (New Delhi: Oxford University Press, 2009), 117–23.

20. There are exceptions, of course, and not surprisingly, they are found in works by scholars familiar with local literary and intellectual life. See, e.g., Amit R. Baishya, *Contemporary Literature from Northeast India: Deathworlds, Terror and Survival* (New York: Routledge, 2019); and Samir Kumar Das, *India's Northeast and the Cultural Historiography of Difference*, NEISP Occasional Paper Series, New Delhi: North East India Studies Programme, Jawaharlal Nehru University, 2016.

21. Wole Soyinka, *You Must Set Forth at Dawn: A Memoir* (New York: Random House, 2007), 112.

22. Bruno Latour, "From Realpolitik to Dingpolitik—An Introduction to Making Things Public," in *Making Things Public: Atmospheres of Democracy*, ed. Bruno Latour and Peter Weibel (Cambridge, MA: MIT Press, 2005), 14.

23. In 2016 the crime rate in Assam in the category of kidnappings and abductions was 18.8 per thousand persons—the highest among all Indian states. See Pankaj Sarma, "Assam Tops All States in Violent Crime," *The Telegraph*, July 22, 2018. This figure was

also cited in a report of the parliamentary standing committee on home affairs, headed by former home minister P. Chidambaram in July of 2018. It makes a connection between this piece of data and the Indian state machinery's peculiar response to Ulfa.

24. Václav Havel, "Letter to Gustav Husak, General Secretary of the Czechoslovak Communist Party," in *Václav Havel or Living in Truth*, ed. Jan Vladislav (London: Faber and Faber, 1989), 34.

25. Havel, 34.

26. I borrow the title for this section from the Occupy movement in the United States. It was one of the key slogans of the protesters.

27. Jelle J. P. Wouters, "Polythetic Democracy: Tribal Elections, Bogus Votes, and Political Imagination in the Naga Uplands of Northeast India," *HAU: Journal of Ethnographic Theory* 5, no. 2 (Autumn 2015): 122. Prior to an election, voter slips are issued and distributed to all enrolled voters by the District Administration. They serve as an identification document for the purpose of voting.

28. Wouters, 122–23.

29. "One Man, One Vote: CEO Warns of Action Against Proxy Voters," *Nagaland Post*, Feb. 22, 2018.

30. Arunabh Saikia, "Did Nagaland's Voter Turnout Fall Because of Campaign to Curb Proxy Voting?" Scroll.in, March 1, 2018.

31. "Proxy Dhama-Dham!" *Morung Express*, Feb. 27, 2018.

32. The ironic expression "the good little democrat's handbook" is Alain Badiou's; cited in Wouters, "Polythetic Democracy," 126.

33. Wouters, "Polythetic Democracy," 132.

34. An earlier version of this analysis appears in my response to a question from Kanchan Chandra. See Sanjib Baruah, "AFSPA: The Darker Side of Indian Democracy," *Seminar*, no. 693, May 2017, 75–76.

35. Ritesh K. Srivastava, "'Iron Lady' Irom Chanu Sharmila Ends Epic Fast Against AFSPA, Aspires to Be Manipur CM," *Zee News*, August 9, 2016, http://zeenews.india .com/news/india/iron-lady-irom-chanu-sharmila-ends-epic-fast-against-afspa-aspires -to-be-manipur-cm_1916651.html.

36. "With Just 90 Votes, Irom Sharmila's Struggle Against AFSPA Reaches Dead End," *Deccan Chronicle*, March 13, 2017.

37. Yengkhom Jilangamba, "Sharmila and the Forgotten Genealogy of Violence in Manipur," *Economic and Political Weekly* 51, no. 36 (Sept. 3, 2016): 17.

38. Jilangamba, 18.

39. Wouters, "Polythetic Democracy," 132.

40. David Scott, "Norms of Self-Determination: Thinking Sovereignty Through," *Middle East Law and Governance* 4, nos. 2 & 3 (May 2012): 201.

41. John D. Kelly and Martha Kaplan, "Nation & Decolonization: Toward a New Anthropology of Nationalism," *Anthropological Theory* 1, no. 4 (2001): 419.

42. James Tully, "Rethinking Human Rights and Enlightenment: A View from the Twenty-First Century," in *Self-Evident Truths? Human Rights and the Enlightenment*, ed. Kate Tunstall (New York: Bloomsbury, 2012), 15.

43. Hans Kelsen, *The Law of the United Nations: A Critical Analysis of Its Fundamental Problems* (London: Stevens and Sons, 1950), 555.

44. Tully, "Rethinking Human Rights."

45. This was the case of the Anglophone territories of Cameroon, for example. The contemporary crisis in that region can be traced back to the contested nature of its decolonization. A United Nations supervised plebiscite in 1961 gave the Trust Territories under British administration the option of joining either a future independent Federation of Nigeria (predecessor to contemporary Nigeria) or the Republic of Cameroon.

46. James Tully, "On Law, Democracy and Imperialism," in *Public Philosophy in a New Key*, vol. 2, *Imperialism and Civic Freedom* (Cambridge: Cambridge University Press, 2009), 139.

47. Rajeev Bhargava, "Should Indian Federalism Be Called Multinational?" in *Multinational Federalism: Problems and Prospects*, ed. Michel Seymour and Alain-G. Gagnon (Houndmills, Basingstoke: Palgrave Macmillan, 2012), 245–75.

48. Sankaran Krishna, "Cartographic Anxiety: Mapping the Body Politic in India," *Alternatives* 19, no. 4 (Fall 1994): 509.

49. William A. Callahan, "The Cartography of National Humiliation and the Emergence of China's Geobody," *Public Culture* 21, no. 1 (2009): 141–73.

50. Aditya Nigam, "Empire, Nation and Minority Cultures: The Postnational Moment," *Economic and Political Weekly* 44, no. 10 (March 7, 2009): 61.

51. Rogers Brubaker, "In the Name of the Nation: Reflections on Nationalism and Patriotism," *Citizenship Studies* 8, no. 2 (June 2004): 117.

52. Frederick Cooper, "*Development, Modernization, and the Social Sciences in the Era of Decolonization: The Examples of British and French Africa,*" in *The Ends of European Colonial Empires: Cases and Comparisons*, ed. Miguel Bandeira Jerónimo and António Costa Pinto (New York: Palgrave Macmillan, 2015), 41–42.

53. James Ferguson, "Decomposing Modernity: History and Hierarchy After Development," in *Global Shadows: Africa in the Neoliberal World Order* (Durham, NC: Duke University Press, 2006), 177, 182.

54. Cooper, "*Development, Modernization,*" 34.

55. James F. Dobbins, *Nation-Building and Counterinsurgency After Iraq* (New York: Century Foundation, 2008), 3, https://tcf.org/content/report/nationbuilding-and-counterinsurgency-after-iraq.

56. Alex Maroya, "Rethinking the Nation-State from the Frontier," *Millennium* 32, no. 2 (2003): 267–92.

57. Lauren Benton, *A Search for Sovereignty: Law and Geography in European Empires, 1400–1900* (Cambridge: Cambridge University Press, 2009).

58. Craig Calhoun, *Nationalism* (Minneapolis: University of Minnesota Press, 1998), 121.

59. Lydia Walker, "States-in-Waiting: Nationalism, Internationalism, Decolonization" (PhD diss., Harvard University, 2018).

60. See my discussion of how the region's present and future is imagined in Indian official discourse in the final section of Chapter 1.

61. "Planned development," writes Tania Murray Li, "is premised upon the improvability of 'the target group' but also posits a boundary that clearly separates those who need to be developed from those who will do the developing." Tania Murray Li, *The Will to Improve: Governmentality, Development, and the Practice of Politics* (Durham, NC: Duke University Press, 2007), 15.

62. See Fernando Coronil, "The Future in Question: History and Utopia in Latin America (1989–2010)," in *Business as Usual: The Roots of the Global Financial Meltdown*, ed. Craig Calhoun and Georgi Derluguian (New York: New York University Press, 2011), 231–92; and Ferguson, "Decomposing Modernity," 178.

63. See Ferguson, "Decomposing Modernity," 187.

64. Cf. Nancy Fraser, "Social Justice in the Age of Identity Politics: Redistribution, Recognition, and Participation," in *Redistribution or Recognition? A Political-Philosophical Exchange*, ed. Nancy Fraser and Axel Honneth (London: Verso, 2003), 7–109.

65. Wolfgang Sachs, "Preface to the New Edition," *The Development Dictionary: A Guide to Knowledge as Power*, ed. Wolfgang Sachs (London: Zed, 2010), viii.

66. Fernando Coronil, "The Future in Question," 246.

67. I borrow the phrase from Guillermo O'Donnell, "Why the Rule of Law Matters," *Journal of Democracy* 15, no. 4 (Oct. 2004): 42.

68. Amartya Sen, "Democracy as a Universal Value," *Journal of Democracy* 10, no. 3 (1999): 5.

69. Stein Rokkan, *Citizens, Elections, Parties: Approaches to the Comparative Study of the Processes of Development* (New York: David McKay, 1970), 49.

70. There were, of course, exceptions. Among pioneers in this critical tradition were Guillermo O'Donnell and Rajni Kothari. See Daniel Brinks, Marcelo Leiras, and Scott Mainwaring, *Reflections on Uneven Democracies: The Legacy of Guillermo O'Donnell* (Baltimore: Johns Hopkins University Press, 2014); and Rajni Kothari, *Rethinking Democracy* (Hyderabad: Orient Longman, 2005).

71. For a discussion of subnational authoritarian regimes in democratic countries, see Edward L. Gibson, *Boundary Control: Subnational Authoritarianism in Federal Democracies* (New York: Cambridge University Press, 2012).

72. John Keane, "Humble Democracy? On the Need for New Thinking About an Aging Ideal," in *Iraq, Democracy and the Future of the Muslim World*, ed. Ali Paya and John L. Esposito (New York: Routledge, 2011), 98.

73. Adrian Little, "Theories of Democracy and Violence: The Case of Northern Ireland," *Theoria*, no. 111 (Dec. 2006): 70–73.

74. See Keane, "Humble Democracy? 98.

75. Engin F. Isin, "Theorizing Acts of Citizenship," in *Acts of Citizenship*, ed. Engin F. Isin and Greg M. Nielsen (London: Zed, 2008), 15–43.

76. Engin F. Isin, "Claiming European Citizenship," in *Enacting European Citizenship*, ed. Engin F. Isin and Michael Saward (Cambridge: Cambridge University Press, 2013), 41–43.

77. James Holston and Arjun Appadurai, "Cities and Citizenship," *Public Culture* 8, no. 2 (1996): 187.

78. Isin, "Claiming European Citizenship," 40.

79. Holston and Appadurai, "Cities and Citizenship," 87–88.

80. Engin F. Isin and Myer Siemiatycki, *Fate and Faith: Claiming Urban Citizenship in Immigrant Toronto* (Toronto: Joint Centre of Excellence for Research on Immigration and Settlement, 1999), 6.

81. Isin, "Claiming European Citizenship," 41–43.

82. See Kevin Duong, "The People as a Natural Disaster: Redemptive Violence in Jacobin Political Thought," *American Political Science Review* 111, no. 4 (2017): 798.

83. Mahmood Mamdani, "Making Sense of Political Violence in Postcolonial Africa," in *Fighting Identities: Race, Religion and Ethno-nationalism*, ed. Leo Panitch and Colin Leys (London: Merlin, 2003), 144–45.

84. Mamdani, 148–49.

85. Seyla Benhabib, "Strange Multiplicities: The Politics of Identity and Difference in a Global Context," *Macalester International* 4, article 8 (Spring 1997): 31.

86. As an alternative to ethnic homelands, I once suggested a model of multilevel citizenship. See my "Citizens and Denizens: Ethnic Homelands and the Crisis of Displacement in Northeast India," *Journal of Refugee Studies* 16, no. 1 (March 2003): 44–66. It is also published as Chapter 9 of my *Durable Disorder: Understanding the Politics of Northeast India* (New Delhi: Oxford University Press, 2005), 183–208.

87. Lloyd I. Rudolph and Susanne Hoeber Rudolph, "Federalism as State Formation in India: A Theory of Shared and Negotiated Sovereignty," *International Political Science Review* 31, no. 5 (2010): 557.

88. Ravindra Kumar, "India: A 'Nation-State' or 'Civilisation State'?" *South Asia* 25, no. 2 (2002): 13–32.

89. Rudolph and Rudolph, "Federalism as State Formation," 566.

90. See Holston and Appadurai, "Cities and Citizenship," 187–88.

# SELECTED BIBLIOGRAPHY

Agrawal, Ankush, and Vikas Kumar. "Cartographic Conflicts Within a Union: Finding Land for Nagaland in India." *Political Geography* 61 (Nov. 2017): 123–47.

Ahmad, Z. A. *Excluded Areas Under the New Constitution. Congress Political and Economic Studies*, no. 4. Allahabad, India: Political and Economic Department of the All-India Congress Committee, 1937. https://archive.org/stream/excludedareas035320mbp/exclude dareas035320mbp_djvu.txt.

Ahmed, Shakil. "Muslims Forced to Live in the Shadow of Partition Policy." *Milli Gazette*, August 5, 2005. www.milligazette.com/dailyupdate/2005/20050805a.htm.

Akoijam, Sunita. "Feeling Nepali: A Manipuri in Kathmandu." *Himal Southasian* 24, no. 8 (August 2011): 56–57.

Amaya-Castro, Juan M. "Illegality Regimes and the Ongoing Transformation of Contemporary Citizenship." *European Journal of Legal Studies* 4, no. 2 (2011): 137–61.

Amrith, Sunil. "Struggles for Citizenship around the Bay of Bengal." In Prakash, Laffan, and Menon, *The Postcolonial Moment*, 107–20.

Anderson, Benedict. "The New World Disorder." *New Left Review*, no. 193 (May-June 1992): 3–13.

Anderson, Perry. *The Indian Ideology*. 2nd enl. ed. Gurgaon, Haryana: Three Essays Collective, 2015.

Appadurai, Arjun. *Fear of Small Numbers: An Essay on the Geography of Anger*. Durham, NC: Duke University Press, 2006.

———. "Grassroots Globalization and the Research Imagination." *Public Culture* 12, no. 1 (Winter 2000): 1–19.

———. "Hope and Democracy." *Public Culture* 19, no. 1 (Winter 2007): 29–34.

———. "Putting Hierarchy in Its Place." *Cultural Anthropology* 3, no. 1 (1988): 36–49.

Arambam, Lokendra. "Narratives of Self-Determination Struggles in Manipur." In Singh, Hanjabam, and Thangjam, *Self-Determination Movement in Manipur*, 83–125.

Arambam, Lokendra, Homen Thangjam, and Shukhdeba Sharma Hanjabam, eds. *Our Common Crisis: What Are We to Do?* Arambam Somorendra Memorial Lectures. Imphal, Manipur: Ashangba Communication, 2016.

*Arunachal Pradesh Human Development Report 2005*. Itanagar: Department of Planning, Government of Arunachal Pradesh, 2006.

Asom Jagriti. "Indian Citizens Versus Foreign Nationals." Memorandum submitted to Prime Minister Indira Gandhi by Ajit Kumar Sharma and Others. Guwahati: Asom Jagriti, 1980.

Athul, M. A. "Northeast: Criminal Nexus." *South Asia Intelligence Review* 17, no. 12 (Sept. 17, 2018): https://www.satp.org/south-asia-intelligence-review-Volume-17-No-12# assessment1.

———. "Tripura: Destabilizing Gambit." *South Asia Intelligence Review* 17, no. 32 (Feb. 4, 2019): https://www.satp.org/south-asia-intelligence-review-Volume-17-No-32# assessment1.

Bagchi, Suvojit. "The Spectre of Eviction That Haunts Assam's Bengali Muslims." *The Hindu*, March 25, 2017.

Baishya, Amit R. *Contemporary Literature from Northeast India: Deathworlds, Terror and Survival.* New York: Routledge, 2019.

Bansal, Samarth. "North-Eastern Flourish at the Ballot." *The Hindu*, April 14, 2016. www .thehindu.com/news/national/northeastern-flourish-at-the-ballot/article8472975.ece.

Barbora, Sanjay. "Introduction: Remembrance, Recounting and Resistance." In *Garrisoned Minds: Women and Armed Conflict in South Asia*, edited by Laxmi Murthy and Mitu Varma, 213–30. New Delhi: Speaking Tiger, 2016.

———. "Road to Resentment: Impunity and Its Impacts on Notions of Community in Assam." In Hoenig and Singh, *Landscapes of Fear*, 110–27.

Bargu, Banu. "Sovereignty as Erasure: Rethinking Enforced Disappearances." *Qui Parle* 23, no. 1 (Fall/Winter 2014): 35–75.

Barker, George M. *Tea Planter's Life in Assam.* Calcutta: Thacker, Spink, 1884.

Barooah, Nirode K. *Gopinath Bardoloi, Indian Constitution, and Centre-Assam Relations, 1940–1950.* Guwahati: Publication Board Assam, 1990.

Barthel, Diane. *Historic Preservation: Collective Memory and Historical Identity.* New Brunswick, NJ: Rutgers University Press, 1996.

Baruah, Sanjib. "AFSPA: The Darker Side of Indian Democracy." *Seminar*, no. 693, May 2017, 70–76.

———. "Assam: Confronting a Failed Partition." *Seminar*, no. 591, Nov. 2008. www.india -seminar.com/2008/591/591_sanjib_baruah.htm.

———, ed. *Beyond Counterinsurgency: Breaking the Impasse in Northeast India.* New Delhi: Oxford University Press, 2009.

———. "Citizens and Denizens: Ethnic Homelands and the Crisis of Displacement in Northeast India." *Journal of Refugee Studies* 16, no. 1 (March 2003): 44–66.

———. "Confronting Constructionism: Ending India's Naga War." *Journal of Peace Research* 40, no. 3 (May 2003): 321–38.

———. *Durable Disorder: Understanding the Politics of Northeast India.* New Delhi: Oxford University Press, 2005.

———. "Generals as Governors: The Parallel Political Systems of Northeast India." *Himal Southasian*, June 2001, 10–20.

———. *India Against Itself: Assam and the Politics of Nationality.* Philadelphia: University of Pennsylvania Press, 1999.

———. "The *Mongolian Fringe*." *Himal Southasian* 26, no. 1 (Jan. 14, 2013): 82–86.

———. "Nationalizing Space: Cosmetic Federalism and the Politics of Development in Northeast India." *Development and Change* 34, no. 5 (Nov. 2003): 915–39.

————. "A New Politics of Race: India and Its Northeast." *India International Centre Quarterly* 32, nos. 2 & 3 (Monsoon-Winter 2005): 165–76. Reprinted in *The Other Side of Terror: An Anthology of Writings on Terrorism in South Asia*, edited by Nivedita Majumdar, 223–35. New Delhi: Oxford University Press, 2012.

————. "Partition and the Politics of Citizenship in Assam." In *Partition: The Long Shadow*, edited by Urvashi Butalia, 75–98. Delhi: Zubaan, 2015.

————. "Partition's Long Shadow: The Ambiguities of Citizenship in Assam, India." *Citizenship Studies* 13, no. 6 (Dec. 2009): 593–606.

————. "Politics of Territoriality: Indigeneity, Itinerancy and Rights in North-East India." In *Territorial Changes and Territorial Restructurings in the Himalayas*, edited by Joëlle Smadja, 69–83. Delhi: Adroit, 2013.

————. *Postfrontier Blues: Toward a New Policy Framework for Northeast India.* Washington, DC: East-West Center, 2007. www.eastwestcenter.org/publications/postfrontier-blues -toward-new-policy-framework-northeast-india.

————. "Rise and Decline of a Separatist Insurgency: Contentious Politics in Assam, India." In *Autonomy and Ethnic Conflict in South and South-East Asia*, edited by Rajat Ganguly, 27–45. London: Routledge, 2012.

————. "Routine Emergencies: India's Armed Forces Special Powers Act." In *Civil Wars in South Asia: State, Sovereignty, Development*, edited by Aparna Sundar and Nandini Sundar, 189–211. New Delhi: Sage, 2014.

————. "Separatist Militants and Contentious Politics in Assam: The Limits of Counter-Insurgency." *Asian Survey* 49, no. 6 (Nov.-Dec. 2009): 951–74.

————. "The State and Separatist Militancy in Assam: Winning a Battle and Losing the War?" *Asian Survey* 34, no. 10 (Oct. 1994): 863–77.

————. "Territoriality, Indigeneity and Rights in the North-East India." *Economic and Political Weekly* 43, nos. 12 & 13 (March 22, 2008): 15–19.

————. "Upending ULFA." *Himal Southasian* 24, no. 10–11 (Oct.-Nov. 2011): 18–20.

————. "Whose River Is It Anyway? The Political Economy of Hydropower in the Eastern Himalayas." *Economic and Political Weekly* 47, no. 29 (July 21, 2012): 41–52.

Baud, Michiel, and Willem van Schendel. "Toward a Comparative History of Borderlands." *Journal of World History* 8, no. 2 (Fall 1997): 211–42.

Benbabaali, Dalel. "Questioning the Role of the Indian Administrative Service in National Integration." *South Asia Multidisciplinary Academic Journal* (Sept. 5, 2008). https://journals.openedition.org/samaj/633.

Benhabib, Seyla. "Strange Multiplicities: The Politics of Identity and Difference in a Global Context." *Macalester International* 4, article 8 (Spring 1997): 27–56.

Benton, Lauren. *A Search for Sovereignty: Law and Geography in European Empires, 1400–1900.* Cambridge: Cambridge University Press, 2009.

Beugrand, Claire. "Deconstructing Minorities/Majorities in Parliamentary Gulf States (Kuwait and Bahrain)." *British Journal of Middle Eastern Studies* 43, no. 2 (2016): 234–49.

Bhabha, Jacqueline. "The Politics of Evidence: Roma Citizenship Deficits in Europe." In *Citizenship in Question: Evidentiary Birthright and Statelessness*, edited by Benjamin N. Lawrence and Jacqueline Stevens, 43–59. Durham, NC: Duke University Press, 2017.

Bhagawat, Mohan. "Don't Neglect Hindu Sentiments: It's the Foundation of India's Culture—Mohan Bhagawat." *Organiser*, Nov. 4, 2012.

Bhargava, Rajeev. "The Crisis of Border States in India." In *Multination States in Asia: Accommodation or Resistance*, edited by Jacques Bertrand and André Laliberté, 51–80. Cambridge: Cambridge University Press, 2010.

———. "Should Indian Federalism Be Called Multinational?" In *Multinational Federalism: Problems and Prospects*, edited by Michel Seymour and Alain-G. Gagnon, 245–75. Houndmills, Basingstoke: Palgrave Macmillan, 2012.

Bhat, Mohsin Alam. "On the NRC, Even the Supreme Court Is Helpless." *The Wire*, Jan. 7, 2019. https://thewire.in/law/nrc-supreme-court-crisis.

Bhattacharjee, Kishalay. *Blood on My Hands: Confessions of Staged Encounters*. New Delhi: Harper Collins India, 2015.

Bhattacharjee, Nabanipa. "'We Are with Culture but Without Geography': Locating Sylheti Identity in Contemporary India." *South Asian History and Culture* 3, no. 2 (April 2012): 215–35.

Bhaumik, Subir. "Repeal AFSPA in India." Southasian Monitor.com, May 8, 2017. https://southasianmonitor.com/2017/05/08/repeal-afspa-india.

Bhonsle, Anubha. *Mother, Where's My Country? Looking for Light in the Darkness of Manipur*. Delhi: Speaking Tiger, 2016.

Biggs, Michael. "When Costs Are Beneficial: Protest as Communicative Suffering." *Sociology Working Papers*, no. 2003–4. Oxford: University of Oxford, Dept. of Sociology, 2003.

Bowen, John R. "Should We Have a Universal Concept of 'Indigenous Peoples' Rights'? Ethnicity and Essentialism in the Twenty-First Century." *Anthropology Today* 16, no. 4 (August 2000): 12–16.

Brake, Jeffrey D. "Terrorism and the Military's Role in Domestic Crisis Management: Background and Issues for Congress." *CRS Report for Congress*. Washington, DC: Congressional Research Service, April 19, 2001.

Brass, Paul R. "Elite Interests, Popular Passions, and Social Power in the Language Politics of India." In *Ethnonationalism in India: A Reader*, edited by Sanjib Baruah, 69–98. Delhi: Oxford University Press, 2010.

Brinks, Daniel, Marcelo Leiras, and Scott Mainwaring. *Reflections on Uneven Democracies: The Legacy of Guillermo O'Donnell*. Baltimore: Johns Hopkins University Press, 2014.

Brosius, Christiane. *India's Middle Class: New Forms of Urban Leisure, Consumption and Prosperity*. New Delhi: Routledge India, 2010.

Brown, Wendy. *Walled States, Waning Sovereignty*. New York: Zone, 2010.

Brubaker, Rogers. *Ethnicity Without Groups*. Cambridge, MA: Harvard University Press, 2004.

———. "In the Name of the Nation: Reflections on Nationalism and Patriotism." *Citizenship Studies* 8, no. 2 (June 2004): 115–27.

Brubaker, Rogers, and Frederick Cooper. "Beyond 'Identity.'" *Theory and Society* 29, no. 1 (2000): 1–47.

Burling, Robbins. "The Tibeto-Burman Languages of Northeastern India." In *The Sino-Tibetan Languages*, edited by Graham Thurgood and Randy J. LaPolla, 169–91. London: Routledge, 2003.

Burra, Arudra. "The Cobwebs of Imperial Rule." *Seminar*, no. 615, Nov. 2010, 79–83.

Buzan, Barry, Ole Wæver, and Jaap de Wilde. *Security: A New Framework for Analysis.* Boulder, CO: Lynne Tienner, 1998.

Caldwell, Lynton Keith, and Kristin Shrader-Frechette. *Policy for Land: Law and Ethics.* Lanham, MD: Rowman and Littlefield, 1993.

Calhoun, Craig. *Nationalism.* Minneapolis: University of Minnesota Press, 1998.

Callahan, William A. "The Cartography of National Humiliation and the Emergence of China's Geobody." *Public Culture* 21, no. 1 (2009): 141–73.

Callimachi, Rukmini. "'Passage from India': Rebels Fight for Christian Nation in Nagaland." *Daily Herald* (Arlington Heights, IL), Nov. 3, 2017 (originally published in 2003). www.dailyherald.com/article/20170311/news/170319735.

Carens, Joseph H. *Immigrants and the Right to Stay.* Cambridge, MA: MIT Press, 2010.

Caroe, Olaf Kirkpatrick. "India and the Mongolian Fringe." 1940. Reprinted in *The North-Eastern Frontier: A Documentary Study of the Internecine Rivalry Between India, Tibet and China.* Vol. 2, *1914–54*, edited by Parshotam Mehra, 111–24. Delhi: Oxford University Press, 1980.

Chadha, Vivek, ed. *The Armed Forces Special Powers Act: The Debate.* New Delhi: Institute for Defence Studies and Analysis and Lancer's Books, 2013.

Chakrabarty, Bidyut. *The Partition of Bengal and Assam, 1932–1947.* London: Routledge-Curzon, 2004.

Chakrabarty, Dipesh. "'In the Name of Politics': Democracy and the Power of the Multitude in India." *Public Culture* 19, no. 1 (2007): 35–57.

Chakravarti, Sudeep. *Highway 39: Journeys Through a Fractured Land.* New Delhi: Fourth Estate, 2012.

Chakravarty, Ipsita. "At Camp Hebron, an Ambitious Project Is Under Way: A Peace Accord to Settle the Naga Question." Scroll.in, Dec. 4, 2015. https://scroll.in/article/769840/at-camp-hebron-an-ambitious-project-is-under-way-a-peace-accord-to-settle-the-naga-question.

———. "How the Fear of Migrants Became the Driving Force of Politics in Assam." Scroll.in, Feb. 19, 2016. https://scroll.in/article/802983/from-votebank-to-spectre-how-political-parties-imagine-the-outsider-in-assam.

Chatterjee, Partha. "Development Planning and the Indian State." In *Empire and Nation: Selected Essays*, edited by Partha Chatterjee, 241–66. New York: Columbia University Press, 2010.

———. "Legacy of Bandung." In *Bandung, Global History, and International Law: Critical Pasts and Pending Futures*, edited by Luis Eslava, Michael Fakhri, and Vasuki Nesiah, 657–74. Cambridge: Cambridge University Press, 2017.

———. *The Nation and Its Fragments: Colonial and Postcolonial Histories.* Princeton, NJ: Princeton University Press, 1993.

Chaudhuri, Sujit. "'A God-Sent' Opportunity?" *Seminar*, no. 510, Feb. 2002. www.india-seminar.com/2002/510/510%20sujit%20chaudhuri.htm.

Chettri, Mona. "Choosing the Gorkha: At the Crossroads of Class and Ethnicity in the Darjeeling Hills." *Asian Ethnicity* 14, no. 3 (2013): 293–308.

Choudhury, Angshuman. "Justice: Contours of the Assamese Insurgency." Hardnewsmedia
.com, July 19, 2016. www.hardnewsmedia.com/2016/07/justice-contours-assamese
-insurgency.

Choudhury, Sashadhar. "An Annotated Interview with Sashadhar Choudhury, Foreign Secretary, United Liberation Front of Asom [Assam]." Interview by Rajeev Bhattacharyya
and Nikhil Raymond Puri, *Perspectives on Terrorism* 7, no. 2 (2013). www.terrorismanalysts
.com/pt/index.php/pot/article/view/257/html.

Civil Society Coalition on Human Rights in Manipur and the UN. "Manipur: A Memorandum on Extrajudicial, Arbitrary or Summary Executions Submitted to Christof
Heyns, Special Rapporteur on Extrajudicial, Arbitrary or Summary Executions." Guwahati, India, March 28, 2012.

Cline, Lawrence E. "The Insurgency Environment in Northeast India." *Small Wars &*
*Insurgencies* 17, no. 2 (June 2006): 126–47.

Clow, Andrew G. "The Future Government of the Assam Tribal Peoples." 1945. In Syiemlieh, *On the Edge of Empire*, 139–227.

Cochrane, Feargal. *Northern Ireland: The Reluctant Peace*. New Haven, CT: Yale University
Press, 2013.

Comaroff, John L., and Jean Comaroff. "Law and Disorder in the Postcolony: An Introduction." In *Law and Order in the Postcolony*, edited by Jean Comaroff and John L.
Comaroff, 1–56. Chicago: University of Chicago Press, 2006.

Cooper, Frederick. "Development, Modernization, and the Social Sciences in the Era of
Decolonization: The Examples of British and French Africa." In *The Ends of European*
*Colonial Empires: Cases and Comparisons*, edited by Miguel Bandeira Jerónimo and An-
tónio Costa Pinto, 15–50. New York: Palgrave Macmillan, 2015.

Copeman, Jacob, and Aya Ikegame. "The Multifarious Guru: An Introduction." In *The*
*Guru in South Asia: New Interdisciplinary Perspectives*, edited by Jacob Copeman and
Aya Ikegame, 1–45. New York: Routledge, 2012.

Cornwall, Andrea, and Karen Brock. "Beyond Buzzwords: 'Poverty Reduction,' 'Participation' and 'Empowerment' in Development Policy." Programme Paper no. 10. Geneva,
Switzerland, United Nations Research Institute for Social Development, 2005.

Coronil, Fernando. "The Future in Question: History and Utopia in Latin America
(1989–2010)." In *Business as Usual: The Roots of the Global Financial Meltdown*, edited
by Craig Calhoun and Georgi Derluguian, 231–92. New York: New York University
Press, 2011.

*Curse of Unregulated Coal Mining in Meghalaya: A Citizens' Report from Meghalaya*. 2 Vols.
Shillong: N.p., 2019.

Curzon, George Nathaniel. *Frontiers* (The Romanes Lecture). Oxford: Clarendon, 1907.

Das, Debojyoti. "Border Mining: State Politics, Migrant Labour and Land Relations Along
the India-Bangladesh Borderlands." In *The Coal Nation: Histories, Ecologies and Politics of*
*Coal in India*, edited by Kuntala Lahiri-Dutt, 79–104. Burlington, VT: Ashgate, 2014.

———. *Cultural Politics, Identity Crisis and Private Capitalism in Coal Mines of Meghalaya,*
*Northeast India*. Case study no. 16. Artisanal and Small-Scale Mining in Asia-Pacific

Case Study Series. Canberra: Australian National University (Crawford School of Public Policy), 2007.

Das, Madhumita. "The Territorial Question in the Naga National Movement." *South Asian Survey* 20, no. 1 (March 2013): 22–43.

Das, Purba. "Casteless, Raceless India: Constitutive Discourses of National Integration." *Journal of International and Intercultural Communication* 6, no. 3 (August 2013): 221–40.

Das, Samir Kumar. *India's Northeast and the Cultural Historiography of Difference.* NEISP Occasional Paper Series. New Delhi: North East India Studies Programme, Jawaharlal Nehru University, 2016.

Dasgupta, Anindita. "Denial and Resistance, Sylheti Partition 'Refugees' in Assam." *Contemporary South Asia* 10, no. 3 (2001): 343–60.

———. "Remembering Sylhet: A Forgotten Story of India's 1947 Partition." *Economic and Political Weekly* 43, no. 31 (August 2, 2008): 18–22.

Davis, Diane E. "Non-state Armed Actors, New Imagined Communities, and Shifting Patterns of Sovereignty and Insecurity in the Modern World." *Contemporary Security Policy* 30, no. 2 (2009): 221–45.

———. "Violence and Insecurity: The Challenge in the Global South." MIT Center for International Studies. Audits of the Conventional Wisdom, Nov. 1, 2006, https://cis .mit.edu/sites/default/files/documents/Davis1106Audit.pdf.

Deb, Siddhartha. *The Point of Return.* New York: HarperCollins, 2004.

Debbarma, R. K. "Where to Be Left Is No Longer Dissidence: A Reading of Left Politics in Tripura." *Economic and Political Weekly* 52, no. 21 (May 27, 2017): 18–21.

Delhi Solidarity Group. "Recent Militant Violence Against Adivasis in Assam: Report of a Fact Finding Report, 10–12 January 2015." New Delhi: Delhi Forum, 2015.

de Waal, Alex. "Counter-Insurgency on the Cheap." *London Review of Books* 26, no. 15 (August 5, 2004): 25–27.

———. "Violence and Peacemaking in the Political Marketplace." *Accord: An International Review of Peace Initiatives,* no. 25 (London: Conciliation Resources, 2014): 17–20. www.c-r .org/accord/legitimacy-and-peace-processes/violence-and-peacemaking-political -marketplace.

Dobbins, James F. *Nation-Building and Counterinsurgency After Iraq.* New York: Century Foundation, 2008. https://tcf.org/content/report/nationbuilding-and-counterinsurgency -after-iraq.

Drennan, Vasundhara Sirnate. "The Naga Conflict: Can an Accord End an Insurgency?" Hindu Centre for Politics and Public Policy, August 7, 2015. www.thehinducentre.com /the-arena/current-issues/article7511878.ece.

Duara, Prasenjit. "Historicizing National Identity, or Who Imagines What and When." In Eley and Suny, *Becoming National,* 151–77.

Duffield, Mark. "Development, Territories, and People: Consolidating the External Sovereign Frontier." *Alternatives: Global, Local, Political* 32, no. 2 (April–June 2007): 225–46.

Duong, Kevin. "The People as a Natural Disaster: Redemptive Violence in Jacobin Political Thought." *American Political Science Review* 111, no. 4 (2017): 786–800.

Dutta Pathak, Moushumi. *You Do Not Belong Here: Partition Diaspora in the Brahmaputra Valley.* Chennai: Notion, 2017.

Easterly, William. "The Cartel of Good Intentions: The Problem of Bureaucracy in Foreign Aid Work." *Journal of Economic Policy Reform* 5, no. 4 (2002): 223–50.

Eaton, Richard M. *The Rise of Islam and the Bengal Frontier: 1204–1760.* Berkeley: University of California Press, 1996.

Eck, Diane L. *India: A Sacred Geography.* New York: Harmony, 2012.

"Elephants, Exploration and Engineering." *Middle East Reservoir Review*, no. 1 (Jan. 1, 2000): www.slb.com/~/media/Files/resources/mearr/num1/exploration.pdf.

Eley, Geoff, and Ronald Grigor Suny, eds. *Becoming National: A Reader.* New York: Oxford University Press, 1999.

———. "Introduction: From the Moment of Social History to the Work of Cultural Representation." In Eley and Suny, *Becoming National*, 3–38.

Ete, Mibi. "Hydro-Dollar Dreams: Emergent Local Politics of Large Dams and Small Communities." In *Geographies of Difference: Explorations in Northeast Indian Studies*, edited by Mélanie Vandenhelsken, Meenaxi Barkataki-Ruscheweyh, and Bengt G. Karlsson, 109–27. London: Routledge, 2018.

Ferguson, James. "Decomposing Modernity: History and Hierarchy After Development." In *Global Shadows*, 176–93.

———. *Give a Man a Fish: Reflections on the New Politics of Distribution.* Durham, NC: Duke University Press, 2015.

———. *Global Shadows: Africa in the Neoliberal World Order.* Durham, NC: Duke University Press, 2006.

———. "Of Mimicry and Membership: Africans and the 'New World Society.'" *Cultural Anthropology* 17, no. 4 (2002): 551–69.

Fidler, David P. "The Indian Doctrine for Sub-conventional Operations: Reflections from a U.S. Counterinsurgency Perspective." In *India and Counterinsurgency: Lessons Learned*, edited by Sumit Ganguly and David P. Fidler, 207–24. New York: Routledge, 2009.

Fraser, Nancy. "Social Justice in the Age of Identity Politics: Redistribution, Recognition, and Participation." In *Redistribution or Recognition? A Political-Philosophical Exchange*, edited by Nancy Fraser and Axel Honneth, 7–109. London: Verso, 2003.

Friedman, John. "Borders, Margins, and Frontiers: Myths and Metaphor." In *Frontiers in Regional Development*, edited by Yehuda Gradus and Harvey Lithwick, 1–20. Lanham, MD: Rowman and Littlefield, 1996.

Gellner, Ernest. *Nations and Nationalism.* Ithaca, NY: Cornell University Press, 1983.

Gerth, H. H., and C. Wright Mills, eds. *From Max Weber: Essays in Sociology.* New York: Oxford University Press, 1958.

Ghosh, Amitav. "The Global Reservation: Notes Toward an Ethnography of International Peacekeeping." *Cultural Anthropology* 9, no. 3 (August 1994): 412–22.

Gibson, Edward L. *Boundary Control: Subnational Authoritarianism in Federal Democracies.* New York: Cambridge University Press, 2012.

Gibson, James L. "Enigmas of Intolerance: Fifty Years After Stouffer's *Communism, Conformity, and Civil Liberties.*" *Perspectives on Politics* 4, no. 1 (March 2006): 21–34.

Gilroy, Paul. *"There Ain't No Black in the Union Jack": The Cultural Politics of Race and Nation.* London: Hutchinson, 1987.

Gohain, Hiren. "Chronicles of Violence and Terror: Rise of the United Liberation Front of Assam." *Economic and Political Weekly* 42, no. 12 (March 24, 2007): 1012–18.

———. "Violent Borders: Killings in Nagaland-Assam." *Economic and Political Weekly* 42, no. 32 (August 11, 2007): 3280–83.

Government of India. *Annual Report 2008–09 of the Union Ministry of Home Affairs, Government of India.* New Delhi: Ministry of Home Affairs, 2009. www.satp.org/satporgtp /countries/india/document/papers/annualreport_2008-09.htm.

———. "The Armed Forces (Special Powers) Act, 1958." www.satp.org/satporgtp/countries /india/document/actandordinances/armed_forces_special_power_act_1958.htm.

———. Census, 1931. *Assam Part I: Report* (by C. S. Mullan). Shillong: Assam Government Press, 1932. Reprint (Delhi: Manohar, 1992).

———. Census, 2011. Ministry of Home Affairs. Office of the Registrar General and Census Commissioner. www.censusindia.gov.in/2011census.

———. *Fifth Report: Public Order.* Second Administrative Reforms Commission, June 2007.

———. *Indian Army Doctrine.* Part 1. Shimla: Headquarters Army Training Command, 2004. www.files.ethz.ch/isn/157030/India%202004.pdf.

———. "Innovative Methods in Fighting Insurgency in North-East India." https://mafiadoc .com/innovative-methods-in-fighting-insurgency-in-north-east-india-_59d2c69 21723dd036915d52f.html.

———. Ministry of Development of North Eastern Region website. http://mdoner.gov .in.

———. National Green Tribunal at Principal Bench, New Delhi. *All Dimasa Students Union Dima Hasao Dist. Committee v. State of Meghalaya & Others.* April 17, 2014.

———. "North East Division." New Delhi: Ministry of Home Affairs. http://mha.nic.in /northeast_new. Accessed Oct. 8, 2014 (site discontinued).

———. *Report of the Committee to Review the Armed Forces (Special Powers) Act, 1958.* New Delhi: Ministry of Home Affairs, 2005. http://notorture.ahrchk.net/profile/india /ArmedForcesAct1958.pdf.

———. *Report of the Committee Under the Chairmanship of Shri M.P. Bezbaruah to Look into the Concerns of the People of the Northeast Living in Other Parts of the Country.* New Delhi: Ministry of Home Affairs, 2014. https://archive.nyu.edu/handle/2451/37861.

———. States Census 2011, https://www.census2011.co.in/states.php.

Graeber, David. "Dead Zones of the Imagination: On Violence, Bureaucracy, and Interpretive Labor." *HAU: Journal of Ethnographic Theory* 2, no. 2 (2006): 105–28.

Guha, Amalendu. *Planter Raj to Swaraj: Freedom Struggle and Electoral Politics in Assam, 1826–1947.* New Delhi: People's Publishing House, 1977.

Guha, Ramachandra. *How Much Should a Person Consume? Environmentalism in India and the United States.* Berkeley: University of California Press, 2006.

Guillaume, Xavier, and Jef Huysmans. *Citizenship and Security: The Constitution of Political Being.* New York: Routledge, 2013.

———. "Introduction: Citizenship and Security." In Guillaume and Huysmans, *Citizenship and Security*, 1–17.

Gupta, O. P. "Rights of Hindu Refugees in India." *Organiser*, Oct. 27, 2012.

Gupta, Shekhar. *Assam: A Valley Divided*. Delhi: Vikas, 1984.

Guyot-Réchard, Bérénice. "Nation-Building or State-Making? India's North-East Frontier and the Ambiguities of Nehruvian Developmentalism, 1950–1959." *Contemporary South Asia* 21, no. 1 (2013): 22–37.

———. *Shadow States: India, China and the Himalayas, 1910–1962*. Cambridge: Cambridge University Press, 2017.

Gwynn, Charles W. *Imperial Policing*. London: Macmillan, 1934.

Habibullah, Wajahat. "Armed Forces Special Powers Act, Jammu & Kashmir." In Chadha, *Armed Forces Special Powers Act*, 22–30.

Hansen, Thomas Blom. "Politics as Permanent Performance: The Production of Political Authority in the Locality." In *The Politics of Cultural Mobilization in India*, edited by John Zavos, Andrew Wyatt, and Vernon Hewitt, 19–36. New Delhi: Oxford University Press, 2004.

Hansen, Thomas Blom, and Finn Stepputat. "Introduction: States of Imagination." In Hansen and Stepputat, *States of Imagination*, 1–36.

———. Introduction to *Sovereign Bodies: Citizens, Migrants, and States in the Postcolonial World*, edited by Thomas Blom Hansen and Finn Stepputat, 1–38. Princeton, NJ: Princeton University Press, 2005.

———. "Sovereignty Revisited." *Annual Review of Anthropology* 35 (2006): 295–315.

———, eds. *States of Imagination: Ethnographic Explorations of the Postcolonial State*. Durham, NC: Duke University Press, 2001.

Harootunian, H. D. "Postcoloniality's Unconscious/Area Studies' Desire." *Postcolonial Studies* 2, no. 2 (July 1999): 127–47.

Harris-White, Barbara, Deepak K. Mishra, and Vandana Upadhyay. "Institutional Diversity and Capitalist Transition: The Political Economy of Agrarian Change in Arunachal Pradesh, India." *Journal of Agrarian Change* 9, no. 4 (Oct. 2009): 512–47.

Hassan, Wail S. *Immigrant Narratives: Orientalism and Cultural Translation in Arab American and Arab British Literature*. Oxford: Oxford University Press, 2011.

Havel, Václav. "Letter to Gustav Husak, General Secretary of the Czechoslovak Communist Party." In *Václav Havel or Living in Truth*, edited by Jan Vladislav, 3–35. London: Faber and Faber, 1989.

———. "Politics and Conscience." In *Václav Havel or Living in Truth*, edited by Jan Vladislav, 136–57. London: Faber and Faber, 1989.

Hazarika, Sanjoy. *Strangers No More: New Narratives from India's Northeast*. New Delhi: Aleph, 2018.

———. *Strangers of the Mist: Tales of War and Peace from India's Northeast*. New Delhi: Penguin India, 1994.

Hegde, N. Santosh, J. M. Lyngdoh, and Ajai Kumar Singh. *Report of the Supreme Court Appointed Commission*. Vol. 1, March 30, 2013, New Delhi.

Hindess, Barry. "Divide and Rule: The International Character of Modern Citizenship." *European Journal of Social Theory* 1, no.1 (1998): 57–70.

Hirschl, Ran. "The Judicialization of Mega-politics and the Rise of Political Courts." *Annual Review of Political Science* 11 (2008): 93–118.

Hobsbawm, Eric J. *The Age of Empire: 1875–1914.* New York: Vintage, 1989.

Hoenig, Patrick, and Navsharan Singh, eds. *Landscapes of Fear: Understanding Impunity in India.* Delhi: Zubaan, 2014.

Holston, James, and Arjun Appadurai. "Cities and Citizenship." *Public Culture* 8, no. 2 (1996): 187–204.

Human Rights Watch. "Human Rights Overview, 2005." http://hrw.org/english/docs /2006/01/18/india12272.htm.

Hussain, Banajit. "The Bodoland Violence and the Politics of Explanation." *Seminar*, no. 640, Dec. 2010. www.india-seminar.com/2012/640/640_banajit_hussain.htm.

Hussain, Monirul. *The Assam Movement: Class, Ideology and Identity.* Delhi: Manak, 1983.

———. *Interrogating Development: State, Displacement and Popular Resistance in North East India.* New Delhi: Sage, 2008.

Hussain, Nasser. "Counterinsurgency's Comeback: Can a Colonialist Strategy Be Reinvented?" *Boston Review*, Jan./Feb. 2010. http://bostonreview.net/world/counter insurgency's-comeback.

———. *The Jurisprudence of Emergency: Colonialism and the Rule of Law.* Ann Arbor: University of Michigan Press, 2003.

Hussain, Shalim M. "Changing the Narrative: 'I Beg to State I Am Not a Bangladeshi, I Am an Assamese Asomiya!'" *The Citizen* (Delhi), May 2, 2016.

Hussain, Wasbir. "Assam: Demographic Jitters." *South Asia Intelligence Review* 3, no. 10 (Sept. 20, 2004): www.satp.org/satporgtp/sair/archives/3_10.htm.

———. "Multi-force Operations in Counter Terrorism: A View from the Assam Theatre." *Faultlines* 9 (July 2001): 39–64.

Hutt, Michael. *Unbecoming Citizens: Culture, Nationhood, and the Flight of Refugees from Bhutan.* New Delhi: Oxford University Press, 2005.

Hutton, J. H. Introduction to *The Lhota Nagas*, by James Philip Mills, xi–xxxix. London: Macmillan, 1922.

Ignatieff, Michael. *The Lesser Evil: Political Ethics in an Age of Terror.* Princeton, NJ: Princeton University Press. 2004.

Isin, Engin F. "Claiming European Citizenship." In *Enacting European Citizenship*, edited by Engin F. Isin and Michael Saward, 19–56. Cambridge: Cambridge University Press, 2013.

———. "Theorizing Acts of Citizenship." In *Acts of Citizenship*, edited by Engin F. Isin and Greg M. Nielsen, 15–43. London: Zed, 2008.

Isin, Engin F., and Myer Siemiatycki. *Fate and Faith: Claiming Urban Citizenship in Immigrant Toronto.* Toronto: Joint Centre of Excellence for Research on Immigration and Settlement, 1999.

Jackson, Robert H. *Quasi-States: Sovereignty, International Relations and the Third World.* Cambridge: Cambridge University Press, 1990.

Jacobs, Julian, with Alan Macfarlane, Sarah Harrison, and Anita Herle. *The Nagas: Hill Peoples of Northeast India: Society, Culture, and the Colonial Encounter.* 1990. London: Thames and Hudson, 2012.

Jalal, Ayesha. "South Asia." In *Encyclopedia of Nationalism: Fundamental Themes*. Vol. 1, edited by Alexander J. Motyl, 737–56. San Diego, CA: Academic Press, 2001.

Jamir, Alemtemshi. "Keynote Address." In *Dimensions of Development in Nagaland*, edited by C. Joshua Thomas and Gurudas Das, 1–8. New Delhi: Regency, 2002.

Jamwal, Anuradha Bhasin. "Politics of Human Rights Abuses." *Kashmir Times* (Srinagar), April 26, 2009.

Jensen, Steffen. "Battlefield and the Prize: The ANC's Bid to Reform the South African State." In Hansen and Stepputat, *States of Imagination*, 97–122.

Jilangamba, Yengkhom. "Sharmila and the Forgotten Genealogy of Violence in Manipur." *Economic and Political Weekly* 51, no. 36 (Sept. 3, 2016): 15–19.

Johnstone, James. *My Experiences in Manipur and the Naga Hills*. London: S. Low, Marston, 1896.

Joshi, Bhanu, Ashish Ranjan, and Neelanjan Sircar. "Understanding the Election in Assam (Part 1)." Working Papers, Centre for Policy Research, New Delhi, April 19, 2016.

Kabir, Ananya Jahanara. "Utopias Eroded and Recalled: Intellectual Legacies of East Pakistan." *South Asia* 41, no. 4 (Nov. 2018): 1–35.

Kalhan, Anil, Gerald P. Conroy, Mamta Kaushal, Sam Scott Miller, and Jed S. Rakoff. "Colonial Continuities: Human Rights, Terrorism, and Security Laws in India." *Columbia Journal of Asian Law* 2, no. 1 (2006): 93–234.

Kalir, Barak, Malini Sur, and Willem van Schendel. "Introduction: Mobile Practices and Regimes of Permissiveness." In *Transnational Flows and Permissive Polities: Ethnographies of Human Mobilities in Asia*, edited by Barak Kalir and Malini Sur, 11–25. Amsterdam: University of Amsterdam Press, 2012.

Kalita, Rakhee. "Writing Terror: Men of Rebellion and Contemporary Assamese Literature." In Baruah, *Beyond Counterinsurgency*, 101–23.

Kar, Bodhisattva. "Can the Postcolonial Begin? Deprovincializing Assam." In *Handbook of Modernity in South Asia: Modern Makeovers*, edited by Saurabh Dube, 43–58. New Delhi: Oxford University Press, 2011.

———. "The Tragedy of Suryya Bhuyan: An Essay." *Biblio* (New Delhi) 13, nos. 5 & 6 (May-June 2008): 26–27.

———. "When Was the Postcolonial? A History of Policing Impossible Lines." In Baruah, *Beyond Counterinsurgency*, 49–77.

Karlsson, Bengt G. "Anthropology and the 'Indigenous Slot': Claims to and Debates About Indigenous Peoples' Status in India." *Critique of Anthropology* 23, no. 4 (Dec. 2003): 402–23.

———. *Contested Belonging: An Indigenous People's Struggle for Forest and Identity in Sub-Himalayan Bengal*. Richmond, UK: Curzon, 2000.

———. *Unruly Hills: A Political Ecology of India's Northeast*. New York: Berghahn, 2011.

Karlsson, Bengt G., and Dolly Kikon. "Wayfinding: Indigenous Migrants in the Service Sector of Metropolitan India." *South Asia* 40, no. 3 (2017): 447–62.

Kashyap, Aruni. *The House with a Thousand Stories*. New Delhi: Viking, 2013.

Kashyap, Samudra Gupta. "Beyond the 'Separate Naga Identity' Lie Similar Aspirations." *Indian Express*, August 9, 2005.

Kaviraj, Sudipta. "The Post-Colonial State: The Special Case of India." *Critical Encounters,* Jan. 19, 2009. http://criticalencounters.wordpress.com/2009/01/19/the-post-colonial-state-sudipta-kaviraj.

Keane, John. "Humble Democracy? On the Need for New Thinking About an Aging Ideal." In *Iraq, Democracy and the Future of the Muslim World,* edited by Ali Paya and John L. Esposito, 83–100. New York: Routledge, 2011.

Keivom, Lalthlamuong. "Ethnic Churning CHIKUMI Style." In Arambam, Thangjam, and Hanjabam, *Our Common Crisis,* 162–84.

Kelly, John D. "U.S. Power, After 9/11 and Before It: If Not an Empire, Then What?" *Public Culture* 15, no. 2 (Spring 2003): 347–69.

Kelly, John D., and? Martha Kaplan. "Nation & Decolonization: Toward a New Anthropology of Nationalism." *Anthropological Theory* 1, no. 4 (2001): 419–37.

Kelsen, Hans. *The Law of the United Nations: A Critical Analysis of Its Fundamental Problems.* London: Stevens and Sons, 1950.

Khangai, Ravi. "The 'Other' Women in the Mahabharata." www.academia.edu/2614172/the_other_women_in_the_mahabharata.

Khilnani, Sunil. *The Idea of India.* New York: Farrar Straus Giroux, 1997.

Khosla, Shyam. "Assam Riots Were Between Indian Citizens and Foreigners, Not Ethnic Clashes." *Organiser,* August 26, 2012.

Kikon, Dolly. "Coal Fuels Dreams of Naga Prosperity." Asian Studies Association of Australia. *Asian Currents,* Sept. 9, 2016. http://asaa.asn.au/coal-fuels-dreams-of-naga-prosperity/#.

———. "The Predicament of Justice: Fifty Years of Armed Forces Special Powers Act in India." *Contemporary South Asia* 17, no. 3 (Sept. 2009): 271–82.

———. "What Is Unique About Naga History?" *Economic and Political Weekly* 50, no. 35 (August 29, 2015): 10–13.

Kikon, Dolly, and Duncan McDuie-Ra. "English-Language Documents and Old Trucks: Creating Infrastructure in Nagaland's Coal Mining Villages." *South Asia: Journal of South Asian Studies* 40, no. 4 (2017): 772–91.

Kimura, Makiko. *The Nellie Massacre of 1983: Agency of Rioters.* New Delhi: Sage, 2013.

Kindo, Constantine, and Daniel Minj. "Territorial Dispute in the District of Golaghat, Assam." In *Conflict Mapping and Peace Processes in North East India,* edited by Lazar Jeyaseelan, 8–53. Guwahati: North Eastern Social Research Centre, 2008.

Kingsbury, Benedict. "'Indigenous Peoples' in International Law: A Constructivist Approach to the Asian Controversy." *American Journal of International Law* 92, no. 3 (July 1998): 414–57.

Kolås, Åshild. "Naga Militancy and Violent Politics in the Shadow of Ceasefire." *Journal of Peace Research* 48, no. 6 (Nov. 2011): 781–92.

Kothari, Rajni. *Rethinking Democracy.* Hyderabad: Orient Longman, 2005.

Krishna, Sankaran. "Cartographic Anxiety: Mapping the Body Politic in India." *Alternatives: Global, Local, Political* 19, no. 4 (Fall 1994): 507–21.

Kudaisya, Gyanesh. "'In Aid of Civil Power': The Colonial Army in Northern India, c. 1919–42." *Journal of Imperial and Commonwealth History* 32, no. 1 (2004): 41–68.

Kumar, Kuldeep. *Police and Counterinsurgency: The Untold Story of Tripura's COIN Campaign.* New Delhi: Sage, 2016.

Kumar, Ravindra. "India: A 'Nation-State' or 'Civilisation State'?" *South Asia* 25, no. 2 (2002): 13–32.

Lacina, Bethany. "Does Counterinsurgency Theory Apply in Northeast India?" *India Review* 6, no. 3 (2007): 165–83.

Laguerre, Michel S. *Minoritized Space: An Inquiry into the Spatial Order of Things.* Berkeley, CA: Institute of Governmental Studies Press, 1999.

Lakshman, Kanchan, and Sanjay K. Jha. "India-Bangladesh: Restoring Sovereignty on Neglected Borders." *Faultlines* 14 (July 2003): 123–58.

Lamb, Alastair. *Tibet, China & India, 1914–1950: A History of Imperial Diplomacy.* Hertingfordbury, UK: Roxford, 1989.

Larmer, Brook. "Can India's Land of Former Headhunters Make Peace?" *National Geographic,* August 26, 2015. https://news.nationalgeographic.com/2015/08/150826-nagaland-india-myanmar-headhunters-baptists.

Latour, Bruno. "From Realpolitik to Dingpolitik—An Introduction to Making Things Public." In *Making Things Public: Atmospheres of Democracy,* edited by Bruno Latour and Peter Weibel, 14–41. Cambridge, MA: MIT Press, 2005.

Lee, Yong S. *A Reasonable Public Servant: Constitutional Foundations of Administrative Conduct in the United States.* Armonk, NY: M. E. Sharpe, 2005.

Li, Tania Murray. "Beyond 'The State' and Failed Schemes." *American Anthropologist* 107, no. 3 (Sept. 2005): 383–94.

———. "Ethnic Cleansing, Recursive Knowledge, and the Dilemmas of Sedentarism." *International Journal of Social Science* 54, no. 173 (Sept. 2002): 361–71.

———. "Indigeneity, Capitalism, and the Management of Dispossession." *Current Anthropology* 51, no. 3 (June 2010): 385–414.

———. *The Will to Improve: Governmentality, Development, and the Practice of Politics.* Durham, NC: Duke University Press, 2007.

Licklider, Roy. "How Civil Wars End: Questions and Methods." In *Stopping the Killing: How Civil Wars End,* edited by Roy Licklider, 3–19. New York: New York University Press, 1995.

Lintner, Bertil. *Great Game East.* New Haven, CT: Yale University Press, 2015.

Little, Adrian. "Theories of Democracy and Violence: The Case of Northern Ireland." *Theoria,* no. 111 (Dec. 2006): 62–86.

Longkumer, Arkotong. "Exploring the Diversity of Religion: The Geo-political Dimensions of Fieldwork and Identity in the North East of India." *Fieldwork in Religion* 4, no. 1 (2009): 46–66.

———. "Moral Geographies: The Problem of Sovereignty and Indigeneity Amongst the Nagas." In *Rethinking Social Exclusion in India: Castes, Communities and the State,* edited by Minoru Mio and Abhijit Dasgupta, 147–67. New York: Routledge, 2018.

Ludden, David. "Investing in Nature Around Sylhet: An Excursion into Geographical History." *Economic and Political Weekly* 38, no. 48 (Nov. 29, 2003): 5080–88.

———. "Spatial Inequity and National Territory: Remapping 1905 in Bengal and Assam." *Modern Asian Studies* 46, no. 3 (May 2012): 483–525.

Lund, Christian. "Twilight Institutions: An Introduction." *Development and Change* 37, no. 4 (2006): 673–84.

Mahanta, Nani Gopal. *Confronting the State: ULFA's Quest for Sovereignty*. New Delhi: Sage India, 2013.

Malkki, Liisa. "Citizens of Humanity: Internationalism and the Imagined Community of Nations." *Diaspora* 3, no. 1 (Spring 1994): 41–68.

———. "National Geographic: The Rooting of Peoples and the Territorialization of National Identity Among Scholars and Refugees." *Cultural Anthropology* 7, no. 1 (Feb. 1992): 24–44.

Mall, Jagdamba. "Must Remain Armed with AFSPA." *Organiser*, May 21, 2016, 17.

Mamdani, Mahmood. "Making Sense of Political Violence in Postcolonial Africa." In *Fighting Identities: Race, Religion and Ethno-nationalism*, edited by Leo Panitch and Colin Leys, 132–51. London: Merlin, 2003.

———. "The Social Basis of Constitutionalism in Africa." *Journal of Modern African Studies* 28, no. 3 (Sept. 1990): 359–74.

———. "What Is a Tribe?" *London Review of Books* 34, no. 17 (Sept. 13, 2012): 20–22.

Maroya, Alex. "Rethinking the Nation-State from the Frontier." *Millennium* 32, no. 2 (2003): 267–92.

Mathur, Kuldeep. "The State and the Use of Coercive Power in India." *Asian Survey* 32, no. 4 (1992): 337–49.

McAdam, Doug, Sidney Tarrow, and Charles Tilly. *Dynamics of Contention*. Cambridge: Cambridge University Press, 2001.

McDuie-Ra, Duncan. *Civil Society, Democratization and the Search for Human Security*. New York: Nova Science, 2009.

———. "The Dilemmas of Pro-development Actors: Viewing State-Ethnic Minority Relations and Intra-ethnic Dynamics Through Contentious Development Projects." *Asian Ethnicity* 12, no. 1 (2011): 77–100.

———. "The 'North-East' Map of Delhi." *Economic and Political Weekly* 47, no. 30 (July 28, 2012): 69–77.

———. *Northeast Migrants in Delhi: Race, Refuge and Retail*. Amsterdam: Amsterdam University Press, 2012.

McDuie-Ra, Duncan, and Dolly Kikon. "Tribal Communities and Coal in Northeast India: The Politics of Imposing and Resisting Mining Bans." *Energy Policy* 99 (Dec. 2016): 261–69.

Mehta, Pratap Bhanu. "The Rise of Judicial Sovereignty." *Journal of Democracy* 18, no. 2 (April 2007): 70–83.

Miller, David. "Sociology, Propaganda and Psychological Operations." In *Stretching the Sociological Imagination: Essays in Honour of John Eldridge*, edited by Andrew Smith, Matt Dawson, Bridget Fowler, and David Miller, 163–88. New York: Palgrave Macmillan, 2015.

Mills, C. Wright. *The Power Elite*. New York: Oxford University Press, 1956.

Mills, James Philip. *The Ao Nagas*. 1926. Bombay: Oxford University Press, 1973.

Miri, Mrinal. "Nation, Diversity and Education." *Man and Society* 7 (Winter 2010): 1–11.

———. "North-East: A Point of View." *Dialogue* (Delhi) 3, no. 2 (Oct.–Dec. 2001).

Misra, Udayon. *Burden of History: Assam and the Partition—Unresolved Issues*. New Delhi: Oxford University Press, 2017.

Mitchell, Timothy. "The Limits of the State: Beyond Statist Approaches and Their Critics." *American Political Science Review* 85, no. 1 (March 1991): 77–96.

Mockaitis, Thomas R. "Low-Intensity Conflict: The British Experience." *Conflict Quarterly* 13, no. 1 (1993): 7–16.

Mohapatra, Prabhu P. "Assam and the West Indies, 1860–1920: Immobilizing Plantation Labor." In *Masters, Servants, and Magistrates in Britain and the Empire, 1562–1955*, edited by Douglas Hay and Paul Craven, 455–80. Chapel Hill: University of North Carolina Press, 2004.

Mukhim, Patricia. "Surrender Policy: Bad in Law." *The Telegraph*, April 8, 2013.

Nakatani, Tetsuya. "Partition Refugees on Borders: Assimilation in West Bengal." In *Minorities and the State: Changing Social and Political Landscape of Bengal*, edited by Abhijit Dasgupta, Masahiko Togawa, and Abul Barkat, 66–87. New Delhi: Sage, 2011.

Narayanan, M. K. "The Devil Is in the Details." *The Hindu*, Sept. 11, 2015.

Naseemullah, Adnan, and Paul Staniland. "Indirect Rule and Varieties of Governance." *Governance* 29, no. 1 (Jan. 2016): 13–30.

Nath, Manoj Kumar. *Ulfa: Xeujia Xopon, Tejronga Itihax* [Ulfa: Green hopes, bloody history]. Guwahati: Aak-Baak, 2013.

Nath, Sunil. "Assam: The Secessionist Insurgency and the Freedom of Minds." *Faultlines* 13 (Nov. 2002): 27–51.

Nehru, B. K. *Nice Guys Finish Second: Memoirs*. Delhi: Penguin India, 2000.

Nehru, Jawaharlal. "Note, Shillong, 19 October 1952." In *Documents on North-East India*. Vol. 4, *Assam (1936–1957)*, edited by S. K. Sharma and Usha Sharma, 287–92. New Delhi: Mittal, 2006.

Neuman, Gerald L. "Anomalous Zones." *Stanford Law Review* 48, no. 5 (May 1996): 1197–1234.

Ngaihte, Thangkhanlal. "Painting a Wide Canvas with a Broad Brush." Review of Sanjoy Hazarika, *Strangers No More: New Narratives from India's Northeast*. *Hindustan Times*, March 10, 2018.

Nigam, Aditya. "Empire, Nation and Minority Cultures: The Postnational Moment." *Economic and Political Weekly* 44, no. 10 (March 7, 2009): 57–64.

Nixon, Rob. "Unimagined Communities: Developmental Refugees, Megadams and Monumental Modernity." *New Formations*, no. 69 (Summer 2010): 62–80.

Noni, Arambam. *1949: The Story of India's Takeover of Manipur*. Imphal, Manipur: Centre for Alternative Discourse, 2018.

North East Network, Guwahati, India. "Written Submission to Committee on Elimination of All Forms of Discrimination Against Women [CEDAW]: CEDAW General Discussion on 'Women in Conflict and Post-Conflict Situations.'" CEDAW, 37th Sess.,

Jan. 15–Feb. 2, 2007. www.ohchr.org/documents/HRBodies/CEDAW/Womenconflict situations/NorthEastNetwork.pdf.

O'Donnell, Guillermo. "Why the Rule of Law Matters." *Journal of Democracy* 15, no. 4 (Oct. 2004): 32–46.

Olsson, Christian. "'Legitimate Violence' in the Prose of Counterinsurgency: An Impossible Necessity?" *Alternatives: Global, Local, Political* 38, no. 2 (May 2013): 155–71.

Onley, James. "The Raj Reconsidered: British India's Informal Empire and Spheres of Influence in Asia and Africa." *Asian Affairs* 40, no. 1 (March 2009): 44–62.

Oppitz, Michael, Thomas Kaiser, Alban von Stockhausen, and Marion Wettstein. "The Nagas: An Introduction." In *Naga Identities: Changing Local Cultures in the Northeast of India*, edited by Michael Oppitz, Thomas Kaiser, Alban von Stockhausen, and Marion Wettstein, 11–29. Gent, Belgium: Snoeck, 2008.

Paasi, Anssi. "Region and Place: Regional Identity in Question." *Progress in Human Geography* 27, no. 4 (2003): 475–85.

Pachuau, Joy L. K., and Willem van Schendel. *The Camera as Witness: A Social History of Mizoram, Northeast India*. Delhi: Cambridge University Press, 2015.

Pandey, Gyanendra. *Remembering Partition: Violence, Nationalism, and History in India*. Cambridge: Cambridge University Press, 2001.

Parratt, John, and Arambam Saroj Nalini Parratt. "Integration or Annexation? Manipur's Relations with India, 1947–1949." In Singh, Hanjabam, and Thangjam, *Self-Determination Movement in Manipur*, 44–62.

Patel, Vallabhbhai. "Sardar Patel's Letter to Jawaharlal Nehru, 7 November 1950." Reprinted as Appendix 2 in Durga Das, *India from Curzon to Nehru and After*, 459–63. New York: John Day, 1970.

Perreault, Thomas. "'A People with Our Own Identity': Toward a Cultural Politics of Development in Ecuadorian Amazonia." *Environment and Planning D: Society and Space* 21, no. 5 (2003): 583–606.

Phizo, A. Z. "Phizo's Plebiscite Speech." Kohima, Nagaland, May 16, 1951. www.neuenhofer .de/guenter/nagaland/phizo.html.

Phukon, Suresh. *Moidamor Pora Moi Lachite Koiso* [This is Lachit speaking from my burial tomb]. Sibsagar, Assam: Rupam Prakashan, 1980.

Pigg, Stacy Leigh. "Inventing Social Categories Through Place: Social Representations and Development in Nepal." *Comparative Studies in Society and History* 34, no. 3 (July 1992): 491–513.

Pillai, G. K. Preface to Chadha, *Armed Forces Special Powers Act*, vii–viii.

Prabhakara, M. S. "Burdens of the Past." *Frontline* 21, no. 18 (August 28, 2004): www.frontline .in/static/html/fl2118/stories/20040910006101200.htm.

———. "Going Round the Mulberry Bush." *The Hindu*, March 20, 2010.

———. "In the Name of Tribal Identities." *Frontline* 22, no. 24 (Nov. 19–Dec. 2, 2005): https://frontline.thehindu.com/static/html/fl2224/stories/20051202002703500 .htm.

———. "Of State and Nationalism." *Frontline* (Chennai, India) 16, no. 21 (Oct. 9–22, 1999): https://frontline.thehindu.com/static/html/fl1621/16210680.htm.

———. "Promises and Problems." *Frontline* 20, no. 5 (March 1–14, 2003): https://frontline
.thehindu.com/static/html/fl2005/stories/20030314001305000.htm.

———. "Sovereignty Struggles in Northeast India: Where Are They Going?" In Arambam, Thangjam, and Hanjabam, *Our Common Crisis*, 94–113.

———. "Territories of Fear." *Frontline* 20, no. 24 (Nov. 22–Dec. 5, 2003): https://frontline
.thehindu.com/static/html/fl2024/stories/20031205003103900.htm.

Prakash, Gyan, Michael Laffan, and Nikhil Menon, eds. *The Postcolonial Moment in South
and Southeast Asia*. London: Bloomsbury, 2018.

Pratt, Mary Louise. "Modernity and Periphery: Towards a Global and Relational Analysis." In *Beyond Dichotomies: Histories, Identities, Cultures, and the Challenge of Globalization*, edited by Elisabeth Mudimbe-Boyi, 21–48. Albany: State University of New York
Press, 2002.

Pugliese, Joseph. "Asymmetries of Terror: Visual Regimes of Racial Profiling and the
Shooting of Jean Charles de Menezes in the Context of the War in Iraq." *Borderlands*
5, no. 1 (2008): www.borderlands.net.au/vol5no1_2006/pugliese.htm.

Raghavan, Pallavi. "The Making of the India-Pakistan Dynamic: Nehru, Liaquat, and
the No War Pact Correspondence of 1950." *Modern Asian Studies* 50, no. 5 (2016):
1645–78.

Rahman, Azera Parveen. "Private Dam Builders Back Out of Brahmaputra Dams." *The Third
Pole*, Feb. 25, 2016, www.thethirdpole.net/2016/02/25/private-dam-builders-back-out
-of-brahmaputra-dams.

Rajagopalan, Rajesh. "'Restoring Normalcy': The Evolution of the Indian Army's Counterinsurgency Doctrine." *Small Wars & Insurgencies* 11, no. 1 (2000): 44–68.

———. "Why Is the Indian Counter-Insurgency Failing Repeatedly?" Observer Research
Foundation, *Commentaries*, April 8, 2014. www.orfonline.org/research/why-is-the-indian
-counter-insurgency-failing-repeatedly.

Rajguru, Prasanta. "Sanskrit Manoxicotar Xondhanot" [Toward understanding the orientation to Sanskrit]. *Amar Axom*, March 5, 2017.

Rammohan, E. N. "Manipur: Blue Print for Counterinsurgency." *Faultlines* 12 (May
2002): 1–22.

Ramunny, Murkot. *The World of Nagas*. New Delhi: Northern Book Centre, 1988.

Ravi, R. N. "Exclusive! How the Naga Accord Was Reached." Interview by Saisuresh Sivaswamy. Rediff.com, August 12, 2015. www.rediff.com/news/interview/exclusive-how-the
-naga-accord-was-reached/20150812.htm.

———. "Nagaland: Descent into Chaos." *The Hindu*, Jan. 23, 2014.

Ray, Debraj. "Aspirations, Poverty, and Economic Change." In *Understanding Poverty*, edited by Abhijit Vinayak Banerjee, Roland Bénabou, and Dilip Mookherjee, 409–21.
Oxford: Oxford University Press, 2006.

Ray, Manas. "Growing Up Refugee." *History Workshop Journal* 53, no. 1 (March 2002):
149–79.

Reid, Robert Neil. "The Excluded Areas of Assam." *Geographical Journal* 103, no. 1/2
(1944): 18–29.

———. *History of the Frontier Areas Bordering on Assam: From 1883–1941.* Shillong: Assam Government Press, 1942.

———. "A Note on the Future of the Present Excluded, Partially Excluded and Tribal Areas of Assam." 1941. In Syiemlieh, *On the Edge of Empire,* 42–80.

Rich, Matthew. "Hill and Plains in the Colonial Imaginary of India's Northeast: Khasi Citizens and Tribal Subjects." Master's thesis, University of Chicago, 2006.

Rio, Neiphiu. "Speech at Consultative Meeting." Niathu Resort, Chumukedima, Dimapur, Nagaland, August 25, 2015. *Eastern Mirror* (Dimapur), Oct. 8, 2015.

Roach, Kent. "Ordinary Laws for Emergencies and Democratic Derogations from Rights." In *Emergencies and the Limits of Legality,* edited by Victor Ramraj, 229–57. Cambridge: Cambridge University Press, 2008.

Robinson, Cabeiri Debergh. "Too Much Nationality: Kashmiri Refugees, the South Asian Refugee Regime, and a Refugee State, 1947–1974." *Journal of Refugee Studies* 25, no. 3 (Sept. 2012): 344–65.

Rokkan, Stein. *Citizens, Elections, Parties: Approaches to the Comparative Study of the Processes of Development.* New York: David McKay, 1970.

Routray, Bibhu Prasad. "China's New Game in India's Northeast." Mantraya.org, July 4, 2017. http://mantraya.org/analysis-chinas-new-game-in-indias-northeast.

Roy, Anupama. *Mapping Citizenship in India.* New Delhi: Oxford University Press, 2010.

Rudolph, Lloyd I., and Susanne Hoeber Rudolph. "Federalism as State Formation in India: A Theory of Shared and Negotiated Sovereignty." *International Political Science Review* 31, no. 5 (2010): 553–72.

Rustomji, Nari. *Imperilled Frontiers: India's North-Eastern Borderlands.* New Delhi: Oxford University Press, 1983.

Sachs, Wolfgang. "Preface to the New Edition." In *The Development Dictionary: A Guide to Knowledge as Power,* edited by Wolfgang Sachs, vii–xv. 2nd ed. London: Zed, 2010.

Sadan, Mandy. "Contested Meanings of Postcolonialism and Independence in Burma." In Prakash, Laffan, and Menon, *The Postcolonial Moment,* 49–65.

Sadiq, Kamal. *Paper Citizens: How Illegal Immigrants Acquire Citizenship in Developing Countries.* New York: Oxford University Press, 2009.

Sahlins, Marshall. "Iraq: The State of Nature Effect." *Anthropology Today* 27, no. 3 (June 2011): 26–31.

———. Preface to *The Counter-Counterinsurgency Manual: Or, Notes on Demilitarizing American Society,* edited by Network of Concerned Anthropologists, i–vii. Chicago: Prickly Paradigm, 2009.

Sahlins, Peter. "Response Paper." American Council of Learned Societies Project on "Official and Vernacular Identifications in the Making of the Modern World." 2003. http://archives.acls.org/programs/crn/network/meetings_nyc_sahlins.htm.

———. "State Formation and National Identity in the Catalan Borderland During the Eighteenth and Nineteenth Centuries." In *Border Identities: Nation and State at International Frontiers,* edited by Thomas M. Wilson and Hastings Donnan, 31–61. Cambridge: Cambridge University Press, 1998.

Sahni, Ajai. "By the Law, for Law and Order." *Tehelka* (New Delhi), June 24, 2006.

———. "Nagaland: Tentative Accord." *South Asia Intelligence Review* 14, no. 6 (August 10, 2015): www.satp.org/satporgtp/sair/Archives/sair14/14_6.htm#assessment1.

———. "Unexpected Calm." *South Asia Intelligence Review* 14, no. 43 (April 25, 2016): http://old.satp.org/satporgtp/sair/Archives/sair14/14_43.htm.

Saikia, Arunabh. "Did Nagaland's Voter Turnout Fall Because of Campaign to Curb Proxy Voting?" Scroll.in, March 1, 2018. https://scroll.in/article/870344/did-nagalands-voter -turnout-fall-because-of-campaign-to-curb-proxy-voting.

———. "In Assam, a Massive Eviction Drive Throws New Light on Old Pressures on Land." Scroll.in, Dec. 1, 2017. https://scroll.in/article/859806/in-assam-a-massive -anti-encroachment-drive-throws-new-light-on-old-pressures-on-land.

———. "Livelihood or Fear: What Really Drives Illegal Coal Mining in Meghalaya?" Scroll.in, Jan. 12, 2019. https://scroll.in/article/908515/livelihood-or-fear-what-really -drives-illegal-coal-mining-in-meghalaya.

———. "'Phaltu sarkar': In Meghalaya, the Ban on Coal Mining Could Cost the Congress Heavily (Part 1)." Scroll.in, Feb. 13, 2018. https://blogs.lse.ac.uk/southasia /2018/02/17/phaltu-sarkar-in-meghalaya-the-ban-on-coal-mining-could-cost-the -congress-heavily-part-1.

———. "This Assam Town Hasn't Forgotten How the Army Took Away Five Civilians and Killed Them in 1994." Scroll.in, Oct. 19, 2018. https://scroll.in/article/898739/this-assam -town-hasnt-forgotten-how-the-army-took-away-five-civilians-and-killed-them-in -1994.

Saikia, Yasmin. "Who Are the Muslims of Assam?" *Outlook* (New Delhi), April 22, 2016.

Saldaña-Portillo, María Josefina. "From the Borderlands to the Transnational? Critiquing Empire in the Twenty-First Century." In *A Companion to Latina/o Studies*, edited by Juan Flores and Renato Rosaldo, 502–12. Malden, MA: Blackwell, 2007.

Sato, Hiroshi. "Normative Space of the Politics of Citizenship in Eastern India." In *Elusive Borders: Changing Sub-regional Relations in Eastern India*, edited by Kyoko Inoue, Etsuyo Arai, and Mayumi Murayama, 83–110. Tokyo: Institute of Development Economics, 2005.

Schmitt, Carl. *The Nomos of the Earth in the International Law of the Jus Publicum Europaeum*. Translated by G. L. Ulmen. New York: Telos, 2003.

Scott, David. "Norms of Self-Determination: Thinking Sovereignty Through." *Middle East Law and Governance* 4, nos. 2 & 3 (May 2012): 195–224.

Scott, James C. *The Art of Not Being Governed: An Anarchist History of Upland Southeast Asia*. New Haven, CT: Yale University Press, 2009.

Sen, Amartya. "Democracy as a Universal Value." *Journal of Democracy* 10, no. 3 (1999): 3–17.

Sethi, Arshiya. "An Overlay of the Political: The Recognition of Sattriya." *Seminar*, no. 676, Dec. 2015. www.indiaseminar.com/2015/676/676_arshiya_sethi.htm.

Shani, Ornit. "Making Universal Franchise and Democratic Citizenship in the Postcolonial Moment." In Prakash, Laffan, and Menon, *The Postcolonial Moment*, 163–81.

Sharma Ajit Kumar and Others to Prime Minister Indira Gandhi. "Indian Citizens Versus Foreign Nationals." Memorandum. Guwahati: Asom Jagriti, 1980.

Sharma, Jayeeta. *Empire's Garden: Assam and the Making of India*. Durham, NC: Duke University Press, 2011.

———. "Heroes for Our Times: Assam's Lachit, India's Missile Man." In *The Politics of Cultural Mobilization in India*, edited by John Zavos, Andrew Wyatt, and Vernon Hewitt, 166–94. New Delhi: Oxford University Press, 2004.

Sharma, Sushil Kumar. "The Naga Peace Accord: Manipur Connections." *Institute of Defense Studies and Analysis, Policy Brief,* Dec. 18, 2015. https://idsa.in/policybrief/the-naga -peace-accord-manipur-connections_sksharma_181215.

Shourie, Arun. "Assam Elections: Can Democracy Survive Them?" *India Today*, May 31, 1983, 54–66.

Siddiqui, Furquan Ameen. "Curse of the Black Gold: How Meghalaya Depends on Coal." *Hindustan Times*, March 2, 2015.

Singh, Aheibam Koireng, Shukhdeba Sharma Hanjabam, and Homen Thangjam, eds. *Self-Determination Movement in Manipur*. New Delhi: Concept, 2015.

Singh, B. P. *The Problem of Change: A Study of North-East India*. New Delhi: Oxford University Press, 1997.

Singh, Gurharpal. "Beyond Punjabi Romanticism." *Seminar*, no. 567, Nov. 2006, www.india -seminar.com/2006/567/567_gurharpal_singh.htm.

Singh, Jaswant. "Assam's Crisis of Citizenship: An Examination of Political Errors." *Asian Survey* 24, no. 10 (Oct. 1984): 1056–68.

Singh, Ujjwal Kumar. *The State, Democracy and Anti-terror Laws in India*. New Delhi: Sage, 2007.

Sinha, S. K. "Report on Illegal Migration into Assam Submitted to the President of India by the Governor of Assam." Nov. 8, 1998. www.satp.org/satporgtp/countries/india/states /assam/documents/papers/illegal_migration_in_assam.htm.

———. "Violence and Hope in India's Northeast." Lecture at the Institute for Conflict Management, New Delhi, June 2001. *Faultlines* 10 (Jan. 2002): 1–21.

Sinha, S. P. "CI Operations in the Northeast." *Indian Defence Review* 21, no. 2 (April–June 2006): www.indiandefencereview.com/spotlights/c-i-operations-in-the-northeast/2.

South Asia Terrorism Portal. "India—Terrorist, Insurgent and Extremist Groups." 2017. www.satp.org/satporgtp/countries/india/terroristoutfits/index.html.

———. "National Socialist Council of Nagaland—Isak-Muivah." www.satp.org/satporgtp /countries/india/states/nagaland/terrorist_outfits/nscn_im.htm.

Soyinka, Wole. *You Must Set Forth at Dawn: A Memoir*. New York: Random House, 2007.

Staniland, Paul. "States, Insurgents, and Wartime Political Orders." *Perspectives on Politics* 10, no. 2 (2012): 243–64.

Stepan, Alfred. *Arguing Comparative Politics*. New York: Oxford University Press, 2001.

Stevenson, Jonathan. "The Role of the Armed Forces of the United Kingdom in Securing the State Against Terrorism." *Connections* 4, no. 3 (2005): 121–33.

Sundar, Nandini. "Interning Insurgent Populations: The Buried Histories of Indian Democracy." *Economic and Political Weekly* 46, no. 6 (2011): 47–57.

Supreme Court of India. *Assam Sanmilita Mahasangha & Others v. Union of India & Others*, Dec. 17, 2014. https://indiankanoon.org/doc/50798357.

———. *Extra Judicial Execution Victim Families v. Union of India & Another.* Writ Petition (Criminal) no. 129 of 2012, July 13, 2016. https://indiankanoon.org/doc/83144198.

———. "Judgment on Writ Petition (Civil) 131 of 2000." July 12, 2005. Bench: R. C. Lahoti, G. P. Mathur, and P. K. Balasubramanyan. https://indiankanoon.org/doc/907725.

Sur, Malini. "Battles for the Golden Grain: Paddy Soldiers and the Making of the Northeast India–East Pakistan Border, 1930–1970." *Comparative Studies in Society and History* 58, no. 3 (July 2016): 804–32.

———. "Spectacles of Militarization." *IIAS Newsletter* [International Institute for Asian Studies, Leiden, The Netherlands], no. 71 (Summer 2015): 28–29.

Suykens, Bert. "State-Making and the Suspension of Law in India's Northeast: The Place of Exception in the Assam-Nagaland Border Dispute." In *Violence on the Margins: States, Conflict, and Borderlands*, edited by Benedikt Korf and Timothy Raeymaekers, 167–89. New York: Palgrave Macmillan, 2013.

Syiemlieh, David R., ed. *On the Edge of Empire: Four British Plans for North East India, 1941–1947.* New Delhi: Sage, 2014.

Talbot, Ian. "India and Pakistan." In *Routledge Handbook of South Asian Politics*, edited by Paul R. Brass, 27–40. New York: Routledge, 2010.

Talukdar, Mrinal, Utpal Borpujari, and Kaushik Deka. *Secret Killings of Assam.* Guwahati: Nanda Talukdar Foundation and Bhabani Books, 2008.

Tarrow, Sidney. "Inside Insurgencies: Politics and Violence in an Age of Civil War." *Perspectives on Politics* 5, no. 3 (Sept. 2007): 587–600.

Teitelbaum, Michael S. "Immigration, Refugees, and Foreign Policy." *International Organization* 38, no. 3 (Summer 1984): 429–50.

Thakur, D. D. "Governor's Report to the President." Reproduced in judgment delivered by Chief Justice A. Raghuvir of the Guwahati High Court in *Nibaron Borah and Others v. Union of India*, March 20, 1991. Reprinted in *News of North East: A Monthly Compilation of Clippings*. Guwahati: Eastern Press Service, May 1991.

Thakur, Shalaka, and Rajesh Venugopal. "Parallel Governance and Political Order in Contested Territory: Evidence from the Indo-Naga Ceasefire." *Asian Security*, April 18, 2018, 1–19. https://doi.org/10.1080/14799855.2018.1455185.

Thiranagama, Sharika. "Claiming the State: Postwar Reconciliation in Sri Lanka." *Humanity* 4, no. 1 (Spring 2013): 93–116.

Thomas, Alan. "Development as Practice in a Liberal Capitalist World." *Journal of International Development* 12, no. 6 (August 2000): 773–87.

Thomas, John. *Evangelising the Nation: Religion and the Formation of Naga Political Identity.* Delhi: Routledge India, 2015.

Tilly, Charles. *Collective Violence, Contentious Politics, and Social Change: A Charles Tilly Reader.* Edited by Ernesto Castañeda and Cathy Lisa Schneider. New York: Routledge, 2017.

———. "Violence, Terror, and Politics as Usual." *Boston Review* 27, no. 3–4 (Summer 2002): http://bostonreview.net/archives/BR27.3/tilly.html.

Tilly, Charles, and Sidney Tarrow. *Contentious Politics.* 2nd ed. New York: Oxford University Press, 2015.

Tsing, Anna Lowenhaupt. "Contingent Commodities: Mobilizing Labor in and Beyond Southeast Asian Forests." In *Taking Southeast Asia to Market: Commodities, Nature, and People in the Neoliberal Age*, edited by Joseph Nevins and Nancy Lee Peluso, 27–42. Ithaca, NY: Cornell University Press, 2008.

———. *Friction: An Ethnography of Global Connection*. Princeton, NJ: Princeton University Press, 2004.

Tully, James. "On Law, Democracy and Imperialism." In *Public Philosophy in a New Key*. Vol. 2, *Imperialism and Civic Freedom*, 127–65. Cambridge: Cambridge University Press, 2008.

———. "Rethinking Human Rights and Enlightenment: A View from the Twenty-First Century." In *Self-Evident Truths? Human Rights and the Enlightenment*, edited by Kate Tunstall, 3–34. New York: Bloomsbury, 2012.

UN General Assembly. "International Covenant on Civil and Political Rights." Dec. 16, 1966. www.ohchr.org/en/professionalinterest/pages/ccpr.aspx.

———. *Report of the Policy Working Group on the United Nations and Terrorism*. 57th Sess., item 162, Provisional Agenda, Measures to Eliminate International Terrorism. August 6, 2002. UN Doc. A/57/273-S/2002/875.

UN Human Rights Committee. "Appendix F: Human Rights Committee Concluding Observations on Caste." August 4, 1997, par. 19. Human Rights Watch. www.hrw.org/reports /1999/india/India994-21.htm.

———. "India: Examination of Second Periodic Report by Human Rights Committee, Recommendations to Bring Indian Laws and Practices in Line with International Human Rights Standards." 41st Sess., March 26–27, 1991, New York. Amnesty International. www.amnesty.org/en/documents/asa20/005/1993/en.

UN Human Rights Council. Report of the Special Rapporteur on Extrajudicial, Summary or Arbitrary Executions, Addendum: Mission to India, 23rd Sess., item 3. April 26, 2013. UN Doc. A/HRC/23/47/Add.1. www.refworld.org/docid/51B98e624.html.

United Liberation Front of Assam (Xomyukta Mukti Bahini Axom). *Xodosya Toka Bohi* (Cadre Handbook). N.p.: United Liberation Front of Assam, n.d.

———. *Xomyukta Mukti Bahini Axomar Doxom Protistha Dibox, Bixex Procar Potro* [Tenth foundation day of Ulfa, special publicity pamphlet]. April 7, 1979. Reprinted in Nath, *Ulfa*, 25–40.

Unnithan, Sandeep, and Kaushik Deka. "North-East Rebel Groups Freely Brandish Arms, Extort Protection Money from Locals and Run Parallel Governments." *India Today*, Oct. 5, 2012. www.indiatoday.in/magazine/special-report/story/20121015-north-east-rebel -groups-freely-brandish-arms-extort-protection-money-from-locals-760072-1999 -11-30.

Vajpeyi, Ananya. "Resenting the Indian State: For a New Political Practice in the Northeast." In Baruah, *Beyond Counterinsurgency*, 25–48.

van der Veer, Peter. "Hindu Nationalism and the Discourse of Modernity: The Vishva Hindu Parishad." In *Accounting for Fundamentalisms: The Dynamic Character of Movements*, edited by Martin E. Marty and R. Scott Appleby, 653–68. Chicago: University of Chicago Press, 1994.

van Schendel, Willem. "The Dangers of Belonging: Tribes, Indigenous Peoples and Homelands in South Asia." In *The Politics of Belonging in India: Becoming Adivasi*, edited by D. J. Rycroft and S. Dasgupta, 19–43. London: Routledge, 2011.

———. "Repatriates? Infiltrators? Trafficked Humans?" *South Asia Refugee Watch* 2, no. 2 (Dec. 2000): 30–63.

Varadarajan, Siddharth. "A Modest Proposal on AFSPA." *The Hindu*, Sept. 6, 2010. www.hindu .com/2010/09/06/stories/2010090661011200.htm.

Vashum, R[eisang]. *Nagas' Rights to Self Determination: An Anthropological-Historical Perspective*. New Delhi: Mittal, 2000.

Vijay, Tarun. "Assam: The Agony of Being a Hindu." *Organiser*, August 19, 2012.

Visvanathan, Shiv. "Manipur Needs Its Life Back." *India Today*, Sept. 1, 2014.

Walker, Lydia. "States-in-Waiting: Nationalism, Internationalism, Decolonization." PhD diss., Harvard University, 2018.

Weber, Max. "Politics as a Vocation." In Gerth and Mills, *From Max Weber*, 77–128.

———. "The Social Psychology of the World Religions." In Gerth and Mills, *From Max Weber*, 267–301.

Weiner, Myron. "The Political Consequences of Preferential Policies: A Comparative Perspective." *Comparative Politics* 16, no. 1 (1983): 35–52.

———. *Sons of the Soil: Migration and Ethnic Conflict in India*. Princeton, NJ: Princeton University Press, 1978.

West, Andrew. "Writing the Nagas: A British Officers' Ethnographic Tradition." *History and Anthropology* 8, no. 1–4 (1994): 55–88.

Wood, Elisabeth Jean. *Insurgent Collective Action and Civil War in El Salvador*. New York: Cambridge University Press, 2003.

Worth, Robert F. "The Billionaire Yogi Behind Modi's Rise." *New York Times Magazine*, July 26, 2018. www.nytimes.com/2018/07/26/magazine/the-billionaire-yogi-behind-modis -rise.html.

Wouters, Jelle J. P. "Polythetic Democracy: Tribal Elections, Bogus Votes, and Political Imagination in the Naga Uplands of Northeast India." *HAU: Journal of Ethnographic Theory* 5, no. 2 (Autumn 2015): 121–51.

Wouters, Jelle J. P., and Tanka B. Subba. "The 'Indian Face,' India's Northeast, and 'The Idea of India.'" *Asian Anthropology* 12, no. 2 (2013): 126–40.

Yadav, Anil. *Is That Even a Country, Sir! Journeys in Northeast India by Train, Bus and Tractor*. Translated from the Hindi by Anurag Basnet. New Delhi: Speaking Tiger, 2017.

Young, Iris Marion. "The Logic of Masculinist Protection: Reflections on the Current Security State." *Signs* 29, no. 1 (Autumn 2003): 1–25.

Zeliang, T. R. "Interview with T. R. Zeliang, Chief Minister of Nagaland." *The Telegraph*, June 15, 2015.

# INDEX

Note: "t" refers to tables found in the text.

Acharya, P. B., 108-9

acts of citizenship, 176, 190-91. *See also* Sharmila, Irom

*adivasi*, use of the term in Northeast India, 120, 199n54

Advani, L. K., 180

affective boundaries of the nation, 12, 142

AGP (Asom Gana Parishad), 133-34, 143. *See also* Assam Movement

Agrawal, Ankush, 120, 122, 219n9

Aier, Wati, 107

Akoijam, Sunita, 21-22

Ali, Jamir, 97-98

All-India Muslim League, 48, 50-52, 128

Amaya-Castro, Juan M., 205n48. *See also* illegality regimes

anomalous zone, 11. *See also* Armed Forces Special Powers Act (AFSPA)

antipolitical politics, 155

anxiety of incompleteness, 75

Appadurai, Arjun, 28, 195n6, 224n13, 240n77, 241nn79, 90. *See also* anxiety of incompleteness

Arambam, Lokendra, 38, 179

armed conflict. *See* "insurgency"

Armed Forces Special Powers Act (AFSPA), 4-7, 9-12, 46, 129-30, 155-59, 173-75, 231n4, 233n38; colonial roots of, 168-72, 175; disturbed areas under, 134, 153-54, 180, 196n20, 225n16, 231n4; immunity under, 4, 173-74; normalization of, 133, 164-

73, 178; resistance to, 12, 155, 157-59, 161-63, 184-85, 190, 232n14 (*see also* Sharmila, Irom)

Arunachal Pradesh, 2, 17-18, 25, 37, 39, 101; agrarian change in, 90-91, 97-98, 217n83; areas claimed as part of Naga homeland, 101, 125; dispute with China over, 18, 32; hydropower in, 94-95; land rights in, 93-94; representation in parliament, 27; reserved and unreserved seats in legislative assembly, 90t; tea plantations in, 91, 94; timber trade in, 86

Asam Sahitya Sabha (Assam Literary Conference), 55. *See also* Assamese language

Assam: areas claimed as part of Naga homeland, 101, 125; armed conflict in, 5-6; Assam-Nagaland border, 119-22; Barak Valley, 63-64, 69-70, 141; Cachar, 62; colonial, 18-19, 25, 27, 30-35, 37, 89; counterinsurgency in, 9, 126-31, 160, 180-2; displacement in, 73, 77; disturbed area designation, 129-30, 134, 153-54, 157; immigration to, 48-49, 51-54, 56-63, 66-71; in the mainland imagination 13-14, 16; migration from, 20, 22; missionaries in, 15; Muslims in, 50-56; Nepali population in, 36-37; oil extraction in, 40-41; population of, 26-27; representation in Parliament, 27; reserved and unreserved

tion; indigeneity; Naga nationalism; Northeasterners

Northern Ireland, 109, 145; the Troubles, 3

North West Frontier Providence (NWFP), 2

NSCN-IM (National Socialist Council of Nagaland-IM): Camp Hebron, 111-12, 116-17, 121; ceasefire agreement with Indian government, 100-102, 107, 118; Christianity and, 106; demands for sovereignty, 108, 125; Designated Camps, 116-18, 123; Government of the People's Republic of Nagaland/ Nagalim (GPRN), 6, 111-12, 117; history of, 103-4, 218n1; military displays, 116; state symbolism, 110-11; tax collection by, 110-13, 115, 117, 119; ties with Naga politicians, 114-15. *See also* Armed Forces Special Powers Act; "insurgency"

NSCN-K (National Socialist Council of Nagaland-Khaplang), 118-19, 218n1

O'Donnell, Guillermo, 11

oil extraction, 9, 40-41, 121. *See also* resource extraction

Olsson, Christian, 196n10, 235n82

Paasi, Anssi, 25

Pachuau, Joy L. K., 159; *The Camera as Witness,* 33

Pakistan, 53, 62; border with India, 71, 73; break-up of, 44, 47-48; migration from, 59-61, 64-65, 70, 156; Nehru-Liaquat pact, 57; Wagah, 73

Pandey, Gyanendra, 47

pan-Indianism, 59, 128, 135, 137, 191, 228n55

Partially Excluded Areas, 27, 32. *See also* excluded areas

Partition (1947), 3, 59-60, 73; attitudes towards Hindu vs. Muslim migrants after, 49, 53-54, 137-38; Hindu refugees of, 26-27, 47-49, 58, 70; impact on Sylhet, 48, 51, 61-63; violence against refugees of, 141-42. *See also* citizenship; immigration

Patel, Vallabhbhai, 61, 169; on Tibet, 19, 39, 43

Perreault, Thomas, 88

Phizo, Angami Zapu, 15

Phukan, Siddhartha, 140

Phukon, Suresh, *Moidamor Pora Moi Lachite Koiso* (This is Lachit speaking from my burial tomb), 146

Pigg, Stacy Leigh, 87-88

Pillai, G. K., 157

Pilot, Rajesh, 139

Prabhakara, M. S., 38, 53, 187n39

Pratt, Mary Louise, 88

President's Rule, 134, 139, 143, 166, 185

protective discrimination, 89, 198n54

psychological warfare, 144-49, 151. *See also* counterinsurgency

Pugliese, Joseph, 202nn102, 114

Quit India Movement (1942), 168

race: in official state discourse, 17, 23, 29, 179; and the racial gaze, 19, 21. *See also* racism

racism, 187; colonial, 17-18, 32-33, 89, 200n79; against Northeasterners, 17-24, 26, 201n89, 232n15. *See also* ethnic violence; hate crimes

Raghavan, Pallavi, 57

Rajagopalan, Rajesh, 130

Rajkhowa, Arabinda (Rajib Rajkonwar), 149. *See also* Ulfa

Rammohan, E. V., 130-31

Ravi, Ravindra Narayan, 109, 113, 116, 123

Reddy (B. P. Jeevan) Committee, 163, 172-73. *See also* Armed Forces Special Powers Act

refugees. *See* Partition (1947)

ALSO PUBLISHED IN THE SOUTH ASIA IN MOTION SERIES

*Paradoxes of the Popular: Crowd Politics in Bangladesh*
Nusrat Sabina Chowdhury (2019)

*Mafia Raj: The Rule of Bosses in South Asia*
Lucia Michelutti, Ashraf Hoque, Nicolas Martin, David Picherit, Paul Rollier, Arild Ruud, and Clarinda Still (2018)

*Elusive Lives: Gender, Autobiography, and the Self in Muslim South Asia*
Siobhan Lambert-Hurley (2018)

*Financializing Poverty: Labor and Risk in Indian Microfinance*
Sohini Kar (2018)

*Jinnealogy: Time, Islam, and Ecological Thought in the Medieval Ruins of Delhi*
Anand Vivek Taneja (2017)

*Uprising of the Fools: Pilgrimage as Moral Protest in Contemporary India*
Vikash Singh (2017)

*The Slow Boil: Street Food, Rights, and Public Space in Mumbai*
Jonathan Shapiro Anjaria (2016)

*The Demands of Recognition: State Anthropology and Ethnopolitics in Darjeeling*
Townsend Middleton (2015)

*The South African Gandhi: Stretcher-Bearer of Empire*
Ashwin Desai and Goolam Vahed (2015)